Winifred Fortescue was born in a Suffolk rectory on 7th February, 1888, the third child of a country rector and connected, on her mother's side, to the Fighting Battyes of India.

When she was seventeen – in order to ease the strain on family finances – she decided to try to earn her own living, and went on the stage, performing in Sir Herbert Tree's company, and later starring in Jerome K. Jerome's *The Passing of the Third Floor Back*.

In 1914 she married John Fortescue, the King's Librarian and Archivist and famous historian of the British Army. The marriage, in spite of a huge disparity of age between them, was a uniquely happy one, and although Winifred Fortescue gave up her career on the stage, she later began a successful interior decorating and dress designing business until illness forced her to close her company down. It was at that point that she began writing, for *Punch*, the *Daily Chronicle*, the *Evening News*, finally inaugurating and editing a Woman's Page for the *Morning Post*.

In the early 1930s, John and Winifred Fortescue, now Sir John and Lady Fortescue, moved to Provence and there she wrote her famous and bestselling PERFUME FROM PROVENCE, and the sequel SUNSET HOUSE. PERFUME FROM PROVENCE became a bestseller once again when it was re-published by Black Swan in 1992. Her autobiography, THERE'S ROSEMARY, THERE'S RUE, was first published in 1939. She died at Opio, Provence, in April 1951.

THERE'S ROSEMARY, THERE'S RUE

'There's rosemary, that's for remembrance . . .
there's rue for you; and here's some for me' – Shakespeare

by

THE HONOURABLE
LADY FORTESCUE

BLACK SWAN

THERE'S ROSEMARY, THERE'S RUE
A BLACK SWAN BOOK o 552 99558 4

First published in Great Britain by William Blackwood & Sons Ltd.

PRINTING HISTORY
Blackwood edition published 1939
Black Swan edition published 1993

Copyright © William Blackwood & Sons 1939

Black Swan Books are published by Transworld Publishers Ltd,
61–63 Uxbridge Road, Ealing, London W5 5SA,
in Australia by Transworld Publishers (Australia) Pty Ltd,
15–25 Helles Avenue, Moorebank, NSW 2170,
and in New Zealand by Transworld Publishers (NZ) Ltd,
3 William Pickering Drive, Albany, Auckland.

Reproduced, printed and bound in Great Britain by
Cox & Wyman Ltd, Reading, Berks.

"And may the gods grant thee all thy heart's desire: a husband and a home, and a mind at one with his may they give—a good gift, for there is nothing mightier and nobler than when man and wife are of one heart and mind in a house, a grief to their foes, and to their friends great joy, but their own hearts know it best."

—ODYSSEY OF HOMER,
Book VI.

"There's Rosemary . . . There's Rue . . ."

"Is the child perfect ? " asked my anguished father.

"Well, she hasn't got all her toes on one foot," replied our old family doctor curtly.

"My God," exclaimed my father in horror, sinking into a chair and covering his face with his hands. "My dread has always been to have a malformed child."

"Of course she hasn't got all her toes on one foot," snapped the doctor, "she's got five on each, and I never saw a more perfect specimen. Ten pounds at birth and not a blemish."

His was a peculiar form of humour, perhaps rendered a whit more acrid than usual because I had been tactless enough to arrive twelve hours earlier than he had predicted—for I was the baby described. All through the night of my coming there was a heavy snowstorm, during which he had been driving about the country in an open dog-cart. He had hardly reached home in the early morning, shaken the clotted snow from his shoulders, changed his soaked boots for warm felt slippers, and mixed himself a stiff tot of hot grog, when his bell rang once more, and after a moment my father stumbled blindly into the room, begging him to drive out at once to our home two miles away.

The old doctor was very fond of my parents, and had doubtless hoped to dine with my father that evening

and then to await my arrival comfortably before a big
fire in his study, afterwards celebrating the event by
drinking with him a glass of his famous port, only brought
forth on great occasions. But I had spoiled all this by
becoming restive in the small hours of that morning
when everyone's vitality was at its lowest, and, in the
whimsical way of women, of course I had chosen the worst
weather of the year.

I was born into a white world on the 7th of February
1888 in the rambling old Rectory of Great Bealings in
Suffolk, and, from the moment of birth, I was destined
to receive more love than any child has a right to expect.
My parents had longed for a girl, having already two sons
and having lost a little daughter, their second child, in
a tragic way.

We lived, as I have said, in a large ill-designed Rectory,
with stables and outbuildings, originally built by a
' Squarson.' We children considered this rambling old
house to be quite perfect. The waste of space involved
by the making of long unnecessary corridors leading to
nowhere in particular, was found by us ideal for playing
hide-and-seek and for exercising our sturdy young limbs.
Waxed linoleum, so much deplored by the supercilious,
was delightful for sliding and tobogganing along the
passages upstairs, as were the maddening little flights
of steps leading from one level to another, which caused
thrilling bumps when you reached them. The hideous
monster stove in the outer hall, designed to heat the whole
house and considered such an eyesore by visitors, provided
exciting trials of endurance. In turn you sat on it after
it had been laboriously lit by the housemaid, and there
you stayed, timed by a stop-watch—a test to see who
could longest bear having his, or her, tail toasted.

That wide twisting staircase under the oriel window
could, said some, be made such a feature of the house
if the banisters of plain varnished deal and the handrail,
stained to imitate mahogany, were swept away and

2

replaced by something worthier. They little knew the joys of swift descent by little balanced bodies, nor of the robbers' cave under the curve of the stairs when you had crawled under, or around, various bicycles and other hidden junk. Those two niches in the wall, flanking the oriel window, might contain some beautiful pieces of Oriental china, but why, oh why, did my parents leave these two *shiny* busts of Shakespeare and Scott ?

These supercilious critics never dreamed that those ridiculous inherited busts were precious to my father, because his girl-wife, thinking that they looked dingy, had with infinite pains painted them with white Aspinall's enamel to brighten them up. So there they remained, and whenever he descended the stairs those shining bumps on Shakespeare's bald head made him laugh.

Near the front door was a square room sometimes known as the Parish Room, because it was here that Daddie presided over the village clothing club and interviewed any of his ' old simples,' as he affectionately called his poorer parishioners. Later it became our schoolroom, where a series of patient governesses tried to instil knowledge into the heads of children filled with only one idea—how best to contrive a quick escape into the garden.

Opening into the inner hall were the drawing-room and dining-room, both large and beautiful rooms ; the former a gay and gracious room full of sunshine (when there was any), typical of Mummie, with low comfortable armchairs, Oriental china bowls filled with pot-pourri made from her own especial recipe, and a Broadwood piano. The chief charm of the room was its apsidal ending, cut by three long windows which opened directly on to green grass and rose-beds.

The dining-room was oblong, with long low windows in its south and west sides which also led into the garden. It was furnished in the handsome but heavy Early Victorian style, with a vast shining mahogany table,

3

mahogany leather-seated chairs, and a huge sideboard with a mirror above it and cupboards below. Upon this were set silver-branched candelabra and a display of silver College cups, rowing and sports trophies. In a corner was an enormous sofa, the joy of our lives as children, for upon it we would roll about with Daddie who invented delightful games.

Upstairs in the corridor of the top landing there was the huge chintz-covered chest—that was full of romance —and blankets. Did I not, at the age of six, greatly daring, hide inside it with a bumping heart hoping that someone might find me and that my skeleton would not be discovered there, years afterwards, like that of the lady in ' The Mistletoe Bough ' ?

The lovely thing was that neither Mummie nor Daddie ever stopped our uproarious games. Very often they joined in them, and then how glorious it was.

The only place of real ' Sanctuary ' for these parents was Daddie's study, immediately over the drawing-room and the same beautiful shape. There we children might not enter without first knocking and being invited to come in—but once inside. . . . It was lined from floor to ceiling with books, and had a delicious smell of tobacco and leather—an exciting male smell. But when the three windows of the curved bow of the room were open, there drifted in a poignant aromatic whiff of the scented geraniums in the window-boxes outside. Mummie used always to put a leaf of scented geranium into her letters to ' special ' people, and so the smells of the study characterised both parents, which was fitting ; for they shared the room as they shared everything in life.

There was a great knee-hole desk in the middle of the study, opposite the fireplace, where Daddie sat to write his sermons. Sometimes I would creep into the room when it was empty, crawl under the hollow beneath the desk, and sit there until Daddie came in and settled down to write. Then I would softly snuggle up and hug his

4

darling knees, knowing that a hand would soon steal down to caress my curls in the darkness. No word would be spoken because it was quite understood that the study was his sanctuary and that I ought not to be there.

Did Mummie, who, of course, had followed him into the room—they were never apart for long—know that I was there ? Mummie had uncanny intuition, especially where I was concerned, and she would perhaps glance down at the black cavity under the knee-hole desk, twinkle, and go on quietly writing letters. She had a funny little Davenport desk (my precious possession now) with a sloping lid that opened ; two twisty legs and a row of little drawers all down the right side. In the top drawer were chocolates, in the second drawer bits of old linen for cut fingers, in the third were precious letters, and in the fourth cooking recipes and doctors' prescriptions. The top drawer interested us most, but probably the second drawer was opened most frequently, for we children were always in the wars ; and climbing trees, bicycle gymkhanas, and other daring sports led to casualties. When Daddie yelled to us to come down from the heights of tall trees, Mummie calmly said : " Be quiet, dearest, if they are going to kill themselves they'll do it without your help." She encouraged all deeds of enterprise and daring, her only fear being that one day her children would realise the meaning of the word danger—and funk. She was gallant from the top of her beautiful little proud head to the soles of the tiny feet so much admired by her husband ; and she wanted her children to be dare-devils too. This, from the testimony of many, we certainly were ; the arch-devils being my elder brother Mervyn and myself. Guy, the second son, just a year older than myself (whose bath and perambulator I shared when an infant as we have shared all joys and sorrows since), was a quiet boy, equally courageous but lacking our dash and impulse ; and Marjory, born four years after me,

was still a queer impish baby when we had reached an
adventurous age.

Mervyn was a beautiful buccaneer, olive-skinned and
slender. Eventually his slim tall body developed and
he became a giant. Though always gentle and patient
with old people and animals, he was both reckless and
selfish as a boy, but filled with a dangerous charm which
always saved him from justice. Being her first-born
he was, of course, the light of his mother's eyes, and
from babyhood he could only be controlled through his
devotion to her. His adventurous spirit fascinated his
brother and sisters, who, when he was at home, followed
him wherever he went and obeyed him slavishly—even I,
a rebel at heart, consented to his experiments.

Once he purloined a sulphur candle from a Kent oast-
house, shut us all into a room with doors and windows
closed, lit the sulphur candle, and left us to our fate.
Mummie, happening to pass the schoolroom as she
wandered round the garden, was arrested by the sight
of her elder son crouching outside the window, his nose
pressed absorbedly against the glass and his stern much
agitated. Always keen to share everything that interested
her children, she drew near and looked into the schoolroom. . . . She was only just in time.

But though Mervyn's experiments were sometimes
dangerous, his inventive faculty could keep us quiet for
hours. He made the two low-shelved cupboards under
the bookcases in the schoolroom into the most enchanting
dolls' houses. Each shelf was a room, and a lift could be
hauled from the ground floor to the attics through aper-
tures cut in the shelves. He also made a ' bundle-coach '
(why ' bundle-coach ' no one knew, except, perhaps,
because all the miniature dolls who inhabited the dolls'
house, and often much of its furniture were bundled into
it on occasion) out of a large biscuit tin laid on its side
and fixed upon a wooden trolly with four wheels. That
bundle-coach accompanied me on all my earliest walks,

and, to my intense joy, proved also to be a watertight boat wherein my dolls could safely sail upon the lily-pools of the little trout-stream in the Church meadow.

Then, one memorable Christmas Eve, he led us all forth into the dark snow-covered garden, and there, in a remote corner under the trees, sparkled a tiny Christmas tree ablaze with lights. Assuredly it had been placed there by the fairies, for certainly it had not been there in the morning—an enchanting little magic tree.

He read to us Greek Mythology and Rider Haggard's fantastic books, which so enthralled my imagination that I never rested until I had learned to read at an unusually early age. An old friend of our family told me that he found me at the age of five, curled up in a big armchair in my nightdress, my hair shaken over a very flushed face, laboriously spelling out ' The Arabian Nights' Entertainments ' when I ought to have been in bed and asleep like other normal babes.

Guy, as I have said, was a quiet little boy with a grave beautiful face and enormous hazel eyes fringed by such phenomenal dark lashes under dark pencilled eyebrows that once, teased and taunted about these ' girlish ' attributes by boys at his preparatory school, he cut them close, and we had to endure the sight of his bald face for months until they grew again, more luxuriantly than ever.

As a little boy he preferred his own pursuits to the riotous games of his sisters and brother. He would lie for hours in a wood watching the ways of birds, and he would collect bees in his small hands, very lovingly, and take them to scented flowers where he thought they would be happier still. Never once did they sting him, but though Daddie was very nervous sometimes, Mummie encouraged him to find more.

One (prophetic) game he invented himself in which he included me. He called it ' High Priests.' Inside the empty dog-kennels he made an altar of a store-box ; then

7

each of us in turn would be robed in one of my stolen nightdresses and a pot of vaseline smeared upon his or her head. When I loudly protested against this greasy rite, I was informed that all High Priests had their heads anointed with oil and that if I refused to submit to it I could never attain to that high office. I bore with the greasy ceremony, but resolved firmly in my heart that I would never take up a priest's vocation—though Guy, afterwards, did.

He was just as unselfish and self-effacing as Mervyn was heedless and spectacular. A lady of the parish once asked him to come for a drive with her when he was yet very young. He raised sorrowful eyes to hers and excused himself, saying, " I'm sorry, I can't come. I've promised to remuse the baby."

This was Marjory, a delicate and exacting infant, at birth resembling a gnome.

She became the family problem with a heart, so Daddie affirmed, the size of a dried pea. One never knew of what she was thinking, and consequently it was impossible to surmise what she would say or do next—something devastating almost certainly.

When very young indeed, during a seaside holiday, when she was being undressed for a bathe in a remote corner of the big tent in which Daddie was disrobing at the same time, Mummie discreetly turned the child's back upon him, whereupon Marjory looked up at her with an impish smile and remarked reassuringly, " You needn't bother. I've seen it all at Bealings."

At the age of nine she was caught spelling out the police news in a newspaper, and when Mummie gently removed it, telling her little daughter that if she read such things she " would rub off all the beautiful bloom of youth before she was ten," the child replied brightly, " The bloomin' bloom is off long ago."

What could be done with a child like that ?

Marjory, it will be seen, was never an ordinary child.

I think I must have been, but I am told that I was a thoroughly healthy tom-boy and that I was an extraordinarily joyous thing ; alive in every nerve and muscle, spilling joy as I tumbled about. I remember that every morning I woke with the exhilarating certainty that something lovely was going to happen that day—and it always did, because to me the finding of a stray hen's egg ; the miracle of mushrooms in a dew-wet field ; kingcups blazing in a marsh ; a ride on the top of a load of fragrant fresh-cut hay ; the discovery of a golden-crested wren's nest hanging like a neat pocket of lichen and moss from the flat, spreading branch of a cedar tree ; the first white violets peeping through the grass under a silver birch ; the gift of square magenta-coloured sweets covered with chipped cocoanut presented by Mrs Sadler, the old woman with the chignon (the only one I ever saw), who made such delicious ginger-beer in the correct stone bottles and advertised it by a notice printed outside her cottage, " Ginger Bere sold hear "—all these things were wonderful and exciting.

II.

Our kingdom was the Rectory garden, to us full of enchantment. It consisted of four acres of green and blossoming loveliness, for the most part uncultivated. Slopes of rough grass, amid which wild flowers rioted at their will, ran down from Mummie's rose-beds to the shade of great bordering trees, under whose green gloom cowered and clustered thousands of primroses in spring. Beneath the fairy foliage of silver birches, white violets hid. One side of the garden was bounded by a little tangle of woodland, known as The Wilderness, where wild cherry trees shook snowy plumes of blossom over glades of grass, and wild honeysuckle raced up the red stems of Scots firs and clung to bushes that crowded round their roots. A clump of spreading yew trees, gnarled with age and interlaced by time, formed a haunt of dark mystery where, high up amid the boughs, we children built little secret wigwams.

The Wilderness was a bird sanctuary—indeed, the whole garden was sacred to wild birds—they seemed to know it and built their nests in every shrub and tree. The air was always full of melody and sometimes, at dusk when all the birds had gone to sleep, Mummie would open the drawing-room windows and then improvise haunting music on her piano to wake them into song again. To Daddie's delight this experiment was always successful. One by one the birds began to chirp, then slowly to whistle, until at last they burst into full-throated chorus and sang to her soft accompaniment until her music died away, when theirs ceased also.

Guy knew all the birds by name and note; their habits and their haunts. I loved the nightingale best, and one was kind enough to perch on the silver birch tree opposite my bedroom window and sing his soul out to another in a distant wood. Mine began softly, his song gradually rising into a passionate crescendo of sound before it suddenly ceased and then, throbbing through the moonlit air, stole the reply.

On nights such as this I could not stay indoors. With beating heart I would steal downstairs through the silent house, draw the bolts of the garden door and slip out into that glory of moonlight.

I can still recapture the delicious feeling of cool night air blowing through my curls and caressing my small body under my thin nightdress, and of dew-wet grass tickling my bare feet. How the scent of white lilac and pheasant-eyed narcissus went to my head, and how I envied that nightingale who could so well express this ecstasy of sensation when all a little girl could do was first to stretch wide her arms, as though to embrace all that loveliness, and then begin slowly to sway them and dance in the moonlight.

Down in the shadow of oak and ash, the primroses seemed to me like the pale reflection of the stars above them, robbed of their shining splendour by the glory of the moon. A mysterious rustling in the undergrowth made me pause nervously until I realised that it was but the stirring of some little night beast. The sudden swirl of a white owl across my path caused my heart to stop—and then it would occur to me that, after all, my bed was a safe warm place, and back to it I would scurry.

In the morning, when I told Mummie of my nocturnal adventures, she never scolded me, but sighing: " How I wish I had been there," she would encourage me to describe to her all that I had seen—and felt. One could tell anything to Mummie and be sure of her sympathy and understanding, and no sensation or adventure was ever perfect unless shared with her. She was me, and I was her.

The boys worshipped her too—it really was worship, for she fulfilled all our ideals. She was so lovely to look upon, her voice was so sweet and low, and she was so full of light and laughter ; understanding us all so wonderfully, although our characters and temperaments were absolutely different. If she had not sometimes deliberately hidden herself from us she would never have had a moment's peace. If a new bird's nest had been found, she must know it and see it ; the first snowdrop must be brought to her ; the cat had kittened ; someone had grazed a knee while tree-climbing ; the tadpoles in the rain-water tank had magically become frogs—how ?—why ?—an organ-grinder was coming up the drive, would she come downstairs, bribe him to stay a long time, and herself dance with us on the lawn ?

Her life must have been a very busy one, for not only

had she the care of a rampageous family of her own, but that of the whole village.

Those village mothers came to ours for everything, and she had only to enter a cottage and the stream of family troubles flowed over her. She was godmother to nearly every baby in the parish, and when she left it, years afterwards, her address book and birthday book were crammed from cover to cover with names, addresses, and dates of anniversaries which she never forgot to honour in some way. Visiting the cottages never bored her. She was genuinely fond of the people and took all their sorrows into her own heart, but she extracted a great deal of amusement from their sayings, for she was brimming over with humour; so much so, that when I accompanied her on these visits it was sometimes sheer agony to me.

Those awful eyes of Mummie's looking at me with their brilliant devil-gleam. The loveliest eyes in the world, large, deep-set, and grey, fringed with black lashes under straight black pencilled brows. They missed nothing: they dreamed over things lovely and mysterious, they danced when she was amused; they shone and sparkled when she was excited; they clouded into still, cold pools when she was hurt or disillusioned; and they narrowed and pierced when she was summing up a character or a situation.

She possessed *in excelsis* that rare and indefinable gift of charm. It sparkled in her inviting eyes, it curled in the corners of her laughing mouth, it tantalised from her cheeky little nose; it vibrated and stirred the heart and the imagination in her very beautiful voice. Her sympathy and intuition, which almost amounted to psychic power, attracted people in all walks of life, as did her original points of view. She had so little time for reading that her outlook on life, her philosophy, her criticisms, and her judgment were never tinctured with the opinion of some other, but always intensely her own, and therefore new and arresting. Spiced by continual experience of human nature, her humour, imagination, and her gift of language made her conversation both witty, fascinating, and fresh. She could capture a roomful of people in five minutes without the slightest effort. The dullest and most silent of people blossomed under the sunshine of her smile and her sallies.

Once I found her gathering the loveliest roses in our garden and asked her for whom they were destined.

" That sour-faced woman in the bun-shop in Ipswich," she replied, " I'm sure she looks like that because no one has ever given her flowers. I've *got* to make her smile." Of course she did, and the bun-woman was added to her long list of ' lame-ducks.'

Mummie never went up to London without taking flowers to the woman in charge of the lavatory of the waiting-room in Liverpool Street Station :

" Think of that woman's life. Eternally wiping seats," she said, with eyes clouded by compassion.

It was perhaps her intense interest in humanity that attracted most. She was a wonderful reader of character, and during our annual seaside holiday we would lose her and then find her sitting before the platform of an old phrenologist who was telling character from bumps at 1s. 6d. per head. (I remember that he told mine and covered me with confusion by saying that my large head was really worth 7s. 6d. He also prophesied a literary career for me, and told me that he would be ashamed of me if I did not develop the talent for writing that he swore he felt in one big bump.) Mummie liked to form her own estimation of his clients and then to compare it with his. She was never so happy as when seated amid a holiday crowd on the shore, or waiting for a train at a crowded railway station, where she could study human nature in the mass and speculate about the home-lives of the people around her. Daddie once said to her—

" In spite of your love of the beautiful, I verily believe that you'd prefer to visit a London slum rather than the finest cathedral."

"Certainly I would," she answered quickly, "the present interests me a great deal more than the past; and live things more than dead things."

When I think of Mummie's training of her daughters I realise how wise she was. Marjory and I adored dolls, and at one moment I possessed a family of eighteen. Mummie encouraged this maternal passion in every possible way, helping us to make clothes for them; decorating wicker cradles with muslin, lace, and ribbon; furnishing baby-baskets with everything needful for a new-born babe. She even dictated to us a list of all the medical and practical requirements for an *accouchement* at home, and my list, written in the large and laborious handwriting of a little girl of seven or eight years old, is in my possession still.

We were taught how to bathe a baby, protecting its head with an encircling arm; how to lift it out of the bath, to powder it in all the cracks and creases and then to dress it correctly, putting on its little belly-binder with a hand under it next to the baby's tumpkin so that the safety-pin fastener could not accidentally pierce it. We were instructed in the art of folding little napkins, and warned that if we did not attend to our babies at intervals those napkins would get soaked.

It was all very real to us, and if we forgot our mother-duties while romping with the boys, Mummie would put her head round the schoolroom door and say warningly—

" I can hear those babies of yours screaming in the nursery. Have you forgotten to change them?" And we would rush upstairs, conscience-stricken, to find our baby dolls lying with great tears on their cheeks—drops of glycerine placed there by Mummie, but to us neglectful mothers, real tears.

When she considered that our babies were old enough

to be vaccinated, she secretly scratched four little marks on their left arms and painted slightly inflamed circles around them. Then we were taught how to bandage the sore places.

All this early training was in preparation for the day when she hoped that we should become mothers of live babies, and I had no other ambition. When asked what I intended to be when I grew up, my reply was always " A mother," and I followed it up in my loquacious way by confiding to my questioner the fact that I intended to have a family of at least eighteen children, and that I should arrange to have them in pairs, or, better still, in triplets, so as to get them the quicker.

III.

From very early days I had a clear picture of the man I should marry, and even knew his name and profession. His name was John ; he was very tall and thin and he had beautiful long fingers and tiny ears. He was a writer of books.

" What kind of books, my Fairy ? " asked Daddie during one of our cosy conversations before the fire in his study where I had somehow insinuated my small person.

" Lesson books," was my prompt and invariable reply.

One could confide in Daddie, sure that he would never laugh at childish dreams and ambitions. Whatever mood he might be in—and he was a moody man—we knew that we could tell him anything, ask him everything, and never fear a snub ; and as we grew up this perfect confidence between us all increased. Before he was ordained priest he had travelled (with his mother) twice around the world, so that he knew the ways of men and was a man of the world as well as a man of God. When changed circumstances made travel impossible, he was obliged to find adventure and the stir of life in books, and these made supportable the life of a country parish. We knew when the *wanderlust* came upon him, for he would read almost savagely ; his great dark eyes would flicker restlessly about him like those of a caged animal ; he became very silent, and would go for long solitary walks. He was a strikingly handsome man, a dark Roman type, with a big powerful frame. At Oxford he had been a noted oar, and he knew how to use the gloves (his own pair were proudly stained with the gore punched from the nose of his instructor), but, although an athlete, he was also a scholar, and he loved the country and country folk, so that he found happiness in his little Suffolk parish with the wife and children he so deeply loved.

Although ' the Rectory children ' we were never over-dosed with church. Daddie liked us to attend one service each Sunday, but he never insisted upon this ; nor were we forced to attend family prayers.

Our pew in the chancel of the church was originally in line with the reading-desk, and because we, in our very early youth, were apt to communicate our impressions of both service and congregation, in pantomime, to friends in pews exactly opposite, it was suggested that during the prayers we should kneel with our backs to the audience, so to speak. Finding the contemplation of a stuffed cushion covered with red baize very boring one day, I decided that, sheltered by the tall oak pew, I could safely crawl along the floor on hands and knees and pay a visit to Daddie in his reading-desk.

This I did with great success, and I think he showed remarkable self-control to continue the prayer he was reading without a pause when suddenly confronted by the shining eyes of his elder daughter laughing up at him from below. A hand stole down to stroke my head and, after this little touch of familiar intimacy, I crawled happily back again.

Mummie was unluckily out of reach, perched up on the organ-seat at the west end of the church. She was a fine musician and her great instrument was the organ. Often she would go on playing dreamily to herself after the out-going voluntary, forgetting time in harmony until startled back to the realities of life by the anxious head of old Jimmy Waters, the organ-blower, whose eyes would perhaps peer round at her with a comically pathetic expression as he puffed out his cheeks exhaustedly; or by the hoarse whisper of some farmer's son saying, " Please mum, mother says you can 'ave a chickun for Wen'sday." Then she would close the organ lid with a snap and, controlling her temper marvellously, would dismiss old Jimmy with smiling thanks or give a polite reply to the farmer's son.

If Mummie and I exchanged glances during the service, as we frequently did, I had to look across a sea of faces in the nave. Old Jimmy would sometimes pop his head round the organ and nod and smile at ' Miss Winnie.' He could do it unperceived, except perhaps by Mummie, whereas if I returned his salutation all the world could see me do it, which was unfair, for I loved old Jimmy and wanted him to know it.

I disliked the publicity of that seat in the chancel, for nothing that happened in the Rectory pew could pass unobserved. When Daddie got a bee in his ear, as once he did when a swarm settled in the chancel roof, all the congregation saw him rush down from the altar to seek the ministrations of Mervyn who extracted it without accident. Mervyn was also seen by all men when, returned from a long absence abroad, he settled down in his corner to listen to Daddie's sermon and absent-mindedly took out his cigarette-case, selected a cigarette and just *didn't* light it, recalled to his surroundings and the enormity of his behaviour by a frantic dig from my sharp elbow-point. Then there was the scandal of Marjory's half-crown—a prized Christmas tip which she accidentally placed in the offertory bag instead of the weekly penny, and then, to the consternation of the kindly church-warden, tried frantically to retrieve. We dared not suck sweets during the service, having been made wary by Mervyn's detection in the chapel choir of his preparatory school. He had been caught in the act, and only the affectionate mediation of the Matron, who had a weakness for demons, and who pleaded to the Headmaster that Mervyn had "sucked them so reverently," saved him from justice.

Those kind of things did not shock Daddie, personally, at all, but he maintained that no man should shock his neighbour. He saw no harm in our playing lawn tennis or dancing on Sundays—healthy exercise of which he approved, but he made the condition that if we did these things we must do them in some place where we should be invisible to his parishioners who might not share his views. In this he was far ahead of his time, and so was Mummie. For instance, she always reserved the most delightful picture-books, our best dolls, the most exciting games, and the most delicious food for Sunday, so that we really thought of it as a feast day instead of dreading it as did most children of our generation.

Of all the Church festivals I loved Easter best, and, curiously enough, all the chief events of my life have taken place at Easter. I was christened, confirmed, and married at Easter.

The Easter services of my childhood remain in my memory, fragrant as the lilies with which my beloved godmother (the wife of our Squire) decked the altar. Into her work she put the love of her soul, so that the flowers she touched so tenderly became emblems and symbols. I see across the years a rocky moss-lined cave in which lies a cross of hyacinths—the empty tomb—the triumphant empty cross—Easter.

We all went to the early Celebration ; walking under a long avenue of blossoming limes in which one heard 'the murmuring of innumerable bees,' and from the chancel, where we sat, we would see through the open door red squirrels racing and jumping among the branches. Once a rioting mob of young horses stampeded into the churchyard during the service, and I saw gleaming eyes, dilated nostrils, tossing manes and flying fetlocks as they shook happy heads and heels in the fresh morning air, glorious Suffolk Punches broken through the hedge of a neighbouring field.

Daddie's beautiful resonant voice, murmuring the consolatory sentences, would recall me to that most moving of all services, though the joyous beasts without had but enabled me to repeat the General Thanksgiving more fervently. When I walked up to the altar-rails, to kneel as close as I could get to Mummie, the service would have been to me neither so happy nor so holy had I missed the secret pressure of Daddie's hand on mine as he gave me the chalice.

Everyone in the parish looked forward to the annual Harvest Festival, called by Daddie the Harvestival, when our lovely little church was decorated with flaming early autumn leaves, fat vegetables, and tempting fruits.

How that congregation of 'old simples' roared out those harvest hymns of thanksgiving, their faces red and shining as the rosy apples from their orchards, given to the church with their best samples of produce to the glory of God—and perhaps, a little bit, to their own ?

In my life I have attended many services, in cathedrals, in London churches, in Royal Chapels, but never again have I felt that inner happiness, that perfect sense of satisfaction, that oneness with the other worshippers that I always experienced in our little Suffolk church. Always I must miss Mummie's wonderful music ; the straight sincerity of Daddie's sermons and the surrounding faces of old friends, rich and poor, who loved them and their children.

Daddie's sermons never lasted for more than ten

minutes, and were practical and full of wisdom. He never preached at his people, but talked to them as man to man, speaking of himself as the most erring of them all ; telling them that he had greater need than they of the Divine forgiveness. He was so humble of heart ; so human, and so humorous. Once he preached a sermon on prejudice, taking as his text—

> " I do not love thee, Doctor Fell,
> The reason why I cannot tell,
> But this alone I know full well,
> I do not love thee, Doctor Fell."

yet no one giggled as he repeated that unconventional text.

The women of the parish admired him not only for his exceptional good looks, but for his great physical strength ; and the men respected him for it. He would roll up his sleeves and go forth into the village to tackle a drunken bully who was ill-treating his wife. No wonder the boys of the village adored him. He invited them to spend one evening a week with him, when he kept them all enthralled with his tales of foreign countries, the adventures and escapades of his youth, and made the Rectory ring with hearty boyish laughter. Not one of ' his lads,' as he called them, but turned out well. His study was filled with their portraits, and those of their wives and babies in after-life, sent from all parts of the world, for into many of his boys he instilled his own desire to travel, and they went into the Army or Navy and some became Colonists.

Daddie delighted in the Suffolk character, indignantly correcting anyone who spoke of ' Silly Suffolk.'

" *Seelig* Suffolk—*holy* Suffolk, because it contains so many churches," he would explain ; and then gleefully recount the story of the supercilious Londoner who, when staying with a friend in Suffolk, said to him—

" Now you hear me make a fool of that yokel there."

Walking up to a man working in a field, he said to him—

" Look here, my man, would you like to take a fool's situation ? "

Without a blink, the Suffolk labourer replied : " Be yew out of place ? Or dew they want tew where yew be ? " Typical of Suffolk humour.

Daddie never sat in judgment on his fellow-men, being ' humble in his own eyes ' ; and perhaps therein lay the secret of the great influence he gained over his parishioners.

Never was pastor more beloved. He was, as I have said, a much-travelled man, and his experience enabled him to understand the many problems brought to him to solve. His sense of humour endeared him to all, and his laugh echoes still in the hearts of many. Few, if any, of his parishioners can have realised that he was cursed with a morbidly active imagination (bequeathed to me), and was consequently of a nervous and apprehensive temperament ; and Mummie's clear conviction that everything is ordered for the best—her selfless service for others, her faith in humanity, and her unvarying serenity and joyousness—were exactly what he needed to steady that anxious mind and to illumine his dark hours. He worshipped the ground she trod, and used to say that she was his strongest argument for Christianity. Mummie and Daddie were lovers till the very end, writing to each other every day during their rare periods of separation ; sharing every great or trivial joy or sorrow ; never really happy unless they were together. They married young, Daddie being only twenty-four and Mummie twenty-two, so that they grew up with their children. An old servant of the family told me that to see Mummie's little girlish figure lying on the lawn, her lion's mane of hair flying loose and gleaming in the sunlight, while her babies rolled over her like obstreperous puppies, and the look in Daddie's eyes as he watched her, was the loveliest sight she ever saw.

As I grew into my teens, their great love used to torment me lest I should never find a like blessedness.

IV.

Always I was haunted by the vision of one man—the
' John ' of my dreams—but did he exist ?   And if he
were indeed as real as he seemed to me, how would he
ever find me, hidden away in this little country village ?
Perhaps it would be necessary for me to go out into the
world to find him.   Always I was looking for him—if I
saw a strange man approaching me in one of our country
lanes, my heart jumped in case it might be He.   When
a party of strangers entered our church, my eager eyes
scanned their faces to see if one among them resembled
my dream-picture of the man I should one day marry ;
if I were invited to a luncheon-party or to a dance, my
excitement was intensified by the hope that to-day I
might see him.   From a large Newfoundland-puppy of a
child, I had grown tall very quickly, and looked far older
than my age at fourteen, when I received my first proposal from an enormous German baron who was learning
farming in the parish.   He was a Saxon of very old family,
and so terribly home-sick that he did no work at all and
practically lived in our Rectory.   Somehow we children
understood him, and contrived to make ourselves understood by him, although, at first, he could not speak a word
of English nor we of German.   I was so sorry for the great
home-sick lump that I suffered his society more patiently
than did my brothers or sister until he became sentimental,
and therefore boring and odious to me.

One day he pursued Mummie into the garden where
she was gathering *Maréchal Niel* roses.

By this time the Baron had learned enough English
to make himself understood, and seizing Mummie's hand
he poured forth guttural protestations of his passion
for me and implored her to give consent to our betrothal.
Mummie could only repeat, " No !   Too young.   No !
No !   Too young "; whereupon the giant broke into

noisy sobs, huge German tears flowing down into his blonde moustache as he bowed his head on her shoulder. Mummie, who had an uncomfortably keen sense of the ridiculous, wondered what the gardener would think should he find a giant German weeping upon the shoulder of the Rector's wife. So, patting the unhappy Teuton in a motherly manner, she presented him with a yellow rose-bud and fled.

After that our moon-struck Baron entirely deserted the farm where he was supposed to be studying agriculture, and daily haunted the Rectory where he followed me about like a great dog, or sat staring at me with eyes that constantly filled with tears. I couldn't imagine what was wrong with the man and grew to hate the sight of him.

Then one day a letter came to my father from the parents of our Baron, saying that their son had told them of his desire to marry me and giving their willing consent to our union. The Baroness, his mother, suggested that I should first go to Germany and live with her for a year or two in order that I might learn practical housekeeping and the management of the Schloss, and she enclosed photographs of an enormous moated castle set amid acres of beautiful trees. She could not resist remarking that German women were known to be more expert in housewifery than were the English, and that it would be well for the future Baroness to be trained early in her duties.

The air of assurance breathed in this gracious and generous letter infuriated my little Mother as much as it amused and delighted my Father—so they told me years later. At the time I was kept in ignorance of the honour conferred upon me. The immediate result of it was that, through the influence of Daddie, the lovesick Baron was transferred to a Southern English watering-place to complete his study of our language. Daddie escorted him as far as London and returned, fuming, because in the presence of a row of snickering porters, our Baron had kissed him noisily upon both cheeks in farewell. I can see Daddie now, rubbing his cheeks with his sleeve, his dark eyes blazing with indignation as he exclaimed disgustedly to us on his return, " The feller KISSED me."

That farm at our gates was an unceasing source of trouble, for a succession of pupils came there, inevitably strolled up our drive, and, having nothing else save turnips and livestock to occupy their minds, became foolish about me.

Luckily I was well used to the society of men and boys. The house was always full of my brothers' school friends and, later, their College friends, and, at the age of nine, I had been sent with Guy to school which a friend of Daddie's inaugurated on the Kent coast. We were the first pupils, but very soon a mob of boys flowed in, and, although I was really under the care of the Matron (sister of the Headmaster) and slept in her room, I was educated with the boys. I had my hair pulled—and pulled *hard*—if I 'told tales'; when we played cricket on the sands I was made to field and never allowed to bat, because I was of the inferior sex ; and I learned to settle differences of opinion with my fists—far better and healthier than being obliged to resort to the weapon of the tongue, which is used with such unhappy results in seminaries for young ladies.

And so, when I reached my teens, the attentions of men rather disgusted me than otherwise. I preferred the company of men and boys until they became sentimental and ruined our happy comradeship. Then they bored and irritated me.

Mummie must have had a vast amount of amusement out of my various affairs, for I always rushed straight to her and poured forth every detail of each day's adventures, and her light mockery, or a sudden biting criticism, was very salutary at times.

At about this time I outgrew my strength and became

anæmic and languid, so that I was educated at home, music and painting masters coming out from Ipswich to instruct me, and a perky little Frenchwoman to teach me French. I also had cooking and dressmaking lessons, Mummie having previously conquered my early aversion to needlework of any kind. At my first (girls') school I was given a dreary piece of calico to hem, which was so stiff that first the thread broke, then I pricked my finger and covered my work with gore, and, finally, the needle snapped in two leaving the small sempstress in a state of suppressed pain and rage. Mummie brought some rich rose-pink silk, soft to the touch and lustrous to the eye, and an elaborate blouse-pattern with forty-eight tiny tucks to control the fulness. These she presented to me saying, " Now make yourself the loveliest blouse with this silk. I will show you how to cut it out."

When I had finished the forty-eighth tuck and was the proud wearer of a really dainty blouse of my own making, Mummie had converted me into a needlewoman and had at the same time implanted in me a desire to make my own clothes.

Marjory was always an orderly little girl, but I was the untidiest child in the world. My bedroom always looked like a jumble sale before the various items are priced and arranged. It was Mummie's despair, and no amount of gentle remonstrance had any lasting effect. Then one day she had an inspiration. She told Marjory and me that we might re-decorate our bedrooms to suit our own individual tastes, choosing the colour of our walls and making our curtains and cushion-covers ourselves.

From the moment my room was re-decorated by myself, no servant was ever allowed to enter it. No maid could, I thought, arrange my cushions on the bed in an artistic way. In future my bedroom was the tidiest in the house. Pride of possession had cured me of my disorderly habits. Mummie had gained her point—in fact, more points than she perhaps realised at the time, for, besides correcting my untidiness, she roused in me a latent passion for house-decoration and also stimulated an interest in period furniture which was to be of great service to me in the future.

Mummie also encouraged my love of scribbling by giving me fascinating subjects to write about in competition with her, and she made me arrange colour-schemes of flowers and leaves to decorate the dining-room table. To her, I owe any success that I have had in colour-combination and design. Her taste was ever more original and striking than mine. Her arrangement of flowers was so individual that one could always recognise her touch. The only talent in me that she failed to foster, and even paralysed slightly, was that of music. She was such a wonderful musician herself that, when she heard her daughter strike a false note on the piano, she would cry out in pain from the top of the house : " *No*, darling ! *Not* G sharp—F sharp," and make me so nervous that there would follow a stream of accidentals.

Mummie must have suffered much from her gift of music, for to her fell the task of training a crude country choir—the Suffolk people are not musical—and of playing the accompaniments for village songsters when our next-door neighbour, dear Admiral Aldrich, organised monthly concerts which were held in the village Recreation Room during the winter. How well I remember those rehearsals held in our Rectory schoolroom ; and those rumpty-tumpty accompaniments to the comic songs which had to be repeated, sometimes twenty times, until the singer removed his collar the better to reach a high note. Mummie got the maddening tunes so badly on the brain that she was unable to sleep, and would go downstairs to her piano in the small hours to play them out of her head. But the villagers loved those concerts so much that it was worth the agony ; the walls streamed with condensed heat, and the light from the swinging oil-lamps shone down upon the beaming rubicund faces of familiar friends who stamped their applause until one wondered if the floor-boards could withstand so much enthusiasm.

From very early days ' Miss Winnie ' was expected to recite to this appreciative audience who thought her amateur efforts marvels of talent.

Daddie gave humorous readings, Marjory danced horn-pipes and Irish jigs learned at her dancing-class ; the Admiral sang ballads in a sweet tenor voice ; really good orchestral music and solos were played by the Downing family, Mrs Downing at the piano, Maud with a violin, Dolly with her viola and Jessie with her 'cello.

Most of the audience did not understand good music, and the village lads at the back of the room were apt to converse with the village lasses during these numbers, and, at the conclusion of a very lovely violin solo played by Maud Downing, her mother closed the piano with a bang and remarked with an acid smile : " Maud tried to play as softly as possible so as not to interrupt the talking."

The village talent was always the most popular, the children, who acted little plays and sang choruses ; the local falsetto quavering forth his love-ballads ; the baritone singing his hunting-songs ; the fat comic bass roaring his absurdities ; and an old sailor who sang sea-chanties.

I wonder if the young people of this twentieth century with their cocktail-parties, their restless life of social activities succeeding one another so rapidly that it seems to me they can only become a bore and can never be appreciated, are as happy in their lives of hectic independ-ance as we were in ours of sheltered peace and few events ? For ours *was* a wonderful youth. As I look back upon it, I cannot remember one sole instance of injustice or unkindness from either Daddie or Mummie. They lived for their children, and we shall never know what personal sacrifices they made for our welfare and happiness. Although by my grandfather's ruin, money had become

scarce, they never refused us if they could possibly consent
when we begged to be allowed to accept invitations to
dances or *festas* of any kind, although, living in the depths
of the country and having no horse or carriage, it was
necessary to hire a cab to convey us to those distant
destinations.

What fun those long drives were in that fusty four-
wheeler smelling of stables and damp leather ; all of us
in uproarious spirits, the boys very smart in their evening
clothes, and Marjory and I, our pretty 'party frocks'
enveloped in shawls. It was very difficult to time one's
arrival at the right moment, for occasionally we were
provided with an ancient hack which could hardly breast
the hills, poor beast, and we feared to be late. Sometimes
we were supplied with a more spirited animal, and then
we risked premature arrival. On one occasion we reached
the house where a dance was being held at least twenty
minutes before we were expected, in spite of Mervyn's
reiterated warnings to our red-nosed driver that we had
plenty of time to spare, and that he need not drive so
fast. I remember now, with a wave of heat up the spine
whenever I recall it, being ushered by a footman into
a large empty drawing-room after we had removed our
wraps, and sitting there, silent and self-conscious, until
our very elegant hostess appeared, greeting us with the
remark—

" I am *so* sorry I was not here to receive you, but I
never expect my guests before they are asked."

Daddie, who was a wonderful dancer, loved to accompany us to our parties, and he was always besieged by
all the prettiest girls in the room, who clamoured for a
waltz with him. I always claimed the first waltz of the
evening with Daddie, for I adored dancing, and he had
taught us all to waltz with a tumbler filled with water
on our heads—an excellent way to ensure smoothness
of motion, for a *douche* of cold water down the neck is
unpleasant. Mummie could never dance without becoming

28

giddy, and so it was Daddie who chaperoned us when Mervyn was not at home.

The problem would always have been clothes, but Mummie was so clever about them that in our case it never arose. For young girls, she believed in quantity rather than quality; and she supplied the village dress-maker with her own simple and charming designs for our summer frocks and a mass of soft washing materials of various pastel shades. These she would vary with different coloured sashes, or petticoats of contrasting shades to be worn under a filmy transparent chiffon. She bought me one really good shady straw hat, and then taught me to trim it myself with *real* flowers from our garden, wrapping damp cotton-wool, hidden by green oiled silk, around the stalks and then hiding these refresh-ing bandages by skilful arrangement of sprays of leaves.

Mummie's invention enabled me to seem the proud possessor of many pretty hats, and few could have guessed that I wore the same old one, bent into different shapes and trimmed with fresh flowers, for every occasion. There was no end to the variations one could have, and youthful vanity stimulated the imagination.

V.

An advertisement in the Personal column of ' The Times ' changed the even tenor of my life. I was then, as I have said, being educated at home, having outgrown my strength. Guy was in London at Westminster School, and Marjory was being governessed at home, sharing her lessons with other children of her own age who lived in the neighbourhood. She was too young, as yet, to be companionable to me, and Mummie and Daddie were always happy together. Sometimes I felt lonely and dissatisfied, and, having been born with a receptive mind and an insatiable curiosity about everything in life, I longed to inform that mind and to appease that curiosity. Our old family doctor told my parents that my languor and anæmic condition came from intellectual starvation. He was of opinion that if I were sent to school again, where I should have companions of my own age and healthy competition in my studies, I should become my cheerful active self once more.

It was then that Mummie read the fateful advertisement. It stated that a certain girls' school of high reputation had a vacancy for one pupil who would be expected to work with girls of seventeen and eighteen. If her references were satisfactory, this pupil would be educated free of all charges save the usual extras. She would be required to start her school year on such and such a date. A personal interview would, of course, be necessary.

Adventurous always, Mummie seized her pen and answered this advertisement on my behalf, enclosing nice solid references. She told none of us what she had done and proceeded patiently to await results—if any. After two weeks of waiting her letter was answered. The delay was explained by the fact that the advertisers had been inundated by hundreds of applicants for this generous offer of free education, and the process of elimination had been slow. I suppose Mummie had unconsciously expressed her charm and delicious personality in her letter, and they had decided that her daughter might be worthy of this vacancy in their school. Anyway an interview was arranged forthwith and Mummie and I travelled up to London. Apparently after being weighed in the balances, I was not found wanting, for, to my great joy, I soon found myself one of the pupils of the Old Cedar House school in Slough—a quaint old-world house with a green garden shaded by spreading cedar trees, bounded on one side by the Bath Road.

There were not at that time a great many girls in the school, but all were delightful. The senior girls with whom I must work were older and far more advanced

than I, and I found that I should have to study very
hard to catch up with them. But my pride was touched
and I determined to slave until I got level, and so I used
to secrete my lesson-books under my pillow at night ;
never drew the curtain of my east window so that the
first light of dawn should waken me, and then, tying a
wet towel round my head I mugged at my books every
morning before the other girls in my dormitory awoke.
I was so happy at the Old Cedar House that my one fear
was that I might be deemed unequal to the work of the
seniors and be sent home again.

The two sister-owners of that school were wonderful
to me. They never breathed the fact that I was a ' free '
pupil. I was treated exactly like the other girls—if
anything I was more indulged. The elder sister occupied
herself only with the domestic management of the school ;
the younger sister undertook the artistic side of our
education, being herself an exceptionally fine technical
musician with a strong literary gift. On our Saturday
half-holidays we were taken to Windsor to do our shopping
and have tea in Fuller's shop, opposite the great grey
Castle which thrilled me every time I saw it, as did the
services in St George's Chapel to which we were sometimes taken as a great treat.

It was arranged that some of us should attend the
Oxford Extension lectures being held at Eton during the
autumn. The lecturer was Mr Ashe King, who came down
from London once a week. His lectures were open to
schools and to the general public, and the hall was packed
when we schoolgirls filed into it. He was to give a series
of lectures on the English essayists, starting with Pope,
and he quoted freely from the Essay on Criticism. At
the end of the first lecture he asked us each to write an
essay for his criticism, choosing for our subject anything
suggested to us by his lecture.

I went back to the Cedar House with my head seething
with ideas. Ever since childhood I had always been

scribbling, inventing silly fairy-tales, describing things that interested me, filling up exercise books, scrawling on the backs of envelopes—little futilities that amused and interested only myself and were seldom finished. Now I was to write my first serious essay, in competition with dozens of other girls and a mob of grown-up people of both sexes, and what I wrote would be criticised by a famous Oxford lecturer. I started composing my essay (in my head) during supper, and was teased for my absent-mindedness by my companions. I continued, as I undressed in the dormitory, oblivious of place and time until suddenly brought back to earth by the sharp voice of the head girl who asked me if I intended to go on brushing my teeth in the moonlight all night.

I chose 'Criticism' as my subject, and in my essay made the rather priggish pronouncement that " a critic should be a judge, not a prosecuting counsel." The essay was short, after much time had been expended in its condensation. I carried it to the lecture hall with me the following week and shyly laid it with a great pile of like manuscripts upon the desk of Mr Ashe King.

He opened his next lecture by announcing that he had read all the essays submitted to him and that he was proud to say that the best essay had been written and the highest marks obtained " by a baby of sixteen years old." He proposed, after to-day's lecture, to make a tour of the hall and to criticise each essay with its writer. My heart throbbed as I thought how wonderful it would be to find oneself that proud " baby of sixteen." My age was sixteen, but surely, surely, she couldn't be me. An usher came round and handed us back our manuscripts. On mine was written *A.* + *Excellent*, and when Mr Ashe King reached my side he peered over my shoulder at my essay, then gave me a resounding slap on the back and called aloud, " Ah ! *here* is my clever baby of sixteen." An awful blush flowed up from my heels to my head, and all I could do at that joyful moment was to stare up at our lecturer with shining eyes. He smiled very kindly and said, " I've found a future writer. When you send me your first book I'll give it such a slap-up review. Go on, my child, and prosper." I do not know if Mr Ashe King is still alive, or if he knows that his "baby of sixteen" ever did produce a book; but it was he who watered the seed of literary desire already sown by an old phrenologist on the sea-shore.

Another great excitement for me was when we seniors were taken up to London to see a Shakespearean play. We were asked to study it beforehand, and its beauty of words and of construction were pointed out to us before we saw it acted by famous actors and actresses. The school was very proud of its acting reputation, and the Cedar House girls got up duologues and little plays which they acted for the benefit of local charities. Always I was given a lovely part, and I revelled in it.

When the school was removed to Wentworth Hall, Mill Hill, and I went with it, our Dramatic Classes were conducted by Miss Elsie Fogerty, who came down from London once a week to teach us Elocution and who soon put me in charge of the Voice Production Practice and gave me important parts in the scenes we studied with her.

At the end of the summer term we played Mr Robert Bridges's " Achilles in Scyros " in the gardens of Wentworth Hall, and I was cast for the Goddess Thetis, wore a long Greek robe and a golden crown; declaimed my blank verse to an audience of parents and visitors, and was 'noticed' by the local newspaper, which stated that " as the Goddess Thetis, Miss Winifred *Bust* was great." I never heard the end of this muddle of my name, for, when in my teens, the villagers at home described me, to my shame and fury, as " a buxom young lady." I felt that no more loathesome adjective could be applied to me, for always I had longed for a sexless willowy figure, and hated curves.

33

I left Wentworth Hall with a very real sorrow and gratitude in my heart.

I was now ' the finished article '—planed and chiselled with some of its angles rounded off, only lacking French polish. There was a talk of sending me abroad to acquire this, but, just at that moment, an old friend of Daddie's, Humphrey Cotton Minchin, who was then Rector of Woodstock and private chaplain to the Duke of Marlborough at Blenheim, fell ill and was ordered a complete rest. The Duke begged him to find someone suitable to take his work during this enforced absence, and Mr Minchin wrote to Daddie imploring him to fill his place for a few months. Guy was then at Oxford—that dear place where Daddie had left part of his heart—and I had finished with schooling for ever. Daddie and Mummie discussed this proposal, and she persuaded him to accept. It would be good for Guy to be able to come over to us when he liked, and for Daddie to go over to see him in Oxford, besides which, the change of place and life would enlarge my horizon. And so a *locum tenens* was found to take charge of Great Bealings while Daddie was away, and we all went to Woodstock. We found ourselves in an ancient grey-walled Rectory overlooking beautiful Blenheim Park with its quiet lake and great Palace of stone. From the moment of arrival I peered out of the wide drawing-room window hoping always to catch a glimpse of the famous American Duchess, ' Consuelo,' riding or driving by. I had heard of her so often from Mervyn and Guy who had seen her frequently in Oxford and who had both fallen instantly in love with her piquante oval face perched upon a long slender neck, her enormous dark eyes fringed with curling lashes, her dimples, and her tiny teeth when she smiled. When I did see her for the first time, riding past the Rectory on a beautiful chestnut accompanied by the Duke's agent, Mr Angas, I also fell an instant victim to her beauty and her smile. For, turning her head in my direction, she caught sight of my eager face, dimpled and smiled, then spoke to her escort who raised his whip in salute of me before replying to the Duchess. She was gone in a flash leaving me hungry to see her again.

That evening, Mr Angas came to visit us and told me that the Duchess had seen me at the window and had asked who I was. " Oh, that's the little Beech-Nut," he had replied, and had then described our family. When she returned to the Palace she forthwith wrote a letter inviting us all to tea with her and suggesting that any of us who played lawn tennis should bring their racquets.

That was the beginning of a new era for me. As I walked up those endless steps to the grand entrance of the Palace I felt that I was walking straight into a fairy-story. Not even those terrifying powdered footmen, who somehow sensed our approach when yet we were afar off, flung open the great doors and then stood at attention like the Fish and Frog Footmen in ' Alice in Wonderland,' could entirely daunt me. Mummie refreshed us by whispering, " If I had only thought of it we could all have been roped together like Alpine climbers before making this alarming ascent." Which remark reduced us all to a painful state of repressed mirth.

It was an afternoon of enchantment for me. Never before had I seen anyone so lovely, so exquisitely dressed, so perfectly simple and sweet despite her great possessions as was this wonderful Duchess.

It was at Woodstock that I overheard Daddie tell Mummie that he wondered how he would be able to afford to go on paying Guy's Oxford fees. Ever since leaving Wentworth Hall I had longed to go out into the world and to earn my living, as secretary or companion— there were not many professions open to women at that time—and so ease the situation at home. But I had no idea how to get started. This sad little conversation decided me to speak to Daddie about it, and then suddenly

I had a brilliant inspiration. I would consult the Duchess about this. She would surely be able to help me—she might even need a private secretary herself. Quickly I sat down and wrote her a letter asking if I might go to see her on private business, and then I waited, palpitating, for her reply. I did not have to wait long. Half an hour later she answered my letter in person, driving up to the Rectory in her electric car, entering the drawing-room and saying simply : " You wanted to see me, Winifred, and so I thought I had better come at once."

What other woman, save only Mummie, would have done as much for a ' flapper ' of seventeen ?

I poured forth my aspirations in a cataract and she listened, smiling sympathetically as I explained my desire to help, to work, to be independent.

" How old are you, Winifred ? "

" Seventeen."

" That seems to me very young to leave your home."

" But she is an *old* seventeen," put in Mummie, loyally backing me up.

The Duchess dimpled and said nothing.

" I thought that perhaps I could be someone's companion or secretary," I suggested, desperately.

" The trouble is that married people have each other, and it is generally only old people or sour old maids who need companions. That would be far too dull and sad for you," answered the Duchess gently, " and you have had no training—have you ?—in shorthand and typewriting, which are part of a secretary's equipment. My secretary is a very learned person and I am terrified of her." So she *had* a secretary.

There followed a despairing silence. My golden dream was fading away. I had no qualifications for any job. I was too disgustingly young and inexperienced. Evidently seeing the look of tragedy in my eyes, the Duchess suddenly made a remarkable suggestion : " Have you ever thought of entering ' the profession.' " She asked me with mock gravity.

" The profession ? " I echoed vaguely, but with hope in my heart.

" I understand that that is the popular name for a stage career," said the Duchess. " I have heard from Mr Angas that you recite very well. You have a good voice and appearance, and I should think it might be a very interesting life."

Mummie's eyes grew suddenly dark.

" Would you dislike it very much for your daughter ? " asked the Duchess turning diffidently to her. " I have a house in London. Perhaps Winifred could stay with me or lodge near me, and I could keep an eye on her," she suggested. " Think it over, Winifred, and talk to your parents and then tell me what you think." A waft of fragrance as she bent and kissed me, and she was gone, leaving me with a hammering heart and a brain on fire. This new idea was discussed for days. Daddie and Mummie were, as always, wonderful. Knowing the prejudice that then existed against the stage and the adverse criticism they would probably have to bear if they consented to this experiment, they yet kept open minds, and were ready to let me make inquiries about Tree's Academy of Dramatic Art, where I could be trained as an actress. I wrote for the prospectus, and from it I learned that I should be obliged to pass an entrance examination. At once I wrote to Miss Elsie Fogerty, begging her to coach me in the prose and poetry I should have to declaim before the judges.

Her answer surprised and delighted me—

" Why, oh why, go to Tree's ? " she began, and then most unexpectedly went on to say that I had much better enter F. R. Benson's Dramatic School, of which *she* was President, and study with my old mistress. Until then I had no idea that Miss Fogerty was connected with any school of acting, and the prospect of working under

her supervision robbed the new adventure of half its
strangeness and gave Daddie and Mummie, who knew
and respected her, great confidence.

I went up to London with Mummie to see Miss Fogerty
at the Albert Hall where the London branch of the Benson
School held its classes. She greeted me with a very kind
enthusiasm, and told Mummie in parting that I " had
every gift for success which ought to make my stage
career a brilliant one "—then added, in parenthesis—" *if*
she doesn't marry first."

I learned that I should have lessons in Voice Production
from the famous Professor Hulbert (father of the versatile
Claude of to-day), dancing lessons from Theodore Gilmer,
who taught the Empire ballet, fencing lessons from a
renowned Frenchman, Elocution lessons from herself,
and be trained to act by Paul Berton, an ex-stage-manager
of Frank Benson who, himself, examined the students at
the end of every term.

As Miss Fogerty already knew my work, an entrance
examination would be unnecessary. The term started
in six weeks' time, and, if I decided to enter the School,
all I had now to do was to arrange where to live in London.
I positively skipped out of the Albert Hall, and I think
Mummie, although, in her heart, she must have had secret
qualms, was almost as excited as I.

Daddie, always nervous and apprehensive, was nevertheless swept along by my wild enthusiasm, backed up
by Mummie's steady encouragement. When he dreaded
the dangers to which a young and inexperienced girl
would be a prey in London, Mummie reminded him of
the Duchess's promise to keep an eye on me ; of Miss
Fogerty's daily supervision ; and suggested that it would
be easy to find among our many friends someone who
would take me in as a paying guest and act as chaperone
during my hours of liberty and leisure.

VI.

At length it was decided that I should lodge in London in the flat of a sister of a friend of Daddie's, a Miss Susie Sonnenschein, who lived in High Street, Marylebone. She was of just the right age, neither too old nor too young, and was quite ready to take me in.

Naturally I was thrilled with this arrangement, and when at last I was in London I lived in a state of joyous excitement. I almost danced along the London pavements and constantly got myself into embarrassing situations because I invariably beamed back gratefully at any man who smiled at me. I thought it so nice of them to do it, and I felt a little flush of power run up my spine when they looked at me—and sometimes looked again. I enjoyed my rehearsal classes, at the Albert Hall, after my first humiliating test before the formidable Paul Berton. I was placed alone upon the platform of the little Albert Hall theatre at the top of the building and asked to recite something to him and the assembled students. All I could think of in my panic was some deadly serious ' poem ' learned as a child about a lifeboat going out to a rescue and the misery of the women left behind. I had recited it, with gestures, at various village concerts, had gained uproarious applause, and been told that I was a born actress, but somehow I realised that it wasn't likely to have a success with this new type of audience. However, with knocking knees, and a parched mouth, I began. At the end of the first verse, which concluded with the lines—

> " Hark ! the alarm bell rings out its sudden imperious cry,
>   Rings out its summons to dare—and to die—
>   At the call of God."

I employed the gestures my governess had taught me, and swung out my arm melodramatically to represent the clapper of the alarm-bell, and finally, with the last words, pointed my finger solemnly towards Heaven. To my indescribable horror and shame, I heard a delighted titter among the students ; and then Paul Berton called out : " Little Amateur ! Come down ! " It was a come-down indeed.

Later, on that awful afternoon, I was again sent up on to that dreaded stage and told to act something in pantomime. Paul Berton asked me to imagine myself returning to my bedroom after a ball and stripping off my cloak and dress. Then I was to sit down at my dressing-table before my mirror and begin to loosen my hair, when suddenly I would see reflected in the glass the stir of a curtain behind me. Being a courageous woman, I should rise and walk quickly towards the window, pull back the curtain—and be shot dead. My body would fall in a heap on the floor—Curtain.

I had never mimed in my life and became terribly conscious of long unmanageable legs and arms. When I strode towards the curtain I seemed not to be able to help jerking my chin with every step I took—this silent acting was terrible—it would help so much more if one might only speak—say something—anything ; every moment I expected to hear that crushing " Little Amateur ! Come down." However, I can't have done it so very badly, because I was allowed to continue my scene uninterrupted until the moment that I was supposed to be shot dead.

Then I realised that I didn't know how to fall down, and stood mutely staring out into the audience waiting for instructions.

" Now you are shot. You must fall and die," shouted Berton from the stalls. And then I made the spontaneous remark which gained me an instant popularity among the students, for I looked at our Ogre and said piteously—

" Oh, Monsieur Berton, I'd far rather *you* died first ! "
There was a roar of laughter in which he joined, and then

he ran up the steps at the side of the stage and gave me a demonstration of the way to fall (without hurting myself) when shot through the heart. I practised that fall for days in my chaperone's flat. I must have weakened all the ceiling on the floor below, and my body was black and blue with bruises, but at last I accomplished it.

Then one proud day I was promoted to study the part of Rosalind in 'As You Like It,' and I swashbuckled round that flat in imaginary doublet and hose and lectured Orlando, impersonated by Florence, the little Cockney maid, and must have made myself a general nuisance. But I loved that part, and determined to get a few hints from Miss Lily Brayton who was playing it, with Henry Ainley as Orlando, at His Majesty's Theatre. I begged my chaperone to take me there one Saturday night, but she had another engagement, and said that if I could find another girl-student to accompany me I might go. I telegraphed to one of the less formidable seniors in the rehearsal class asking her to meet me at a certain hour outside the door of the pit of His Majesty's Theatre ; ate an early dinner and hurried thence. To my consternation she wasn't there. What must I do ? I knew that I ought to return at once to the safety of the flat and miss the performance, but my adventurous spirit revolted against so dull an ending to what had promised to be a glorious evening, and so, greatly daring, I decided to go in alone. With beating heart I took my place in the pit *queue* and began to study my part from a little pocket Shakespeare I had brought with me. One of those terribly sad maimed men with cymbals attached to the stumps that once were legs, a trumpet in his mouth, and a drum slung round his neck, began to give a grotesque musical performance in the street, hopping on a board to make the cymbals clash. He horrified yet fascinated me whenever I stole a glance at him above my book. I longed to escape him, but that would mean losing my place in the *queue* and not seeing this wonderful performance of 'As You Like It' which all London was talking about.

Suddenly a man's voice in my ear remarked : " Very enterprising, isn't he ? " A man—a strange man—had spoken to me. Perhaps one of those night-marauding men my chaperone had warned me about. He was close at my side. He would get a place beside me in the pit. He would probably speak to me again. Ought I to answer him and snub him ? What could I say ? Ought I to preserve a haughty silence ? I decided upon this last and more dignified course of conduct, and, with a heart beating in my nose, opened my little Shakespeare again and appeared to immerse myself in study.

Then I heard the voice again—

" Forgive me, but you would find it much easier to read your poet if you held your book the right way up." Maddening man ! He had seen that, in my agitation, I was holding my book upside down.

I shot him an indignant glance and met the twinkling blue eyes of a fair-haired man. But he was not THE man of my dreams.

" You know I am rather surprised that your parents let you come to a London pit alone on a Saturday night," was his next remark. " Any cad might speak to you."

At that I could not resist looking him full in the face and shooting my right eyebrow up into my hair. He got my meaning at once : " Ah ! but *I'm* not a cad," he answered my ironic eyebrow.

Then my sense of justice made me blurt out the indiscreet truth : " My parents are in Suffolk and my chaperone doesn't know that I am here alone," I retorted with dignity.

" Suffolk ! you know Suffolk ? " and then he began to talk familiarly of houses and people I had known all my life. This was reassuring, so that when the pit doors opened and the people began to stream in and I found myself in the last place—but one—and the strange man stood above me, and, indicating the only remaining place, asked courteously, " Do you mind if I sit here ? " I only gave a smiling shrug, and there we were, side by side, for the rest of the evening.

I think my intense concentration upon the play, and the copious notes scribbled in my little pocket-book, piqued and amused him, for during the interval he asked for my Shakespeare to read while I wrote. The moment my pencil paused he invited me to some new form of entertainment. Would I go with him and see such and such a play—I might bring all the students of the Benson School (for I had admitted that I was a student) with me if I would only come too. Would I go and see him play in a big cricket match at Lord's ? Would I allow him to get me an invitation to his cousin's ball ? Didn't I want to know his name ? The monuments to his family were in Petworth Church in Sussex and their name began with P. Would I not at least tell him *my* name. Having answered all his requests with a brief negative, I looked up at last and replied, " Great personages always travel about incognito when they are engaged in their private amusements."

This finally shut him up ; he laughed ruefully, and the next Act began. I felt quite a woman of the world and able to cope with a pit-load of strange young men.

Of course he wanted to drive me home (and find out where I lived) at the end of the play, but my little youthful priggish remark, " If you really are the gentleman you have been trying to persuade me that you are, all the evening, you will stay quietly on the pavement while I get on to my bus," put an end to that impulse. He shrugged his shoulders rather sulkily, bowed, and obeyed me. When I got home tingling all over with that delightful feeling of daring and achievement that one gets when one has deliberately done something that one ought not to have done, I found that the strange man had underlined the words " Who ever loved that loved not at first sight " in my Shakespeare, and in my little note-book he had scrawled, " Sweet little Unknown, if we are destined never to meet again, accept my heart-felt wishes for your career." I did see him once again at a big ball. He ran round like a mad rabbit trying to find somebody who knew someone in my party, so as to get an intro-duction, and failing, refused to dance and stood near the places where I was resting with my partners. At one moment I was alone in the ballroom waiting for my next partner to appear, and he suddenly dashed up, seized me in his arms with fierce determination and said—

" I don't care a damn whether we are introduced or not, you are going to dance this with me."

Before he had finished speaking my real partner appeared, and suavely saying, " *My* dance, I think," swept me away from the impetuous stranger.

In the crush of departing people I suddenly felt my hand captured and squeezed in a strong clasp, then hurriedly relinquished—and that was the last I ever saw—or felt—of my neighbour in the pit; though I did have the curiosity to find out that name beginning with P. on the monuments in Petworth Church.

What fun it all was and how I would love to feel again that wild youthful excitement and *joie de vivre*. Even crossing a street, entering a shop, climbing upon a bus, racing into the Albert Hall for a fencing lesson, tripping down to the dance-practice rooms with a tweed skirt pulled over my ballet skirt, to learn how to move grace-fully with our Professor Gilmer (how well I remember the embarrassment of catching my heel in my under-frills as I raced down a tube stairway and became hope-lessly entangled in yards and yards of torn yellow lace which seemed to have no beginning nor end).

Daddie, coming one day to the Albert Hall during one of his rare visits to London, asked the old hall porter if I were in the building.

" Would that be the young lady 'oo wears 'er 'at on

44

the back of 'er 'ead an' always looks 'appy ? " the old man inquired.

" It sounds rather like her," Daddie replied.

Of my fellow-students during my training at the Albert Hall under the formidable and remarkable Miss Elsie Fogerty, only a few have made any position on the stage. Jack Hulbert was then an enormous awkward leggy youth who haunted the rehearsal class in the hope of being cast for some part. Even then he had that talent for comedy and farce which he has since developed so remarkably.

Dion Titheridge, the brother of the lovely little sprite Madge, came sometimes, and I once acted with him in some adaptation of classics which were arranged for the education of boys at Public Schools. We did the scene at Lochleven Castle from Kenilworth (I was Mary of Scots) and the story of Launcelot and Elaine from Malory's ' Morte d'Arthur.' I played Elaine, and Dion Titheridge played Gawaine, my brother, very beautifully.

Those little plays were very good experience for us all, particularly as we had to finish our scenes at a given time or our audience of schoolboys would have drifted away to their scheduled classes.

Our final examination at the Dramatic School was conducted by F. R. Benson himself. We were allowed nothing of any sort to help us—no scenery, no ' properties,' no character dresses. I had to act my selected scenes in my brown fencing tunic and shorts, and so was very sore when at the last moment Paul Berton cast me for a comedy part in an American playlet he had written himself, instead of letting me play Rosalind in ' As You Like It.'

I was admitted to be the best Rosalind there had ever been at the School ; so that I naturally wanted to play her before a great Shakesperian actor ; and my boyish attire would have been a great help.

However ' Pa,' as we called (the then) Mr Benson, was

pleased with my American heroine and I got honours in the final examination just the same. The time of decision had now come. I had been allowed to study at the Albert Hall in order to find out if I had any real talent for the professional stage. The results of the final examination and a report from Paul Berton saying, " The nearest approach to ' The Sacred Ten ' that I have seen for some time . . . I have great expectations from that pupil in comedy " . . . and Miss Fogerty's comment, " Winifred's work is the most promising I have seen for years. She has every gift for success and a splendid power of work which ought to make her future a brilliant one . . ." decided my parents to let me take up the stage as a career.

VII.

Berton was anxious for me to find a ' walk-on ' and an understudy in some West End theatre and still to continue my training with him, having classes at the Guildhall, where he taught once a week. The problem was, as usual, money. I refused to allow Daddie to finance me in London because that would have defeated my whole object. I thought that if I could get a paid job in a theatre that would solve my problem. I was told that James Welch might have a vacancy in ' When Knights were Bold,' which had been running at Wyndham's Theatre for over a year and playing to packed houses. Accordingly Mummie (who was staying with me in London) and I haunted the stage-door of Wyndham's Theatre one afternoon. We arrived there in good time before the *matinée* began, hoping to waylay the famous ' Jimmy ' before he entered the stage-door. To my keen disappointment he arrived in a flurry one minute before the curtain was due to go up, shot past us without even seeing that we were there, and vanished through the stage-door.

Mummie, always undefeated, at once suggested that we should go across to the *matinée* at the Hippodrome and come back again at the end of the performance to try our luck once more. This we did, but owing to mis-information from the stage-doorkeeper at Wyndham's, when we returned it was to find the alley deserted and the stage-door closed. Mummie was certain that Jimmy Welch must still be inside the theatre so she beat peremp-torily upon the door with her sunshade and, to my amaze-ment, it was opened by Jimmy himself. My excited incoherence and youthful ardour must have impressed him, for he very kindly consented to give me a short interview and led me back to his dressing-room while Mummie waited outside with her victorious sunshade.

He asked me why I wanted to go on the stage and said he was afraid that if I did I might find that " the con-versation of the green-room might shock my finer senses." He then inquired whether I wanted the stage " as a stick or as a crutch," and went on to say that if a girl had no home of her own to go to, life became very difficult and dangerous when she was out of work.

I told him that I wanted it as ' a stick,' and that I had a lovely home to flee to when I liked. Then he objected that my height would dwarf him—he was a tiny little man. At this moment his wife, Miss Audrey Ford, came into the dressing-room, and when he introduced me as a stage-aspirant she clasped her hands together and exclaimed, " Oh! Jimmy. Our frocks ! " She saw me at once, in imagination, robed in one of the mediæval frocks worn in the dream hunting-scene, and her ecstatic remark decided my fate. I was engaged, and then sent upstairs to see the Business Manager. He informed me that I should represent a mediæval lady in Act 1 and a nun in Act 2, and that I should be paid 15s. a week for six evening performances and 2 *matinées*. Further, I was instructed to be at the theatre at ten o'clock next morning for my first rehearsal.

I left that theatre feeling a prospective Sarah Siddons and millionaire rolled into one, and oh the joy of telling Mummie of the success of our perseverance and seeing her grey eyes sparkle and her cheeks flush pink. Nothing that affected me in any way could ever leave her untouched. We were one person.

I went down to the theatre next day quivering with excitement and apprehension in every nerve. I was longing, yet dreading to see a full rehearsal, and the thought of being actually one of the players, if only a very humble one, went to my head like wine. I found the stage dark and deserted and, for one panic-moment, feared I had misunderstood my instructions until the silence was suddenly broken by a noisy and despairing yawn. Peering through the shadows I saw a little dark man slouching in a chair with his feet on the back of another.

I approached him timidly—

" Please, I was told to come to the theatre for a rehearsal at ten o'clock," I began nervously.

" Oh, you're the new girl," he replied, dragging himself up from his chair. " Come on then and begin."

" But where is the rest of the company ? " I inquired eagerly.

" Do you mean to say you expected the whole company, stars and all, to come down here at ten o'clock in the morning to rehearse with a new walker-on ? " he demanded scornfully. " But you're green, of course."

I felt very green—stage-green—and very, very new.

Another man strolled out of the shadows. " The new girl, Mr ——" introduced the stage-manager. " This is our Musical Director," with a nod to me.

Thus began my first rehearsal.

The stage-manager, reading from a ragged script, informed me that I entered R., crossed the stage slowly in the hunting-procession waving a scarf dreamily and singing a hunting-chorus. Then I made exit L.

" What are the words of the song ? Can I have the music ? " I asked.

" Oh, I can't remember the words, you'll pick them up from the others," said the stage-manager irritably. " How does that music go, Mr B——? "

Mr B——, who although a Musical Director had apparently no sense of pitch, whistled two bars which sounded like a doleful tuneless dirge and then snapped out—

" Oh damn it all, she must pick it up as she goes along." And that was Act 1.

The second Act was much the same, save that at some point I had to fling myself upon my knees and throw up my hands in a supplicating gesture—at what point neither of the two men could remember. And that was my first rehearsal.

I was then sent upstairs in search of the wardrobe mistress who would supply me with my mediæval and nun's dresses. I found a little yellow Jewess sitting in a long dim room hung with tawdry gowns, sewing quietly. I introduced myself diffidently and she shot a quick appraising glance all over me with humorous beady eyes, and then selected a long sheath-like dress of green brocade which I was to wear with a tall pointed hat with a gauze veil floating from its tip. Her lightning judgment of my measurements amazed me, for the frock fitted me perfectly. I voiced my astonishment, and she gave a smile of pleasure and remarked briefly, " 'Abit, me dear."

That night, which was to be the occasion of my first appearance upon a London stage, found me shaking with nervous excitement. I had scarcely eaten all day and had been repeating my vague instructions from the stage-manager over and over again, " Enter R. Cross the stage slowly waving a scarf dreamily and exit L." I devoutly hoped that I shouldn't make a fool of myself, and felt perfectly certain that this was inevitable. But before I walked on to that terrifying stage I should have to face the even more fearful ordeal of entering a dressing-room full of strange women and displaying my utter ignorance of the art of making-up my face.

I was told the number of my dressing-room by the stage-doorkeeper, and I climbed those dark stone stairs with wobbly legs, clasping my tin box of grease-paints and powders that I had bought that afternoon in Soho. Devoutly I prayed that the girls inside that room might be kind to my inexperience. I knocked timidly once—twice—and then a thin shrivelled little woman with bright snapping eyes opened the door and stared at me in blank astonishment (afterwards I learned that she was the dresser of Room 3).

" Wot can I do for yew, Miss ? " she asked alertly.

" I was told that I was to dress in Room 3," I replied shyly, entering the room.

" Ow ! yew're the new—young *lidy*," she remarked, accentuating the ' lidy ' rather acidly.

There were seven women seated in that room busily engaged in rubbing on grease-paint and blackening their eyelashes before small square mirrors—a glaring electric light placed above each. All these women were half undressed, and before I had entered the room I had heard a buzz of animated gossip. Now a hostile silence fell upon it. Not one of them so much as turned her head in my direction. The dresser indicated the darkest and draughtiest corner before a cracked looking-glass, as my place. I humbly took it, removed my dress, put on a kimono and began fumbling with my grease-paints, casting sneaking glances at my neighbour—a handsome voluptuous woman, with a head covered with an incredible number of little sausage curls posed on a ' Pompadour ' pad. I tried to see which paints she was using and how she applied them, but my head swam with the heat of the room and my fingers trembled ridiculously so that all I did was to pick up and put down first one stick of grease-paint and then another without using any of them.

My neighbour had apparently been covertly observing me under her waxed eyelashes and suddenly could stand it no longer, for she proved to have a kind heart.

"Why, bless the child!" she suddenly burst out. "I don't believe she knows how to make-up." "I *don't*," I wailed dismally. "Oh, *would* you please help me ? "

"Here, give me your paints," she said briefly, and, emptying them on to her dressing-table, she quickly selected a pale flesh-pink (absolutely wrong for my tint of skin as I learned some months afterwards). She smeared my face all over with this as a groundwork and then proceeded to rub a shade of toothpowder pink in round circles over my cheek-bones ; after which she smeared sky-blue all over my eyelids right up to my eyebrows and put a dot of scarlet in the corners of my eyes, using the same scarlet for lips. Finally she lit a candle and melted a block of black grease, which she applied in blobs to my eyelashes until they stuck out round my eyes like the petals of a daisy, stiff and separate.

She herself was a blonde, and she made-up my face exactly like her own, although my hair was chestnut and there is a golden tint in my skin. The result appalled me when I looked in the glass. I resembled a terribly vulgar French doll, and when she had rolled my hair into two gigantic puffs on each side of my face I hated my appearance so much that I wondered if the stage-manager would ' give me the sack ' directly after my first performance.

But I managed to thank my kind-hearted neighbour, and at least that awful make-up made me feel like someone else, so that it temporarily took away some of my nervousness.

It returned, however, in greater force when, just as I had been given my place in the hunting-procession, the stage-manager rushed up to me and hissed in my ear: "*Reverse* all I told you this morning." However, I got through somehow without making a particularly great ass of myself, and, once on the stage, I gained confidence quickly when I saw that the audience were only interested in Jimmy Welch and his supporting stars.

Between the Acts I sat silently in my corner covertly watching the behaviour of the other girls and our little Cockney dresser, who continually rushed from the room on their errands, returning with curious packages which proved to be *delicatessen* from Appenrodt's and bottles of beer. My large neighbour had ordered a greasy potato salad soaked with mayonnaise sauce, and the way she conveyed slices of potato, impaled upon a long hat-pin, to her mouth, thus avoiding soiling her fingers which were plastered with wet-white, fascinated me.

Looking up suddenly she caught my eye upon her, and, evidently imagining that she caught an envious glitter therein, she stabbed her hat-pin into a succulent slice, and after first casting a defiant look around the room, offered it to me. To my surprise it was perfectly delicious, and I soon became a regular patron of Appenrodt's. I hope my kind-hearted protector has long been married to her musician who was then playing the trombone in the Covent Garden Orchestra, for soon she and I became friends, and, while rolling up those prodigious curls and waxing her eyelashes, she gradually confided to me her complete life-story. She also explained to me my frigid reception in the dressing-room on my first evening and the reason of the hostile demeanour of the other girls towards a complete stranger. It appeared that the wardrobe mistress who had outfitted me for my scenes, when questioned by the others in my room about ' the new girl ' who was to be their room-mate, had replied with enthusiasm, " Ah, you've got *a real lady* this time."

Whereupon they one and all decided to ' down me ' and ' put me in my place ' and ' send me to Coventry,' imagining, I suppose, that I should ' put on frills.' Also they imagined that I was taking up the stage as a profession merely to occupy my idle time and sample a new sensation. When they found that I was really a very

scared and humble-minded person, only too grateful
for their hints and help, and that my great ambition
was to be self-supporting, to earn my own living and
ease the situation at home, they one and all became
friendly and helpful.

During my interview with him Jimmy Welch had said
that " the conversation of the greenroom would shock
my finer senses," but never once at Wyndham's Theatre
did I hear one word that could have shocked a convent
of nuns. Good-natured gossip about members of the
company ; happy flirtations ; new cooking recipes ;
advice upon the remodelling of old clothes ; holiday
hints ; and chiefly the difficulties that had to be overcome
in humble homes where the week's small salary supported
more than one person—these were the usual subjects of
conversation.

I was very proud when I received my first pay-envelope.
So proud, that I would not put my very first earnings
into my hand-bag, but carried the envelope clasped in a
hot fist which I uncurled at intervals to take a peep at
the precious packet. This was my undoing, for, while
travelling home on the underground railway, dreaming
of the day when I should be a star, be paid by cheque,
and be able to shower presents upon my family, I suddenly
realised that I had arrived at my station and that the
train was at the point of moving on. I sprang to my feet,
forced my way through a crowd of strap-hangers, and
jumped for the platform. As the train roared off into
darkness I found, with a sick shock of loss, that my
precious packet was no longer in my hand.

I have often wondered since who found my first little
salary. It was very bitter to lose it.

VIII.

After some time at Wyndham's Theatre, it dawned
upon me that I was learning nothing at all and that to

gain experience I must try for another walk-on in a new and bigger production, and, if possible, understudy a part as well. Paul Berton advised me to try His Majesty's Theatre where Sir Herbert Tree was shortly putting on an adaptation of ' Faust ' by Stephen Phillips and Comyns Carr.

I will not describe the difficulties I had to surmount before I was ultimately engaged as a witch, a Court lady, and an angel at 25s. a week.

Marie Löhr was the Marguerite, Henry Ainley took the part of Faust, Rosina Filippi the aunt, and Tree, himself, was Mephistopheles, surrounded by an enormous company of village maidens, students, witches, Court ladies, and angels. I had complained that the rehearsals at Wyndham's were not rehearsals at all, now I was to learn what a real rehearsal in a big theatre could be. We rehearsed for weeks on end, and the final week of dress rehearsals and lighting rehearsals nearly killed the company. We would begin at ten o'clock in the morning (sometimes even earlier) and continue until five o'clock next morning. Sir Herbert had luxurious rooms in the dome of the theatre whither he retired for meals and repose, while we perfected the scenes already rehearsed. Even the stars were exhausted, although they went out to restaurants for meals. The walkers-on, known as the crowd, could not afford to do this, and, in any case, it was impossible, for their scenes might be called at any moment. It was hopeless to ask if one could be spared for ten minutes or a quarter of an hour, for the stage-manager, Mr Cecil King, never knew which Act Sir Herbert might want to rehearse next. And so we sent our dressers out to buy buns and rolls, which we devoured standing up in the wings. I used to feel that my inside was dropping out from so much standing, and used to prop my tumpkin up against a bit of scenery while waiting to be called back on to the stage. In the final Brocken scene, a wonderful effect of lighting was gained by steam

54

turned on from the kitchens of the Carlton Hotel next
door to the theatre. It swirled up in clouds and wreaths
of vapour, and different coloured limelight lamps were
focussed upon it. I was one of the crowd of witches,
and, having the longest hair, was placed on the foremost
rock, so that I got the full benefit of the steam, and my
flimsy witch's rags were always sopping wet at the end
of the scene. In this condition we all had to rush up
into ' the flies '—the gallery encircling the inside roof of
the theatre—and become a choir of invisible angels,
singing a heavenly chant of triumph through the storm
and thunder to signify good triumphing over evil as
Marguerite was wafted up to Heaven. We felt far from
angelic—more like devils. We were soaked to the skin ;
packed tightly together amid dirty sweating scene-shifters
while we sang our angelic chorus to the accompaniment
of twenty cannon-balls rolling down a trough of tin ;
periodic explosions of gunpowder, and sixty electric
hammers beating on a sheet of iron—very realistic thunder
—agony to the ears.

Rehearsals were sometimes enlivened by unrehearsed
incidents. ' Flying ladies ' had been engaged to soar as
witches (on wires) above the rocks in the Brocken scene.
They were hooked on to their wires and then attached
to rope-pulleys, operated by scene-shifters in the wings.
They were hauled up to a certain height and then given
a violent shove to swing them right across the stage
where other scene-shifters were hidden ready to catch
them. But on the dress rehearsal a man on the opposite
side failed to catch his flying lady and the rope, swinging
back, she dangled, screaming and kicking frantically in
the centre of the stage, and the dramatic effect was
ruined.

In the same scene, Mephistopheles had to declaim from
a pinnacle of rock at a dizzy height, and Sir Herbert,
fearing to fall, had himself attached to a wire-pulley
concealed up in the flies. Once attached to his wire it

was drawn taut. During the first trial of this safety-expedient, stage-thunder was rolling so noisily that the man operating the pulley on high failed to hear Sir Herbert's injunction to stop winding. He continued to wind until the desperate Sir Herbert was suspended in mid-air, shouting to the stage-manager that this device had been devised to save his life and not to hang him by the waist until he were dead.

Another stage-effect that had to be suppressed was a kind of invisible moving staircase on which Faust and Marguerite, in the final scene, were posed in prayerful attitudes and propelled slowly Heavenward. But the machinery failed to function as it should and their progress upward was achieved in a series of spasmodic jerks, so that Marguerite, facing Faust, constantly lost her balance and fell upon his chest, with disastrous result, for, before they achieved Paradise, both were in an irreverently hysterical condition—as were we all.

Sir Herbert's energy was terrific. He was a marvellous producer and spared neither himself nor his company at rehearsals. As we neared the day of production, he became a bundle of nerves, flew into violent rages about trifles, and would dismiss every member of the staff in turn. They never took any notice of these dismissals, being fond of, and thoroughly used to him, and they always turned up to rehearsals next day.

One morning towards 4 A.M. Sir Herbert turned towards the orchestra and commanded them to repeat a certain passage for about the twentieth time.

Silence.

"Mr Schmidt! Adolf Schmidt! I said, repeat that passage!" shouted Tree.

Silence.

He walked down to the footlights and peered into the void that had once been full of orchestra—Mr Schmidt had taken upon himself to send his exhausted musicians home to bed and himself had left the theatre.

Tree raved, and then Miss Rosina Filippi spoke up bravely—

" I think he is quite right, Sir Herbert. *I* am going home now, too, without permission if you do not dismiss us all at once. Your company is exhausted. How do you expect to get good work out of us if you never give us any sleep ? "

Having said this, she rolled across the stage with that peculiar gait of hers and disappeared into the wings. Sir Herbert stared after her for a moment in dumb astonishment and then abruptly dismissed the company.

As a producer he was a genius, but he was a hard task-master. Once, during a rehearsal of the Brocken scene which lasted into the small hours of the morning, one of the little dancing witches suddenly collapsed in a heap on the stage. Henry Ainley who, as Faust, was standing near, picked her up in his arms and carried her out into the wings.

Tree, who was sitting in the stalls the better to criticise the scene, called out irritably—

" What has happened, Mr King ? Why don't they go on ? "

Mr King replied, " One of the ladies has fainted, Sir Herbert."

" Then don't *let* the ladies faint—it interrupts," shouted Mephistopheles, and the rehearsal continued.

On the first night a company of ghosts assembled at the theatre, too utterly weary even to be nervous. Poor little Marie Löhr was sobbing all through her scenes from sheer fatigue, but as Marguerite has to weep a great deal it was very effective. I had caught a chill from my steamings in the Brocken scene ; a funny lid seemed to open and shut in my head ; the faces around me seemed faces in a dream and voices, spirit-voices. I did not know until the next day, when Mummie (who had of course come up from Suffolk for the first performance of

' Faust ') took me to see a doctor, that I had a temperature of 103°.

I narrowly shaved pneumonia, but my illness did one good thing ; for the management of His Majesty's Theatre arranged that the steam from the Carlton kitchens which had so soaked the poor witches, should be turned on *after* they had left the stage. My salary was paid in full all through my absence from the theatre, and my place kept for me. Sir Herbert was generous in many ways. Our fares, by rail, or by hansom cab, or ' growler ' if the train service had ceased, were always paid when the rehearsals lasted into the small hours, and that was something. But we of the ' crowd ' often became very hungry before the day of production, because, in those days (1908) no one was paid for rehearsals, and one had to go on living—somehow—while they lasted, sometimes for weeks. It was a disaster for us if, after long rehearsal, the play proved a failure and was taken off almost at once, for there were always arrears to be paid to patient landladies and washerwomen. How often for several weeks after the first night of a play did I hand over my complete salary. It was a continual struggle to get level. Of course I could have applied to Daddie for help, but my pride forbade that. Also, when I told Jimmy Welch that I had a lovely home to flee to, I had not then learned the absolute necessity for a beginner to remain on the spot. A telegram might come from some manager summoning one to his theatre to try out a part and, if one were not in London, then there were hundreds of other girls on his waiting-list only too eager to snap up that part. No, one had to hang on, somehow, during those periods of unemployment or perhaps lose some wonderful chance.

At the end of my training at the Dramatic School I had changed my lodging ; for my parents felt that I must now be independent and that the late theatre hours would upset the little *ménage* of the kind woman who had so far chaperoned me. Accordingly, a room was taken for me in the Twentieth Century Club, not very far from Notting Hill Gate. It was full of militant suffragettes who were still at that moment fighting for the vote and always getting imprisoned after some demonstration.

I was then too young to be anything but amused and interested in the various types that lodged in that Club, and the Directress told Mummie that it was a joy to her to watch the happy assured way in which I marched into the communal dining-room and seated myself in any vacant chair at any table I fancied, regardless of fierce feuds and exclusive *cliques*, smilingly sure of the welcome that I always got. I was the Club baby, and spoiled by everyone, and so full of my own happy affairs and ambitions ; so abounding in joyous vitality that apparently no one had the heart to give me the snub I surely often deserved.

Even the Club servants were delightfully kind to me, and once during a terrific thunderstorm in the night, when I ran out of my bedroom in my nightdress to console a timid neighbour, I stumbled over the night-porter who was sitting outside *my* door in case I might be scared— bless him !

When I came in late after the theatre he would creep down to the kitchens and filch some delicacy from the larder to assuage my youthful hunger, or brew me a delicious cup of hot chocolate. We had great fun during these marauding parties—the night-porter and I.

After the run of 'Faust,' we were informed that Tree was putting on a children's fairy-play for Christmas. Knowing that I was built upon too generous a scale to be able to represent either a child or a fairy I was perhaps the only member of the company who did not importune him for a part in the new production.

One night, after the Brocken scene, Mr Cecil King, the stage-manager, came up to me and told me that

Sir Herbert wished to speak to me in his dressing-room directly after the performance.

I was terrified, and at once began to review every detail of my past conduct—the things left undone that ought to have been done and the things I had done that I never ought to have did. There was one wicked act that stood out in my memory and I feared that somehow it had come to Sir Herbert's knowledge.

Because of the sin of unpunctuality, Sir Herbert had decreed that if any of the ' walking-on ladies ' were late for the first Act their weekly salary must be confiscated. He had further ordered that the stage-manager (Mr Cecil King), assistant stage-manager (Mr Stanley Bell), the call-boy (Claude Rains), and various spies deputed for this special purpose, should post themselves upon the staircase at the entrances of corridors leading to the dressing-rooms so that no late-comer could enter unobserved.

By some cruel fate, just after this new rule was issued, my tube-train got stuck in a tunnel when I was on my way to the theatre.

When at last the electric current was restored and I could look at my watch, I realised that I should be at least a quarter of an hour late for the first scene of Act I, and that I should lose my precious salary, already owing to the Twentieth Century Club. Arrived at Piccadilly Tube Station, I tore down a back street, avoiding the crowded Haymarket at theatre-hour, and reached the stage-door of His Majesty's in a frightened breathless condition. The grumpy old door-keeper was happily a friend of mine, and, hearing the opening chorus through the swing-doors, I begged him to reconnoitre for me before I ventured to put my head round them. This he did, and returned to tell me that my case was hopeless, for, although the two stage-managers were both on the stage by this time, the call-boy, his duties over till the next scene, was posted at the foot of the staircase up which I must pass to reach my room.

I pleaded with my ally still to keep watch in case the sentry's attention wandered for a moment, which happily it soon did, and I shot noiselessly past him as he turned to answer some question of the stage-manager.

One flight of stairs was safely mounted, but at the next bend I saw a youth sitting upon the stairs smoking a cigarette and reading an evening paper. Impossible to pass him, but, determined not to be defeated, greatly daring I sped down Sir Herbert Tree's private corridor to my left, passing the open door of his dressing-room where Campbell, his dresser, was fortunately too much absorbed in tidying the room to notice me pass. At the end of the corridor I knew that I should find Sir Herbert's private electric lift. I flipped into it, pressed the button marked 5, and sailed up gaily past the spies on the lower floors and alighted on Floor 5. Once again Fortune favoured me, because the end of the corridor was just above the bend of the staircase where the next spy was placed, and while he was busily engaged in kissing our dresser six steps below me, I gained my dressing-room.

Inside it sat one girl who had been excused from singing because of a bad head-cold. She was sitting before her mirror, deeply depressed because as fast as she painted her nose pale cream she had to wipe it and it became once more a vivid red. She looked at me with pity in her streaming eyes and remarked—

" Poor devil ! A week's salary gone, I suppose." Triumphantly I told her of my adventure and escape, but she dashed my spirit at once by informing me that the spies had orders also to visit the dressing-rooms so that even yet I might be caught.

I began to undress and had hardly donned my witch's rags when we heard heavy footsteps coming down the corridor.

" *You're* done for ! " ejaculated my depressing companion.

But having already dared so much, I felt that I might

dare more, and, flinging open the window, I crawled out on to the parapet of the roof, pulling the window shut behind me. I shall never forget the terrifying but exhilarating sensation of being perched up there in the cold night air, looking down upon the tiny pedestrians and the tops of buses from that dizzy height. In those days great flares were lit at intervals along the parapet, so that my figure in its fluttering rags with long hair streaming in the wind was visible to people down below who happened to look up, and I saw arms gesticulating towards the weird figure crouching on the parapet. I suppose they thought I was about to commit suicide.

When the spy entered our dressing-room he found only one girl, crying with sheer terror at my escapade, but knowing that she was suffering from a head-cold, he put down her tears to inflamed lachrymal glands, and, having poked about the room, looked behind curtains and into cupboards, he departed, feeling that his job was well and truly done. Then I reappeared through the window and danced a triumphant *pas seul*, having diddled the lot.

But now, weeks later, being told that Sir Herbert wished to speak with me in his private room, I was panic-stricken. *Could* he have heard of this adventure of mine and was I about to be dismissed in disgrace ? Shivering in my witch's rags, I knocked at his door and was bade to enter. There he stood, straddling before his fire in scarlet Mephistophelean majesty, but instead of lecturing me he looked me over with a benign eye and said—

" I have noticed that you are one of the few ladies of this company who make-up as conscientiously to walk once across the stage as if you were playing a leading part. Many of the girls rush across with the crowd without taking the trouble to put on any make-up at all. They think that among so many they escape my notice. I see everything."

At this point, Henry Ainley entered the room, and

drawing Sir Herbert aside, laughingly whispered something to him.

"No, Harry," replied Sir Herbert. "I will *not* give Lady X. a piece of my cloak as a souvenir. I refuse to play Joseph to her Mrs Potiphar."

Henry Ainley laughed and departed. Then the Chief again turned to me—

"I want you to try the part of 'Beauty' in my new production 'Pinkie and the Fairies.' I don't suppose for a moment that you will be audible beyond the foot-lights, but you can come down to rehearsal to-morrow morning and try it," he startlingly remarked, handing me a small scroll of paper. I put out a shaking hand and grasped my first part.

I don't know what I said to him, or how I got out of the room and upstairs, but I do remember the chilling silence with which my news was greeted by the other occupants of our dressing-room—a hostile silence of jealous and disappointed friends, which made me acutely miserable and dimmed the glory of that moment.

On my way home I bought a box of voice-lozenges and devoured the whole of them during that hectic night, in the intervals of repeating over and over again my few lines which I must speak in public the next day. I dreaded the moment when I should be tested before the whole company assembled upon the stage at His Majesty's ; for rehearsals had been in progress for over a fortnight, and Sir Herbert had engaged an all-star company con-sisting of Ellen Terry and Augusta Haviland as the Aunts, Marie Löhr as Cinderella, Viola Tree as the Sleeping Beauty, Stella Patrick Campbell as 'Molly,' and other well-known people besides a mob of children as fairies, elves, rabbits, frogs, &c., led by Iris Hawkins as 'Pinkie ' and Philip Tonge as her play-fellow, 'Tommy.'

I was so frightened when the awful moment came that I declaimed my first two lines in a clear ringing voice (trained so carefully by Professor Hulbert), then heard,

to my overwhelming joy and relief, the voice of Sir Herbert
who was listening in the stalls—

" She'll do, Mr King."

IX.

From that moment my theatrical life changed. Instead
of ' Chorus at 9 A.M.,' only the notice ' Principals at
11 A.M.' applied to me.

The atmosphere in the theatre was delightful. Perhaps
the presence of so many children gave a gaiety and infor-
mality to the rehearsals.

The sweet personality of Miss Ellen Terry captivated
us all. She was so kind to all beginners, and I shall
ever gratefully remember how she drew me aside after
that first rehearsal and discussed my tiny scene with me.

" Don't be intimidated by all the stars in the firmament,"
she heartened me. " When you make your first entrance,
sweep down to the centre of the stage, brushing everyone
aside. For those moments the stage is YOURS, so don't
allow yourself to be elbowed into the wings by any
important personage."

This advice from so great an actress gave me courage.
Until that moment I had been trying to appear as incon-
spicuous as possible, and was therefore making nothing
of my small opportunity.

I look back to that period of rehearsals very happily,
for I made many new friends. Dion Clayton Calthrop,
that clever artist, author, and expert on historical costume,
had been engaged to dress the play, and ' Mr Bill ' (as he
was called for some reason) was very popular with us all
and very kind to me. Often he would take me to lunch
in some little quaint Soho restaurant, or home to tea with
his wife. He was so gay and so young, was Mr Bill, and
his delicious fancy danced and flickered over passing
incidents to the delight and refreshment of us all. He

was a veritable 'Peter Pan'; he never grew up, and I believe his inner life was lived with The Little People whom he portrayed so well, for never was there anyone so unworldly—or, better, so other-worldly.

But Mr Bill was enough of this world to understand that, to a young girl who was to play her first part in a big West End theatre, her dress was to her of vital importance. The wardrobe mistress had suggested that Beauty might wear a 'stock' dress — perhaps one of those worn in the production of 'The Merry Wives of Windsor,' and an old dress of Mrs Kendal's was brought forth for me to try. Mr Bill must have seen my face fall for he at once said: "As I am dressing this play, I prefer to design all the dresses myself, and I have other ideas for Beauty's frock." He over-persuaded the authorities, and a really lovely straight mediæval dress of silver tissue shot with sky-blue was made for me, and a little wreath of white moss-rose buds to band my smooth-capped hair. But when the moment came for us all to try on our dresses and be inspected by Sir Herbert, after one glance at mine he said, " It is far the loveliest of all— and hers is an unimportant part. The dress must be vulgarised somehow or there will be trouble." And so, to my disappointment and Mr Bill's real grief, this was done by the addition of a yoke and girdle of flashing rubies and my hair uncoiled and arranged in two huge plaits twisted with rubies. " We will pretend that the Beast was a *nouveau-riche*," laughed Sir Herbert.

It was a very charming play written by Mr Graham Robertson, the artist, to amuse his little god-daughter 'Binkie.' Pinkie, in the play, was a friend of The Little People, who one night invited her and her playmate, Tommy, to a fairy party in the wood near her house at midnight. The children were allowed to invite anyone they pleased, and they chose characters from their favourite fairy-tales: Cinderella, The Sleeping Beauty, Beauty, the Beast, and others. Pinkie's cousin Molly was also included. She was eighteen, and just not too old to be persuaded that fairies did exist.

The Queen of the Fairies was a tiny girl dancer, little more than a baby, and so small that she made her first appearance folded inside the bud of a water-lily which suddenly rose out of a pool and uncurled its petals to reveal the sprite hidden within it, who then descended and danced the daintiest *pas seul*. That tiny little girl has since blossomed into the famous *ballet* dancer, Elise Craven.

The woodland scene was very lovely ; a pine-wood on the slope of a hill with a moonlit sky showing through the boles of the trees, and fireflies flickering among the branches. The slope was planted with hundreds of real ferns and alive with scudding rabbits, and a little cascade of water trickled down through the ferns into a rock-pool below. Cinderella made her entrance in a fairy coach drawn by six white ponies and drove through the wood down on to the stage ; and I can never forget the beauty of the willowy form of Viola Tree, as the Sleeping Beauty, wrapped in filmy draperies of rose and purple, dreamily wandering down that woodland path, fanning herself with a huge poppy and singing a lullaby in that sweet voice of hers as she went.

Graham Robertson's wistful words, accompanied by the delicious music of Frederic Norton, made sweet and haunting songs and the Sleeping Beauty sang the loveliest of all.

The first night of ' Pinkie and the Fairies ' was a tremendous affair, and a wonderful experience for me, because every friend I had in the world either wrote to me, sent me a telegram, or flowers, and my dressing-table was heaped with them. And at the end of that week I had another thrill, for Sir Owen Seaman, then editor of ' Punch,' gave me a little notice all to myself—

" Beauty really is a beauty—and at last we have an actress who *can speak*."

My life was now entirely happy, for I felt that I had actually got my foot upon the first rung of the ladder of fame, and every day I made new friends. Marie Löhr invited me often to her flat in the old Adelphi Terrace, where I met her mother, Kate Bishop; and Stella Patrick Campbell carried me off to her home in Kensington Square where I often saw the famous 'Mrs Pat.' During rehearsals we made up luncheon-parties at the Pall Mall restaurant, and always I was meeting new and distinguished people— authors, artists, playwrights, politicians, and 'idle rich,' who, having a *flair* for the theatre, sought introductions to stars like Marie and Stella. And always I hoped that among their number I might one day meet my Man.

It was during the run of 'Pinkie' that I heard of rooms in Shepherd Street, Mayfair—a little hexagonal sitting-room with a tiny bedroom (once a powder-closet) opening out of it—and after consultation with my family it was decided that I should move into this ancient eighteenth-century house so as to be nearer the theatre and to my 'Fairy Godmother,' as I called the Duchess, who, since the Woodstock days, had never ceased to take an interest in the career which she herself had proposed for me, and who now lived alone at Sunderland House, just opposite Shepherd's Market.

The old house in which I was to live was originally occupied by Mr Shepherd himself, and a little wooden bust of the great man was fixed upon its roof. In my time the house was rented by a dear Devonshire woman named Mrs Fowler, known to everyone in the neighbour- hood as 'The Little Mother,' because of her great heart. I had the two rooms on the second floor; a beautiful mannequin from one of the leading London dressmakers rented the two rooms on the first floor; a tailor's cutter, whose perfect manners and respectability lent a tone to the whole house, occupied a bed-sitting room on the ground floor; and a gouty old sea captain lived in a hole at the top of the back stairs. He was never seen, but often heard when the Little Mother was tending his afflicted feet.

One of the rooms on the top floor was rented by a majestic Major Domo who was hired by the Houses of the Great to superintend their balls and receptions during the season. Once he presented me with the *menu* of a banquet at Buckingham Palace and seemed quite wounded that I did not frame it. The Little Mother was immensely proud of him and his activities, and he shed an aura of aristocracy around her house.

She was not so proud of the gallant Major who had taken the bedroom on the landing opposite that of the beautiful mannequin. He lay in bed most of the day, clothed in pyjamas of sky-blue silk, with his door wide open so that he might watch the exits and entrances of the lovely lady. Towards evening he would dress himself with elaborate care, saunter down the stairs, hail a taxi (new and smart innovations in those days), and drive away. The Little Mother confided to me that he was sheltering from his creditors and that he had lived in her house for over a year and never yet paid her a penny. When I remarked that, if he was so hard up, it was strange that he could afford a daily taxi, she replied, " Poor gentleman ! He daren't go out on foot or he'd be caught by one or other of his creditors."

The Major was a thorn in her side, yet she had not the heart to have him extracted. Eventually he disappeared in the night, and, for all I know, the money owing to the Little Mother remains unpaid to this day.

" Poor gentleman, it must be hard to be placed in such a difficult situation when you have been used to the good things of this world," was her only comment upon his flitting.

Another thorn was ' Martha,' a terrible woman whom someone left, as a baby, on the Little Mother's doorstep. Of course Martha was taken in, sheltered, and taught to help a little in the house. But in her riper years she had taken to drink, grown ungratefully lazy and sluttish, and constantly disgraced us all.

Martha had an insatiable curiosity and a passion for answering the front door bell. She would gallumph up the back stairs, forestalling the Little Mother with her spotless apron, shining white hair and apple-blossom cheeks, and would present herself to callers in her dirty rags, with a smutty face, red nose and bleary eyes, and the black cat (her familiar spirit) perched on her shoulder and rubbing his arched back against her chin.

I used to love the incongruity of the pair when Martha opened the door to one of the Duchess of Marlborough's powdered footmen, resplendent in livery and silk stockings, bringing a box of her lovely clothes for the lady on the second floor.

What a thrill those boxes always gave me, and what a help those beautiful frocks were to me later on when I toured the provinces in modern plays, and had to provide my dresses myself. She was indeed a Fairy Godmother to me, and her wonderful thoughtfulness, so apparent in every act of kindness that she performed, transformed my life at various critical periods. However busy she might be, she was always accessible to me. I knew that in any difficulty I had only to cross the road, ring the bell of Sunderland House at any hour, and I should immediately be taken up to her room. Sometimes I would find her in bed, a vision of lace and loveliness, a mass of correspondence littering the coverlet, and she would look at me with those wonderful eyes of hers full of interest and gentle concern and say—

" Well, Winifred, what is it ? "

I was sure of wise and humorous counsel from that clever brain, always prompted by a great heart.

Since we had left Woodstock she had bade farewell to Blenheim Palace for ever, and her loneliness now tore my heart. She had everything in the world except the things that matter most. After she had kissed me farewell

I hated to hear those little heels of hers clicking away from me across the marble floors into the dim desolation of that great French palace, fragrant with lilies and incense and lovely with antique brocades and priceless porcelain.

It was a joy to see her at one of her great receptions at Sunderland House, standing at the head of the double staircase greeting guest after guest always with the appropriate word or gay jest, receiving the homage of foreign ambassadors and speaking fluently to each in his own tongue as he kissed her hand.

But it was an even greater joy to see her among her poor. She had a Recreation Club for factory girls in the East End; she had founded a laundry to employ the wives of prisoners doing time, and a *crèche* for their babies while the mothers were at work. She told me a wonderful story of a prisoner who, having finished his sentence, came to thank her for her kindness to his wife and children during his captivity. He pleaded for a sum of money to buy the necessary equipment for some art or craft to enable him now to support his family. The Duchess gave him the money, with which he immediately bought a new set of burglar's tools, used them carelessly, and was returned to prison, from whence he wrote to ask her if she would again protect his family during his enforced absence. This time she didn't. She knew the life-history of each girl at the Club, and of every woman she helped, remembered their many relations by name and never failed to inquire as to their welfare. This, in the midst of the life of social engagements inevitable for one of her position in London.

Prebendary Carlile was a constant visitor and suppliant at Sunderland House where he could always find sympathy and help for his destitute. The Duchess herself pleaded innumerable causes from public platforms, and although in those days so nervous that she could neither eat nor sleep until the ordeal was over, she always captured her audience.

The Little Mother of Shepherd's Market also fell under her spell, though at their first meeting she was faintly hostile. I had had trouble with my ears and had been slightly deaf for some time. The Duchess swept me off to see her own throat and ear specialist. My deafness proved to be caused by adenoids, hitherto unsuspected, because I neither snored nor talked as though I had a gooseberry in my mouth. The Duchess stayed in the room during the subsequent operation, then drove me back to Shepherd Street and herself put me to bed. The Little Mother, not knowing that I had returned, entered my room to put a hot-water bottle in my bed, and found her place usurped by a tall and lovely lady. Her blue eyes blazed for a moment and her cheeks flushed.

Then the Duchess immediately disarmed her with a gracious word of apology for entering her house unannounced, explaining that as a slight hæmorrhage had started it was vital to get me into bed as quickly as possible. One dimpled smile and a pleading look in the soft eyes, and the Little Mother was her slave for ever.

How I loved my quarters in No. 11 Shepherd Street. The little hexagon sitting-room, with its deep presses (why do we call them cupboards?) hidden behind the panelling; the dim old mirror, in its tarnished gilt frame, over the fireplace; the crooked cabinet in the corner filled with Toby-jugs and bits of old Devon pottery, visible through its glass door; the rickety chintz-covered sofa near the fire with the bump in the middle of it where a spring had broken, and the quaint little fire-grate with its hobs and its small black kettle always there ready to brew a comforting pot of tea. Then the bow-window leaning out over the cobbled street below, supported by two painted posts planted in the pavement. What lively scenes I witnessed from that window: dog-fights, cat-fights, Punch and Judy shows attended by the shouting, dancing youth of the Market; street brawls; footmen from the Houses of the Great having their pates

powdered in the little barber's shop opposite ; lost ladies,
beautifully attired, mincing over the muddy cobbles in
search of their carriages, picking their way through heaps
of vegetable refuse from the Market ; the organ-grinder
with his monkey, and the chair-mender who came at
intervals ; a roaster of chestnuts and potatoes, which
often provided me with a delicious supper or were bought
and held inside my muff to warm cold hands on wintry
days ; smart young officers striding from the Junior Army
and Navy Club (once in Whitehorse Street) to some
romantic *rendezvous* somewhere in Mayfair. The peep-
show never ended.

And the music one heard ! Barrel-organs, cornet
soloists, German bands, flautists and penny-whistlers,
and sometimes the dreamy strains of some perfect
orchestra, or a popular dance-band playing in some great
house for the delectation of dancing *débutantes*.

I loved my little rooms in Shepherd's Market.

Some years ago I passed the old house and was startled
to see workmen tearing down its walls. Brick after brick,
permeated with such memories, fell in a cloud of romantic
dust.

Demolition . . .

Sudden tears started to my eyes to see such desecration,
and I was glad that the Little Mother had long since
left London and gone to live with a daughter in the
country. It would have hurt her, too, to see the dear
old house destroyed.

X.

The run of ' Pinkie and the Fairies ' was all too short
for the happiness of us all. It was only put on as a
Christmas production. During the rehearsals, Sir Herbert
Tree was in Egypt getting local colour for the great
Egyptian spectacle he intended to put on in the late
spring ; but he was back for the first night, in time to

present an enormous bouquet to the diminutive Fairy Queen; and to organise the Pinkie Bus Service—motor-buses to collect from, and return to their homes the chorus-children who appeared in the play. The buses were brightly painted and had the names of the stars acting in 'Pinkie' stencilled upon curtains hung inside the windows so that the play was advertised throughout London as the buses rolled through the streets carrying their freight of merry chattering children.

While the Egyptian play was being thought out, Tree revived 'The Dancing Girl,' who was Marie Löhr; taking the principal man's part himself.

I was given a small *rôle* as one of the many smart women who talked social nothings at the reception, so that I was glad when Mr Harrison asked me to play Constance in 'She Stoops to Conquer' at the Haymarket, and Sir Herbert released me to 'better myself.'

But I proved to have 'worsed' myself, for, having been 'tried out' and given the part, Miss Ethel Irving, who was to play Kate Hardcastle, coming in late and seeing me standing on the stage, asked who I was and what I was doing there. Being informed that I was the chosen Constance, she said abruptly—

" Too tall. She'll dwarf me."

As she and her husband had a financial share in the production, the part of Constance was taken away from me and given to Miss Beatrice Ferrar, and I was given her understudy and the part of the maid.

Very bitter, that disappointment. When one is young, how terribly cast down one is by all reverses of fortune. The whole of one's horizon is blackened and not one rift is visible in the sky.

The second tragedy that befel me was that on the first night, a Saturday, not one small bunch of flowers did I receive from any friend, and on Monday Miss Irving's dresser came to my dressing-room with her arms full of wilting sprays and bouquets of flowers which had been addressed to me, but sent in error to Miss Ethel Irving's room as a matter of course, and had been swamped in the sea of blossom which already inundated the floor of the star actress. When the moment came to detach the cards of good cheer from the bouquets so that the senders might be thanked for their kindness, my bouquets were discovered.

Miss Irving was very sweet and really distressed about this mistake, and she gave a little luncheon for me at the Pall Mall Restaurant to make up for it. I remember still the shout of laughter that went up when I refused the proffered champagne, and youthfully remarked that I didn't like it because it ' made my neck ache.' It does still, and although I live in a country of vines and make my own good wine, I never drink it and much prefer ginger-beer.

The run of ' She Stoops to Conquer ' ended almost before it had begun. Our notice went up at the end of the first week. The play had been badly cast ; an incongruous mixture of ancient and modern acting— Miss Irving and Robert Loraine representing the modern style, and Mrs A. B. Tapping as Mrs Hardcastle, Holman Clark as Mr Hardcastle, Miss Beatrice Ferrar as Constance, and George Giddons as Tony Lumpkin, interpreting the play in the true spirit of old comedy. The public were bewildered by the mixture of twentieth century and eighteenth century acting ; and then came a violent fall of snow which discouraged the frequenters of pit and gallery, and the play also was frost-bitten.

We were all very much depressed, and, of course, I wished that I had stayed at His Majesty's.

Then one day Mr Vedrenne, one-time partner of Mr Granville Barker, sent for me. He was very kind and encouraging, but assured me that I should only waste my time in London, understudying and playing small parts. He told me that I must get my experience by playing leading parts on tour, because I was ' too important-looking' ever to be engaged for secondary (juvenile) parts in London—

"Leads—or nothing—for you, my child," he said emphatically.

Then he told me that Mr Trevor Lowe, who had played the waiter in 'You Never Can Tell,' was taking out a tour of Bernard Shaw's plays, and Mr Vedrenne was of opinion that the parts of Gloria, in 'You Never Can Tell,' and of Raina, in 'Arms and the Man,' would suit me perfectly—

"Go and see Trevor Lowe. I think he will agree with me," said Mr Vedrenne kindly. He wrote me a letter of introduction; an interview was arranged with Mr Lowe, who engaged me at once and informed me that rehearsals would begin that week.

How I loved the rehearsals of my first big part, Gloria, in 'You Never Can Tell.' It was so delightful to be working hard all the time; to be 'on' in every scene instead of speaking a few lines in one of them and then—final exit.

We were not bad as a company. Dolly, Gloria's impudent sister, was played by a chubby little girl, Dolly La Ferme, half English half French. It was her first experience of theatrical life on tour—as it would be mine—and her parents confided her to my especial care. Valentine, the dentist-lover of Gloria, was played by Graham Colmer, a young man who had made his mark in the O.U.D.S. We three were new to 'the profession,' but the rest of the cast were seasoned actors and actresses.

When Mr Trevor Lowe had booked all our dates for a sixty-week tour, and we were pretty nearly ready to start on it, he came down to one of our last rehearsals looking very white. He told us that he had had an angry letter from Mr Bernard Shaw asking why he had never been invited to superintend the rehearsals of his play; saying that he had heard that Mr Lowe had engaged " a bunch of amateurs who couldn't even speak the King's

English," and that if, when he came to see us act, he
found the report to be true, he would forbid the tour.

No wonder Mr Lowe looked pale. He was not a rich
man and had recently married Miss Sydney Fairbrother,
having just gone into management with bright prospects.
If this sixty-week tour were cancelled at the eleventh
hour he would be practically ruined, for he would have
to pay the fees of the theatres he had booked. When
Trevor Lowe engaged us all, Mr Shaw was helping Mr
Keir Hardie in an election campaign somewhere in Wales,
and Trevor Lowe naturally concluded that the famous
author would be unable to be present at our rehearsals,
so he did not invite him to attend them. Whereas Mr
Shaw had returned after only a few days in Wales, and
had since been fuming in his study until this very natural
outburst. On the day appointed for the Shaw rehearsal,
Mr Lowe was too nervous to be present, and a trembling
little company were left to the mercy of the great man.

He appeared, wearing the familiar snuff-coloured
Burberry with a floppy scarlet bow-tie, a squash felt hat,
and his beard bristling with indignation. But as the first
scene proceeded he became convulsed by his own impudent
witticisms, as voiced by the sprightly twins, and was
soon in paroxysms of good-humoured laughter. Thence-
forward the Acts went with a swing, and never have I
enjoyed a rehearsal more. No one could have been
kinder or more understanding than Mr Shaw, who is a
born producer and knows so exactly what he wants and
how to get it done. We worked together for some delightful hours. So encouraged was I by his sympathetic
demeanour towards me that I asked him if I might endow
Gloria with a sense of humour. I said I was sure that
Gloria's prig-attitude was only assumed, and that after
the kiss-episode on the terrace she surely would have grown
more human.

Mr Shaw paused for one surprised moment, then laughed
and said : " Well, my child, Gloria has been played in

about six different ways, and I don't see why you shouldn't interpret her in a seventh." And so I did. At the end of the rehearsal he told us that we were " a very clever little company," and must do him credit in his native Ireland where we were going directly after being tried out in Swansea. Trevor Lowe was enchanted by this triumphant sequel.

XI.

We were due to start on my birthday, 7th February, and Mr Lowe, who was not accompanying us on the tour, had nevertheless promised to travel with us to Swansea, watch our first performance, and give us a final polishing-up before we embarked for Ireland.

When we all met at Paddington Station there was no sign of our popular manager. Then suddenly, to our utmost consternation, we saw two red-eyed women clothed in deep mourning approaching us. His wife and mother . . .

Trevor Lowe had died suddenly—a stroke. It was the most appalling beginning to our tour, and that train steamed out of Paddington carrying in it many heavy-hearted people, for we had all grown fond of our kind and considerate manager.

The arrival at Swansea, late in the evening in pouring rain, did nothing to raise the depressed spirits of his little company, and Dolly and I were also very anxious because, being new to the life, we had not secured theatrical lodgings in advance as had the experienced ' pros ' who always book their rooms for weeks ahead with the best landladies.

We therefore stood, forlornly, on the wet platform wondering what to do next. The old man who played the benevolent waiter came to our rescue by giving me the address of lodgings he intended to occupy himself—

" A man can always fend for himself, my dears," he

reassured us in answer to our protests. "Those digs used to be tip-top when I was here some years ago."

Perhaps they were once, but it certainly must have been many years ago; for, when we arrived on their dirty doorstep, the squalid appearance of that house sent my already depressed spirits to zero. Dolly was audibly sniffing—tired and home-sick and scared. An angular female with dirty hands and wisps of grey hair plastered with sweat to a lemon-coloured visage, opened the door to us and regarded us as sourly as the fruit whose colour her complexion resembled.

We parleyed with her and she led us into the sitting-room which she was prepared to let to us. Smoke-begrimed cotton lace curtains looped up with dirty pink ribbons from dingy smeared windows, a mangy catskin hearth - rug over the fireless grate, a cracked mirror decorated with post-card portraits of the Brothers Beeno with their banjos, and toothy ladies in pink tights, fly-blown paper fans, flowers, &c.; a centre table covered with a faded plush cloth spotted with the grease of years. Sordid beyond belief.

Then we were conducted to our bedroom which looked equally dirty. With an assumption of dignity and experience which I was far from feeling, I asked the landlady if the sheets had been well aired—

"Well aired? They've been *slept in*," she retorted fiercely.

This shattering assurance deprived me of the courage to demand the clean sheets that were our due. I was very young, and just as tired, home-sick, and scared as Dolly, but being 'the leading-lady' I must never show it.

I asked if we might have some supper at once for we had only eaten a few sandwiches during that long train journey to Wales.

"Fish, I can give yer," snapped the Virago. Fish— anything—but quickly ere we faint.

When at last our fish arrived it was served up lying on the greasy paper-bag in which it had been carried home. The plates were marked with dark finger-prints ; the forks had bits of somebody else's dried egg stuck between their prongs ; the tea was a dark maroon colour and the milk was sour.

We crawled up to our bedroom, enveloped ourselves in travelling rugs, hooding them over our heads and got under our bed-quilts, *not* between those slept-in sheets.

The last sounds I heard before I dropped into the sleep of the over-weary were the subdued sniffles of poor little Dolly and the pattering of relentless rain against those smoke-begrimed windows.

Swansea may have developed into a clean and prosperous city, but in those days it was a dirty depressing place, only enlivened by the song of Welsh miners who went to their work singing, most beautifully, in parts. The theatre was—oh ! but the theatre was, then, indescribably filthy. So dirty was the floor of our dressing-room (for all the women were packed into one gas-lit room) that we were obliged to spread newspapers over it to save the skirts of our dresses.

Our audience consisted of miners and their wives who sat sucking oranges or suckling their young in the stalls. The youthful males of Swansea made a sound with their irreverent mouths, as though drawing corks from imaginary bottles when Valentine kissed me in the Terrace scene. The witticisms of Shaw fell flat upon such an audience who obviously considered the play to be ' a dud.' If only our kind manager had been beaming encouragement at us from the stage-box how much happier we should have felt.

Instead it gaped blackly at us like an open tomb.

After that first awful meal in our lodgings, I decided that we must cook our own food or get ptomaine poisoning. Accordingly, I bought a quantity of eggs and a saucepan. I remembered very little of what had been

taught me at my cooking classes of long ago ; but any
fool can boil, scramble, or poach eggs. I might even
attempt an omelette. So I fed poor Dolly on eggs until
one morning she came down to breakfast complaining
that everything around her looked yellow.

Luckily we had reached the end of the week, and that
night were to entrain for Holyhead and embark for
Ireland where I hoped we should find clean rooms and a
decent landlady who could cook. By the time we had
played both a *matinée* and evening performance, packed
our theatrical baskets at the theatre and our private
luggage in our lodgings, we were all tired out. It was
bitterly cold and very windy when at last we stumbled
into the train, I clasping in my hand some well-advertised
preventive of sea-sickness, which must be taken an hour
before getting on to the boat. I took it an hour before
we were due at Holyhead, but the train was over half
an hour late, so that my drug had begun to work before
we arrived and everything was very hazy around me.
However I managed to get undressed and comfortably
installed in my first-class cabin on the boat, when I heard
a thunderous knock on my door and the steward's voice
shouted, " You must get out of this, miss. You're all
booked third class."

The ship had started and was rolling horribly in the
gale. I staggered out of my bunk, slipped on a wrap and
went out into the passage to expostulate. There must
be some mistake. No decent theatrical company was ever
booked third class, particularly in the old days on those
Irish boats. But the purser was firm. It appeared that
this unprecedented thing had actually been done in our
case by the two little Jews who had taken over the tour
when Mr Trevor Lowe died. I went down to the third-
class saloon, which was strewn with recumbent figures
of private soldiers, shawled women, squealing babies, all
rapidly turning green with the violent lurching of the
boat.

One look and one sniff of that saloon were enough for me.

" I shall pay the excess fare myself and travel first class," I said with as much majesty as the movements of the vessel would allow, and I stumbled back to my cabin and into my berth.

It meant that the whole of my first week's salary would be swallowed up in one gulp, but I was past caring. My poor companions in adversity who could not afford to pay the excess fare nor stand that third-class saloon, spent their night huddled together on the deck, beaten upon by wind, sleet, and spray; so I was told next morning by a pathetic little frozen company through blue lips and chattering teeth. What a shame it was.

XII.

At 6 A.M. we disembarked at Rosslare and got into the milk-train to Cork, stopping at every small station on the way while engine-driver and guard conversed with cronies on platforms ; the train sometimes waiting for some peasant to arrive, complete with goat ; or for some cows to be milked in a neighbouring field, the milk then decanted into cans and deposited in the luggage-van. A leisurely business. After a six-hours' journey we reached Cork in full sunshine and began to thaw a little. I had written ahead to book rooms recommended to me by a member of the company who had occupied them recently. Dolly and I found them deliciously clean and bright, and were welcomed warmly by a delightful landlady with her spotless children clinging to her skirts. She gave us a wonderful meal, beautifully served upon a *white* table-cloth, and we heard to our joy that the house was within five minutes' walk of the Opera House where we were playing. She told us that her husband was a sergeant in the Irish Constabulary, so that we should be well guarded.

The Opera House was a beautiful theatre, and I was told, to my relief, that the leading lady had a dressing-room to herself—a luxury I had never before experienced. The audience on the first night was so appreciative that the play went with a roar ; but we found it a little difficult to play to Irishmen who knew and loved Shaw plays, anticipated the coming jokes, and were already laughing before they were uttered. The laughed so much that they delayed our performance and we emerged from the theatre nearly an hour later than usual.

Next morning we were heartened by enthusiastic notices in the local paper. The critics liked us and enjoyed our rendering of the play so much that they came back to the theatre every evening of that week. We were so popular in the town, our landlady informed us, that the Irish Constabulary drew lots to decide which of them should patrol the beat near the Opera House so as to see us going in and coming out.

She continued to be a joy, washing our clothes and our hair-brushes for us, and doing countless little things for our comfort. Her many children instead of being the noisy nuisances these little people often can be, were so well brought up that they never disturbed our peace yet were ever at hand to go out to buy stamps, post letters, and run all kinds of errands for us.

During the daytime we explored the surrounding country. On my first afternoon, seeing a gigantic Irish Constabulary-man on duty, I approached his back and began to address it—

" Could you please tell me . . ." I began. He wheeled round and confronted me, and he was so beautiful and had such devilish Irish blue eyes that I suddenly found myself blushing and stammering, " any—any—any nice places we could go and see—in—in Ireland ? " I concluded shyly and stupidly.

He twinkled down at me from his great height and suggested Blarney Castle, so several of us hired a most dilapidated looking jaunting-car tied up with string in various important places, drawn by a leggy moth-eaten mare, and, taking our picnic luncheon with us, we started off. It was naturally always important that we should never start on an expedition unless we were certain of returning in good time for the theatre, and the stage-manager much preferred that I and my understudy should never go together, so that if some unforeseen happening made me late for the play my understudy could carry on in my absence.

In Ireland it was very difficult to gauge distances— Irish miles are apparently much longer than English ones, and no Irishman ever has the faintest idea of time. However, we could see from a map that Blarney was not so very far distant from Cork, although to us swaying from side to side and perched precariously in that extremely rickety and dangerous vehicle it seemed to be farther than it was.

We lunched near the Castle and then climbed to the top, fully intending to kiss the famous Blarney-stone. But when we saw its position we became less enthusiastic.

While I was wondering whether I had the courage to attempt this dangerous feat, an American voice far below hailed me thus: " Say, ma'am, it's easy to see you're not an Amurrican."

Maddening taunt. For the honour of England I must risk my neck. So, after begging my companions to hold my legs very firmly, I sat upon the edge and, grasping two supporting stanchions, lowered myself gradually down, crooked my neck under the coping and kissed that famous stone. It was a giddy performance.

Levering myself up again was even more difficult, especially as I was full of lunch, but in the end I did it, much to the relief of my companions who had been leaning against my legs *en masse*.

No one else seemed anxious to repeat my performance

and so we descended the tower. My American strode up
to me as we came out into the open and, taking a long
insolent cigar out of his mouth, said—

" Bravo, ma'am, you're a sport. If ever you come to
Amurrica I shall be vurry glad to take you around Niagara
Falls."

I wondered if he had kissed that Blarney-stone himself,
but looking at his paunch I decided that this would be
almost physically impossible.

The Irish were charming to us. One knew that at least
three-quarters of their compliments were entirely insincere,
but the warmth of heart that prompted them was real
enough, and no one seemed able to do enough to make
us feel welcome and happy. A host of new friends,
including the dramatic critics who had haunted the
theatre every night, came to see us off at the station, and
we left Cork very regretfully.

Our next date was Dublin, and there we had the same
typically Irish reception and an equally happy week. I
escaped with little Dolly one day to visit (the then)
Queenstown Harbour where several warships lay at
anchor. Longing to see over them I asked a lounging
Irishman what were the visiting hours. He rolled a
wicked eye at me and replied, quick as lightning, " Sure,
it'll be an honour an' a pleasure to show anyone as beheuti-
ful as yerself over the harbour at anny hour of the day or
night." He gave a beckoning nod to a group of equally
grimy and villainous-looking men who immediately
launched a battered old dinghy, got into it themselves,
and then he held out his hand to assist us to embark. I
felt a moment's hesitation. Six double rows of astonish-
ingly white teeth gleamed up at me from those sooty
faces in a delightfully gay smile of welcome, and Dolly
and I decided to risk adventure.

Our self-invited guests were as charming as though
they had hired the boat for our pleasure. They pointed
out places of importance on the shore ; they abused

uniformed officers on the decks of warships when they
politely informed me that their visiting hours were long
past ; and at length the most voluble of our companions
actually did secure us admittance to a destroyer in charge
of a very young and chubby naval lieutenant who seemed
delighted to see us and implored us to take tea with him
as he was bored to death.

He brewed us some extremely black tea in his tiny
quarters while our escort sculled around the harbour,
promising to return in half an hour. I devoutly hoped
they would, for Dolly and I had to get back to Dublin
in time for our work. But they kept their word, and
we all parted on the quay the best of friends, having
thoroughly enjoyed our joy-ride together.

Belfast, our next town, prepared us in some small
measure for the type of audience we should get when
we crossed over to Scotland, for the population of Belfast
is, of course, half Scottish.

Whereas the Irish audiences had delayed our performance by anticipating jokes, the Scots delayed it by
their slowness of perception. They missed very few of
Shaw's witticisms, but the points took time to pierce
their leisurely brains, so that they laughed late ; and we
discovered early that unless we played very slowly and
gave our audience time for realisation and laughter, half
the play would be lost. During the first scene, the bright
dialogue of the twins was continually being drowned by
the laugh accorded to the previous joke.

" Play slower—Give 'em time to take it in—Don't
speak into a laugh," hissed the stage-manager from the
prompt corner, and we soon got used to the new type of
audience. I remembered, then, Jimmy Welch's answer
when I asked him if he didn't get tired of playing the
same part hundreds of times in succession.

" No," he replied, " it's always interesting and sometimes thrilling. It is like salmon-fishing. Every day
you fish for salmon, but each fish you hook has to

be played differently, for no fish ever behaves in the same way."

I found it increasingly fascinating to notice which points each audience would take and which lose; and only in Ireland and Oxford was every single Shavianism appreciated. Oxford was the most wonderful experience because my father and brothers were all Oxford men, and Daddie and Mervyn were known to be very fine oars.

I had hardly arrived in my rooms than I was waited upon by three captains of boats—those of my father's and brothers' colleges, Worcester, Corpus Christi, and Merton. They came to welcome me and to make me free of the three college barges—for it was Eights Week and the whole of Oxford *en fête*.

Our first night was a tremendous affair, and the theatre packed to the doors. Even the gangways were crowded.

I had never before been *cheered* at my first entrance on the stage, and I found it a most exhilarating experience, and acted as I had never acted before. It is a wonderful sensation to know that one is 'getting over the footlights' and to play upon the emotions of a sympathetic audience.

I telegraphed to Mummie asking her to allow Marjory to join me and share the Oxford festivities, and the child put up her hair for the occasion and arrived next day. We could have had every meal triplicated during that extraordinary week had we so desired. A great many Suffolk boys of our acquaintance were up at Oxford then, besides friends of Mervyn and of Guy, and at every entertainment we met more friends of these friends, so that our engagements accumulated in snowball-fashion. The excitement of it all so went to Marjory's head that she complicated both our lives tremendously by blushingly accepting every invitation given to us, and it became increasingly difficult not to wound some hospitable heart.

I don't think either of us had ever been given so many flowers and chocolates in our lives before, and the whole company at the theatre, including managers, scene-shifters, electricians, and call-boy, were glutted with our surplus.

Little Dolly also had a great success at Oxford. Her chubby face and cheeky part appealed to the younger members of the University, and she was included in many of our invitations. Then, having made the acquaintance of several boys, she was whirled off in a vortex of her own.

Graham Colmer, who played Valentine, being an old and distinguished member of the O.U.D.S., was likewise *fêted* everywhere. His gaieties and mine were rather interrupted by rehearsals for ' Arms and the Man,' which we were to play for the last three nights.

Graham Colmer was cast to play Bluntschli and I was to play Raina, and I thoroughly enjoyed representing the little minx. It is a picturesque and amusing play, but my part was rather an anxious one because of the quick changes of costume ; from a nightgown, with my hair down, in the first Act, to a bustle and chignon in Act II., and thence, very quickly, to short curls and a peasant's dress in Act III. My hair was so long that it took ages to arrange it, especially with nervous shaking fingers. I dreaded every moment to hear the yell of the call-boy—

" ACT THREEEEEEE—BEGINNERS, PLEEEEEAASSSEE ! "

' Arms and the Man ' had a terrific success at Oxford, and we had lovely notices in all the local papers and magazines. I even got personal praise from a woman-hating Don who acted as dramatic critic for the 'Varsity magazine. Instead of lacerating me with his piercing pen, he spilt quite a lot of complimentary ink upon Raina.

XIII.

That sixty-week tour was a very happy one, chiefly
because everyone in the little company was so nice and
so kind. Life on tour can be made miserable by petty
jealousies and intrigues, but we were, mercifully, free of
them. Had the women of the company been less warm-
hearted and generous they might easily have resented
my very beautiful clothes, given to me by my Duchess.

During the *matinées* I always had a tea-party in my
dressing-room between the Acts. My dresser would rush
out and buy cakes and buns, and we all had great fun
together.

I had made myself responsible for little Dolly, and so
we usually shared rooms, but I am certain that, in general,
it is better for each member of a touring company to
live entirely independently—the life is so tiring, acting
and travelling incessantly and meeting the same people
in the theatre night after night for weeks and months on
end can easily get on one's nerves. It would be boring
to chronicle a sixty-week tour in detail, and, although it
is twenty-seven years ago since I was ' on the road,' I
do not suppose that touring conditions have changed
very much. I imagine that all actors and actresses,
before starting on tour, write to various addresses recommended to them as excellent theatrical lodgings in each
town. That often those rooms or those landladies have
become dirty or slovenly and a week of misery has to
be endured. That each member of the company is exhausted on Saturday night after two performances and
the packing of personal possessions in lodgings and stage-
clothes and properties at the theatre (unless the luxury
of a competent wardrobe mistress to travel with the
company is provided) ready for the departure to
another town either that same night or early next
morning.

I cannot believe that those Sunday train-journeys are any less boring than they were in my day. Boxed into reserved carriages for hours, shunted into sidings until attached to another train ; unable to obtain food, since the refreshment *buffets* in the stations were generally closed ; everyone feeling tired and jaded—and looking it.

And how I dreaded early morning arrivals in a new town. I used to be at my worst in the morning, and my soul died within me when I reached my new lodgings to find an unmade bed with dirty sheets, traces of the last occupant, in what was to be my bedroom ; and the remains of a hurried breakfast in my new sitting-room. Then I used to sink down in a chair surrounded by my baggage, and wonder what on earth made me leave my very happy and lovely home to follow this hideous profession.

Nearly always I was saved from despair by finding a fat letter from Mummie awaiting me on the mantel-piece among the post-card portraits of theatre and music-hall stars. Before starting on tour I gave her my touring list of dates and towns and addresses of lodgings booked in advance.

She was wonderfully clever at timing her letters so that one awaited me each week on arrival. Only sometimes, if I had not been able to secure rooms in advance, she posted her letter to the theatre and I had to wait for it all through a dreary twenty-four hours.

Very often she sent flowers from our Rectory garden, the first snowdrops packed in moss, then aconites, prim-roses and squills with perhaps a tiny bunch of white violets. Their heavenly faint sweet scent and the smell of wet earth and leaves that clung to the moss, would bring pictures of home so vividly to me, even amid my sometimes sordid surroundings, that I often watered the little spring flowers with home-sick tears.

" Now, miss, wotudyerlike fer yer dinner before yer

go down to the theyater ? I cud cook yer a nice red chop wiv some chips—and perraps yer'd fancy er termarter ? " Some such question would drag me back from our fragrant garden to the prosaic present. I was no longer living in a sheltered home, I was working for my bread—or red chops and chips.

Still it was all ' experience '—valuable experience, and the unpleasant episodes were doubtless very salutary for one who had always been loved, sheltered, and spoiled from her youth up.

The Shaw tour gave me some very valuable theatrical experience. We did not travel our own scenery, and relied upon the stock sets found in every theatre, so that very often all our entrances and exits were changed by the new positions of doors. I found this very disconcerting at first, but I soon got used to it and even found it exciting.

My greatest thrill on that tour was when my complete family, with the exception of Mervyn, who was then in Borneo, came to see me act, and our business manager gave them the stage-box to witness my performance.

Between the Acts, the family surged round to the stage-door and visited me in my dressing-room. I sent the call-boy to fetch various members of the company and introduced them all round. Little Dolly at once fell in love with Daddie, and cheeked him deliciously to his great delight.

When at last the tour ended, she and I still kept in touch with each other although she never acted again, preferring the safe shelter of a very happy home. Later she married Harry Cartwright, a well-known football player, and has produced three large daughters, all much taller than she, one of whom is my namesake and goddaughter ; herself, now, a married woman.

XIV.

Back in London once more, again began the search for work. The Duchess gave me an introduction to Mr Norman Forbes in his flat one morning, and he asked me to act something for him, a truly ghastly request at 9.30 A.M. I suddenly became so paralysed with shyness that I couldn't remember one word of anything I had ever learned by heart, and to encourage me he turned his back on me saying, " If I don't look at you, you won't be nervous."

I remember frantically wondering how he could possibly judge of my acting powers with his back turned.

What I acted—or recited—I cannot now remember, but apparently my voice pleased him, for I was sent down to the Lyceum Theatre and there given the small part of a Court lady, companion and *confidante* of Louise de Valois, and the understudy of Miss Dorothy Thomas, who played Louise.

Working at the Lyceum was excellent experience ; for the audiences there were like no others in London. They cheered their hero and heroine for minutes on end, and they hissed and booed the villain whenever he appeared on the stage. If he didn't get his venomous hisses he became at once discouraged. When good triumphed over evil there were roars of applause, and shouts of laughter if an actor forgot his words or anything went wrong with the shifting of scenery.

In my part I had to take continual messages to the King from Louise, and every time I entered and left his presence I had to make a deep Court curtesy with my bent head almost touching the ground. One day I had to have a slight operation on one ear which left me very giddy. The specialist who performed it advised me not to act that night, but I disregarded his counsel and went down to the theatre as usual. Whilst performing my

first Court curtesy to the King a sudden vertigo seized me,
I swayed, and was obliged to steady myself by putting
one hand on the floor and feared I was going to faint.
But the startling roar of mirth from the audience brought
my senses back swiftly, and then Matheson Lang, realising
that something was amiss with me, stretched out a gracious
hand, and, when I put both mine upon it, he levered me
to my feet. Thenceforth, every time I made an entrance
that night I was greeted with a roar of laughter as the
audience recalled my poor little wobbly curtesy.

The mixed cast was interesting. Matheson Lang,
Dorothy Thomas, and Frederick Ross had all been carefully trained under great actors, and then there was the
stock Lyceum crowd, some of whom could not even speak
the King's English much less pronounce the French
names of the characters in the play or enunciate the
occasional French sentences they were called upon to
pronounce.

One gentleman of the French court, resplendent in
satin doublet and lace ruffles, accosted me thus after a
dress rehearsal—

" Are yer goin' out now ter feed fer faice, Miss ? "
For a moment I stared at him uncomprehendingly ; then
realised that he was merely asking me if I were going out
to lunch.

It was fun crossing Covent Garden Market every day,
and I made friends with many of the costers whose crude
compliments amused me vastly. One day I was walking
past stalls of ripe strawberries, watching two rather
sour-looking angular women appraising the baskets of
fruit. A fat old coster sitting on a barrel remarked to a
friend as the two critical spinsters passed him—

" Two mouldy old strawberries, Jim."

Then, as I ran past him towards the theatre, " But
'ere's the cream," and he shied a strawberry at my hat.

It took me some time to realise that the volleys of
small tomatoes, green pears, and other missiles that

were aimed at my flying form (for in those days I usually ran or skipped to an appointment) as I crossed the great Market, were only intended as compliments. The costers were merely ' saying it with fruit.'

It was also the greatest fun to be in London again ; to be taken out to luncheon by my many friends and acquaintances ; to have tea-parties in my rooms and to visit the dressing-rooms of my various theatrical friends in the theatres in which they were acting, and be given free tickets to see their performance when their *matinées* did not coincide with mine.

Stella Patrick Campbell was acting with Sir George Alexander in ' The Importance of Being Earnest ' at the St James's Theatre, and she often carried me off to her home in Kensington Square, where I delighted to go.

I was fascinated with her mother's beauty, her voice, and her unaccountability. She was always very kind to me and loved playing with my hair, which she would twist and plait and arrange in fantastic fashion.

She was to me an absorbing study, ' a bundle of con-tradictions, a mass of incongruities ; ' for one hour sweet, gentle and considerate, and during the next she would become utterly unreasonable, dismissing the servants for the slightest peccadillo and pleased with nothing. Her neatness amazed me. Somehow one would have expected so great an artist to be careless about detail, but she was meticulously neat in all her habits. But domestic details maddened her, and I can see her now, entering Stella's bedroom, her great tragic eyes smouldering, and declaim-ing passionately—

" They tell me there is no more toilet paper in the house. How CAN I be expected to act a romantic part AND remember to order TOILET PAPER ! "

She was acting, then, herself and would jump into a taxi in the morning and drive out into the country for fresh air and exercise, returning with bunches of wild flowers and branches of blossoming trees which she

arranged exquisitely in her drawing-room. One day she
came back with five mongrel puppies which she had
bought from a street vendor because she said they had
unhappy faces. These she insisted upon taking down to
the theatre with her lest they be lonely in her absence.

One night when I was staying for the week-end with
Stella we had both been back from our respective theatres,
had supped together and gone to bed before Mrs Campbell
came home, and Stella became anxious.

At last her mother appeared with a wild distraught
air and told us dramatically that, feeling stifled by the
stupidity and insensibility of all the members of the
company with which she was acting, she had driven out
to St John's Wood to visit a parrot of her acquaintance
who had a soul and had comforted her greatly.

She would confide in me her sorrow that Stella had
also taken to the stage. " I never wanted her to act—
but she insisted upon going on the stage when she was
twenty-one, and prefers friends of her own making—
beautiful fools such as So-and-So and So-and-So and
Peggy Beech—I'm sorry, darling, I was thinking I was
talking just to myself," she apologised with a disarming
smile when I burst out laughing to hear myself included
in the list.

One could never be angry with her ; she was just a
spoiled child when in one of her rages, and although I
have heard it said that her tongue could be cruel it was
never cruel to me. If one could only make her laugh
and show her how ridiculously she was behaving the
storm was over in a moment, for she has a delicious sense
of humour and a deep wisdom. When in a happy mood,
no one could be more winning, and charm radiated from
her every look, tone, and gesture.

I loved to see her ' playing with a room,' and she could
transform ugliness into beauty with her magic touch
just as she did in ' The Matriarch,' when she descended
with a mass of luggage upon the poor lodgings of her

relations and at once proceeded to beautify them with treasures of brocade, lovely pieces of stuff, and embroidered Oriental shawls from her capacious trunks.

She was such a joy to the eye and the ear. I can see her now, wandering about that delightful little house in Kensington Square, wearing some lovely draped garment of exotic colour; suddenly becoming impatient with the weight of that mass of blue-black hair, drawing out the great tortoise-shell dagger that held up the heavy coil on the base of her beautiful head and shaking it loose so that it fell around her like a dark cloak—murmuring, and grumbling, or chuckling over some joke in that musical slightly husky voice of hers as she paced about with the movements of a panther. Then, upon the sudden entrance of a visitor she would gather up that weight of hair in those lovely hands of hers and with swift deft movements roll it, coil it upon the nape of her neck and then stab the dagger through the lustrous knot. All this without a trace of self-consciousness or the aid of a mirror.

XV.

Just then I was in a great state of excitement because Mervyn, who had by this time entered the Colonial Civil Service and become a District Commissioner, was coming home on leave from East Africa and I longed to exhibit him. When he did arrive, he flatly refused to take a room in an hotel, preferring a mattress on the floor of my little panelled sitting-room in Shepherd's Market so that we should not lose one moment of each other's society while he was in London. He had business at the Colonial Office and the Oriental School of Languages before going home to the parents in Suffolk.

Next day he had various appointments to keep, and I had promised to go over to Kensington Square to see Stella, so it was arranged that he should fetch me from there and take me out to luncheon. Mrs Campbell was up and dressed, but I found Stella still in bed, with curtains drawn, shutting out the sunlight, reading Browning's poems by the light of an electric lamp with a violet shade and smoking Egyptian cigarettes, looking like some Eastern princess with her magnolia skin, shadowed eyes, and her long straight dark hair spread out upon the pillow.

Of course I could talk about nothing but Mervyn, and made her laugh over his odd choice of cheese, pickled onions and beer for supper, and the length of him stretched upon a mattress in my sitting-room with his head in the bow-window and his feet touching the door.

When he called for me at Kensington Square, by some mistake the parlourmaid sent him straight up to the second floor where I was still sitting on Stella's bed, and we were suddenly startled by his voice calling my name just outside the door. I rushed out to him and introduced him to Stella from the landing, to their joint amusement, and then followed a queer little dialogue, Mervyn inviting the invisible Stella to join us at luncheon, and asking her advice as to where he should take us as he had been so long abroad that he had forgotten all the good restaurants in London. Stella chaffing him in her low sweet voice and asking him what dress she should wear to honour the occasion. I was made to carry out a selection of frocks on to the landing, and he chose a dim purple one with dull gold embroidery, delighting her because he had instinctively chosen her favourite colour.

To my great disappointment Mervyn was as tongue-tied as a shy schoolboy when Stella, looking quite lovely, eventually emerged. She and I had to do all the talking all through luncheon and during the intervals of the *matinée* to which we all went afterwards ; and I feared that this meeting of two people that I loved had proved a failure, for Mervyn was so glum and silent.

When we had left Stella at Kensington Square and

were driving back to Shepherd Street in a taxi, Mervyn, who had been so unusually quiet, suddenly turned to me and said violently, " Win, I MUST marry her. I can't go back to Africa without her. She's everything that I have always wanted. I fell in love with her voice before I even saw her. When can I see her again ? You *must* help me."

The *coup de foudre*—this great giant had had innumerable flirtations but had never before fallen in love. Now it was really serious, and, knowing his strong will and impulsive temperament, I was frankly terrified. If Stella refused him he was quite capable of sacrificing a promising career and sitting on her doorstep in London until she promised to marry him.

Then began a hectic fortnight. Mervyn proposed to Stella by letter that very night and went in person for her answer next day. Naturally she refused an almost complete stranger, and he was in black despair for hours, then continued his siege with redoubled fury. Flowers and letters were sent by special messenger and prayers for an audience. Stella was flattered and attracted by this huge volcanic creature and his unconventional behaviour, and she consented to meet him again—and again—and yet again until she, also, lost her balance and fell head over ears in love with him. He was so strong, so simple, and so brilliant, besides being so beautiful —he was so totally unlike the London type of men she was accustomed to meet, polished courtiers and men of the world. She had always longed to be the whole universe and the firmament above it, to one man, and every woman loves to be taken by storm. By the end of that exhausting fortnight (exhausting for me because I was between two burning fires and perpetually got scorched on both sides) Stella at last consented to leave the stage, marry Mervyn, and go back with him to East Africa.

They both implored me to break the news to Mrs

Campbell, who would certainly not be pleased, having more ambitious views for Stella. After much persuasion and cajoling I consented to do it, and it was arranged that Mervyn should take Stella out to supper the next night so that I should find her mother alone when I went to Kensington Square after my play was over.

I timed my arrival rather late so that Mrs Pat would have returned from the theatre and have had time to eat some supper. She was still eating it when I arrived.

When I broke my news to her, she first regarded me with a pitying stare as though she feared I might be delirious ; then, picking up a large cucumber from the supper table, she viciously sliced off its bitter end as though she wished it were my head. Then she began to point out to me the madness and the impossibility of the proposed alliance. Between each biting sentence she ate a chunk of cucumber, and, before she had finished lecturing me, the whole of it had been devoured.

" Your brother may be a very delightful and brilliant man, but you don't know Stella as I do. She is accustomed always to be the centre of the stage both in social and theatrical life. (Another slice of cucumber.) She could never take a back seat, efface herself, and help a man with his career. There is an undercurrent in Stella of which everyone but her mother is unaware. She may think her 'world well lost for love,' but she would soon get bored with the life of East Africa, pine for London, and make your brother's life miserable. It would be pure folly for her to attempt such a sacrifice—for to her it *would* be a sacrifice and not the crowning joy of her life as marriage ought to be. (This with a satirical smile.)

" Then your brother has scarcely any private means— only his salary in the Colonial Civil Service. I own that it is a good one, but if anything happened to him ? I can't give Stella an allowance. I have worked very hard to give my two children an exceptional education and advantages, and now, in the late twenties, they must fend for themselves.

" I know exactly what will happen if Stella marries your brother. He will die after one week leaving her with seven babies." Here she cut another piece of cucumber into seven neat pieces.

" Darling," I interrupted her, " isn't that rather quick ? "

Her flood of eloquence was stemmed for a moment and a smile curled her mouth, then, having finished the cucumber, she moved over to a comfortable chair, lit a large black cheroot and continued to lecture me in the same strain for an hour.

In spite of that refreshing cucumber and cheroot, all she said depressed me greatly. I longed for the happiness of Stella and Mervyn to be assured, but Mrs Campbell's wise arguments made me wonder if this marriage would assure it.

Having kept my promise to them, I kissed her rather chilly cheek and returned to my rooms in Shepherd's Market, quite exhausted, but relieved that the dreaded interview was over and that I had done my part. Stella and Mervyn must now fight for what they imagined to be their own happiness. This they did with vigour, and very soon Mrs Campbell succumbed to Mervyn's charm, and the beauty of his hands, and his smile which attracted her greatly.

But although she eventually was obliged to accept the position, her attitude towards it was ever reluctant and discouraging. Always she hoped that the fires would flicker out as quickly as they had blazed into being. She did not know Stella who, if opposed, became obstinate, or Mervyn who found difficulties stimulating.

In the end it was decided that Stella and Mervyn should be married at the end of his home leave so that they might travel out to East Africa together, but, most unfortunately as we all thought, H. B. Irving suddenly offered her the part of Princess Clementina in A. E. W. Mason's play, which ' H. B.' intended to produce in the provinces and then bring to London, he himself playing Wogan.

Clementina is a lovely romantic part, and Stella was thrilled with the offer—but—it would mean that Mervyn must travel back alone and she go out to him later to be married in East Africa.

Mervyn became plunged in gloom, and not all Stella's enthusiasm over the money she would earn by playing a star part could pull him out of it.

While this was going on I received a letter from Mr Austen Brereton, H. B. Irving's manager, asking me to go and see him. He offered me the understudy of Princess Clementina, saying that the part would suit me and that, as I was ' a coloured edition ' of Stella, I could wear her frocks if necessary without much alteration.

I demurred that, as I had just been playing a leading part on tour, it seemed to me bad policy to return to the provinces as a mere understudy—a step backwards instead of forwards. He replied that he was a gambler and so would advise me to accept his offer, which might lead to my big chance.

Back in London Stella added her persuasions to his, saying that it would be such fun if we toured together, sharing rooms, and so on.

But just at that very time I had a letter from Mr Montefiore of the Coronet Theatre at Notting Hill, saying that he was putting on a West End repertory season and would like to engage me to play a variety of parts. I went to see him. He said that if I came to the Coronet I should have every chance of playing leading parts since, in a suburban theatre, only one West End star would be necessary in a cast. That one star might easily be a man, and then I could play leading woman opposite him. Mr Montefiore was opening his season with a play of Madame Albanesi's with Marion Terry, Aubrey Smith, and Norman Trevor starring in it. I could understudy and play a young girl's part in this production. Perhaps —in the next—and he buoyed me up with bright hopes.

I asked for time to think the matter over, and I took counsel of various actresses of experience. One and all advised me to go to the Coronet and not to the provinces with H. B. Irving—and I took their advice. Had I followed that of Mr Austen Brereton, I should have played Princess Clementina in London, for, on the opening night, a piece of scenery fell upon Stella's foot, breaking a small bone, so that she was laid up for weeks, and her understudy played that lovely part throughout the run of the play. Cruel luck for Stella, and for Mervyn who had, of course, gone back to Africa alone. (In a flash I saw again his distraught face and remembered his parting words to me at the station which then seemed so extraordinary—

" Take care of my darling—*and don't let anything fall on her*.")

Cruel luck, also, for me.

XVI.

I enjoyed the rehearsals at the Coronet Theatre. Miss Marion Terry, Aubrey Smith, and Norman Trevor were all so delightfully kind to me and I made a lasting friendship with Viva Birkett, who afterwards married Philip Merivale. She, also, was playing a small part and was afterwards cast to play the lead in Cecil Raleigh's drama which followed the Albanesi play and which we weathered together. Then came a letter for her from Mr Gaston Meyer, begging her to go at once to Liverpool to play her original part of Sylvia in F. Anstey's 'The Brass Bottle,' which had such a tremendous success in London, as the actress who had been playing Sylvia on tour had fallen ill. Viva was already booked to play Mrs Darling in ' Peter Pan ' at the Duke of York's Theatre, and so she very generously recommended me for the part, and Mr Meyer, who was in an awful hole, joyfully accepted her suggestion.

The part of Sylvia was put into one of my hands and my ticket to Liverpool in the other, and I was told to study the part in the train because I should have to play it that evening with the full London company.

I was very proud, but very nervous. Luckily the journey to Liverpool is long, and, having a carriage to myself, I could repeat my part aloud and get my inflections right. But when at last I reached the theatre my knees were knocking together and my dry tongue clave to the roof of my mouth. However, everyone was perfectly charming to me. The company had assembled early so as to give me a quick ' run through ' before the curtain went up, and fortunately I had many exits and entrances so that I could study my next sentences in the wings. Also the other members of the company had acted in ' The Brass Bottle ' so long that they knew the play by heart, and were ready to prompt me if my memory failed, which happily it did not.

I made great friends with Mr Rudge Harding, who played Mr Pringle in the play. When he found that I was country-bred and loved birds and flowers he warmed to me at once, being himself a great naturalist. He promised to take me into the fenced copses in Richmond Park where wild birds nest in hundreds, when we all returned to London, for he possessed a private key giving him entrance to all the enclosed places so that he could study bird life in all his leisure moments. He was rather like a queer bird himself—with the pose and demeanour of a staid penguin, which was perfectly appropriate to Mr Pringle and very funny in a fantastic farce. He was such a dear, and such an excellent actor. I found it terribly difficult to keep a perfectly grave face during some of the ridiculous situations in the play when the audience rocked with laughter sometimes for three or four minutes on end, and I fear I was sometimes guilty of a twinkle or a twitching mouth. But nothing could move Rudge Harding's stolid imperturbability. He was a conscientious actor, a great artist, and the kindest-hearted man in the world.

It did not surprise me in the least to hear soon after the war broke out in 1914, that Rudge Harding had said that, being too old to fight, he had no more the heart to paint his face and mum to amuse the London people while men were being killed every moment in France, and that he had offered his services to the Red Cross. After the war he was given the post of Superintendent of the Star and Garter Home for disabled officers at Richmond, where he did splendid service, and spent his leisure hours with his beloved birds in Richmond Park.

During the tour of 'The Brass Bottle' he and Mr Holman Clark with his attractively ugly face and curious lisp both 'uncled' me very kindly in their characteristic ways. Rudge Harding took me out for country walks outside the various towns we visited, and taught me much about birds and trees. He also gave me many fussy bachelor counsels about hygienic food, precautions against damp sheets in lodgings, and the excellent effect of senna tea upon the intestines. He was beautifully courteous and absolutely sexless in his behaviour towards the women of the company, who respected him highly but thought him rather dull. Not so Mr Holman Clark with his knowing twinkle and appreciative eye, they all 'fell' for him. He was of the 'cake and compliments' type of 'uncle,' and was very popular. The chorus-ladies described him as 'an old rip' because he pinched their cheeks and criticised their hats and gave them chocolates. His performance as the Geni was quite wonderful, and I shall never forget his green face, rumbling voice, and grotesque uncanny gestures.

It is very nervous work acting in a play which depends

for its great effects upon fantastic trick-illusions which may go wrong or sometimes never happen ; and the travelling of all the expensive properties, reflecting mirrors, and other contrivances which were used for the trans-formation scenes, was a very anxious business for the stage-manager.

If a breakage occurred on a journey and could not be mended or replaced before the next performance, we had to change the scenes or gag.

' The Brass Bottle ' tour ended a little prematurely for me with a nightmare experience.

We were playing in Edinburgh, and one wet cold after-noon, whilst standing in puddles of water watching the Guard march up the Castle hill, I caught the chill of my life. I was staying in huge palatial rooms, dim and dark, with an enormous mirror at each end of my sitting-room. I had a great four-post bed with dark tester and hangings which depressed me to the soul. In that great bed I was destined to spend the greater part of our week in Edinburgh. I struggled through my work at the theatre that night and somehow walked back to my rooms through icy blinding rain.

My first surprise was to find the great stone staircase in complete darkness and the house strangely silent, for, in general, theatrical landladies keep late hours for the convenience of their lodgers, and prepare them a hot supper after the play. With difficulty I found the key-hole of my bedroom door and groped about trying to discover the gas-jet in the darkness. Failing to find it I undressed in the dark, feeling too ill to search for biscuits or something to eat, and then, walking delicately, like Agag, felt my way towards the great bed.

Suddenly I had to stifle a scream as my bare feet trod upon something cold and slimy which, from a solid mass, divided itself under my weight into separate fingers like a dead hand. Feverish as I was, a cold sweat broke out all over me and I made one leap for the bed to escape that invisible horror. But an hour later I was in such intense pain that I had to get out of bed again to go in search of my landlady to see if she could give me anything to alleviate it. Creeping out of the other side of the bed to avoid that hidden horror on the floor, I at last found the door after barking my shins and bumping my head. I called her name across the passage until a door opposite mine opened and an awful apparition stood framed in it, holding a candle. A tall emaciated old man with a long straggling white beard, clad in a flannel nightshirt reaching far above his bony knees, regarded me with a terrifying glassy stare. I stammered out my request and, saying that he would tell his wife, he left me to find my way back to bed, murmuring weakly to myself, " *Que c'est ridicule un homme en chemise.*"

Presently he returned with something which I drank without question while he stood like some awful spectre waiting for the empty glass. As he departed I stole a quick glance in the direction of that slimy horror on the floor and saw—two pounds of raw sausages.

Why my landlady should have strewn my floor with sausages I was too ill to conjecture, but not too ill to laugh hysterically into my pillow over the scare they had given me.

The rest of that week I spent in a semi-comatose condition, for she had given me a tremendously strong dose of opium, to which, as I afterwards heard, she was an addict.

I slept all next day, and I remember being awakened with difficulty by a wild-eyed woman who shook my shoulders and implored me to get up as she didn't know my part and my clothes didn't fit her.

This vaguely seen woman was my understudy. She got me up and dressed me and I don't know how I was taken to the theatre or how I contrived to play my part, for I haven't the faintest remembrance of anything that happened and must have acted quite mechanically. Next day was exactly the same. I slept through it till evening, was awakened, dressed, I acted at the theatre, was taken back and put to bed where I slept again, dreaming wonderful dreams, floating in the air above houses and cathedrals and mountains and valleys in an atmosphere of crystal light. Nothing mattered any more, no sorrow or anxiety could touch me. I was completely happy in a fantastic world.

This state of things lasted for a week. The doctor who was called in said that my landlady had given me a dose strong enough to kill a weaker person.

The awakening was quite terrible. Never shall I forget that feeling of nausea. I could touch no solid food and had to abandon the tour and go home to recuperate.

XVII.

It was wonderful to be at home again. Of course everyone had heard that I was coming back and I was welcomed at the tiny station by Pigg, the porter, Bacon, the ticket-collector, and Mr Fryett, the stationmaster (those three queer names are genuine and their association was a continual joy to us).

The villagers were at their doors to wave to ' Miss Winnie ' as she drove past. They had forgiven me for going on the stage, and had got over the disappointment of my first appearance in church after I had taken this terrific step, NOT attired in pink tights and spangles as they had obviously hoped and expected. Their idea of the stage was founded upon the local pantomime or occasional itinerant circus, and our washerwoman confided to Mummie one day, " I thought of goin' on the stage meself but me legs was too fat."

Those happy intervals of rest at home whilst out of work were only marred by the anxious feeling that, by being there, I might be losing some splendid opportunity of work.

When I had recovered I went back to London to resume my search for work, and there one day I had a letter from the wife of an old friend of my father's, Colonel Mount Batten, who was at that time Lord Lieutenant of Dorset. She invited me to come down to Upcerne Manor for a rest in the country, since I was not acting at the moment, and asked me to bring very few clothes as they were spending a quiet summer.

So I packed a small suitcase containing the usual necessities and only one evening frock, put on a smart little blue serge suit and shady hat for everyday wear, and started on my journey.

The Colonel met me with his dog-cart at Sherborne Station and during our drive to the old manor-house told me that he was so glad I had come down to support his shy wife through the various social functions at which, as his lady, she was expected to appear. This was disconcerting. Thanks to my Duchess, I had a cupboard full of lovely filmy frocks which would have been entirely appropriate to wear at these County garden-parties, but I had obeyed the instructions of my hostess and had left them behind. I blurted out all this to the Colonel who merely gave me a sidelong glance and remarked—

" It don't much matter what *you* wear, me dear," which statement might have been taken amiss had it not been accompanied by an appreciative and encouraging wink. I loved the old Colonel and his wicked eye.

We reached the old grey manor-house in time for tea— a delicious time to arrive I always think.

My hostess rose slowly, and with a greeting of " Well, Winifred, how nice to see you here," came forward and gave me her usual shy and formal kiss. Then she introduced me to a rather beautiful old man who proved to be her father, Mr James Sant, once Court painter to Queen Victoria, but better known as the artist who painted " The Soul's Awakening "—that picture of an anæmic and earnest young woman with the eyes of a fanatic, clasping a Bible, and gazing heavenward. When I first met him Mr Sant was very old and rapidly becoming childish, so that his instant desire to paint my portrait may only have been another symptom of approaching senility.

I suffered much from dear old Mr Sant. He insisted that I should sit for my portrait on lovely sunny September mornings when I longed to be blackberrying in the fields or nutting in the woods.

Another trial of patience was that the portrait threatened to become an old painter's permanent pastime, for every day he changed the pose or the colouring. One day I was portrayed with chestnut curls bound by a blue ribbon ; the next day with black hair and a velvet picture hat. The final picture, finished long afterwards in London, rather resembled a death-mask of Charles I.

Sometimes Mr Sant's reminiscences, recounted to me during these long fuggy hours indoors, were interesting or amusing. He told me of the tyranny of Queen Victoria over her household, and of her Spartan habits. Apparently she never felt cold, and sat placidly in a glacial atmosphere at Windsor Castle whilst he tried to paint her portrait with fingers so stiff with cold that he could hardly hold the brush.

One bitter winter's day the Queen remarked to a shivering blue-nosed lady-in-waiting who was attending the sitting—

" You look cold, Jane."

Greatly daring the poor lady affirmed through chattering teeth, hoping for the relief of a fire—

" I *am* cold, Your Majesty."

The Queen merely smiled a little disdainfully, but gave no order for a fire to be lighted.

Later, during Mr Sant's period of office, she ordered him to paint a portrait of one of her ladies and when it was finished, not approving of some detail of decoration he had put in, she bade him change it. He refused, saying that as an artist he saw it in that way. The Queen never forgave him for his defiance of her wishes.

He also told me a true story of two married friends of his, " the ugliest man and woman in the world." They knew they were ugly, but the wife determined that she would have a beautiful son, and, during the nine months of his making, she went daily to the National Gallery and stared at the picture of a beautiful boy, feasting her eyes upon it and praying that she might have a son exactly like him. When her child was born, he was an exact replica of the picture.

Someone else once told me that the mother of Charles Kingsley did the same kind of thing. She wanted a son who would become a writer and who would love birds, beasts, and flowers as she did, and so, during her pregnancy, she lived on the moors in Devon, studying the wild life around her and writing. Her son developed all the same tastes.

I have often wondered how far it is in a mother's power to combat unpleasant family traits and tendencies in her unborn child and to substitute the talents and virtues she admires. I suppose she would have to possess a very strong character and a great power of concentration to get what she wanted, and I imagine that a boy would be far more malleable in the making than a girl who, from the first spark of consciousness, would probably, in the perverse way of her sex, instantly start combating the plans for her formation and decide to be exactly the opposite.

XVIII.

During that Dorset visit I had to accompany my hostess to various garden-parties at all the great houses of the neighbourhood, always unsuitably attired in my little blue suit, while other women trailed about in chiffon and lace.

The last function I was expected to attend was a garden-party given by Thomas Hardy at Max Gate. I was very much excited about this, having been swept off my feet by his picturesque prose, and I expected to find him living in a long low farmhouse in a lonely place overlooking the country he describes so wonderfully.

Mrs Mount Batten, Mr Sant, and I drove over to Max Gate, and I was bitterly disappointed to find only a small modern red-brick villa with a square of grass lawn entirely hedged in by a tunnel of pruned nut trees, so that not a glimpse of view could be seen.

As we entered the porch my eye was caught by the small reproduction of a famous Italian Venus in alabaster, standing on a little wooden bracket from which was suspended a post-card inscribed in rickety capitals with this warning—

" WHEN DUSTING, PLEASE *BLOW* BUT DO NOT TOUCH."

Old Mrs Hardy bustled forth to greet us and swept us into a room with a long table spread with a Dorset farm-house tea : ' cut-rounds ' and jam and scones and large Mad-Hatter-sandwiches. I had to feed old Mr Sant and admire the Herkomer portrait of Thomas Hardy which hung on the wall dominating the room and dwarfing all others around it. Each person entering the room was led up to ' The Herkomer of Mr Hardy ' by his little wife, who seemed to me to be continually breathless with the effort to climb after her illustrious husband up the ladder of fame. I liked her homely welcome, and her post-card, and her cosy cut-rounds, and above all her panting pride in her rather formidable husband. To me he made the rather sinister impression of an ancient moulting eagle, with his piercing restless dark eyes and lean naked neck rising in folds above a low collar, and his bald peering head moving ceaselessly from side to side as he rallied his guests.

I was rescued from the hot tea-room by Mr Albert

Bankes, of Wolfeton, an old friend of the Colonel's whom I had met often before at Upcerne Manor, and he led me out into the garden to introduce me to his wife. It was then at that very ordinary moment that I had the greatest shock of my life.

Standing alone at a corner of that small grass lawn was my Man, THE man of my early dreams. There he stood, silent and aloof, a very tall thin figure ; one scholarly hand nervously caressing a well-shorn chin. In my dream-picture of him that beautiful hand had always been holding a pen, but I recognised it at once.

Across the stretch of grass, over the heads of the guests chattering there, our eyes met. His were curiously brilliant eyes, deep-set under fierce black eyebrows, and as he looked at me my knees almost gave way and I turned dizzy and faint, for, without a shadow of doubt, it was HE and none other. In all that crowd he stood out, startlingly different from all others. Not strictly handsome in the conventional sense, but handsome, I thought, in a hungry sort of way, and every bit of him showing *race*, as the French say. That arrogant pose of the small head on its long neck ; that high brow, that clean-cut sensitive face, those small close-set ears, that curiously beautiful mouth, the long slender hands and small feet ; that air of bored, impatient superiority.

All were familiar to me, for he had been my constant companion for years in my dreams. The miracle was that he was there—in the flesh—at last.

I suddenly realised that Mr Bankes was speaking to me and that a tall fashionably dressed woman was standing by his side looking me up and down with a rather vague stare.

"My wife," he said. "Florrie, this is Miss Winifred Beech, my young friend of whom I have often spoken to you."

"Oh yes," she replied, then immediately she raised her voice and called "John ! " to someone in the distance.

For a moment I thought her the rudest woman I ever met; hardly had she been introduced to me than she intended to rid herself of my company and push me off on to someone else. And then I saw—THE man striding towards us.

JOHN—the ' Man sent from God.' With a vague gesture she waved us together, speaking no word of introduction, and then drifted away to talk to someone else.

We were alone together . . . I stood still in the hot September sunshine deprived of speech and the power to move. Nothing seemed real any more except those brilliant eyes looking at me so quizzically from under those startling brows.

Then he spoke—

" Let us get away from all these boring people," he surprisingly said, and, turning abruptly, led the way across the lawn to the shady nut-walk.

" I know of a place," he added confidentially, twinkling at me over his shoulder.

I followed him instantly. I would have followed him to the end of the world if he had asked it ; but he only led me to the end of that leafy tunnel where a bench was placed opposite an ancient slab of stone posed upon a boulder.

He pointed silently to the seat, his eyes still dancing, and obediently I sank down upon it. I was very glad to sit down, for my limbs did not seem to belong to me any more. Everything seemed to be taken from me— nothing seemed to belong to me any more. I was a mote whizzing about in radiant space. The proud in- dependent young woman who had always felt so sure of herself, knew what she wanted, and generally got it ; who had hitherto felt perfectly self-sufficient and con- sidered herself capable of managing her own life without the aid of any other person, had suddenly been trans- formed into a boneless blithering nonentity with no will of her own and only one idea left in a swimming head—

that she had found her man ; only one desire in a spinning
world—to stay with him always. And even then, though
I had only been in his presence a few moments, a sharp
pain began to tear me inside my heart as I realised that
in an hour or two he would have gone his way and I
mine ; that I might never see him again—I *must*—MUST
see him again. Having found him at long last I could
not bear to lose him now.

How tragic it is that when we feel deeply and long to
express ourselves, we are dumb. That when we most
want to appear to advantage we become self-conscious,
tongue-tied, and *gauche* in the extreme. What an agony
of youth this is. Perhaps this man, so much older than
I, realised a little of my shyness, for he talked to me of
his work—he was a writer (I had always known that),
a writer of military history (' lesson books,' I thought).
He told me of the gallant exploits of soldiers whose deeds
he had unearthed from original manuscripts, and suddenly
my tongue was unloosed, for he was talking of my mother's
family, the Fighting Battyes of India. I told him this,
and he rose to his feet and made me a beautiful bow,
saying that he was proud to talk with one of their blood.
He knew that their regiment was The Guides, but did
not know that The Guides would not fight without a
Battye in their midst and that this had long been a
tradition.

While we were talking, two old ladies strolled down
the nut-alley towards us and paused by the ancient slab
of stone.

" Can you tell us, perhaps, the history of this interesting
stone ? " one of them asked my companion.

He told them the most fascinating story of its origin
while I hung upon his words. Then they went away
delighted, and he continued his conversation with me.

A few minutes later a man and a woman strolled up to
the stone and asked him the same question. He told
them a totally different story, equally interesting, equally

circumstantial, which completely satisfied them, and they also went off.

I was rather mystified, but refrained from making any comment until the third party of people had been told yet another story about this stone and had left us in peace, and then I asked gently—

" And which is the true story, please ? "

Whereupon he screwed an eyeglass into his eye and peered at the stone, saying—

" I must have a look at it. I haven't really noticed it and I know nothing whatever about it. But those people seemed satisfied with what I told them—and the great point is that afterwards they *went away*."

He shook out the eyeglass with a swift movement of the head and looked at me with such a delicious twinkle that I burst out laughing, and from that moment felt perfectly at my ease with him. Like nearly all the men that I have known, he was at heart only a mischievous boy, and this little episode swept away the bridge of years between us once for all, and I found myself prattling away, telling him about my work and asking him about his. He told me that he was soon going out to India to write the story of the Durbar, and hoped that he would also have time to visit some of the battlefields he must still describe in his History.

I choked down the " Oh ! TAKE ME WITH YOU " that flew to my lips, and constrained myself to listen dumbly with an ache in my heart because soon he would be going so far away.

He talked on and on, in that deep musical voice, using a vocabulary of words which, from the lips of anyone else, would have sounded pedantic. He described a woman as ' comely,' and used phrases such as ' be it so,' and ' wot of '—good old English that I had read in my Bible, where so much perfect prose is to be found. He asked me my name, and then proceeded to call me ' Mistress Winifred.'

I listened as in a dream, losing all realisation of where I was and all count of time, until, rudely awakened by a voice calling, " Winifred ! Winifred ! Where can you have hidden yourself ? "

It was the voice of Mrs Mount Batten, in search of me. It was nearly six o'clock. We had been talking for over two hours. She entered the nut-alley and met us with rather an acid smile ; she said that she had been looking for me everywhere ; that Mr Sant was tired and wanted to go home.

I told her that I had been hearing about the exploits of the British Army on various battlefields.

We all filed down the alley and out on to the lawn where Mr Sant, very cantankerous because of my desertion of him, and Mr and Mrs Bankes were awaiting us.

My heart had turned sick at the prospect of being parted from this man that I had found at last.

Then I heard a quiet voice behind me. It was his.

" Since I leave Wolfeton on Monday morning it seems that this must be farewell," he said gently.

I turned and looked at him dumbly.

" But I wonder if you would like to come down to Windsor one day and allow me to show you its treasures ? " he asked diffidently. " If you would so honour me it would make me very happy. Just write to me and tell me the day that best suits you."

The nut-alley suddenly swirled up into the sky, and the guests upon the lawn whirled after it. Again that queer sensation in the knees. What was happening to me ? I looked into those brilliant eyes and saw that reassuring twinkle which steadied the world again.

" Oh—please—oh *Yes*—oh—can I ? But I don't know your name—only ' John,' " I stammered like an awkward schoolgirl.

" John Fortescue," he answered quietly. " Oh, what a LOVELY name," I said impulsively. " You like it ? " he asked amusedly. " I am very glad of that. Well, I count upon you to write that letter to John Fortescue living at Windsor," and with a lovely bow, which began at the head (instead of the tail), as all good bows should begin, he walked away.

I do not remember much about that drive back to Upcerne Manor, save that Mrs Mount Batten teased me for having 'monopolised the lion of the afternoon,' and when I looked at her quite blankly, she said—

" Didn't you know that you were talking to the King's Librarian and Archivist—the famous historian of the British Army ? "

" No," I answered softly, " I only knew that he was —John."

" Only knew that he was John ? " queried Mrs Mount Batten, tartly.

" Yes, Mrs Bankes just called ' John ! ' and he came," I said stupidly, wishing that she would stop talking about things that didn't matter at all and leave me alone with my wonderful reality.

Old Mr Sant then began to reminisce about his experiences as Court Painter at Windsor and to describe the pictures there to his daughter, and I was left in peace with my dreams. This man that I had met at last had been a familiar figure in them all through my life, but now my mind-picture of him was intensified, for I had seen him in the flesh—though there wasn't much of it ; for he was (thank Heaven) very lean—like a pure-bred Arab horse, I decided, clean-limbed and straight, with the same fine points, those sensitive nostrils, those brilliant eyes ; that proud poise of the head, and that nervous alertness.

I think that his mouth made the greatest impression upon me. In my dream-picture of him he had always been sitting in the recess of a small pointed window set in the thickness of a wall ; writing at a great table ; so that I only knew his face in profile and that long artistic hand. I had never seen the complete modelling of the mouth. The upper lip was winged, the lips slanting up into an inverted V. The lower lip was shaped like a natural V and the corners of the mouth were lost in two deep furrows slanting downwards from the cheek-bones ; an unusual mouth, a very beautiful mouth.

But it was the signs of struggle in his face that attracted me most. The high forehead was lined, and the face furrowed with the effort of repression—an æsthetic scholarly face, not a trace of self-indulgence anywhere, yet the mouth and eyes were those of a passionate man. He must have had a hard life—the set of the jaw and of that mouth when in repose told me of battles fought—and won. I longed to have the privilege of fighting Fate with him—and for him ; of taking care of him—serving him and protecting him.

I wondered if I had made any impression upon him save one of ignorance and *gaucherie*—whether, though he must have found me very crude and stupid, he had at least thought me to be a little ' comely.' I had noticed that all the afternoon he had talked to my eyes and stared at my hair. That blush again and that weakness of the knees—and here we were at Upcerne Manor and old Mr Sant wondering querulously what fish we should have for dinner.

Dinner was a dream-like affair. Of course I sat next to Mr Sant—I expect I ate something—I hope that I was polite—but all the time I was thinking only of John Fortescue, living at Windsor, and longing, longing for the moment to come when I could go up to my room and be alone with my thoughts of him.

When at last I was released, I sat before my log-fire trying to recapture every word that he had said to me, every tone of his voice, every change of that expressive face, and every gesture of his hands—he talked so much with his hands.

In my mind I began to compose the letter I had promised to write to him.

" Dear Mr Fortescue "—how formal that sounded when I had known him all my life—here the dream got mixed up with the reality, and I thought it was time to undress and get into bed.

XIX.

The rest of my Dorset visit seemed unreal to me, though I have one painful recollection of attending a Hunt Ball during which large horsey men trampled on my feet and galloped with me across the Dorchester Town Hall as though they were taking fences. It was there that I saw for the first time one of the dearest women in the world, Helen Ilchester, known to a wide circle of friends as ' the beloved Birdie.' She came in late, with a laughing crowd of young things and rioted through Kitchen Lancers so joyously with them that I longed to be of her party. I liked her attractive deep voice and chuckle, and her total unconcern when the small tiara she wore slid down over one eye as some hulking man charged into her back. But I was not destined to know and love her until three years later.

Soon after this I went back to London, but, finding no hoped-for telegram from a theatrical manager and seeing no immediate prospect of work ahead of me, I rushed home to confide the wonderful news to Mummie that I had at last found the Man I had always described to her. She listened in silence and looked frightened while I told her about him. Two spots of colour burned in her cheeks and her eyes had an expression I had never seen in them before.

" Mummie," I attacked her fiercely, " why don't you say something ? I've been bursting to tell you all about this—I couldn't write it—and now you don't seem glad at all." She took me in her arms, stroked back my hair and stared into my eyes. Then she kissed me quickly and went out of the room, leaving a hurt and puzzled daughter alone.

She told me long afterwards that I had terrified her. For years I had described to her my vision of this man, and when I came back from Dorset rushed into her room and poured forth this wonderful story, full of joyous confidence, she was shaken with a dreadful apprehension that my dream might be shattered and my life's happiness with it. The fact that I had persistently refused to marry any other because of this man of my imagination, had shadowed those last years for her, because she had feared he did not exist and had dreaded that my life would become embittered if I did not find him. Now that he was found, the dread became the greater, lest he, a man of the world and a famous man, many years my senior, might immediately forget this chance meeting with a girl at a garden-party. Later, I told her of my invitation to Windsor, which she said would be delightful for me if it could be arranged. Her cousin, old Montagu Battye, the last of that famous band of brothers to survive the Indian Mutiny, was one of the Military Knights of Windsor. He and his wife would surely receive me there if I wanted to go down and see the Royal Library. So I wrote that promised letter to ' John Fortescue living at Windsor,' and in three days received a red-crowned envelope addressed to ' Mistress Winifred Beech ' in a beautiful scholarly hand.

I rushed up to my bedroom with it and noted all these details with passionate interest before I opened my precious letter. It was couched in courteous and whimsical terms—he wrote the same beautiful English that he spoke—he was much looking forward to my visit, he suggested dates and asked me to avoid choosing a ' week's end ' because he had many shooting engagements—he gave me the hours of trains to Windsor, promised that he would be at the station to meet me, and implored me " not to shroud my face in a veil in the way some women have, so that even the most zealous of men find difficulty in recognising them," adding, however, that even if I hid my face he felt sure that he " could not fail to identify my figure though having seen it but once."

Roman pie, followed by an apple pie and Devonshire cream, were proposed for our luncheon. I was begged not to bring a chaperone with me, for, the writer reminded me, " Am I not old enough to be your great grandfather ? " and added that he would enjoy me so much more alone.

In conclusion he promised me, if I " would do him the honour to wait upon him," that, whilst showing me the ancient Castle and its treasures, he would refrain from asking me any date save that of my birthday.

I read and re-read my letter, then took it to Daddie's study to read it to the parents who stopped talking confidentially as I entered. They knew I had had a letter important to me because I had rushed straight up to my room with it like a dog with a bone, instead of tearing it open in the presence of the family as was my wont.

Daddie was charmed with the writer's style and envied me my visit to Windsor. Mummie preserved that unaccountable silence. Two days later I had a letter from a manager asking me to present myself in London for an interview. This fitted in very well with my plans, for I could not easily have visited Windsor from Suffolk. For the first time my work came second in my mind, and the letter from the manager, which a few weeks ago would have sent me nearly off my head with excitement, now was deemed a good excuse for getting back to London as a better ' jumping off ' place for Windsor.

I answered John Fortescue's letter and fixed a day for my visit. Another thick, red-crowned envelope arrived before my departure for London, confirming the arrangement and the final sentence thrilled me—

" If Mistress Winifred proves all that I think her to

be, I shall put into her hands, at parting, my first little book."

What ' little book ' ? I am ashamed even now to own that I had never even heard of that child's classic, ' The Story of a Red Deer.'

XX.

I went back to London with the same sensations I always experienced on the first night of a play—Catherine wheels inside, a vague swirling head, wobbly knees, a dry mouth—all this because in a few days I should see again the man who now never left my thoughts. When the actual day came I felt quite light-headed. I shall never forget the thrill I had on seeing once again the Brocas clump of trees below Eton and the first view of Windsor Castle that one gets from the train above the shining curve of the river ; nor that greater emotion that seized me as I caught sight of a familiar thin figure waiting for me on Windsor platform, one hand nervously fingering the cord of his eyeglass.

He greeted me with that beautiful courtly bow, but I missed the reassuring twinkle, for he was as shy as I was. We walked up to the Castle, he, jerkily telling me the history of the various buildings as we passed through Henry VIIIth's Gateway and climbed the Lower Ward. His quarters, he told me, ran under the Library, and one entered them under the Norman Gateway. He pointed out the old portcullis, still in place, and told me that in the room above the great gate, his Royalist forbear, Edmund Fortescue, was imprisoned by Cromwell and had scratched his name and the arms of the family on the stone wall. This room, since it did not form part of his suite, he would show me after luncheon.

We entered the little dark doorway of his dwelling and found ourselves in a tall narrow passage—the last remaining portion of the old curtain wall that, in old days, led from Edward IIIrd's Gatehouse, now John Fortescue's sitting-room, to the Castle proper.

Then he led me into the Gatehouse itself, and, to my bewilderment, it was vaguely familiar to me, although, to my certain knowledge, I had never entered it before.

A very lovely hexagon room with a beautiful vaulted ceiling of stone, a wide open stone fireplace with a strip of faded Renaissance embroidery stretched across the overmantel ; a high dado of light-oak panelling surrounding the walls, ending in a narrow shelf which was decorated with ancient pewter plates. Above the woodwork were massed engraved and mezzotint portraits of famous soldiers. A bookshelf was inset in one wall and narrow lancet windows were built into the thickness of two others. Under one of them was a light-oak writing-table and chair, and in the centre of the room stood a hexagonal table. Oak chairs with dim Prussian blue cushions to match the carpet and curtains completed a really perfect room.

Of course I raved about it, and this broke the shy reserve of my host who was as delighted as a boy by my enthusiasm, for he had decorated and arranged it himself. All the time I was wondering why that room seemed familiar to me.

Luncheon was served by a sturdy personage who was introduced to me as an old Rifleman. His wife cooked the very excellent food that was served soon afterwards, but I was far too excited to eat enough to satisfy my host, who told me that he had expected me to ' mop up ' all the Devonshire cream which he had had sent from his home in Devonshire expressly for me. (In spite of this, I noticed that he seemed to have a weakness for it himself.)

After luncheon while smoking delicious Egyptian cigarettes in the hexagon room, he asked me about my work, and I told him of my rather disappointing prospects.

" More drudgery," he commented. " Poor Mistress

Winifred. But in every profession one must drudge and
drudge doggedly before one can attain excellence. I, a
second-rate writing man, can tell you that. If you knew
of the hundreds of pages of manuscript that I have torn
up and thrown into that waste-paper basket, especially
designed for the purpose (he pointed out a tall wide
wicker basket, the top level with his desk, standing upon
a tripod of stout cane), you would take heart. A man who
cannot drudge is naught." He told me that luck always
changed ; that a pendulum, having swung backwards,
must then swing in the opposite direction ; that he, himself, had been nothing but a failure until success came to
him at the age of thirty or thirty-five ; that on his return
from India, where he was going almost immediately
with the King and Queen, he expected to see my name
advertised in huge lettering outside some theatre in the
West End of London.

Such a prediction had no longer power to stir my
ambition. All I felt was a sick sense of loss. He was going
away, going away very soon. When he came back he
might even have forgotten to look for my name on a
play-bill.

" Don't look discouraged, little Mistress Winifred,"
he went on gently, misinterpreting the look in my eyes.
" Youth always wants everything at once—patience,
patience and you will attain your heart's desire."

My heart's desire—and he didn't even know what
it was. Then, suddenly, he rose to his feet, opened a
drawer, and, taking from it a huge bunch of keys, suggested
that we should make a tour of the Castle.

" I do not propose to waste time in showing you what
the ordinary visitor sees on payment of a fee," he informed
me. " I want you to get an idea of the general topography
of the Castle. I shall show you first a map ; then the
basement, the Steward's Room, and the kitchen. You
will prefer to see twelfth century walls and fourteenth
and fifteenth century vaulting, to the Georgian gilding

of the Corridor and State-rooms, though you shall have a peep at my little pale Henrietta Maria and the naughty little Duchesse de Lorraine in the Vandyck Room, and see some lovely remnants of Grinling Gibbons carving. I will lead the way if you will permit me, and you must forgive me for taking you through my bathroom, which is Elizabethan—and a passage-room."

I followed him up some narrow stairs and through the bathroom to another door which he unlocked and we found ourselves in " the Castle proper," as he termed it. Down a short length of corridor and he opened a door and said tersely, " My Office."

Inside a rather bleak room I saw another great writing-table piled with books and papers and a curious kind of lectern which he told me he used for writing, as often, when obliged to consult the mass of books which lined the walls from floor to ceiling, it was less exhausting to write, standing, than to get up from a chair fifty times in an hour. He pointed to a line of scarlet volumes on a shelf. " There is my History," he said quietly. " God knows if I shall ever finish it."

We visited the huge kitchen lined with hundreds upon hundreds of shining copper pans and saucepans ; electric cooking stoves and heating-tables were set into the walls, and at one end a gigantic open fireplace with the original spit upon which, in olden times, a whole ox was roasted. My guide lifted the great basting-spoon which was as tall as he.

" The kitchen is quiet and deserted now when the Court is away," he said, " but you should see it during a Royal visit, white with bustling chefs and humming like a hive."

The beautiful vaulting in the Steward's Room impressed me greatly and the wooden plaque with its ' Code of Behaviour,' painted upon it in the reign of Charles II., enjoining those who ate in that room to good manners and kind speech.

We walked through dim stone passages and peered through windows set in walls fourteen feet thick, until at last we reached the stairway leading to the Round Tower.

" When the Castle was rebuilding in Edward IIIrd's reign it was recorded that the King built a little wooden house for himself and his Philippa inside the shell of the Round Tower," explained my guide. " I had seen a primitive plan of this wooden house in the Library and always wondered if it still existed, and the other day when workmen were repairing one of the rooms, I happened to say that I would much like to know if the original beams were hidden under that ceiling. Whereupon the foreman remarked : ' That is easily found out, Sir,' climbed a ladder, knocked a big hole in the plaster—and underneath I saw a solid oak beam.

" I rushed to the Queen to appraise her of my discovery, and she was as keen as I to find out how much of the wooden house still existed, and allowed me to give the workmen orders to demolish that ceiling.

" We found the original beams underneath it in as good condition as when the wooden house was first built. The work of demolition was continued until three-quarters of the great dining-hall was uncovered, and there the work had to stop because, to gain the whole depth of the hall, it would have been necessary to destroy a suite of maid's rooms underneath, and the Queen refused to sacrifice the comfort of her staff to ancient history—for which I rather loved her, although, of course, I regretted that we could not restore the whole room to its original proportions.

" However, ' finding is keeping ' as the old proverb says, and that hall is now my Archive Room," he concluded with a twinkle. " You shall see it."

It was a wonderful room, and later I saw the primitive plan of it in the Library.

When we reached a certain door, he unlocked it, ushered me through it, and exclaimed proudly—

" *Das ist mein Reich* "—and we entered his kingdom—the Royal Library and Print-rooms which were his charge. I was drawn at once to the windows by the beauty of the view looking over the North Slopes. He laughed and said—

" Quite right, Mistress Winifred, you have at once discovered the most beautiful thing I can show you here. The works of God are ever more beautiful than the works of man," and he allowed me to gaze in peace at the wonderful expanse of sky, green grass, and tree-tops, the silver ribbon of river and Eton College Chapel shining white in the sunlight.

When I could tear myself away from that view, he showed me so many treasures that my head whirled. The little clock given to Anne Boleyn by Henry VIII. with their monograms entwined inside a heart engraved upon its weights ; the extra shirt worn by Charles Ist upon the scaffold, for which he asked lest he should tremble with cold and be thought to be afraid—the finest example of drawn-thread work in England, worked upon fine linen, coloured buff with age, and laid upon a background of purple velvet.

" I am very fussy about detail," the Librarian informed me. " I wanted to give the idea of ' lying in state,' and that is why I chose purple velvet. You can have no idea how difficult it is to display a shirt without making it look ridiculous. It took me a whole morning to arrange it, and a day to find that little piece of pasteboard upon which to write its history. A white card would have ruined the whole effect, but at last I found an old piece mellowed with age to the same tint as the shirt."

I was allowed to hold the precious Sobieski Book of Hours in my hands while his long fingers turned the exquisitely illuminated pages to point out to me the work of many patient monks over a period of years. I was shown the glass goblet from which Queen Elizabeth drank, one of the earliest specimens of glass, of a queer

dark colour, contained in a leathern case. I was led
into a little bow-windowed recess known as Queen Anne's
Closet, where she was sitting with Sarah, Duchess of
Marlborough, when Daniel Parkes brought her the dispatch
from the Great Duke telling her of the Victory of Blenheim,
and my guide showed me the white banner which forms
the annual rent of Blenheim Palace, brought every year
to the King at Windsor by the reigning Duke on the
anniversary of the battle of Blenheim. Then I was asked
to examine various bindings of the Librarian's own
design, and very beautiful they were. For rebinding
ancient manuscripts he had used white pigskin, which
mellows to the beautiful tone of old vellum, and whose
rough surface was, to me, far more attractive. His
half-bindings were in such perfect taste—backed with
morocco leather of a deeper tone than the linen, or canvas,
sides—the blocking perfectly proportioned and the
lettering beautiful also. There were some glorious
Levantine leathers used for the foreign classics.

On the sunless north side of Queen Elizabeth's Gallery
I noticed that the shelves contained only very shabby
faded books, and, following my eyes, the Librarian told
me that it was the hard cold light that had faded and
actually burned the bindings, so that he was obliged to
put the less important books on the north side and had
placed red blinds to kill the violet rays of light which
did far more damage than full sunlight.

I was rapidly getting mental indigestion, and when,
while showing me a relic of Henry VIII., my guide suddenly
asked me the number of the King's wives, I disgraced
myself by blurting out "Eight," and was told that it
was time for a walk in the Home Park to blow away the
cobwebs.

Blushing and humiliated, I followed him the length
of Queen Elizabeth's Gallery and through the outer
rooms. He unlocked the end door and led me through
the State-rooms, pausing a moment before his favourite

pictures, through the great Corridor, downstairs, and out into the Courtyard, where the Guard was just being changed.

"The Coldstream Guards: my family regiment," he said ; and I saw a light in his eyes that I would have given worlds to inspire.

During that walk through the Park and down by the river he told me more of his life and his work. He talked of books and tried to draw me out about my reading, but I was feeling so much that my usually voluble tongue was tied and when I did manage to unloose it, it seemed only to utter futile and ignorant things. I became more and more self-conscious and unhappy, and wondered, in agony, whether I had pitiably failed the test he was surely giving me. "If Mistress Winifred proves all that I think her to be I shall put into her hands, at parting, my first book." I felt certain that I should leave the Castle empty-handed.

Tea was suggested, and we turned back under the yellowing lime trees and once more entered the Norman Gate.

He had ordered a wonderful schoolgirl tea for me, and the Devonshire cream appeared once more, but I could hardly touch anything. He ate nothing at all, sat in an armchair, and, having asked permission to smoke, puffed at a cigarette, regarding me quietly out of those deep-set brilliant eyes and rallying me on my lack of appetite.

How could I eat when in half an hour my train would be carrying me away from him ; when I knew that he was soon going to India, and I should not see him for months—perhaps never again—for I feared that I had bored him to death, and that he could only be relieved to see the last of me. I sat in the blaze of light that flooded the room, with darkness in my soul.

"One day you must shake loose that mass of curls for me," he said abruptly. "I love beautiful hair."

He rose, and crossing to his writing-table took up a slim quarto volume lying there, opened it and began to write on its fly-page. And then, seeing him in profile, framed in that lancet window, his head bent and a pen in his hand, I realised in a flash why that hexagon room had seemed so familiar to me the moment that I entered it—it was the picture I had always seen in my dreams, that man, writing at that table, in the embrasure of that lancet window. My vision and this moment's reality were identical.

I stilled the cry of recognition that rose to my lips, and, at that moment, I was too shaken by this sudden revelation of the extraordinary truth to realise that the green-covered book he put into my hands was 'The Story of a Red Deer,' and that, after all, I had passed my test.

XXI.

Of course I wrote John Fortescue a small conventional letter, thanking him for the wonderful day at Windsor and for his book, and I received in reply a letter bidding me be of good cheer, to work hard and justify his faith that I should succeed in my chosen profession and be able to give him good news of my progress when he returned from India.

So he wanted to see me again after all—I had not known it was possible to feel so miserably forlorn ; that I could so suddenly lose all my interest in my work and all my soaring ambition ; that I could be obsessed only by one idea or, rather, by one person. I was furiously angry with myself for feeling like this, but it was too powerful to be controlled, and I was thankful when the *Medina* sailed for India with the King and his Household. While John Fortescue was in England, I could settle to nothing. He had told me that he kept a bachelor flat in Brook Street, opposite Claridge's Hotel, and came up to London

for certain days in each week to consult archives and
original manuscripts at the Record Office, War Office,
India Office, British Museum, &c., so that I knew he
pervaded London, and that by some marvellous chance
our paths might cross again before he sailed. Because
of this remote possibility, I had been living in a state
of suppressed excitement, with a hurrying pulse every
time I caught sight of a tall thin figure in the distance
that might prove to be his—but never was.

I was furious that I had lost my independent spirit
and the ambition to succeed in my chosen career, and
because I could not banish the tormenting thought of
this man from my mind. I missed Stella terribly. She
had long since followed Mervyn out to East Africa. He
met her at Mombasa where she was the guest of the
Governor, being *fêted* and made much of until her marriage
could take place in the cathedral. After the wedding,
she and Mervyn had had a *safari* honeymoon and had
ridden in stages to Mervyn's district. They had gained
their hearts' desire ; but I was lonelier than ever.

Well for me that, at this moment of unrest, I had a
letter telling me that Mr Anstey Guthrie, author of ' The
Brass Bottle ' and ' Vice Versa,' wished to make my
acquaintance. He had followed our tour in the provincial newspapers ; had read my notices and was anxious
to meet ' Sylvia.'

Famous authors are never in the least like the mental
pictures one forms of them. I had expected to see a big,
bluff, hearty man with a loud laugh, and I was rather
dreading him. Instead, a ·small, scrupulously neat, and
very shy one greeted me with an old-world courtesy
and actually thanked me for having rushed up to Liverpool
to take the part of Sylvia, thereby rescuing his play.

I was so overwhelmed by being *thanked* for being
given a good part that I at once became as embarrassed
as he, and when he asked me, extremely diffidently, if
I would play Sibyl Elsworth in an adaptation of his

story 'The Fallen Idol' at St George's Hall, I was quite overcome. He told me, in nervous gasps, that Maskelyne & Devant wanted a short play 'as a vehicle for their illusions,' and thought that the fantastic situations in his book would give them excellent scope for transformation tricks and grotesque effects, and so he had been persuaded to dramatise it for them. Rehearsals were to start almost at once, so that he would be very glad if I could give him an answer as soon as I had thought the matter over.

I gave it there and then, and he asked me to go and see Messrs Maskelyne & Devant the next day.

I saw Mr Anstey again at the first rehearsal, when it seemed to me that the author was always the last to be consulted about any proposed cuts in the dialogue or changes of any sort, and I admired the way this small man insisted that his was the right of final decision.

When at last the final scene was over, Mr Devant came up to me and told me that he would like me to go with the author to choose my dress for the most important scene.

When I told Mr Anstey that he was expected to accompany me to some big Store to help me select my dress, he giggled hysterically and blushed up to the roots of his hair protesting, amid shrill chuckles, that he had never been inside a woman's shop in his life. He begged me to excuse him, saying that he had perfect confidence in my taste, and was sure to like anything that I chose. But I wouldn't let him off. I insisted that he must come too, and threatened not to go myself if he refused to accompany me, so that in the end he reluctantly gave in. I shall never forget that adventure. Mr Anstey was frankly terrified. He was very short-sighted and always wore *pince-nez*, and when we entered the ground floor showroom of Peter Robinson's he collided first against one beautiful, elaborately attired wax mannequin, then another; apologised profusely, bowing many times to them, and removing his hat. Then he turned to me in great confusion and found me leaning against a counter in silent convulsions of laughter ; looked back at the ladies he thought he had offended, and, seeing them still standing in rigid positions of affected ease, realised his mistake, gave one shrill delicious giggle which rapidly developed into a roar of laughter, and stood helpless.

This was the beginning of a great friendship. As we stared at each other, tears of mirth coursing down our cheeks, we realised then, I think, that we were kindred spirits and every trace of shyness between us was washed away for ever by that blessed flood of laughter.

It was a bad beginning to the solemn business of choosing a dress in the more elaborate model gown department upstairs, and we had neither of us fully recovered from our attack by the time the lift deposited us upon the first floor where we were confronted by a formidable (human) black satin lady and found ourselves almost unable to articulate our requirements.

When I had made her understand what we wanted and she had sailed majestically away, Mr Anstey hissed in my ear—

" Don't you think you could manage this affair much better alone ? I am a bachelor, you see " (indeed it was very evident). " I feel so out of place here—I shall surely disgrace you—that splendid satin lady terrifies me. . . ."

I seized his arm firmly and said, " Say to yourself ' It all comes off at six '—the finery I mean—Mummie always says that to herself when grand saleswomen try to intimidate her. The satin draperies are provided by the firm. You are NOT to desert me—we've got to go through this together."

The formidable lady swam back to us carrying a load of French models on her arm, and asked me if my husband would like to come into a dressing-room with me to see me try them on.

This was fatal. I gave one glance at Mr Anstey, who had been standing nervously tapping his finger-tips together, saw his agonised expression and his awful blush, and I collapsed once more. What that woman thought of us before we left the shop I really do not know—or care. When, between gasps, I had contrived to make her understand the position, she icily indicated a crimson plush sofa upon which Mr Anstey might sit while I tried on model after model in the dressing-room, emerging elegantly attired to show myself to the small solitary figure enthroned upon the gigantic divan.

Every time I did this, he giggled helplessly and, tapping his finger-nails together with a sharp clicking sound, ejaculated : " Awfully jolly— awfully jolly——" and the mannequin retired once again to the dressing-room to try the effect of another model.

When I had repeated this performance about five times, always hearing the same comment, seeing that the satin lady looked almost as desperate as I felt, I walked up to Mr Anstey and whispered—

" Do, PLEASE express a preference or we shall be here till the end of our lives. You can't think *all* the dresses are ' awfully jolly.' "

" But they are—I mean to say *you* look awfully jolly in them," he protested eagerly.

" But you *must* like one better than another," I urged. " Do, please, criticise the next. Say *why* you like it or don't like it," I pleaded.

I tried on yet another—a complicated affair decorated with flat white buttons.

When I paraded before the author he said—

" Awfully jol—I mean—*do* I quite like those extra-strong peppermints glued on the side ? "

Hopeless. But a gallant effort nevertheless. In the end I chose the dress I myself preferred, and he heaved a great sigh of relief, saying : " But I told you before we came here that I knew nothing about such things and begged you to make your own choice, knowing that I should like it." After this we were both quite exhausted, and I was looking about Oxford Circus for a bus that would take me back to my rooms for a late luncheon when my companion suddenly looked up at me—

"Couldn't we celebrate this famous purchase by a little lunch together somewhere? Would you? Of course if you have no other engagement . . . It would be awfully jolly if you could," he jerked out diffidently.

"Thank you so much. I think it would be *awfully jolly*," I replied with a twinkle which, when he saw it, started him off into another giggling fit.

We were both in happy mood. We talked of the play, the players, and the managers; and Mr Anstey wanted to hear all about 'The Brass Bottle' tour, so that the time flew, and it was nearly four o'clock when at last he drove me back to Shepherd Street in a luxurious taxi.

This was the first of many delightful luncheons with my new-found friend, and, as week after week passed by and still we rehearsed without any definite date being given for the production of the play, the kind author little knew how welcomed and needed those luncheons became. Rehearsals were not paid for in those days, and my slender store of money had nearly run out. I was too proud to ask Daddie to send me some, for I intended to earn my own living and thus relieve the financial strain at home, and so I ate very sparingly when alone.

My fellow actors and actresses were likewise feeling the pinch of these endless rehearsals, and one day a member of our small company came up to me and said desperately: "You seem to be friends with the author. Can't you get out of him the date of production? We're all very hard up and perhaps he could hustle things on."

I promised to do what I could, and the following week when Mr Anstey again invited me to luncheon at Frascati's, I tackled him as we were walking down Regent Street—

" Mr Anstey, can you tell me definitely when your play will be produced ? " I asked him bluntly.

" I really cannot say," he replied. " I'm as much in the dark as you are. ' They move in a mysterious way their wonders to perform ' at St George's Hall."

I only smiled faintly at this quotation, for I felt too sick at heart, and walked on silently by his side. Silence, in me, was so unusual that he sensed something was wrong, and with that extraordinarily intuitive sympathy that I learned to love in him, he said—

" Something is troubling you. I wish you would tell me. Is it anything to do with your part ? You don't intend to leave the company ? Has anyone been rude to you ? Can I do anything ? I have been so enjoying these pleasant rehearsals, and I hoped you were too."

I stood stock-still on the crowded pavement and blurted out—

" Mr Anstey, we are all VERY HUNGRY."

He dropped his stick, his *pince-nez* fell off, and he turned quite white. Replacing the *pince-nez* and looking at me with the utmost consternation, he stammered out, " I—d-don't understand."

" We are all very poor and very hungry. Rehearsals are not paid, you know, and we have got to live—some-how—while they are going on. We have been rehearsing for weeks on end and are all at the end of our resources," I told him quietly.

The poor man was quite horrified. He had never thought of this possibility, and was shocked when I told him the truth in this brutal manner. His eyes grew moist, he took off his *pince-nez* and polished them feverishly with his silk handkerchief, a passer-by stumbled over the fallen stick, and Mr Anstey, stooping hurriedly to pick it up, in so doing dropped the *pince-nez*. I bent down to help him. We bumped heads, and I displaced his bowler hat over one eye. We were blocking the pavement, and a few curious people stopped to see what we were doing.

In desperation Mr Anstey hailed a passing taxi and we tumbled into it.

Then he said: " I ought to have realised—this is terrible—I never thought—I must do something—I am really shocked." I tried to comfort him, saying that we could all hold out a little longer, especially if strengthened by the announcement of a definite date for the production of the play ; and he promised to speak to Messrs Maskelyne & Devant before the rehearsal next day.

The knowledge that he would do this was a great relief to me, though I was full of remorse to have caused my kind friend such evident pain.

The rehearsals dragged on for several more weeks, but every Friday in future we were each given an envelope containing a sum of money which I have always been certain came from the pocket of the author of the play.

XXII.

These long rehearsals and the anxiety about finance had at least served to distract my thoughts a little from one haunting face, although every morning I searched my newspaper for shipping news. The Durbar was over ; the King and Queen had toured a part of India and would soon be home in England. Soon—soon . . .

One evening I was invited to dinner with old Mr Sant and his daughter in their house at Lancaster Gate. Afterwards the old painter asked his daughter to play some gay martial music on the pianola and to accompany it with her kettledrum—a queer instrument for a woman to play, I thought. She told me that her father, being now very deaf, adored this form of entertainment because he could hear it. She placed a new copy of ' The Tatler ' in my hands in case the music bored me, and the concert began.

Miss Sant was an expert drummer, and, although

nearly deafened by the din, I could nevertheless admire the deft agility of her wrists. In the pauses between her selections, I idly turned the pages of my magazine until suddenly confronted by the photograph of a group of people taken on board the *Medina* during her homeward voyage. The King and Queen surrounded by the chosen members of their Household, backed by the *Medina* crew. Towering above all I saw the head of John Fortescue.

Again that sudden sense of shock. I was thankful to be sitting down when I saw that picture, and that the attention of my host and hostess was otherwise engaged, for had they spoken to me then I could not have replied ; had they looked in my direction they must have seen what I could not conceal.

From that moment the wild unrest again filled my spirit. Every time the postman knocked and my landlady brought me my letters I feared that she would see the trembling of my lips and hands. When I saw that there was no letter from the one person whose handwriting I longed so passionately to see, there would fall a chill and a darkness upon my mind and heart. I lived from postal delivery to postal delivery, telling myself fiercely and contemptuously in the intervals that I was an optimistic fool ; furious because none of the reasoning and self-discipline of the past weeks had killed that hope— almost a certainty—that I should see this man again.

And then, one morning there *was* a letter. It told me that I was the first person to be informed of his arrival. He wanted news of me and of my work. Might he one day wait upon me, tell me his news, and hear mine ?

All the stars sang together that night, and, alone in the darkness of my little powder-closet bedroom, I pictured that meeting and rehearsed the things that I would say. Yet, when the blessed moment came and he stood before me, once again I was tongue-tied and awkward, because all the things I longed to say could not be said. I had to act the part of a mere acquaintance, when I had known and loved him since my early childhood. He did not know, nor could I explain.

And so I stiffly and shyly answered his questions as to my welfare and my work during his absence, and listened to the tale of his adventures in India—the Durbar, the pageantry and colour of it all ; the marvellous jewels of the Indian princes ; the bravery of the Queen when a near tent caught fire and was burned out in five minutes, she, with her terror of fire, motionless and white as a marble statue ; and the matchless courage of the King, who, when the Indian police could not guarantee his safety if he attended the Calcutta races, insisted upon riding, at a foot's pace, around the edge of the race-course, close to the seething crowd of Indians who kissed the dust his horse had trod ; of the King's tiger hunt when the tiger suddenly turned in the direction of the King's Librarian, and of his definition of Calcutta when asked by a lady at one of the State balls his opinion of the city. Looking around in search of the pretty faces he so liked to see, he had replied whimsically : " Well, I should describe Calcutta as a City of the Plain." He told me of the beauty of Miss Venetia Baring on the great day of the Durbar, her slender figure swathed in soft satin of a tender blue. How, on stepping forth from her car, someone had drawn her attention to a great stain of car-grease on the very front panel of her beautiful gown. With admiration for her self-control, rare in so young a woman, he told me that, after one dismayed glance at her ruined gown, she had remarked quietly : " I am resolved that nothing shall spoil my pleasure to-day," had borrowed a safety-pin from someone and pulled a fold of drapery across the stain to hide it. " Most women would have made a scene and even wept," he said. " Not so Venetia." I felt a despicable surge of jealousy within me.

" You and Venetia Baring would like each other," he

stated—and—I wondered. Just then I almost hated this unknown woman. She had shared a sea-voyage with John Fortescue ; together they had seen the wonderful pageant of the Durbar. He admired both her looks and her character. She was a member of the Royal Household too. But then came the comforting remembrance that, a few days after his return, this man had sought me out of his own accord. He was here, now, before me.

He was glad to be home again, and, the Durbar book finished, free to continue work upon his History of the British Army. He looked at his wrist-watch, then rose to his feet and bade me farewell—

" I have to live to a time-table, Mistress Winifred, or this History of mine will never be finished," and he heaved a great sigh and went on his way. That evening Mrs Fowler scolded me for lack of appreciation of the dainty little dinner she had prepared for me to eat before going to St George's Hall.

XXIII.

The run of ' The Fallen Idol ' was as short as the rehearsals had been long. The play absolutely depended upon the success of difficult tricks and illusions, which very often did not come off at all. This made acting in it an agonising business. I had continually to exclaim upon miracles which constantly were not performed, and I would wait with eyes on stalks to see if they were happening or not, and then gag frantically if there was a delay in the working of trick machinery or if it failed to operate. It was worse than my experiences on ' The Brass Bottle ' tour.

The author became indignant because every day he was asked to cut yet more of his amusing dialogue so that more tricks might be substituted, and the poor little play became so mangled that at last he had no longer the heart to witness its performance, and though we were very sorry for him, I think we none of us had many regrets when the announcement of its termination upon a certain date was put up on the notice-board near the stage-door.

During that last fortnight, a girl who was a leading member of the stock company at St George's Hall, and who had been kept on to understudy me and shared my dressing-room, had been suffering from a terrible streaming cold. One night I came in early and found her already there talking earnestly with my dresser, who had a bowl of liquid powder called ' wet-white ' in one hand and a sponge in the other. Catching sight of my understudy's face and her bare chest and shoulders reflected in her mirror, I saw that they were scarlet with rash, and my dresser was endeavouring to cover this with paint.

The girl told me that she had eaten shell-fish and was covered with nettle-rash ; it was nothing more. On the final night, to my surprise, she embraced me fervently in farewell.

I stayed on in London for some days afterwards, writing to and being interviewed by managers with a view to future work, and being *fêted* by my friends, who all seemed glad that at last they could see something of me. One great thrill I had, when the man who was ever in my thoughts took me to a picture theatre to see a cinematograph reproduction of the Durbar, telling me the names of all the celebrities and Indian Princes as they appeared upon the screen. Of course I searched always for his face, but only once did I see the top of his hat ; for, as his carriage came into view, the picture was flicked away and another stage of the procession was shown. He laughed at my indignation—

" Small fry are of no interest to the British public, Mistress Winifred. The cinema operator is quite right to hurry them off."

During the interval he talked of his work at the Record Office, of the new despatches he had discovered during the day which would be invaluable for his History of the British Army, and of all that he was doing and intended to do in the Library at Windsor.

During the days that followed I saw him often for short periods of time, always limited by his accursed wrist-watch. He had told me that he was obliged to live according to a strict time-table, rising at a certain hour, eating at fixed hours, working for a certain number of hours, walking for a number of others, else his History would never be finished. In the midst of an interesting conversation he would instinctively look at that wrist-watch (which I learned to hate), and, seeing that the time he had allowed himself for relaxation was over, would get up swiftly, brace his shoulders, make his excuse, and depart, leaving me to live through the succeeding days until I saw him again.

'The Fallen Idol' finally crashed in Lent—the season in which most plays come to an end, and I was wondering if I could go home for Easter or if I had better stay in London searching for work. John Fortescue would be living permanently at Windsor as the Court would be in residence at Easter, and, when he said good-bye to me, he counselled me to go down to Suffolk, saying that all theatrical managers were sure to be out of London for the Easter holiday, and that I looked tired and dragged, and as if I needed the fresh air of the country and my mother's care. This depressed me more than anything. Evidently I was looking pale and hideous, and I certainly felt very far from well. I had a sore throat and a raging headache, and could eat hardly anything poor little Mrs Fowler brought to me.

On Saturday I resolved to make an effort and go to the early service in Down Street Church. It was an effort, a very great effort to dress myself, and a still greater to walk even the short distance to Down Street.

Everything around me seemed unreal, and I remained upon my knees, or rather crouched upon my haunches with my head upon my hands, feeling giddy and sick, throughout most of the service until it was time to go up to the altar-rails. When I rose, my legs seemed strangely wobbly, but this angered me, and by sheer force of will I got there, and back, and out into the street and back to the house in Shepherd Street.

Having crawled up to my rooms on the second floor, I thought I was going to die, and I lay down on the rickety little sofa. My nose and eyes were streaming, and I imagined that I had developed the world's worst cold—or influenza. Little Mrs Fowler nearly finished me by bringing me some richly scented fish for my breakfast.

Of course I couldn't touch it, and I decided then that if I were going to die I would rather expire under the family roof-tree and be interred in my own village church-yard. I had a sudden weak longing for Mummie—to get to Mummie as quickly as I possibly could.

I tottered into my bedroom, threw a few things into a suitcase, then lay on the bed to recover from the effort, and at last the few necessaries I should require were packed, a few at a time, with long intervals of rest. I said good-bye to my dear little landlady, who looked at me with concern and said—

" Well, Miss, you *have* got a cold, a real howler you have and no mistake. I don't like your taking that cold journey, that I don't, but no doubt when you get to your Mummie she'll tuck you up in bed at once and give you some hot onion gruel."

At Liverpool Street I found a third-class carriage, empty save for one pale, spectacled youth. I can't remember much about the journey, save that my companion stared at me covertly with goggling eyes and an open mouth, constantly asking me if I would like the window up—or down—if I felt too cold or too hot—if he could do anything for me. I suppose that I looked quite ghastly, and the poor boy was in terror lest I should collapse and die and he be held responsible for my murder if found alone in the carriage with my corpse.

Daylight had faded when we reached Bealings. The platform was deserted save for Fryett the stationmaster strolling slowly along it carrying a lantern. When he saw a figure descend from the train he hailed Pigg the porter, who emerged from the goods office and flapped his arms energetically to restore circulation, for it was bitterly cold. I had telegraphed the hour of my arrival from Liverpool Street, so that Mummie could order me some form of vehicle to bring me home (for Great Bealings was situated nearly two miles from the station), and I found a high dog-cart awaiting me outside. I had not told her that I was ill. In this I was driven home, shivering and burning alternately, and when at last I walked into the hall of the Rectory my appearance (so I was told afterwards) gave my family a shock. I was put to bed at once, and next morning awoke to find Mummie bending over me, her face full of concern.

" What is the matter, Sweet ? " I asked her feebly.

" That is what I am wondering," she answered grimly.

Our old family doctor was sent for, and he told Mummie that I was suffering from a virulent attack of black measles, and that my life was in danger. Apparently people seldom recover from the black variety, for the rash goes inwards as well as outwards and attacks the lungs and internal organs, which often become septic.

My understudy had presented me with her microbe as a parting present, and I had caught a chill on the top of it. This was the worst transformation trick ever performed at St George's Hall, for it changed me from a very healthy animal into something less satisfactory, and I was to feel the effects of it for the rest of my life.

I narrowly escaped pneumonia and was delirious for days on end, always imagining that I was upside down and putting my head at the foot of the bed and my heels on the pillow.

Mummie told me afterwards that I puzzled her by repeating over and over again : " Is this h'all, H'Albert ? Gawd's truth ! This here's a bloody feeasco," which was the sergeant's version of Queen Victoria's remark when she was taken on board the wrong ship to review the remnant of troops which had been engaged in the battle of Balaclava, and, by mistake, was shown only four soldiers of another regiment. John Fortescue had told me the story, but Mummie had never heard it and could not imagine what I was raving about.

Mummie pulled me through black measles and then proceeded to pour concentrated beef-tea into me at all hours of the day. She said I had consumed the essence of about half a ton of shin of beef before I was up and about again, and whenever I woke I always found her bending over a little saucepan heating over my bedroom fire.

I had asked her to write and tell Mr Anstey what had happened to me, and when I was strong enough to sit up, by every post he sent me some ' surprise.' Never was a patient so spoiled. He wrote me delightfully long and amusing letters, sent delicious black - and - white drawings of dragons and knights in armour, tiny turreted towns in the background, and always animated doglets in the foreground, designed by himself and treasured by me to this day. All through our friendship I used to implore him to write a children's book and to illustrate it himself, but his answer was invariably—

" I never had a drawing lesson in my life. I can't draw. I should only be laughed at. I do these things to amuse myself and my friends, but I should never have the cheek to publish them."

This, in spite of the fact that Mr Peter Davies, seeing Mr Anstey's sketches framed on my walls, raved over the originality and action in them and begged me to per-

suade him to write and illustrate a story for children and
then allow him to publish it.

Among the shower of gifts that arrived from Mr Anstey
every day, I was most delighted by these vivacious
sketches of his. They were so full of humorous detail
that one could pore over them for an hour and still find
some other quaint conceit. He was like a kind of fairy
uncle to me, and I began to call him ' Uncle Anstey '
and gradually became his ' Peggy-niece.' There were
so many Winifreds abbreviated into Winnies, Wins,
and Fredas at school and afterwards at the Dramatic
School that I became ' Winnipeg ' shortened soon to
' Peggy ' and ' Peg.'

I think that I must have become very difficult during
my convalescence, for, with returning strength, came
the longing to get back to London. There I could see
John Fortescue again. He wrote to me now and then,
surprising me by the confidential tone of his letters.
Surely so reserved a man would never talk of his life
and work, his hopes and his fears, so intimately to one
who meant nothing to him ?

In any case I realised that in work lay my salvation,
and quite evidently I must have fretted myself into a
fever on hearing that Jerome K. Jerome had seen me act
and wished to cast me for the part of Vivian in his
wonderful play ' The Passing of the Third Floor Back.'
Rehearsals were soon to begin in London. He wished
me to visit him in his home near Marlow and to read the
part to him, as he was already fixing up dates for the
tour.

It was a part that I longed to play, but poor Mummie,
having so nearly lost me, was terrified that if allowed
to go back to London after so short a convalescence I
should catch cold and develop pneumonia.

At last I got my own way and returned to London,
and I travelled down to Marlow and found Mr Jerome
living in a modern baronial hall with pitch-pine galleries

and staircases and large stained-glass windows. The man himself was a delightful surprise in these rather pretentious surroundings, for he was modest, simple, and kindness itself.

He took me into his study where I read the part of Vivian, he reading the part of The Stranger. The play always touches me deeply. I know that as a play it has glaring faults of construction, that it has been said that the series of 'conversions' coming swiftly one after another are inartistic and some think ridiculous. But there is a wonderful spirit irradiating the whole, and the person who can witness that play and come out of the theatre unmoved must, in my opinion, be in some way wanting.

Feeling my scene with The Stranger so sincerely, I suppose I read my lines sympathetically, for Mr Jerome told me that I was " exactly what he had been looking for," and gave me the part, asking me always to wait quietly in the wings, apart from everyone, before my big scene with The Stranger so as to get into the spirit of it.

Then he led me into the hall and introduced me to his family, who were just going to have tea.

Mrs Jerome was a tiny gentle little woman with dark hair and wistful blue eyes always full of enthusiastic admiration for her husband and adoration for her family, two daughters, one married and very delicate, the other, Rowena, in those days a healthy fair-haired tom-boy.

I was introduced as the new 'Vivian' and Rowena rushing up to me told me impulsively that she was to play 'Stasia,' the little maid-of-all-work in her father's play, so that we should be touring together, and " what fun it would be." Remembering Miss Gertrude Elliott's pale-faced, hollow-eyed representation of the poor little drudge, I found it hard to picture this plump, flaxen-haired rosy girl in the same part. But make-up can do wonders, and perhaps a coat of pale grease-paint, shadowed eyes, and a smut or two artistically smeared upon that laughing round face might give it the necessary mask of pathos. Certainly her father's child ought to be able to interpret one of his best characters.

The Jerome family were all charming to me, and I travelled back to London well pleased with my afternoon.

XXIV.

Rehearsals are always rather wearing and nerve-racking, and so, when possible, I ran home to Suffolk for week-ends, and, on one occasion, persuaded Uncle Anstey to go with me. My family were delighted with him and he with them, and he immediately adopted Marjory as another niece, promising to treat her to a week or two with me in the provinces when the tour started.

She chose the Scottish dates, never having been in the North, and she shared with me a horrible experience with a mad landlady, an hysterical she-devil who continually invaded our sitting-room to assure us that she was 'saved' and 'just converted,' and to reproach me for being 'a scarlet woman' who 'exhibited herself to lustful men to gain a shameful wage.' When I foolishly attempted to reason with her she became noisy and violent and shouted, " You lie, woman."

I decided that we could not remain in that house, and so I shut Marjory into her bedroom and told her to pack her clothes while I tackled the Virago and her two idiotic daughters single-handed. When I had done this I packed my own things, got a cab, and then went down-stairs, money in hand, to count out the bill. The manager of the theatre (to whom I had appealed for advice) had counselled me to pay in full, even though we had had scarcely any cooking or attendance, so as to avoid having to listen to the woman's foul language. He told me that mine was the fifth complaint that he had heard of those rooms, and that he always warned people against them when they came to him for an address.

In the hall I came upon a strange scene. Our landlady was seated upon Marjory's suitcase, her elder daughter upon a hat-box, and a burly policeman upon my trunk. When I asked the meaning of this outrage, the Virago informed me that she was 'protecting herself,' for how did she know that we weren't thieves?

Of course when I opened my hand and disclosed the money inside it, the policeman slunk away looking an awful fool.

As we left the house, the Virago and her two 'acidulous virgins' were noisily and offensively counting their spoons and forks.

It was a nightmare while it lasted, and I was almost too tired after it to act in the evening. We had had no breakfast, and I had to tackle that beast *and* find new lodgings on an empty tumpkin. We got nothing to eat until 3.30 P.M. when, thank Heaven, we found, at last, comfortable rooms and a dear, motherly old landlady.

I shook *inside* with nervousness for two days afterwards, and imagined the madwoman would come and boo me during my scenes. I could not sleep either—she had got on my nerves.

A very reliable actress had given me all the addresses for my rooms on tour, and, until that week, I had splendid ones. I could only think that the weak brain of this woman had been unbalanced by the exciting effect of an overdose of Religious Revivals.

However, this deplorable incident was soon forgotten, and, in Glasgow, Marjory and I were very happy in spacious sunny rooms belonging to a delightful Scotswoman who took an immediate fancy to Marjory and even forgave her when, deafened by the song of seven canaries singing in unison in our sitting-room, in desperation she draped their cages with the white crocheted antimacassars which decked our plush armchairs, to enable us to hear each other speak during luncheon.

In another town I had the front set of rooms and the back set was occupied by music-hall artists—a man, his wife, and a troupe of performing cats. I was told by my landlady, who had, of course, been given a free ticket by her lodgers to see their performance, that these cats were quite wonderful, but, as the music-hall show began at the same time as ours at the theatre, it was impossible for me to go to see them.

However, after our *matinée*, which the cat-trainer and his wife attended, our landlady came into my room with a message from them inviting me to go into theirs and witness a little private performance in gratitude for the pleasure mine had given to them.

Of course I went joyfully, and I shall never forget that little scene.

There were cats all over the room, all doing their individual tricks to earn their supper. This was the way their beaming trainer told me that he had taught them to love their work. The moment it was over they were rewarded by a bit of fragrant fish.

In one corner a little black cat was sitting sad and solitary on her hind-legs weeping into a black-edged handkerchief clutched between her front paws and pressed close to her mourning face. Only her whiskers were to be seen protruding from each side of it. In another corner, two tom-cats on their hind-legs were having a silent and energetic boxing-match, their front paws encased in miniature boxing-gloves. On the sofa cushions lay a voluptuous chinchilla lady wearing a lovely brocade garment, while a tiny black cat stood by her head on its hind-legs fanning her with a gaudy fan of peacock's feathers attached to his front paws.

In front of the fire a ginger kitten was solemnly turning endless somersaults all by itself; and on the centre table a little tortoiseshell was repeatedly leaping through a hoop suspended from the ceiling, while a white cat caught tiny coloured balls in his mouth, thrown from afar.

All the artists went through their performances with silent precision and intense concentration until their trainer spoke to each in turn when he or she answered him with a respectful yowl, ceased acting, and looked with expectant eyes towards his fishy fingers. It was a joy to watch the love and pride in the faces of that man and his wife as their cats performed, and to see the eager way the cats, having finished their fish, leaped purring upon the shoulders and lap of their master and mistress.

I don't much like cats, and, in general, I hate watching performing animals, being always haunted by the fear that their tricks have been learned painfully, taught by terrorism; but these cats really were attractive, and, quite obviously, had been trained by love.

In nearly every town ' The Passing of the Third Floor Back ' had a tremendous success, and there can be nothing much more delightful than acting in a popular play. My scene with The Stranger closed the most important Act, and it was always our ambition completely to silence the audience. If the curtain dropped upon utter stillness, which was maintained for several seconds after it had fallen, we knew that we had conveyed our message and caught up our audience into the true spirit of the play.

It was the most difficult entrance I have ever had to make, coming into that quiet fire-lit room with bare feet, hair unloosed, and groping hands, as though sleep-walking and drawn from my bed by something—or Someone—stronger than I; to walk noiselessly down to the fireplace, sink down upon my knees, and plead with a Presence felt, but not seen.

Mr Jerome did not travel with the company, but constantly visited us and often rehearsed my big scene quietly with me, when he thought that the provincial audiences were sucking the spirituality from my performance. It is so terribly easy to broaden one's style, and everyone has a tendency to rant in the provinces, I don't know quite why ; but Mr Jerome's kindness and interest in my work saved me from that pitfall.

We had such fun together, the Jeromes and I, going for expeditions into the surrounding country, and having cosy tea-parties in the dressing-room which I shared with Rowena.

Little Mrs Jerome was tremendously proud of her daughter's performance and obsessed by the idea that Rowena was delicate and must be fortified and nourished continually between the Acts. Personally I never saw a healthier specimen, and was vastly amused by the egg-drinks, glasses of port, and other stimulants poured down the throat of my rosy little friend.

She was her father's darling and their relationship was a very pretty thing to watch ; they were such perfect companions, laughing and teasing each other and always so happy to be together.

During the tour we began to rehearse a farce of Mr Jerome's which he hoped to produce in London when ' The Passing of the Third Floor Back ' finished its run.

I shall never forget my depression during the first reading of the play by the author to the assembled company. Personally I think that the day of farcical comedy is over. Our humour now is far more subtle, conveyed by suggestion—a lifted eyebrow, the twist of a mouth, or even an eloquent silence ; and I have long since found it difficult to laugh at the blatantly obvious. I had hoped to find this farce of Mr Jerome's so excruciatingly funny that it would even wrench laughs out of me, but as he read it my smile became more and more like stretched elastic for I found the situations forced and not funny. His little family, who were present at the reading, laughed loyally at all the expected places, and their mirth prevented the play from falling entirely flat ; for, to my consternation, I saw that the rest of the company (all seasoned actors and actresses) were likewise failing to find it amusing.

I was all the more disappointed, because I had been cast for a really delightful part, straight and sincere—the one foil to all the farcical characters in the play.

I did not see how it could succeed in London, even if it survived the provinces. We were going to try it out in Brighton, and my entire family decided to come down for the opening night—a great event for me. It was thrilling to welcome them all in my lodgings and to present them proudly to the company and the Jerome family, who promptly got up a *gala* evening in their honour at one of the hotels.

But they did not find the play very funny and were as doubtful of its success as I, although we didn't do so badly in Brighton.

When we reached London the play was put on at the Vaudeville Theatre, preceded by Bernard Shaw's ' Great Catherine,' in which Gertrude Kingston starred, under the direction of Mr Norman MacKinnel.

We had a trial performance before him, and the deep gloom with which he witnessed the play damned it forever in my eyes, as I had a great respect for his judgment. To play our scenes to that frowning face and never once see it relax into a smile was, to say the least of it, depressing.

He had taken us on the recommendation of Miss Kingston, who had seen us play at Brighton, and thought that an amusing farce might successfully replace the tragedy which was then being played before ' Great Catherine,' and, as she imagined, was killing it. We killed it just as surely, and after a very short run both plays were taken off.

My personal notices in the newspapers were good, and I was not sorry to have a rest after touring the provinces for so many weeks. But all the same it was very sad to be disappointed of a run in London.

Of course I went home ; and I found the family much

happier in mind, for Stella had given Mervyn a beautiful
son, Patrick Mervyn, born (in the Scottish Hospital) at
Nairobi. Both she and the baby were doing splendidly,
and an English ' nanny ' had been found.

Guy was working hard in his curacy at Aylesbury
(playing at ' High Priests ' in earnest now), and seemed
very happy and fond of his Vicar, Canon Constantine
Phipps, and his family ; and Marjory was at home ; very
popular among the girls and boys of the neighbourhood.

XXV.

Nearly three years had passed since my whole outlook
on life had been changed by the sudden finding of my
Man. I saw him from time to time in London, and when
I was on tour he wrote to me regularly—long intimate
letters. From Windsor, telling me of all he was doing
in the Library ; describing the Easter and Ascot parties,
even to details of the dress and jewellery of the women ;
from London, telling me of his research work at the
Record Office and elsewhere, of the friends he had met
at his Club, and of visits to his relatives ; from country
houses where he had gone to shoot, describing the autumn
scene and good or bad days in the coverts. Letters
written in his own perfect prose and humorous inimitable
style ; affectionate letters begging for news of me, of my
work and my play, my prospects, hopes, and fears. Sometimes would come an exciting registered packet. When
I was in bad lodgings on tour one came from Aix-les-Bains,
where he was having baths. It contained two very
beautiful hat-pins, chosen with perfect taste, and I forgot
my sordid surroundings.

Surely I *must* mean something to him ? Such a man—
and so hard-working a man would never write to a woman
so often, so confidentially and at such length, unless he
were fond of her ? And then, on my twenty-sixth birthday

came another little registered packet in which I found an old-fashioned gold chain linked together with a simple ring to form a bracelet. Round this was wrapped a birthday message which told me that the bracelet he sent me had once been his father's watch-chain. He asked me to wear it sometimes and to think of the giver who so often thought of me. Wild surmise then became happy certainty, for I knew that so reserved a man with so great a family feeling would never give away a family possession unless . . . unless . . . UNLESS . . .

But it was not until a month later that I heard from him again. He asked me if I could arrange to meet him in London, for he had something of importance to say to me. . . .

When we met, his expression and his manner were so changed that I was shocked and chilled to the soul. His face was set in stern rigid lines ; the mouth tightly compressed as though by pain. Gone was the twinkle I so loved ; and the affectionate bantering greeting—" Well, my little Mistress Winifred, and how's things ? "—was never uttered.

In cold and formal phrases he told me abruptly that after long and deep consideration he had decided that it would be better for both of us never to meet again nor correspond. . . .

The shock of it was so sudden, so cruelly unexpected— after those years of exchanged confidences—that bracelet —that message—this summons to London which I had obeyed with a heart beating so heavily with joy and hope—that now I could not speak. I stared up at him with a face so ashen and eyes so stricken with anguish, so he told me long afterwards, that at last he learned my secret, and with a shaking voice he began to reason with me. He had feared that I might grow too fond of him—this was what he felt he must say to me—he was old enough to be my father—my grandfather—he was a man of set and solitary habits who had dedicated his

life to a big job. In that life there could be no place for
youth and joy. He ought to have thought of this long
since, but, truth to tell, he had found the sympathy
and sometimes the companionship of Mistress Winifred
so very sweet ; for he was a lonely man. But now he
knew that he must never blight so young a life as mine.
I should forget him soon in my successful work, and
one day, some lucky man . . . He had been talking
softly, as though reasoning with himself, not looking
at me at all. Now he turned towards me, and what he
saw brought him swiftly to my side. On his knees before
me he dried my face with his handkerchief, murmuring
things I had waited all my life to hear. At last I understood the meaning of his long silence. Three wasted
years. . . .

Now, as he told me of his life and his work—the fear
that racked him lest, if he marry me, he should cloud
my youth—I resolved to match him in unselfishness.
It might well be that a young wife would upset and render
unhappy his life—distract his thoughts from his great
work. Perhaps he had asked me to be his wife in a moment
of impetuosity—because I had been taken off my guard,
and so had shown him that I loved him. I must give
him the chance to retreat. And so I told him that *because*
I loved him so much I would not marry him. But he
would not accept this, and now reasoned with me in
another sense.

Shaken to the depths of my being, feeling sick and
faint, somehow I rose to my feet.

" Think it over quietly for a week," I said to him,
" then tell me your decision, and be sure that I will
accept it whatever it may be. I only want *your* happiness."

" I consider myself bound," he told me tenderly.

" But you are not bound. You are free," I said.

He kissed my hand.

" I shall never forget that you said that, my Darling.
Farewell—for a little while."

Then I went home to Suffolk and told Mummie and Daddie that I was the biggest fool God ever created. I had been given my heart's desire—and I had thrown it away.

When they had heard my story, I saw again that curious fierce look in Mummie's eyes. She did not speak, but Daddie said quietly—

" You did the only straight thing, my Win. Whatever his decision you will always feel that."

But has virtue ever been its own reward? I have often wondered that, for so often, when I have followed the dictates of my conscience, I have got nothing out of it but a bleak sense of desolation, or of loss, or the conviction that I have acted like a fool.

It was Saturday evening. I had given John a week —seven days and seven nights to be lived through, somehow . . .

Well—in a week this long suspense would be over, and I should know my sentence.

The early post on Monday brought me nothing. Our second delivery of letters came, generally, at half-past two, and I hovered foolishly in the garden near the drive up which the postman would soon appear on his red bicycle. Yet when I saw him coming I could not trust myself to greet this old friend casually and take the letters from him. He would see my shaking hands—my voice might tremble ; and so I went into the house.

There followed what seemed an interminable delay. The man was loquacious and our parlourmaid was pretty. Would they never cease chattering? Again I was possessed by the nervous rage which little things could now induce.

" A letter for you, Miss Winnie."

" Thank you, Frances."

A letter addressed to me written upon the blue-grey hand-made notepaper John Fortescue always used, lay uppermost upon a pile of letters on the salver she held.

I forced myself to pick it up casually, and, when the maid
had gone, I dragged myself upstairs by the banisters
for all strength had suddenly left me. Locked in my
own room I held that letter in my hand, lacking the
courage to open it. It was a thick letter. Perhaps it
contained sheets of explanation why the writer had
decided that our friendship must end.

A curious stillness enfolded the house. Mummie must
have heard the parlourmaid tell me that there was a
letter for me, and, because I had not rushed upstairs
with hers as was my wont but had vanished into my
room, she had surely guessed from whom my letter
came. I must break this hush of suspense. I must
read my letter and know my fate. This sitting
motionless in a chair staring at an envelope was pitiable
cowardice.

I opened it.

At first the beautiful scholarly handwriting swam
before my eyes and made no sense. I had to wait for
some time longer before I could read what he had
written. . . .

The moment after I had left him he had composed a
telegram telling me that his decision remained firm.
Then, thinking of the inquisitive eyes of a village post-
mistress, he had torn it up and sat down at once to
tell me all that was in his heart—which really was
all mine if I cared to keep so old and battered a
thing. He implored me to consider the disparity of
age between us ; the kind of life that I should lead
with a man trained to hard and unremitting work ;
a man of naturally solitary habits, who had long left
youth and joy behind him. He dreaded that, married
to him, my young life would be crippled and maimed.
I must think on these things. If, when I had weighed
them well, I still felt that I wished to entrust the
sacred care of my youth and happiness to him, then—
he was mine—and I was his. . . .

XXVI.

Daddie did not believe in long engagements and often used to quote the old saying, " Long acquaintance, short engagement." Well, John and I had known each other for three years, and so there seemed no point in prolonging our separation. We decided to wait until Lent was over ; then came the official announcement that the Court would go down to Windsor for Easter which, in the ordinary course of events, would mean that John must be in attendance there.

As he was the only member of the Household who knew the history of every stone of the Castle, he was always very much in demand during the Royal visits to Windsor ; for he was an admirable guide, and generally took guests in charge, especially on wet days when they invaded the Library to be amused. Also Queen Mary took a tremendous interest in the arrangement of the Castle apartments and collections, tracing the history of pictures, miniatures, furniture and relics, and being very keen that all treasures should be catalogued and sometimes photographed. So that John—who was in charge of the Library, consisting of about 150,000 books ; the Print-rooms containing approximately the same amount of prints and engravings, besides 18,000 drawings ; the Stuart Collection of relics ; the jewels, and the War Museum, not to mention the Archives—was a necessity to her during her researches.

He told me that he felt that it would be selfish to ask so good a master and mistress as the King and Queen for leave of absence (to be married) during the Court Visit when he knew that he could be of use to them ; and he suggested that we should wait until it was over. Of course I agreed, and we fixed 30th April as the day of our wedding.

The next few weeks were full of excitement. Wonderful

presents flowed in every day; old silver, lace, jewellery, pictures, and furniture of all kinds, for, when asked to choose what we would prefer, we always said ‘a bit of furniture,’ knowing that we should have to furnish a little home in London.

King George and Queen Mary gave John a beautiful silver rose-bowl of unusual design, quite plain save for a deep removable border formed like a crown, and, of course, the inscription and Royal Arms. His messmates of the *Medina* sent him a large silver salver (after Paul Lamerie) with their names engraved on the back of it. Ever afterwards we had our coffee served upon it. There are pathetically few left now of those whose signatures are inscribed upon that salver. Among my personal wedding-presents was one very great treasure—the bound manuscript of John's book, written for children, ‘The Drummer's Coat,’ sent to me by his widowed sister, Lady Mary Bridgeman, to whom he had given it. The manuscript of ‘The Story of a Red Deer’ (since burned with the old Castle Hill—a double tragedy) was the property of John's nephew, Hugh Ebrington, for whom it was written; so that I could never have the joy of that possession.

It was a very thrilling time, for John seemed to revel in showering gifts upon me. When he asked me what stones I should prefer for my engagement ring, I told him that I loved pearls above all other jewels, and cared not a jot that they were considered unlucky. He came down to Great Bealings bringing with him *two* engagement rings; an oblong sapphire surrounded with brilliants in an antique setting which had taken his fancy, and a lovely half-hoop of pearls that he had not considered quite worthy of me, and so, to be on the safe side, had bought the two.

Then there was the business of clothes to be dealt with. My Duchess, who had long since become ‘Consuelo’ to me, gave me a magnificent cheque for this purpose, and I went up to London and spent a delirious morning choosing the loveliest *lingerie* and fluffy *negligées* to wear when dining alone with my husband ; the place where I knew I should always prefer to dine.

My forthcoming wedding was destined to be a disappointment to many. I know Mummie had dreamed of seeing me ' clothed in white samite, mystic, wonderful,' with lilies in my arms. What mother in the world does not see a vision of her daughter draped in the traditional bridal garments ? The villagers had expected a grand wedding in our own little church, which the whole of the county and half London, including, I am sure, the King and Queen, complete with jewelled crowns and full Coronation attire, would attend. Great was their consternation when it was known that the marriage would be of a strictly private character and held in London. Worst of all was the fact that their ' Miss Winnie ' would not be married in white.

One of my greatest friends among the cottagers whispered the request that even if the wedding could not be held in Great Bealings, at least they might all be allowed to ' see me in my white.' Then I confessed to her that I should only wear a little blue picture-frock, but that I would arrange to parade in it before them, and at the same time introduce them to my husband.

To make this possible, Mummie arranged a double reception to be held in our parish room a week before the wedding. The children of the village were to be invited to a party in the afternoon and their parents in the evening. There would be a huge wedding-cake for them, and, of course, John and I would act as host and hostess. Friends and relations would be invited to tea at the Rectory, where they could see a certain number of our wedding-presents (I never can imagine why anyone should want to see wedding-presents, but apparently the majority of people do). Our gifts could never be concentrated in one place. Some were sent to John at

Windsor, others to his flat in Brook Street, a certain number to Castle Hill in Devon, whilst mine came to the Rectory.

John's relations—and, being the ninth child of a family of fourteen, their name was Legion—were all anxious to make my acquaintance, so that he suggested that I should come up to London for a week to meet as many of them as lived there. Consuelo invited me to stay with her at Sunderland House during this ordeal, and Mummie insisted that I should go, assuring me that she could perfectly well make all the arrangements for the village teas alone.

John's relations were perfectly charming to me, and his youngest brother, General Charles, whom John always described to me as his 'special' brother, told me that there had only been one thing wrong with John—the fact that he had never married ; but now I was going to put that right.

Together John and I made the tour of his immediate family, lunching, tea-ing, and dining with one member of it or another every day ; and finally I was presented to his two ancient aunts, both well over ninety, Lady Blanche Haygarth and Lady Camilla Fortescue. Lady Blanche Haygarth, sister of John's mother (and widow of General Haygarth who was wounded on the Field of Waterloo and carried away among the dead, but recovered and lived to a ripe, if cantankerous, old age), was a wonderful old lady, whose limbs were now infirm, but whose mind was as bright as a diamond. It was fascinating to hear her talk of her youth. She had met the famous Duke of Wellington, and she had known the third Napoleon, who had proposed to, and been refused by, her sister (John's mother), but had evidently borne no malice, for, when she married, he was among the wedding-guests and signed the register. 'Aunt Blanche' was rather a formidable person, with a very sharp tongue with which she sometimes stabbed her relations and friends, and she lacked the charm and beauty of her sister, Lady Constance Leslie, though she always looked perfect with her frills and cap of old lace and her lovely hands.

Lady Camilla Fortescue, the other old aunt, I loved at sight. Some people, I know, considered her to be either formidable because of her reserve, or boring because of her deafness. She adored John, and he warned me that I must be prepared for a hostile reception since she entirely disapproved of his choice of so young a wife, and was shocked that I had been on the stage. When I entered her drawing-room she came stiffly forward to receive me, and, drawing me forward to a window where the light fell full upon me, said very severely—

" I suppose you know, my dear, that this is a *very* serious thing that you are undertaking—the care of John ? "

" No one could realise that better than I, Lady Camilla," I replied earnestly, looking her straight in the eyes.

Then, to my secret consternation, John made some excuse to leave me alone with ' Aunt Cam,' and she pulled me down on to a sofa by her side and began to search in a pocket of her voluminous black silk skirt.

" I have found a little wedding-present for John's wife," she said as she at last extracted a small packet and began to untie the string. The careful knots eluded her, and I could hardly restrain my impatience while the old fingers fumbled and tugged, and at last I fear that I completely forgot my manners and cried out : " Oh, please—PLEEEASSSEE be quick. I can't bear this suspense." She looked up sharply, smiled and handed me a little leather case in which I found a lovely old ring— a half-hoop of five large turquoises which had kept their colour through the years. Whereupon, forgetting all formality, I threw my arms around the old lady's neck and fairly hugged her.

When released, she looked at me, beaming all over her face, and, straightening her lace cap, exclaimed—

" My dear ! I shall *have* to love you ! "

And ever afterwards John's wife became as sacred as John in that house in Hertford Street ; and one of his relations told him that " Since Peggy came into the family, Aunt Cam speaks of the stage as though she, too, had trod the boards."

John had always lunched with Aunt Cam every Sunday before going on to tea with Aunt Blanche, and I was very anxious not to upset any habits of long-standing, particularly engagements with relatives, and so, after our marriage, I accompanied him. Aunt Cam and I were always very happy talking together—our one great subject—John. She told me of his childhood, even a disgraceful story of his return from a preparatory school when given a holiday tip by his uncle, he remarked that it was " damned good of him," and that it would be " b——y useful." When these remarks were greeted with shocked silence, the small boy carefully and distinctly repeated them lest his Aunt and Uncle might have missed these manly words, learned from the lips of an usher at school (which usher was afterwards removed).

During the few weeks of our engagement John spent his week-ends with my family in Suffolk. His very first visit was an anxious one for me, because neither Mummie nor Daddie had ever seen him before. I felt quite certain that he was everything that Daddie most respected and admired, but I was rather nervous of Mummie's reception of him. I remembered too vividly her curious manner and the look in her eyes when I first told her that I had found THE man—MY man—and how much it had puzzled and hurt me. She knew how restless and unhappy I had been during the past three years while John, thinking that he was too old a man to make me happy, had said nothing of his love for me. She had bitterly resented this silence. It had terrified her, for she had feared that this unknown man had for ever robbed me of my joy in life, my peace of mind, and my keen interest in my stage career, and that, while he had become my whole life, I was but an incident in his.

How would she receive him now? When we entered the Rectory she came out to greet us, her little face flushed, wisps of wavy hair blowing in the wind, her lovely grey eyes very bright, her sleeves rolled up and her arms covered with soap-suds. She and Marjory were washing the priceless Waterford glass of the Beech family, which no servant was ever allowed to touch, so that John and I might make our choice of it for our wedding-present. The small soapy hands made a good excuse not to take John's in hers, but she bade him welcome very graciously, and then passed him over to Daddie, who came hurrying downstairs to greet him. Her eyes had swept over John, and then held his with one of her piercing glances. He had regarded her with a disarming twinkle, and then had given her his beautiful courtly bow. Soon he was in the midst of an animated conversation with Daddie, whom he had obviously captured at sight. He was holding apart the drawing-room curtains with both arms outstretched, the better to see the lovely quiet view of our little Norman Church under the distant over-arching trees, with the foreground of green and blossoming garden. His long slim body and very beautiful hands were silhouetted against the sunlight. I felt terribly proud of him, and I saw Mummie and Marjory staring at his back with all their eyes.

In the evening, after dinner, we were alone together for a few moments, and screwing in the eyeglass and looking at me whimsically he said—

" Am I a success with your family, Sweetheart ? "

When I assured him of this he said—

" And which of them do you think likes me the most ? *I* know."

" Daddie ? " I asked.

" No."

" Marjory ? " (She had confided, rapturously, to me

164

that he had secretly given her a kiss and a ten-pound note
" to buy her wedding-frock," and she was already his
slave.)

" No."

There was a pause.

" Your Mother," he said with a quiet laugh.

" *Mummie ?* " I said incredulously.

" Yes. I made an immediate conquest there. She's
angry about it, but she can't help herself."

It was quite true, though I had not apprehended it,
but it made of my romance a perfect thing. Had Mummie
disapproved of John, loving her as intensely as I did, my
future life must have been miserable.

John was very shy about our wedding. Being a member
of the King's Household and belonging to so enormous
a family, if we were married in London our wedding
would become a pageant. If it were held in our little
Suffolk church, as I longed for it to be, all the county
would expect to be invited. John did not mind a congregation of simple villagers, but, marrying so late in
life, he dreaded being ' on show,' and besides he had always
had a horror of big weddings, saying that " when two
people found their happiness in each other, they should
enter life together in quietness and humbleness of heart,
not prancing forth to the vulgar strains of Mendelssohn's
Wedding March before the curious eyes of a mob of people."

John's brother, Seymour Fortescue, an ex-Equerry
of King Edward, had quarters in St James's Palace, and
he wanted us to be married in the Chapel Royal. John
firmly declined. He had a fancy to be married privately
in the Royal Library at Windsor, but the Special Licence
was far too costly. His London flat being in Brook
Street, he was of the parish of St George's, Hanover Square
—one of the most fashionable churches for weddings in all
London, and therefore to be avoided.

The only way to secure a really quiet wedding was to
choose some other church in London, and at length it

was decided that he should dump a suitcase of clothes in his eldest sister Susan's flat in Burton Court, which would then give him the right to have his banns called in the church of Holy Trinity, Sloane Street.

Accordingly he and I went to see the Rector, to make arrangements and to ask his permission for Daddie and Guy to perform the marriage service for us in the little side chapel of his church.

He was perfectly charming and seemed only too eager to make us as happy as possible.

" What about music ? " he asked. " Would you like my organist ? "

" There will be no music," replied John.

" And the flowers ? " queried the Rector. " Will you be responsible for the decoration of the chapel ? "

" Why should we want flowers ? " asked John.

" Well, music and flowers would make the ceremony more cheerful for the bride."

" I don't want cheerfulness. I want despatch," John told him firmly. After which we took our leave. Out in the street John turned to me and said—

" The poor man seemed rather low and depressed. Was it Lenten fasting, do you think ? "

" It was our wedding," I told him.

XXVII.

Consuelo very sweetly suggested that I should be married from her house, and the night before our wedding gave a little dinner-party in our honour. To my consternation John arrived wearing a dark green eyeshade and confessed that his eyes had been troubling him all day. We dined by candle-light in consequence, and very soon afterwards, being obviously in a great deal of pain, he excused himself and went back to Brook Street.

Fortescue had lent us Castle Hill for the first part of

our honeymoon, after which we were to go on to Clovelly Court, lent to us by John's cousin, Christine Hamlyn. I spent a sleepless night, repeating my responses in the marriage service and wondering frantically what I should do, so far from his oculist, if my Historian's precious eyes should continue to give trouble.

He, also, it transpired, had a sleepless night, and in the small hours knocked up a chemist and begged for some soothing lotion. The eyes continued to get worse, and so, after a few hours, he went to his oculist.

" How soon can you patch up these eyes of mine ? " he asked.

" Ten days of constant treatment at the very least," responded the specialist.

" I'm afraid that you must do it before noon to-day. I'm getting married at twelve o'clock," John informed the amazed man, who did his very best and sent him away with many lotions and salves.

John had chosen the workmen's dinner-hour during which to be married, for the same reason as his subtle choice of a church. He wished to avoid all publicity, and, so far, the Gentlemen of the Press had been unable to discover either the date or place of our wedding. Two reporters were hot upon the scent, although they never knew it. The representative of ' The Western Morning News ' actually climbed the staircase of the block of flats in Brook Street, crossing John who was on his way downstairs to get married. The reporter rang John's door-bell and asked his man if he could tell him " if the Hon. John Fortescue was being married to-day ? " In all sincerity he was assured that this was impossible, because Mr Fortescue had just gone out wearing a blue suit and brown shoes. Outside Holy Trinity Church an awning had been put up and a carpet laid down for an important wedding in the afternoon, and, as John walked up to the side door of the church, a reporter of some other newspaper accosted him—

" I beg your pardon, sir, but could you tell me if this awning is put up for the wedding of the Hon. John Fortescue ? "

" Yes, I can assure you that it is not," replied John gravely—with perfect truth.

" Thank you, sir, you've saved me from wasting my time kicking my heels here," said the reporter gratefully, and walked off.

Our wedding took exactly seven and a half minutes, as John informed me proudly afterwards, and only eleven people were present, including ourselves and clergy.

After the register had been signed by everybody, and Consuelo had decorated us all with tiny waxen sprays of orange blossom, John and I drove with her to Sunderland House for a quick luncheon before catching our train to Devonshire. The Fortescues carried off my family to Lowndes Street. I could hardly bear to see Mummie disappear. She would not say good-bye, for it wasn't good-bye—that could never be said between us until one or other of us died—and even then . . . ? She had just kissed me rather fiercely and I had whispered, " I'm still yours, you know."

All through that journey my poor Man had to bathe his inflamed eyes with lotions, but as we came into Devonshire he forgot the pain while pointing out to me familiar landmarks. When we changed our train at Exeter, he was received by the station officials as though he were royalty, and I realised, for the first time, what the name Fortescue meant in Devon.

It was evening when we drove up to Castle Hill. The approach to the great white house, which was built in the style of a French *Château*—a central block with two long wings extending on either side—did not greatly impress me, for the drive swept up to the back of the house. But once inside, I could admire the beautiful staircase, one of the proud features of the house, rising from the midst of a lofty flower-filled hall ; the gracious

curves of the circular library, where a great fire blazed
a welcome and the warm air was scented by burning logs
of pine and bowls of lilies-of-the-valley, and, as John
quietly led me to one of the French windows, opened it
and ushered me out on to the terrace in front of the house,
I was struck dumb by the beauty of the view before me.
My eyes swept over formal terraces cut by flower-beds
and approached by stone stairways flanked by tall clipped
yews—down over a green valley laced by a silver stream,
and up a slope on the farther side, where a wide grass
ride swept between noble trees to a distant arch of stone.
An arm stole round my neck.

" My home pleases you, Sweetheart ? " said a deep
voice at my side. " It's—not amiss—is it ? "

" Oh—JOHN ! " was all that I could say, but it was
enough. He knew that I must love it as he did.

XXVIII.

Never shall I forget that glorious first of May. John
led me next morning through the woods which back
the house, on and up amid the green gloom of wonderful
trees, until suddenly we came out into the sunlight
and stood above a sea of primroses, acres of little pale
yellow stars washing in yellow waves downhill to a bluebell
wood far below.

" The Easter Close," John said simply, and it seemed
to me that no more fitting name could have been chosen
for that perfect place. . . .

" You are crying, darling ? " . . .

That spring was one of the loveliest that I had ever
seen : every flowering shrub was loaded with blossom ;
the thorn trees were snow-white ; the golden wild azaleas
flamed to a height of fourteen feet and scented the air
with heady fragrance ; the woods and copses were carpeted
with bluebells ; the meadows yellow with cowslips and

primroses ; foxglove spears guarded the hedges ; golden marsh marigolds and yellow iris fringed the streams. John practically lived out-of-doors. I found that he was a keen fisherman ; he knew every likely pool where trout might lurk, and caught many. The rest from writing and the open-air life soon cured those over-strained eyes. We went for a wonderful drive across Exmoor on a day of dramatic contrasts of light and shade when the brilliant sun was obscured at swift intervals by great billowing clouds driven across a vivid blue sky by a keen and pungent wind. We stood at the top of Five Barrows Down and John said to me : " When I die, I should like my ashes to be blown over Devon from this spot."

Seen from the top of Dunkerry, the moor around us was splashed with deep violet cloud-shadows hurrying across its surface of tender greens and browns before the Atlantic gale. Only down in little sheltered Porlock a hot stillness brooded over the white thatched cottages. John pointed out to me the course of many a run he had had with the stag-hounds, and, on our way home, the last run of the red deer in his story and the stream which had borne its gallant weary body away.

He took great delight in presenting his wife to all the tenants on the Estate, and we had a substantial Devonshire tea with the two old sisters of a gamekeeper, since dead, who had been the friend of all the Fortescue sons, and had shared with them many a sporting day. John became a different man with these true simple friends. They still called him ' Master John,' and with them he lost all his shyness, chaffed them, and talked with them of old days in broad Devon dialect while devouring an incredible quantity of cut-rounds, home-made jam, saffron cake, and Devonshire cream.

It was during these lovely lazy days that he thought out the plot of his child's story, ' The Three Pearls,' and began to write it ' in his head.' He would appear in the doorway of his dressing-room, his face covered with soap-suds and a razor in his hand, to ask me queer questions, such as :—

" What is the name of those things women wear on their heads when their hair is getting thin ? "

" Do you mean a false fringe ? " I asked.

" Yes—but there's a name for it," he persisted.

" A ' transformation ' ? " I suggested.

" Ah, yes ! That's it—a transformation. My old Queen in my story wears one," and he went off chuckling to himself. Many feminine details of this sort were supplied by me, and he thoroughly enjoyed writing that book.

We spent a few days at Clovelly Court. The slopes of the wooded Hobby Drive were clothed with bluebells, so dazzlingly blue that the sea, far below, looked grey in contrast. We climbed about the precipitous little village, so famous now that description is superfluous, and John told me that in the early days of cars, Christine Hamlyn, Lady of the Manor, had gone to London to choose one.

" Has that car got a really strong engine ? " she demanded of the salesman. " For you must realise, young man, that when I leave my house I must often climb a gradient of one in ten."

Clovelly was full of memories of John's childhood. Here he came with his brothers, escaping the formalities of Castle Hill to romp with his unconventional Fane cousins, riding, bathing, fishing, shooting, and sailing over to Lundy Island. He recalled some of the happiest days of his life.

But I loved best Hartland Abbey, the home of Marian Stucley, Christine Hamlyn's sister, hidden in a wooded hollow some miles from Clovelly, with its chain of lovely walled gardens, once cultivated by monks, its shady woodland walks, and little excitable trout-stream cascading through the valley in a series of waterfalls and still pools, until at last it dashed over the cliff and into the sea.

Our honeymoon lasted but a fortnight. John would

not spare longer from his History. I understood this
very well, and so I did not seek to dissuade him. Every
day at Castle Hill he had left me for an hour or two,
following out his theory that everyone should spend some
part of every day in solitude. I had seen him striding
through the gardens, puffing furiously at his pipe, and
had known that he was fighting some action with the
British Army, for that History of his had become the
motive of his life. Until it was finished he could know
no real peace. Well, I had come into his life to help and
not hinder his life's work. When I married him I always
expected to take a second place—the great History must
always be first. And because I was so proud of his work
and never jealous of the time he gave to it, in the end I
became the more important.

One cold and windy day at Castle Hill, when he left
me alone for a while, I curled up on a sofa with a book,
and after a time fell asleep. When I awoke I was still
alone, but I was covered warmly with John's great
shooting-cape. A trivial thing to touch me as it did, but
it showed me that even during those hours which he
dedicated to his History he had thought of me.

XXIX.

John told me repeatedly that his one terror was that
he might 'cloud my young life with his sad and serious
mode of living': " I've a big job to finish, Sweetheart,
and I must mug at it continually—two big jobs in fact,
my History and my work at Windsor. But there is no
reason why you should not play while I work. I propose
taking a small house in London as your headquarters
and that I live chiefly at Windsor, spending my weeks'
ends in London with you. The King has no other
suitable house to give us at present, but he has kindly
offered to enlarge my present quarters in the Castle to

make it possible for you to visit me whenever you feel inclined."

He must have seen my blank expression, for he went on to tell me that he was convinced that lasting happiness in marriage could be ensured by frequent absences. He was by nature a solitary man, and I think he feared a complete upheaval of his disciplined and ordered life by the sudden intrusion of a young wife. He had told me that his theory was that everyone in the world should have at least an hour or two of their very own daily " to commune with themselves."

I did not at all want to commune with myself. I felt that I had had a great deal too much of this already during the three years that he had wasted thinking that he was too old to marry me. All I wanted now was to be with him always, to look after him, and, if possible, to help him somehow with his work. But I realised that I must in nowise upset him or his way of life, and therefore I accepted his suggestion with, I must admit, a heavy heart.

However, I started the search for a small house, and, in the interim, we hired a furnished one in a quiet Square off Knightsbridge where I and our wedding-presents could be temporarily housed and looked after by the servants let with the house. John went back to Windsor, and I was left alone. I very nearly ran home to Mummie. Never in my life had I felt so lost and lonely. In addition to missing John every moment of the day, I suffered from uneasy evenings and short nights, for I had been on the stage for so long that I had grown into theatrical habits. Towards six o'clock I always became restless because, for years, I had had an early meal and then gone down to the theatre. It seemed so extraordinary to have no work to do—only to have a bath, get into a tea-gown, and dine in solitary state at eight o'clock. If I went to bed early I lay awake until midnight, the hour when I should have gone to bed had I been acting.

By day I searched for houses, and eventually found one in Brompton Square.

John came up from Windsor to see the house—liked it at once, as I had, and when we had had it properly surveyed, we took it.

While various alterations and decorations were being carried out, he suggested that I should pay a visit to our Windsor quarters, which had now been enlarged to accommodate me also. His flat in the Castle ran under the Library and opened into a spare store-room for books which, in its turn, opened into the corridor leading to his office and the Print-rooms and Library. This store-room had now been cut in two with a passage between the two rooms, one of which was to be John's dressing-room and the other a servant's room. He wanted me to come down and tell the Head of the Lord Chamberlain's Office how I would like these rooms and my own bedroom decorated when the Office of Works had finished the structural alterations.

I found it great fun to choose my furniture from the Castle Stores and to make the acquaintance of the various officials of each department, who all vied with each other in their effort to please me and give me what I wanted. One and all had considered the King's Librarian to be a confirmed bachelor, and he had created a sensation in the Castle by suddenly producing a bride young enough to be his daughter. But, in many ways, he seemed younger than I. His great fear was that he might one day 'stop growing' as, he told me, so many of his contemporaries had done and had forthwith become old. He could wear me out very quickly when we went for walks together, striding ahead with his long tireless legs (' my seven-league husband ' as Lord Annaly once called him) ; his quick eyes noted every tree, the habit of every bird ; he found wild flowers that I had missed, and all the time he was pouring forth an odd stream of information about everything around us. His mind was an encyclopædia, and he missed nothing. We would cross the two Castle Courtyards, traverse the Home Park, and go out into the Great Park where deer grazed under great oak trees and bracken grew waist-high. The Court were not in residence on my first visit, so that we could wander anywhere and everywhere about the Castle and its precincts, for John had all the keys. While he was working in his office he would turn me over to his Library Assistant, Mr Barry, who knew the contents of the Print-rooms by heart, and would spend hours showing me the Leonardo da Vinci drawings (the largest collection in the world), the Michael Angelos, the Holbeins, and other priceless treasures.

The evenings John and I spent together in Edward IIIrd's Gatehouse were very happy, for he would read aloud to me Jane Austen, Dickens, Trollope, while I did some form of needlework ; or we would merely gossip and laugh together, or plan the arrangement of our little house in Brompton Square.

Then I would go back to London alone to supervise the workmen and just count the hours until I saw John again.

When he came up to London he delighted in buying me 'surprises,' and one day, to my amazement, suggested taking me to Liberty's to get me some material for evening dresses. I fully expected that when we entered the showrooms he would become as nervous and miserable as Uncle Anstey had been, but to my surprise he seemed to be perfectly at home there, leading the way and acknowledging the salutes of bowing shopwalkers. When we reached the Silk Department he quite embarrassed me by the work he gave the salesmen, choosing bales of lovely materials and insisting that each should be displayed apart from all others. " Colour is purely relative," he stated ; " it is impossible to judge a colour truly with others around it." The sweating salesmen had to heave heavy bales of stuff out of the way until a wide space had been cleared where John's selected materials were displayed, and he was far more difficult to please than any woman.

Once outside, I rallied him upon his complete ease of manner in a woman's shop, whereupon he replied airily—

" Oh I always go there on ' remnant days ' to buy strips of stuff to mount the treasures in the King's collection."

Those three dresses had a great success. He came with me to my dressmaker and superintended their draping, and I well remember wearing an azalea-tinted gown soon afterwards during a visit to Melbury where we went to stay with Birdie Ilchester, who proved to be one of John's dearest and best friends. By some odd chance the dining-room table that evening was deco- rated with azaleas of exactly the same colour as my dress, and old General Pultenay whispered to me as I passed him on the way to the dining-room—

" Is the gardener a friend of yours ? "

That visit to Melbury, so soon after we were married, was, at first, a rather terrifying experience, for there was a large house-party consisting of very critical *mondaine* people, all very curious to see the wife John Fortescue had chosen so late in life. I longed for the afternoons when we would go away together to one or other of the lakes in the Park, John carrying his fishing-rod that I had given him—' a little love of a rod,' he described it—and I a landing-net.

He gave me my first lesson in fly-fishing on ' Lucerne,' the largest of the lakes, lending me his precious rod for a few moments with strict injunctions to throw my fly gently on to the surface of the water and on no account to catch the hook on a submerged bit of wood. I threw it—and the fly disappeared. I tried to raise my line, but found that it resisted me. John cast despairing eyes to heaven and exclaimed : " Oh, *darling !* Just what I feared—you've entangled your line. The hook must be caught in some sunken bit of wood."

" Well, it's a very lively bit of wood," I retorted, " it's

moving about." With the proverbial beginner's luck I had caught the best fish of the day. After which triumph I preferred to rest upon my laurels.

No one could feel shy or lost very long in the house of Birdie Ilchester ; one of those rare women who realise the importance of little things and who, though always busy, yet find time to think of and plan for the happiness of all around them.

John, in common with all her friends, adored her.

" Of her, I never heard a ' catty ' remark from a woman nor a cynical comment from a man," he said when talking of ' the beloved Birdie.' " She has the mind, humour, straightness, and broad outlook of a man ; combined with all the best qualities of a woman."

I believe she was the very first person, outside his immediate family, to whom he confided the secret of his approaching marriage with me ; a fact never quite forgiven by her mother, Theresa, Lady Londonderry, who reminded me, rather acidly, that John was of *her* generation, not Birdie's, and that therefore he should have told her his news first. John was also very fond of her husband, Stavy Ilchester, a writer himself : " one of those rare country gentlemen who has troubled to learn the history of his family and possessions, and to record it," he would say.

Very soon after my arrival at Melbury, Birdie's three children, Harry, Mary, and John, adopted me as their own.

I was very proud of the children's adoption of me, and because they treated me as a contemporary and not as ' a grown-up.' Whenever possible, I stole away to share their walks and games, and, from that moment, I was completely happy at Melbury, which had been for some time like a second home to John. He used always to go there twice or thrice a year and loved the shooting, especially the sporting Abbotsbury shoot, where the bag included every kind of game from hares to water-fowl.

I went to Abbotsbury with the shooting-party on one

occasion, being anxious to visit the Swannery which has
been in the possession of the family since the days of
King Canute. (Among the Melbury archives is a deed
signed by his X in place of signature.)

Birdie met us later and we had a picnic luncheon in
Mary Lady Ilchester's lovely tropical garden of Abbotsbury, where Himalayan rhododendrons, mimosa, and
camellias of every kind, besides many other rare and
exotic trees, shrubs, and plants grow happily in the open,
and arum lilies bloom in the pools as they do in the South
of France. An enchanting day.

XXX.

During the first few months of our marriage we were
more social than we were ever after to be, for John had
a big work to finish, and once he had presented his wife
to all his nearer relations we settled down to a quiet
life. But during those first months we spent many of
our week-ends in different parts of England. We went to
Coln St Aldwyn in Gloucestershire to stay with John's
sister Lucy St Aldwyn, who had married the formidable
Michael Hicks-Beach, in the days when he was Chancellor
of the Exchequer, and known as ' Black Michael ' ; a
strikingly handsome man in his youth, with very blue
eyes, fine features, and curly black hair and beard which
had grown grey when I first met him. He was one of
the few living men who had known Disraeli. At first
he intimidated me with his formal courtesy and aloof
manner, so that at the end of our visit in the beautiful
old grey manor-house, I was appalled when John pushed
me into a non-smoking carriage alone with Michael,
who was also travelling up to London, and then tucked
himself away into another carriage where he could enjoy
his pipe in peace.

Michael, ever courteous, thought it his duty to converse

with his new sister-in-law, and began to ask me questions as to John's progress with his History.

" John is too prejudiced," he began. " He can never be fair to the politician."

Whereupon, forgetting my fear of ' Black Michael,' I blazed forth—

" How DARE you say that ? John is absolutely fair and just. He even criticises his pet heroes when they deserve it. It is you politicians who can never give justice to the Army," and with cheeks flaming with temper, after one withering look at my brother-in-law, I picked up my book and pretended to immerse myself in it so as to end this disgusting conversation. Michael took up his ' Times ' and began to turn its pages. We both read silently until Paddington was reached, and I thought to myself, impenitently, " Now I've done it. I shall never again be asked to Coln St Aldwyn. I've been terribly rude to my host—a man old enough to be my great-grandfather—but he deserved it—DARING to say that John was prejudiced and unjust—and TO ME ! "

Arrived at our station Michael rose to his feet and with majestic politeness opened the carriage door and assisted me to alight. I avoided his eyes, feeling sure that in them I should read icy condemnation of my behaviour. John jumped out of his carriage and hailed a taxi. The moment had come when I must say farewell to my brother-in-law and thank him for my visit.

Nerving myself for the ordeal I walked up to him, held out my hand, and looked him straight in the eyes, which, to my great astonishment, were dancing with amusement.

He took my hand in both his, and pumped my arm up and down heartily as he said—

" Good-bye, Peggy. Come again *soon*. And *stay a long time*."

Apparently these formidable men like to be stood up to.

Later, I was to find out that 'Black Michael' was intensely human and very soft-hearted under that assumed majesty of manner, and we became great friends. Perhaps I saw a side of him not shown to many. One Christmas when we were all staying at Castle Hill he made me *l'amende honorable* for that infuriating conversation in the train. I was sitting alone on a huge Chesterfield before the hall fire when Michael, coming down that lovely staircase, walked up to me and, vaulting over the back of the couch as lightly and easily as a boy (he was then over eighty), sat down beside me and once again began to talk of John.

" John has been one of the great satisfactions of my life," he told me. " He was one of those nervous brilliant boys who never quite come off. He muffed many of his examinations, and could not settle down to any profession. Then suddenly he came into his own rather late in life, for he had no success of any kind until he was half-way through the thirties. I always put it down to indifferent health and over-sensitiveness, but was certain he would make his mark one day, and I was right. When he finishes that classic History his country will inevitably give him the Order of Merit—I'd far rather have had the O.M. than my Earldom—John can't avoid getting it."

Nevertheless, when the great History was at last triumphantly finished, his country gave John nothing at all save the posthumous title of 'The Historian of the British Army,' which was, perhaps, the greater honour.

This little conversation endeared Michael to me, so that when he sneezed once, twice, and then thrice that evening, I cheekily remarked to him—

" You just saved yourself."

" Saved myself from what ? " he inquired.

> "'Once a wish,
> Twice a kiss . . .'"

I quoted gaily.

"Then I regret that third sneeze," he assured me, whereupon I hugged him.

On his birthday that year I chalked a little black X on a piece of paper and sent it to him in a tiny registered parcel marked PERISHABLE. In return, I got a sheet of paper upon which was written—

> " *Kisses returned. Long may you happy live.*
> *But why mark ' Perishable ' the love you give ?* "

His children, Michael, Susan, and Victoria, were all my seniors by several years, and delighted in teasing me by addressing me as 'Aunt.' It was always a happiness to go to Coln and to live among these delightful people, and Lucy, John's sister (described by him as " one of the bravest women in the world "), was kindness itself to me.

From Coln, we went on to Fairford to stay with John's youngest sister, Francie Gordon Duff. Coming at almost the tail-end of the family, she was yet a child when her elder brothers were grown-up and many of them gone abroad. She was almost of another generation, and because of this had wider interests, a larger circle of friends, and more advanced ideas. She was as thrilled as a girl over any new event or idea, and her tremendous sense of the ridiculous, coupled with a highly educated intelligent mind and a quick sympathy, made her a wonderful companion. John delighted in her, and was very proud of her slim figure, her energy, intelligence, and humour. If anything amusing happened in our lives, he would immediately say—

"I must remember to tell that to France."

He loved making her laugh until she wept, and he was very fond of her boy John, destined for the Rifle Brigade, and of Helen, her elder daughter, who had the makings of a very good painter, and Jeannie, her baby, who was then a little girl of twelve.

The house we visited most, because it was so near Windsor, was Stoke Place, the property of Howard Vyse, who had been at the same preparatory school as John.

When we first arrived at Stoke Place I saw a young man in a bath-chair drawn up on the terrace; and hardly had I been introduced to 'Vyse' than he drew me aside and told me that his younger son, George, had been semi-paralysed by a fall from his pony in his early teens, but that his brain was brilliant. This I soon found out for myself, for the moment my John appeared the young man's face lit up as he shouted joyously: " *Well*, Mister Johnnie," and they began to chaff each other with great spirit. George delighted in John's visits when he could sharpen his intelligence with this battle of wits. When apart, they carried on an animated correspondence, often in ridiculous rhyme, and George treasured John's letters, particularly one in which John made arrangements for the family to visit St George's Chapel and begged George to leave his dog, Hector (whose manners were not irreproachable), at home, lest he " defile the polished corners of the temple."

Often when we went to Stoke Poges Church, made famous by Gray's " Elegy," John would stay in the garden with George, wheeling his chair about the paths or sitting with him on the terrace, both chattering for all they were worth. As we walked off, we would hear shouts of laughter ringing through the garden, and once on our return George produced 'a poem' that they had concocted together to celebrate the nuptials of an early love of his to a detested rival. John and he had composed two lines apiece. George began—

> " I knew a Jobson once, his hair was orange,
> His face was speckled like a turkey's eggs "—

" Now, Mr Johnnie," said George, " I defy you to find a rhyme for 'orange.' "

> " Nor could silk petticoats, the best from Gorringe,
> Disguise the bandied horror of his legs,"

flashed John without a moment's hesitation.

George was a wonderful person; although his legs were

powerless and his hands partly paralysed, he could get a right and left with a gun. The gardener, old ' Empy,' his devoted slave, would hold the gun and George would pose it, sight his bird, and push the trigger with his wrist. His gallant spirit had so far mastered his infirmity that he even illustrated, quite delightfully, children's books, holding pen or brush between his two flat palms or in his teeth. So well did he do his work that it was accepted joyfully by publishers who appreciated not only his draughtsmanship but the humour of his drawings.

So far I had only seen the King and Queen in the distance, driving in the Home Park. They had come to Windsor for the day. I dropped a respectful curtesy from afar ; later, when I was back in London, and they saw John, they asked him why he had not brought me up to their carriage to present me to them.

One morning when the Court was in residence at Windsor for Ascot week and I alone in London, I got a letter from John telling me that Queen Mary had come to our quarters in the Norman Gateway to call upon me, had seemed rather put out that I was not there to receive her, and had only stayed a few moments. John explained to her that, according to his compact, I was staying in London while the Court was in residence because of that ancient rule which excluded all actresses, musicians, and singers, and all people engaged in commerce, from being received by their Sovereign. He said that he did not wish to cause any awkwardness for Their Majesties by the near presence of the wife of a member of their House-hold whom, for this reason, they could not receive. Queen Mary told him that the King hoped that I would come down to Windsor whenever I liked, and that, of course, they intended to receive me privately. John thought that as Their Majesties had graciously said this, I had better come down to Windsor for the coming week-end.

I went. The King and Queen were informed of my arrival, and both came to call upon me. They were all that is gracious and charming, and for some time we sat and talked in the Gatehouse sitting-room. Almost the first remark the Queen made to me was to ask me if I had been in our Windsor quarters when last she came to call.

" No, Madam, of course I was not," I protested vehemently. " Had I been here when Your Majesty was kind enough to come to see me, I should have appeared at once to receive you."

Fixing me with an accusing eye, she said—

" Your needlework was on the floor."

" My needlework, Ma'am ? " I queried, puzzled. Then sudden comprehension came to me—

" It must have been *John's*," I assured her.

" JOHN'S ? "

" Yes, Madam, he excels me in every kind of stitch on canvas—*petit point*, *Point de Flanders*, *Point de Venise*. . . ."

The astonishment of the Queen when she heard for the first time that her learned Librarian was also an expert needle-man, was genuine. Then I remembered John's letter telling me of Her Majesty's last visit, and that he had said she seemed put out about something and had not stayed long. Seeing needlework upon the floor beside an armchair she had imagined that John's wife, in an access of shyness, had thrown it there and fled into hiding. Naturally she had been surprised and felt offended. Now all was explained, and she was heartily amused by her mistake.

Both the King and the Queen wished to see the enlargement and improvements made by their permission in John's bachelor quarters to accommodate a wife, so John accompanied the Queen, and I the King, on the short tour of our rooms. When I reached John's new dressing-room with King George, I was startled to see the butt-end of our man-servant protruding from under the bed. He was a countryman from Daddie's village, and, being overcome with shyness and fright, had tried to hide himself hurriedly under John's bed during the visit of his Sovereign, but had found his chosen hiding-place partly blocked by uniform cases. The King looked at me and raised his eyebrows questioningly, but I was too shattered to reply.

When Their Majesties had seen all there was to be seen, we all came to a halt in the narrow space by the front door, once the old ' curtain wall ' leading from the Gatehouse to the Castle proper, and now the passage from sitting-room to dining-room. The Queen had her back to the kitchen door, and I was terrified lest the cook, not knowing of Her Majesty's presence, would suddenly burst forth with a plate of raw meat on her way to the larder which was just behind where the King was standing. It was a quarter to five, and the Queen had told me that at five o'clock she was due for tea with Princess Alice (Countess of Athlone), who was living then in Henry VIIth's Tower, just across the way. If she left at once she would be too early for her appointment, but she had already seen all there was to see in Norman Gate, and it was hardly worth while to re-enter the Gatehouse sitting-room for so short a time. While she hesitated, we all stood in that passage, and the pause and silence made me nervous. I looked at John, who was standing at attention and did not catch my glance. I looked at the King, who smiled kindly at me but gave no sign. Nor did the Queen. Then it suddenly flashed across me that, as I was hostess, perhaps it was *my* duty to break this silence and to speed my parting guests, and so I suddenly dropped a curtesy and thanked Their Majesties for their gracious kindness in coming to see me. The King laughingly took my hand and shook it heartily, then the Queen did likewise and both of them went out of the front door, the King still laughing and waving his hand to me as they passed under the Norman Gate. Then I went into our sitting-room where I found John lying back in an armchair, shaking with silent laughter.

"What *are* you laughing at ? " I inquired in astonishment.

"Nothing, darling, oh! nothing," gasped John. "Only I daresay that you are the first woman in Europe who has ever dismissed *two* Sovereigns."

"What do you mean—*dismissed ?* " I asked blankly. "No one seemed to be doing anything, and I couldn't stand that silence any more. Surely as hostess it was my place to thank my guests for visiting me ? "

"Yes, darling, your manners as a hostess were irreproachable, ONLY it is customary and traditional for the Sovereign to do the dismissing."

"So *that* was why the King laughed ? " I said. "Anyway he wasn't offended, for he waved to me as he walked away."

XXXI.

In August, two months later, war broke out, and John wrote from Windsor saying that he would be happier if I were safely with him, since there was a possibility of panic in London—food-hoarding, bread-riots, &c.

This danger was never very imminent, but I know that we had each learned to dread even those short weekly separations, and the declaration of war with Germany served as an excellent excuse for their termination with dignity.

I joyfully packed up my things and travelled down to Windsor by the first possible train.

With secret joy, I noticed John's face changing day by day. The 'hungry wolf' expression was gradually disappearing; the lines of stress became less marked; when we were together his eyes were happy, and I could make him forget for a time the strain of his work and the wearing anxiety for his beloved Army in France. During the magnificent retreat from Mons this was more difficult. He scanned his 'Times' as he drank his morning coffee, his sensitive hands stroking his lean jaw, his eyes anxious and intent.

" Why do I waste my life in writing the history of the British Army ? " he groaned one day. " I am told that my book is widely read by soldiers and politicians alike. Yet we repeat the same blunders century after century, and the Nation is never ready. At the end of every war the Army that has saved us is weakened by the politicians, and, when the next war breaks out, as usual we are unprepared and the Flower of our Army is destroyed while we train new troops. What is the use of sweating one's life out recording past blunders if no lesson is learned from bitter experience ? " And he would rise wearily to his feet and make his way towards the door leading to his office until recalled by me.

" John ! You've forgotten something. . . ."

He would turn a discouraged and somewhat impatient face towards me which would then break up into my special smile.

" What an exacting woman mine is," he would say as he returned to kiss me.

His Windsor doctor told me that he was thankful I had come into John's life.

" He has been over-working, under-feeding, and over-walking for years," the little doctor said. " It is high time this was put a stop to. Your mission in life, Mrs Fortescue, must be to *interrupt*."

" A very popular form of mission it will be," I grimaced. " No one is allowed *near* his room when he is writing."

" Well, you must go into it every morning at eleven, and, if you can't drag him out to have some strengthening drink—beef-tea, Ovaltine, egg-nog—then plant it on his desk and see that he drinks it."

Accordingly every morning I mixed a drink and walked with it down the long corridor under the Library till I reached John's office. A snarled " COME in " answered my first knock, and the fierce scowl that greeted me would have scared stiff anyone who did not know him as I did—teeth bared savagely and bushy black eyebrows meeting across the lined forehead. Then—

" Oh, it's you, Sweetheart," and a flicker of my special smile before the head was again bent over the manuscript and the quill pen scratching rapidly over the paper before him.

I left the drink, and when I came to his office at one o'clock to remind him that luncheon was waiting, I was relieved to find the glass empty. In a year he had learned to come and fetch his drink at eleven o'clock, and would remain standing with me for five minutes while he drank it. In two years, this break had lengthened into fifteen minutes. He was learning to relax a little, and would sink quite gratefully into an armchair, sip his drink slowly, smoke one cigarette, and then go back to work.

Backed and encouraged by his doctor, I threw myself heart and soul into the work of demoralising my husband ; undermining the Spartan habits of years ; softening the rigid self-discipline that he had imposed upon himself since, as a tiny frightened little boy, he had forced himself to walk under a leather, collapsible, tube-ventilator which, during Atlantic gales, writhed above one of the dim upstairs corridors of Castle Hill like a dark sinister snake. Sweating with terror, fists tightly clenched, the child would stare up at it and walk to and fro under it in the moonlight for a number of times fixed by himself.

Later, at Harrow, he made a vow that before the school-bell ceased ringing in the early morning his feet should have touched the floor, and, when he married me at the age of fifty-four, he would still spring out of bed, half-asleep, eyes shut and body swaying drunkenly, the moment his soldier-servant knocked on the bedroom door to rouse him at 6.30 A.M. When I grumbled at this startling and uncomfortable habit of his, he confided to me his Harrow vow, and I instantly made a Windsor one that

I would break his. The only way that I could ever
influence him to change his mode of living was by telling
him that it upset mine; that being woken suddenly at
6.30 A.M. gave me a headache for the rest of the day;
that personally I liked a light but normal luncheon,
and the sight of my husband eating nothing but brown
bread and butter and drinking glasses of milk while I
enjoyed an omelette or a grilled cutlet, took away my
appetite; that a walk of fourteen miles on a hot August
afternoon exhausted me, and that if he insisted upon these
forced marches, he must march alone; that tea was, to
me, the cosiest and most companionable meal of the day,
now robbed of all its charm because my husband scorned
it and rushed straight back to work in his office the
moment he returned, hot and tired, from his walk.

Gradually he discovered that an extra half-hour in
bed did not interfere seriously with his daily programme
of work; that after a hard morning's writing he could
enjoy a normal luncheon; that it was far more of a relaxation to go for shorter walks and take his wife as a companion since, when gossiping with her, his mind stopped
working out incessant military problems; and finally
that ' the five o'clock ' was really a delightful institution,
and that he could lap up Earl Grey tea and devour toasted
crumpets and cake with the best.

My greatest triumph was when I persuaded him to
take me for a picnic tea on the river. He was excited
as a boy over this novel idea, and appeared in spotless
flannels and an ancient ' boater ' straw hat which rather
spoiled the effect (it was later replaced by a Panama
bought from Mr Locke).

The Royal pages, footmen, and porters seemed positively
electrified by the vision of the King's formidable Librarian
and Archivist clad in white flannels carrying a picnic
basket and laughingly conversing with a linen-frocked wife
as they made their way across the Home Park to the river.

John henceforth developed a taste for the river, finding

that he had not lost his proficiency as an oar, and that sculling lazily along the reaches of the Thames was a far less tiring form of exercise than seven-league walks.

Another happy picnic party we sometimes met on the river during Eton term-time was Harry Verney with his Greuze-wife, Lady Joan, and their children. We knew so many of the Eton boys, and, on half-holidays, the mantelpiece of Edward IIIrd's Gatehouse was decorated by a row of top-hats, and our cook kept hard at work cutting sandwiches, baking cakes, sizzling sausages, scrambling, boiling, and frying eggs and bacon to provide those substantial teas expected by Eton boys. Once John was asked to lecture to the History Specialists of the College, and so he invited the boys to come up to the Royal Library and talked to them there, illustrating his lecture by showing them treasures and treaties. One or two of the boys could be shown papers signed by, or concerning, their distinguished ancestors. The afternoon was a tremendous success ; John did not realise how great until next morning when the post brought him a ' round Robin,' signed by all the boys, beginning : " We, the History Specialists of Eton College "—thanking him for his lecture and begging him to give them another. I have that rare document still—for surely it must be rare for schoolboys to *beg* for more instruction ? Anyway, John was as pleased as a puppy with two tails when he got it, and it is one of the few tributes he ever kept.

Life in the Castle during that last half of the year 1914 was much the same as usual, save for the saddening strains of the Guard's band which seemed to be for ever playing " Auld Lang Syne " followed by " God save the King " at the railway station below, as draft after draft of cheering soldiers were sent out to Flanders. Heard from our Norman Gatehouse, the distant music, rising up to us in the autumn air, sounded indescribably mournful and the cheers of the young unschooled soldiers going, gaily, straight into the mouth of hell, sadder still.

We now lived in an eternal atmosphere of war, for John's work dealt with past wars, and now his leisure hours were spent in reading newspapers and consulting maps of Flanders. During our walks in the Home Park and the Great Park he talked of strategy, of salients and re-entrants, of enfilading a column, and so on, illustrating his meaning with diagrams drawn upon the ground with the point of his stick so that I might understand the positions of troops and their ultimate chance of victory or defeat.

Early autumn in Windsor was very beautiful. Seen from the bend of the river at sunset, the red rays of the setting sun falling upon its grey walls and towers, with the flaming foliage of ancient trees around its base, the Castle looked on fire ; the russet oaks and bracken of the Great Park ; the golden limes of the Home Park ; the silver river winding in the valley ; the white-lace tracery of Eton Chapel, and, below the north slopes, the outline of Queen Anne's Garden still to be seen through the turf of the fields below, revealed by the drought of summer.

But later autumn—and winter—could they be spent in a drearier place ? The playing-fields of Eton and the lower slopes of the Home Park were flooded ; the Castle was shrouded in mist, muffling even the thudding steps of the sentry as he plodded up and down the North Terrace ; I watched cawing rooks sail by to leafless trees ; and the dampness rising from the stagnant water on the flats below the north slopes chilled me to the bone ; streamed down stone walls and even rusted my hairpins overnight.

When John emerged from his office his face was drawn and anxious, his mind preoccupied ; things were going badly on the Western Front. When we walked through the town we met white-faced women in deep mourning. The Guards were suffering heavy loss, and many of the officers' wives, lodged in Windsor and its outskirts, were already widows. Everyone was depressed, everyone apprehensive save John, who never, even at the blackest moment, doubted that we should win the war.

I had waited three endless years for my happiness with him; we had had but "three unclouded months of glorious extravagance," as he put it, before our life, like that of everyone else, was maimed by the agony and uncertainty caused by a world convulsed by war. Rigid economy became the rule; our planned holiday to St Jean de Luz (the base from which John had chosen to visit ancient battlefields and so combine work and play) became impossible; for, in time of war, every man must be at his post. My adventurous spirit longed to explore new countries, and now it was extremely doubtful if we should be able to leave England for years to come, for John never shared the optimistic view that the war would be over in a year. Petty personal disappointments of which I was secretly ashamed at such a time, though it was very bitter to me that when my radiant dream at last came true it should so soon be shadowed by this ghastly war.

By this time John and I were well established in the little house in Brompton Square, dividing our time between London and Windsor, but now always happily together. Our first guests to dinner were my sister-in-law, Lucy St Aldwyn, and her husband, Michael. Of course I was terribly fussed and important beforehand, arranging the flowers, making the house look as attractive as it could for Michael and Lucy's first visit, and planning the food we should give them. After tea, in the midst of my preparations, Susan Fortescue called to see me, and was much intrigued by the *festa* attire of the dining-room table, which she had given us as a wedding-present— an old circular Trafalgar table inlaid with brass.

" Are you having a dinner-party, Peggy ? " she inquired.

" Yes, Michael and Lucy are coming," I answered proudly, for they seldom dined from home.

Susan's jaw dropped. " Has anything gone wrong with their kitchen stove ? " she blurted out anxiously.

Could any remark be more damping to a young hostess ? Luckily it made me laugh as much as it did Michael when I told him at dinner.

Our life in Windsor Castle when the Court was away was quiet but unusual. A Military Governor had been put in command, and every day the police sent us up the password in a sealed envelope to gain us re-admittance should we wander outside the great gates when they were closed and barred at dusk. I lived in terror lest, when challenged by the sentry, I should forget the word or repeat the password of an earlier date, and be denied entrance.

I worked in a *crèche* for unwanted babies and some-times in a Y.M.C.A. canteen in the Great Park, where one day I had the great pride of being asked to ' walk out ' by a smart young corporal who bought cigarettes from me. I told him that the Christian young men always sent us home in a car, and hoped that he would never discover my identity. But, as bad luck would have it, he was sent up in charge of some men to whom John, with the King's glad permission, had promised to show the Castle, and I had to receive them dressed as myself and not in an overall. I shall never forget that poor boy's really awful blush when he recognised me. I had to devote myself to his especial entertainment that afternoon until I made him happy again.

Later, as more and more wounded were shipped home from France, the Windsor hospital was so packed with casualties that the Matron telephoned to the Castle for voluntary helpers, for she and her nurses could not cope with the work. Taking our cook and ' tweeny ' with me, I went down daily to do odd jobs and sometimes, to the joy of the men, John would come down for an hour in the late afternoon when his duties in the Castle were over.

A continual stream of visitors, chiefly soldiers, now came down from London to consult him, particularly at the time when conscription was first discussed. Lord Roberts rode over to talk about this, being as indignant as my Man over the delay in enforcing it. As they said farewell after an animated conversation, and the Field-Marshal mounted his horse under the Norman Gateway, I became conscious of a grizzled sentry trying to remain rigid in his box, but in such a state of agitation that I could not miss it. Suddenly Lord Roberts spied him, laughed happily, and hailed him by name. The man, sweating with excitement and pride, saluted, the whole of his face alight with joy and love. He had served under the Field-Marshal in South Africa, and the little man actually remembered his name. No wonder his men adored ' Bobs.'

XXXII.

Officials in London had long been trying to persuade John to write an Interim History of the War. Twice he refused on the ground that such a history could only be ephemeral, that no story of any value could be written for at least a hundred years, when the facts on both sides had been examined, and the chief actors in the world-drama were dead. But these persistent people continued to press him, and at length he was over-persuaded. They said that he was too old to fight (a fact that I knew festered in his soul and gave him no peace), and that he should be mobilised to write the history of the war, " since he was the only man in whom the British Army had confidence to do them justice."

So in the year 1916, with a great sigh, he laid down his own classic History for the necessarily ephemeral interim history of the war, and we were both heavy of heart. True, the official History carried a salary with it, but the whole thing seemed to me nothing but a tragedy.

At first it was only intended that he should write a short history of the Western Front, but this alone proved a gigantic task. Tons of despatches and documents rolled into our little London house. Hundreds of maps were strewn around his writing-desk. It took him six weeks to make abstracts of abstracts before beginning to write the story of the first battle of Ypres. We were inundated with letters from parents wanting the heroic deeds of their dead sons to be chronicled, often enclosing their photographs—infinitely pathetic. War-diaries of various regiments and of private individuals flowed in by registered post, and it was my duty to return them to their anxious owners when the historian had read them. It was a nightmare time, and the general agitation of our lives was heightened by the anxiety of officials that blunders in the Field should not be referred to. My husband's manuscript had to be read by many people, and suggestions were always being made that such and such a paragraph should be blue-pencilled. He, who had always told the truth without fear or favour, chafed under these inhibitions. I became furiously indignant and implored him to drop the beastly work.

I HATED that official history of the war which, like a great spider, was gradually spinning an ever larger web around my exhausted Man and sucking up all his time and his vitality.

Although sometimes disgusted, he was always feverishly interested in the work, though often I caught him gazing wistfully at the incomplete line of red volumes on his shelves, entitled 'A History of the British Army.' He enjoyed enormously the visits of the keen young officers fresh from the Front, and his talks with those of the Higher Command. But the task became heavier and heavier and heavier, the scale of the maps smaller and smaller as the line of the Western Front extended ; and then Gallipoli was added to his burden. The East was also to be included. It seemed that for the rest of his

life he would be toiling at the Official History of the War,
and that his own great History would be permanently
shelved. We were told that the General Staff used *only*
his History during the war, and a multitude of officers
took their favourite volume with them to the Front and
read it in dug-outs ; for, as Mr Pember of All Souls,
Oxford, once said to me—

" Your husband as an historian is so dramatic and so
thrilling. Most historians make me yawn, but on every
page of his history John Fortescue hits me in the eye."
The increasing demands that John would come and
lecture to new recruits, proved that words of his and
the stored historical knowledge of years, were precious
in their influence. And then, one memorable morning,
came the greatest proof of all. I received a little packet
from the Front. Some time before, John had been asked
by the Editor of ' The Times ' to write for him the histories
of the various regiments. The Colonel of the Coldstream
Guards was so proud of this history of his regiment that
he had the article reprinted, bound in scarlet paper, and
a copy of the pamphlet given to every recruit going out
to the Front. My parcel contained one of these pamphlets
—stained and torn with a curious jagged hole pierced
right through it surrounded by a dark stain. It was sent
to me by a sergeant of the Coldstream Guards who had
found it in the breast pocket of a Devon recruit who
had been shot through the heart. Tenderly and reverently
I turned the tattered pages and found all the glorious
deeds of Coldstreamers throughout the centuries underlined with coarse blue chalk, and their motto, which
concluded the article, underlined twice. This ragged
little pamphlet is one of my most treasured possessions,
for it proved so pathetically and conclusively how well
worth writing was this great history of a great Army.

And now the precious months and years were being
wasted upon an ephemeral and unsatisfactory thing
which tired out the historian and nearly broke his spirit.

XXXIII.

In London, while John toiled in his garden study, I, in common with every other Englishwoman, did various kinds of war-work. I packed parcels of food-stuffs for prisoners of war in a great concrete-floored building in Brompton Road ; I acknowledged gifts of socks and cholera-belts which were accumulated in Devonshire House (never shall I forget one ' belly-band ' measuring fifty-four inches round the waist knitted in double-Berlin wool in the Belgian colours, sent by some kind old lady, nor how Queen Mary laughed when it was shown to her on a day when she came to hearten us all). I took the blind soldiers of St Dunstan's for walks—a terrifying thing to do, for they loved most to walk through the most populated thoroughfares of London, saying that they felt less lonely and cut off from the world when they were jostled in a crowd. Above all, they loved rides on the tops of motor-buses—short rides and many rides, so that they might have the excitement of climbing often up and down the stairways. Fortunately for me every bus-driver and conductor was sympathetic, the drivers stopping longer at each halt until I got my charges safely upon the pavement, and the conductors helping me to guide them there in safety.

Once when walking down Baker Street an old Sergeant clutching my arm on one side whispered hoarsely to me :
" O, what an 'evingly smell, Miss ! "

Surprised, I said : " There are no flowers here, Sergeant, only a public house."

" I KNEW it," he shouted ; " BEER ! "

It was very hard not to take him in and give him a drink, but alcohol was, of course, strictly forbidden for those suffering from head wounds, and so, instead, I took my little party to ' Lyons' Pop,' a haunt they loved, where they could hear music while drinking their coffee.

My family had, of course, been swept into the war-stream. Mervyn was alone in East Africa; for Stella had so pined and fretted for London and the life of the Stage that he had sadly sent her back to England with their baby Pat. His letters showed that he had been striving feverishly to be given permission to leave his post of District Commissioner and be transferred to the Army in Flanders, but he was far too valuable where he was, having a marvellous gift of tongues. He could speak no less than fourteen native dialects, had written a text-book of the Tidoeng language, and, after only six months in East Africa, had been made examiner for Suahili for all Africa. Only he, could understand the Governor's code telegrams, based on one or other native dialect. The natives adored him, and, when thousands of native refugees were sent by sea from the West Coast to the East, to Mervyn was entrusted the heavy task of disembarking these poor terrified blacks through heavy surf, and of forming and provisioning a camp for them. His work was tremendously complicated by epidemics. First came Spanish influenza, which killed off the natives like flies; then a rare form of plague attacked the camp, and he spent hours of each day watering tents and their occupants with strong disinfectant and burying the dead.

Guy had at last been liberated from his curacy and detailed to the Artillery. He had gone to the Front. Marjory, having attended many lectures and passed all her examinations, was now a full-fledged V.A.D., and was working in a canteen in France.

In spite of Mummie's gallant demeanour, Daddie noticed that she was wilting under the war-strain. She was in perpetual anxiety about Mervyn, Guy, and Marjory; worried about my health and a mysterious poison I had contracted while doing my war-work; shaken by Zeppelin raids and scares of invasion, and depressed by the great empty Rectory from which all her children had gone. Daddie was offered (and accepted) work in Sussex, the care of three tiny Down churches, Barlavington, Burton, and Coates, not far from the village where lived Mummie's favourite sister. None of the three villages where stood the little churches could boast of a Rectory, but Daddie secured the lease of a house in Petworth, once part of an old hostelry, with the delicious name of Kitchen Court. Daddie was enchanted with the little house tucked secretly away in a corner. One ducked under an archway and found oneself in a diminutive courtyard to which sloped ancient uneven roofs of mellowed russet tiles. A tall Elizabethan chimney towered above a crooked gable-end under which sheltered the front door, clothed in a shock of creepers. Inside, the rooms were surprisingly spacious, and opened out into a sunny strip of secret garden which was enclosed by a tremendous wall splashed with huge shocks of aubretia and flecked with wall-flowers of every hue.

To this haven of peace Daddie brought Mummie in triumph.

Sometimes it seemed to me that the war-work I was doing was very little—that I was not ' pulling my weight,' but then Mummie reminded me that the care of such a husband as mine was in itself important to the country.

Certainly he needed my care and encouragement then. His early prophecy proved correct—the war was not going to end quickly—and every day, by every post, came more and more masses of material for the official history, to be read, sifted, analysed, weighed and written up. How he contrived to combine the writing of this history with his work at Windsor and not break down under the strain I could not understand, for his health had never been good ; he was very tall, and described himself as under-engined, having a very poor circulation. It was a difficult task to tempt him to eat as he should ; impossible to persuade him to relax, but, thank heaven, I could generally make him laugh.

Meanwhile, that obsolete rule which excluded all

members of artistic professions and those engaged in commerce from being publicly received by their Sovereign had been swept away by the wise and kindly King George, and I was now invited to official functions with the rest of the world.

When the rule was abolished, Courts having been abandoned during the war, I was presented publicly to the King and Queen at one of the Garden Parties at Buckingham Palace. On that same occasion Miss Ellen Terry was also presented, and I had the joy of seeing her exquisite curtesy. Her eyes had been troubling her, and under her delicious lace-frilled poke bonnet she wore large smoked-glass spectacles. When she was led up to the King, he at once asked her if she would remove them for him, and she swept them off with one of those perfect gestures of the hands (Miss Marion Terry told me that even in old age her sister still practised making chalk circles on the wall to keep her wrists supple), and then, as the King said, " Ah ! *Now* I see the one and only Ellen Terry," she sank down before him amid a foam of dove-grey silk and lace, making the loveliest curtesy the Court had ever seen.

Soon after the Garden Party there was to be a cinematograph performance at Windsor to be given in the Waterloo Chamber, and for the first time I was invited. It was a very nervous business for me, but when I entered St George's Hall with John, Sir Derek Keppel, Master of the Household and our very good friend, rushed forward to welcome me with both hands outstretched.

" Mrs John ! I am so, *so* glad. John, old man, this is splendid ! " which made me feel much happier as I braved the battery of curious eyes watching my first public appearance at a Court function ; for all the inhabitants of the Lower Ward, the Canons and their wives and daughters and a host of Windsor residents were gathered there.

The entry into the Waterloo Chamber was a further

ordeal. The servants, and the host of Castle officials with their families, were already seated, as were the King and Queen, Princess Mary, and Princess Alice. Next, the Members of the Household trooped in, John among them, and then I, as the only wife of a member of the Household present, had to make my entry alone, followed by the invited guests. Because I was so scared I walked very slowly, with assumed nonchalance, to my seat, profoundly grateful for my stage-training, which had taught me not to seem conscious of my arms and legs.

Next morning when I paid a visit to the Library I was surprised and deeply touched when dear old Barry, John's assistant, came up to me and told me that the Castle servants as a whole had asked him to tell me what happiness it had given them to see me in the Waterloo Chamber last night, and that nothing had given them so much pleasure for years.

They showed this, personally, on the first night that I was invited to dine with the King, for I had an almost royal progress along the corridors, passing at intervals footmen and pages who beamed and bowed very low. Every guest was shown a map of the dining-table showing his or her place—the King in the middle of one side and the Queen opposite to him. Blind with nervousness, and never having been able to read a map or quickly to place the points of the compass, this chart meant nothing to me. I need not have been apprehensive, for by almost imperceptible signs those kind servants indicated to me my place when the time came to follow the King and Queen into the dining-room.

At this dinner I was lucky in my neighbours, having the late Lord Rosebery on one side, who happened to ask me what I had been reading lately. When I said 'Pride and Prejudice'—not knowing he was a Jane Austen 'fan'—he replied, "Oh, I wish I didn't know Jane Austen by heart," began to quote from her various characters, and was delighted when he found that in most instances I could continue the quotation. We became almost too hilarious. On my other side was Lord Herschell, the gay and brilliant 'Dick,' cut off, in his prime, some years ago. He was such a delightful mixture. When he came to stay with us in London he would stew for an hour in a bath highly scented with bath-salts, and took his ' Continental breakfast ' in bed, reading the works of Guy de Maupassant. Yet he had sailed as a deck-hand before the mast, unshorn and unwashed for weeks, roughing it with the hardiest. He was a very fine musician, had navigated a 20,000-ton boat into the Bay of Naples, was a wonderful linguist, interested in criminology, a good all-round sportsman, and at Bembridge, where he took a house after his marriage, he built a wall on the property with his own hands, aided by a French servant ; kept the household supplied with fresh fish, and grew French vegetables for the table. So that Dick and I had plenty to talk about during dinner.

It was a very plain little dinner, I remember. Mulla-gatawny soup. Turbot, shrimp sauce. Vegetable cutlets, green peas, new potatoes. Asparagus. Cold baked custard in china cups. Dessert.

Directly war broke out, the King and Queen rationed themselves and their family, but it was not until Admiral Campbell had lunched alone with the King and Queen some time afterwards that he expressed his opinion that the Household should also be rationed.

"Personally I object to living on the fat of the land when my Sovereigns are lunching upon a cutlet and a rice pudding," he protested indignantly to Sir Derek Keppel, who agreed, but was of opinion that the King's Chef would resign if he had no scope for his art. " Well —let him," grunted Admiral Campbell. (Of course he did not, but exercised his art by varying and enhancing the simple fare thereafter provided.) When wine was also rationed we were told that one of the servants draped the cellar door with crape, and the Queen told me one night that her only regret was that when boys from the Front came to be decorated for gallantry they could not be *fêted* with champagne.

After dinner the Queen and all the women present sat in the White Drawing-Room while the King smoked with the men in the Red Drawing-Room, alongside. In King Edward's time, John told me, there was no such division of sexes, and nobody sat down while Queen Alexandra flitted among the company.

But during the war, the King and Queen must have been only too thankful to sit, at the end of those exhausting days. Often Queen Mary would look grey with fatigue after visiting hospitals or munition factories, for neither she nor the King ever spared themselves during those nightmare years. Always she was knitting something for the soldiers at the Front while she talked to her guests, who were brought up to her sofa, one after another, by the Lady-in-Waiting.

I remember that she conversed with me on the subject of intensive hens. She began the conversation by asking me if we liked our little house in Brompton Square, and I told her that Lady Cowdray had persuaded us to keep intensive hens upon the roof of John's study. I made the Queen laugh when I told her of the excitement of our small household when the first hen laid its first egg. At the sound of that wild conceited cackle John had rushed up from his study, colliding with me on my way from the drawing-room ; the cook and ' tweeny ' thundered up from the basement ; the house-parlourmaid from the dining-room, all converging upon our little roof-garden, agog to be the first to discover the treasure. I described the method of exercising hens in close captivity ; the hanging of green leaves in a net just within reach of them if they jumped high in the air ; the hiding of grain amid cedar-shavings, so that the poor ladies must scrabble and hunt for it. So did we keep our hens healthy and

slender. The Queen told me that she longed to keep hens
under the structure placed on the roof of Buckingham
Palace to protect it from bombs. Her Majesty said that
she doubted very much if it were bomb-proof, but was sure
that it might be put to some practical use.

I remember, very vividly, one dinner at Windsor
during the war. King George had gone to Newmarket,
so that Queen Mary was hostess, supported only by
Princess Mary (still in the governessed stage) and Prince
George (then a very cheerful midshipman) besides the
members of the Royal Household. Princess Beatrice
and the Marquis de Soveral were staying in the Castle,
and some young officers of the Scots Guards had, to their
great pride and excitement, been invited to dine ; so that
it was very little more than a family party.

After dinner, while the Queen was knitting on a sofa
and talking to me, she suddenly noticed Prince George,
who was performing odd balancing tricks with a poker.

" What is Georgie doing ? Acting ? " asked Her
Majesty, smiling.

" No, Ma'am, I don't think so," I replied. " He's
just bored and trying to amuse himself. But, Your
Majesty, *couldn't* we act ? Charades—or Dumb Cranbo—
or something ? I'm sure John would join in."

To my delight the Queen encouraged my suggestion,
asking Lady Airlie (who was the Lady-in-Waiting) to
peep into the adjoining Drawing-Room to see if the men
were still there, or, the King being absent, if they had
slipped down to the Smoking-Room. Lady Airlie returned
with John, looking slim and wonderful in his Household
uniform ; a twinkle in his eye. She concluded that
Her Majesty would, of course, form part of the audience,
and I was sure that I detected a look of disappointment
upon the Queen's face as she took her place at the opposite
end of the room.

John and I were deputed to pick sides, and he chose,
first, Princess Mary, and I, Prince George. Then John

suggested that we should strive to portray a Biblical scene—the arrival of Jehu when Jezebel looked out at him from an upper window. John was Jehu ; the Scots Guards officers were the steeds that he drove so furiously, and they galloped gallantly across the room to the chair upon which Lady Airlie, as Jezebel, had climbed. She peered out over its gilded back as she ' tired her head,' covering that wonderful coronet of white hair with her long evening gloves.

I shall never forget that vision of John, peering whimsically up at her through the eyeglass as he mimed the appeal : " Who is on my side ? Who ? " nor the arch glance Jezebel gave him before she toppled herself off that gilded chair to represent being thrown out of the window.

There being no star parts left in the cast for Princess Mary, Prince George, and me, we tried, on all fours, to impersonate the dogs that licked up all but the palms of the hapless Jezebel's hands and the soles of her feet.

The audience laughed at us immoderately, but I cannot remember whether they managed to guess what scene we were trying to enact.

When it was over, I whispered to Prince George : " *Do* go over and ask the Queen to come and act too."

" Mamma ? " he queried in surprise.

" Yes," I replied, " I am sure that she is longing to join in the fun."

And I was right ; for, when he ran over to the Queen and whispered urgently in her ear, she smiled very sweetly and came over to us at once.

Lady Airlie suggested that we should now act some scene of Elizabethan days, and that Queen Mary should impersonate Elizabeth, the Virgin Queen. John, seeing at once that Her Majesty seemed depressed by this idea, expressed his opinion that some more original rôle should be chosen for her, and suggested that we should do the exit from the Ark, he and I representing Mr and Mrs Noah, and the rest of the company, birds, beasts,

and insects. Whereupon the Queen's face brightened,
and, with the greatest animation, she said—

" And I will be the homely flea ! "

" No, Ma'am," I said. " In that green and gold dress
you would make a wonderful grasshopper."

" But I'm not sure that I know how to hop," Her
Majesty demurred, and forthwith began to practise high
and elegant hops.

When the moment came for her entrance, her performance was so spirited and so excellent that the enraptured
audience gave her a long round of applause.

We had a happy and uproarious evening, and Queen
Mary was the life and soul of it.

XXXIV.

For nearly three years John laboured on at the official
history, still going to Windsor by day to do his work
there when the King was not in residence, and living
there when the Court came down. He became more and
more tired, and then, one terrible day, he began to com-
plain of pain in his eyes.

With fear in my heart I took him to an oculist, first
writing to the eye-specialist to extract a promise that
if there were anything seriously wrong, the news should
be told to me and not to my husband. I was young
enough to bear a heavy blow, but if it fell upon him,
with his life-work (his own History) still unfinished, I
dreaded the consequences.

After a long examination, the oculist forbade the
poring over minute maps (tiny in scale because of the
enormous length of the fighting line). Soothing lotions
and complete rest were prescribed. In a private interview
later in the day, the oculist told me that my Man was
going blind.

I can never forget those next months. First I insisted

that he should resign the official history. He told me that if he did this, our income, already reduced by taxation, would be smaller still. I replied that I would rather live in one room and see him finish his History of the British Army.

He could not free himself from the official history under six months, for a successor had to be found to take on the job. In the end it was decided to give different sections to different men, for no other man would undertake the whole.

In the meanwhile he was not allowed to read or write. I learned to type ; I began to learn shorthand ; I pretended that I was a worse fool than I am, and could not write certain letters unless he dictated them to me, trying, without letting him know my purpose, to train him to dictation when he should no longer be able to see to write. Also I encouraged him to lecture to the troops. His facility of language, varied vocabulary, and his wonderful memory, led me to believe that he would lecture extremely well without notes ; and I knew that the habit of expressing his thoughts in words would be invaluable to him when the time came to dictate the remaining volumes of his History to me. The only thing that broke me was the certainty that I could never acquire the knowledge and skill required for expert map-work. Too often I had watched John working with Mr Cribb, his wonderful cartographer, and I knew that neither my geography nor my military knowledge was anything like adequate.

The lecturing proved a great success. The new recruits of various regiments were eager to hear the early history of their regiments, and John's simple language, his twinkle, and his attractive personality won their admiring attention. Colonels all over England, finding that the lectures stimulated *esprit de corps*, begged him to go to Blackpool, to Cambridge, to Plymouth, anywhere and everywhere, to talk to their men.

I remember his return, at 3 A.M., after one of these expeditions. He had lectured to hundreds of men in the North, and their Colonel had hospitably offered to put him up for the night. But, as ever, he preferred to come straight home, so back he travelled to London after the lecture. I was keeping anxious vigil with a blazing fire burning—for it was mid-winter,—some Benger's food ready made, and a hot bath and bed waiting for him. But when at last he arrived he was too exhausted to make use of anything but the bed, and was so dazed and weary that I had much ado to prevent him getting into it with his boots on, like Mr Squeers.

These lectures, besides doing much good among soldiers, kept him interested and employed. The doctor told me that we ought to find a house with a garden, so that when my husband's eyes prevented him from writing (he had by this time resumed writing a little every day) he could work out of doors instead of wandering about noisy London streets. And so we set forth one day to Hampstead in search of a house on the Heath.

An awful day we spent, inspecting terrible mansions and baronial halls with always a turret, imitation stained glass windows, liver-and-red tiled halls, and a 'smoke-room' with plush-seated cosy corners under fret-work canopies. Pure poison.

Late in the afternoon John lost his temper and decided to go home. I being of a more 'cussed' nature refused to accompany him. I would continue the search alone, and, if humanly possible, FIND a suitable house before dark.

We therefore went our several ways, he to Hampstead Tube Station and I back to the house agent.

" I want an *old* house, with a garden, and on the Heath," I reiterated firmly. " These houses you gave me are in every particular exactly what we *don't* want."

The agent looked bored. He shrugged his shoulders and smiled superciliously. Such a house was not to be found in that locality, and, if it existed, the rent would be far beyond the modest figure that we were prepared to pay.

Silence. Deadlock.

But I stood my ground and waited for him to exert his brain a little.

Suddenly, from a dark corner, a little ancient bespectacled man rose up, climbed a ladder reaching to a top shelf, and took down a mighty tome. This he laid upon the counter, dusted it with a bandana handkerchief, peering at me mysteriously all the time, opened it, and silently turned the leaves. Then he paused, placed a grimy forefinger upon a certain spot and remarked to his chief—

" I think you must 'ave forgotten this, sir. The tenants wants to sub-let." At the same time he turned the book round and placed it before my eyes.

There, written in old English handwriting with queer long ' s's,' was the description of my dream house. It was built in the reign of George III. by an eccentric Admiral who constructed two decks on the roof, a main-deck and a quarter-deck, and mounted cannons all round them from which he fired salutes on the King's birthday and to celebrate Naval victories. His cabin, built like the stern of a ship, still existed high up in the air. There was a lovely garden of an acre, since terraced and paved and generally beautified. Through the garden ran a tunnel which was said to communicate with the Heath, and was the alleged escape-way of Dick Turpin. Constable, the painter, evidently fascinated by the house, had immortalised it by his picture entitled " The Romantic House at Hampstead," which now hangs in the National Gallery.

Even before seeing it I knew that I had found my house. Could I see it at once ? No, it was after the prescribed visiting-hours. Would the agent please telephone to the tenants and say that a lady would be very much obliged if they would stretch a point and let her see over the house that evening? Objections. Difficulties.

Then once again the little old man in the corner settled the question by quietly unhooking the telephone-receiver and asking for a number.

The tenants would receive the lady if she went at once. The lady went at once.

By that time it was dusk. I lost myself in a maze of little by-roads, all twigs of The Grove and all entitled Grove-something-or-other. The house itself had been re-named Grove House, and I asked an old inhabitant where it was.

" Yer mean the old Admiral's House? " he creaked.

I followed his complicated directions, and, at the end of an avenue of crooked old lime trees, I saw a tall white house with a queer excrescence bulging from it on the third floor.

The Admiral's cabin! It MUST be the Admiral's cabin.

Excitedly I rang the bell and was admitted. In spite of ghastly futuristic decoration I felt at once the charm of this old house and its possibilities. Little odd stairways sprang from the central staircase. The rooms were all queerly shaped, some with rotund bow-windows, some with beautiful alcoves adorned with what must surely be Adam work. The slim dining-room, whose mustard-yellow walls were desecrated by an enormous frieze of magenta and black cabbages meant to represent roses, opened out into a covered verandah, adorned by the branches of a vine and leading into an oval paved rose-garden. The old windows, with frames untouched by Vandals, although draped with Reckitt's-blue curtains, also looked out into the garden.

I peered through them, and, though the ground was covered with snow, I could see that the form of the garden and the proportion of its terraces was perfect. This MUST be my house—and my garden. The house seemed to me to be mutely pleading to be restored to its old Georgian dignity ; the garden to be tended and loved. Well, I would do both.

A return visit to the house next day, with John, did nothing to damp my enthusiasm, but greatly increased it. He was enormously attracted by it too . . . but . . . the heavy premium asked made the project seem impossible, and we went home like two punctured tyres. I refused to see any more of the ' desirable residences ' sent me by the agent. I just sulked and brooded over my frustrated and so passionate desire for that one old house. And then one morning the telephone bell rang, and, when I answered it, a squeaky familiar voice asked—

" Are you that lady wot inquired about the old Admiral's 'ouse at 'Ampstead ? Well, I'm an old resident of 'Ampstead an' I'm proud of that old 'ouse. I want someone to 'ave it 'oo'd appreciate and love it. You said you wanted something old and romantic. No one else 'as asked for that these many years. So while the boss is out I want to give you a 'int. You can use the 'ammer pretty freely on that premium."

Before I could regain my breath to thank him, the queer old man had hurriedly hung up the receiver.

We did use the hammer pretty freely on that premium. We signed the lease of our dream house and took proud possession of it.

Our occupation of Admiral's House was marked by three air raids in succession—the worst known in London. From old Admiral Barton's quarter-deck (the upper roof) John and I watched the fiery passage of tracer-shells, fired from the 9-inch Naval gun on the Heath, and the pointing fingers of searchlights. I hate a noise—I mind thunder far more than the lightning of a fierce storm— and now I dreaded the awful roar of that gun on the Heath, and the woof-woof-woof-WOOOOOOFFFF of the shells as they tore the air above us. The old house shook, and our servants were absolutely terrified and wanted to 'take cover' in the tunnel in the garden. John said that the only way to avoid panic was to behave exactly as usual, and so we dined in our slim panelled room, waited upon by a green-faced parlourmaid whose shaking hands we deliberately ignored.

The second night some officers of the Air Force asked permission 'to watch the fireworks' from our roof, flaming tracer-shells shooting like comets into the sky. We went up with the officers, and they were able to distinguish German planes from ours by the sound of their engines. We stayed up there watching this beautiful sight until a fragment of falling shell lopped off a branch of a neighbouring tree, when our guests suggested that it was 'no longer healthy' to remain in so exposed a position, and we went indoors.

It was very curious to hear the hundreds of pattering feet on the roads and pavements around us, all rushing to crowd around the great gun on the Heath directly the 'Take Cover' Signal sounded. People seemed to think that they would be safer there.

But from the moment that we took possession of dear Admiral's House, life became happier.

During this period, the last three months of the official history expired. One of my happiest memories will always be the morning of my Man's liberation. He woke with a radiant smile transfiguring his whole face, turned to me, and said : " I've been dreaming of Nepaul ! " Nepaul was the next incident to be tackled in his OWN History, and that quiet little sentence told me very eloquently how much he had grieved for and longed to continue his unfinished life-work.

All this time I had been silently but fiercely rebelling against the verdict of the oculist, and now I determined to seek a second opinion on John's precious eyes. We consulted another man, and when, during a private interview with me after the examination, he appeared doubtful, we visited a third, Richard Cruise, then a very young man.

A few keen questions; a few tests with marvellously modern apparatus, and he prescribed lotions, temporary reading-spectacles—a new eyeglass. Then came the confidential word with me—quite another verdict given in terse confident tones—

" Your husband will never go blind. His eyes are terribly overstrained, but are the best type for the close research-work that he does—short-sighted eyes. If he continues to work at this pitch he will have bad inflammation and pain, but—he will never go blind."

I went blind for a time. . . .

The great History would, please God, be finished after all.

XXXV.

The splendid air of Hampstead; the delight and interest of a big shady garden; the release from the nightmare official history; and the pure happiness of getting back to his own History of the British Army, completed the cure of those weary eyes.

We often looked back upon this more or less peaceful period of our married life in England as the happiest of all. Excessive taxation had not then robbed us of our sense of security. We could enjoy the spacious rooms of ' Animals ' (as we had learned to call Admiral's House, since the visit of two small boys who told their mother afterwards that they had been to tea at ' Animals' House '), and we could work or play in our really lovely garden with light hearts, unvexed by surmise as to whether we could continue to pay rent and rates.

The same intense concentration and tireless effort that he put into the writing of his History was applied violently to anything John did. He would hoe a path so energetically that in ten minutes he was streaming with sweat; he would delve for dandelions in our lawn as though his life depended upon their destruction, and when he tidied up our herbaceous border he was so active with fork and trowel that we lost several plants.

Once a friend who came to see us found him seated upon a sack digging furiously in the soil with a trowel and unearthing some rare bulbs. When she gently told him this, he peered up at her through the eyeglass and said innocently: " You don't say so ? I thought they were defunct croci." And she collapsed upon a wheel-barrow in helpless convulsions of laughter. On another occasion when I came home from Lower London, I found him looking muddy but triumphant: " Sweetheart, I've had such an afternoon," he told me. " I've rooted up and burned masses of that poisonous little strawberry-leaved weed." I rolled an apprehensive eye in the direction pointed out by a slender dirt-begrimed finger. Yes, it was as I had feared. My bed of potentilla, grown from seed by myself and bedded out a month before by my own hand, had completely disappeared. I looked upon a clean patch of soil neatly dug over and raked.

I know that I, also, must have made many mistakes, but perhaps, owing to my Suffolk caution, I made less than he did. I preferred to pester my gardening friends by letter and by telephone for information. Then one day Miss Ellie Willmott, the famous gardener who was also an old friend of John's, gave us, with apologies, a little book entitled ' Gardening for the Ignorant.' This we both studied sedulously, rushed for in any doubt, and really learned something, although it was evidently written for people far less ignorant than we, for it by no means solved all our minor problems.

Work in the open air did marvels for John's over-strained eyes, and with joy I saw them improve week by week. Now, when they began to ache, he sensibly threw down his pen and went out into the garden. It had been neglected for a long time while the house was unlet, and, to John's delight, there was much cleaning and cutting back to be done.

When we had tended it, planted a myriad rose trees
and foxgloves in the beds of the sunk paved garden, and
some thousands of bulbs in the grass and under the
trees, the garden of Admiral's House became, I verily
believe, the loveliest in London. That others shared
my opinion was proved by the number of requests
that came to us for its loan as a setting for stage or
film photographs.

Having gained our consent, the company acting in a
production of Monsieur Beaucaire drove up to Hampstead
in a huge motor-coach which broke down, irreparably,
on the Hill, so that its occupants were obliged to walk
the rest of the way to our house on foot, clad in their
very beautiful eighteenth-century costumes and wigs,
to the immense joy and excitement of the inhabitants
of Hampstead, who followed them in a cheering crowd.

Once safely inside our high garden walls, a scene of
enchantment followed, for these graceful figures in their
pale silks and brocades *might* once have walked in that
lovely paved rose-garden, for their costume was of the
same period as the house. John and I watched a dream
of the past come true.

Mr Hamburgher, then Director of the Dover Street
Studios, wrote to me one day asking if he might make
some pictures of Karsarvina, the Russian dancer, in our
garden one morning. Of course we gave our thrilled
permission, and she arrived with her maid, the photographer, and Mr Hamburgher, carrying an enormous
box of chocolates as a thank-offering to me. I had
prepared a dressing-room for her, and very soon she
appeared, wearing a short Greek tunic, and at once
began to move gracefully about among our roses in the
paved garden. Suddenly she turned to Mr Hamburgher
and said pleadingly—

" May I do my little jomps ? "

" Sure," he replied with a chuckle. " Do whatever you
like, Madame, it's sure to be stunning."

After that she seemed like a white feather, blown by the wind, leaping high in the air and seeming to float there a moment before she touched earth with one tiny foot, only to eddy away again in the breeze. Finally she bounded towards a rose tree, and, balancing on one toe, the other pointing to the sky, she sniffed a trailing rose, picked it with the loveliest sweeping gesture, held it to her lips, and then with a forward spring towards John, laid it at his feet.

I know that he never forgot that moment.

Mr Hamburgher, a fat cigar swivelling from corner to corner of his smiling mouth, whispered to me : " Now would you credit that that sprite over there is a married woman with a baby nearly as big as herself ? "

" Married ? " I echoed, for it was difficult to believe that this exquisite elfin thing was human after all : " Now who was the clever man who succeeded in capturing her ? "

" A great big Scot," grunted Mr Hamburgher.

" A Scotsman ? " I said in astonishment. " How did he do it ? "

" He just sat down to it," was the reply.

We had amassed a capable staff of friendly servants indoors, governed by a cosy Scottish housekeeper who was also an excellent cook. In after years, when ' Ichabod ' had been written for us by the finger of Fate over the doorway of that tall Georgian house, ' rearing up in the dusk like a white lighthouse,' as our neighbour, Mrs John Galsworthy, once described it, we were to look back, regretfully, to those cheerful breakfasts eaten in our paved rose-garden beneath the giant syringa which grew luxuriantly on the terrace above ; to the delightful little luncheons served in the vine-covered verandah outside the dining-room when we ate delectable food, daintily presented, inhaling the while the fragrance of great tubs of heliotrope and of the roses beyond. Those small dinners we used to give—

" Six is the ideal number," John used to say, " then

general conversation is possible," and, as a rule, we invited only two guests at a time, which I liked best of all.

Our guests were nearly always men, and always men with jobs ; writing men, artists, musicians, sailors, and, of course, soldiers. (John Galsworthy, Anstey Guthrie, Philip Guedalla, Edward Elgar, Hubert Hall, Sir Herbert Lawrence, Henry Campbell, Charles Cust, John Tweed, Lord Ilchester, Sir Ian Hamilton, Sir John Hall, Sir William Garstin, and their like.) If they had intelligent and charming wives, these were always joyfully welcomed, particularly Birdie Ilchester, Mrs John Galsworthy, Lady (' Johnnie ') Hall, Mrs Leo Maxse (that darling musician whom many mourn to this day). One of our best-loved guests, who alas ! came but rarely, was Luke Paget, erstwhile Bishop of Chester, who drank cup after cup of forbidden black coffee among our roses with the glee of a naughty boy.

Queen Alexandra loved to escape the formalities of her life, and paid us many impromptu visits. On her first, one Sunday morning, John and I, rendered desperate by the untidy state of our hen-houses neglected by the gardener who considered vegetables to be more important, were dressed in our grubs and cleaning out these parasitic dwellings, when old Morley, our butler (an ex-Rifleman), appeared with twinkling eyes and announced the arrival of Queen Alexandra and Princess Victoria. I sat back on my haunches and laughed at him. He was a humorist and loved his joke. But he remained firm. They really WERE awaiting us in the drawing-room.

" JOHN ! " I exclaimed, aghast. " What do we do now ? "

" Go down and receive them just as we are," he answered decidedly. " If we wait to clean up, the Queen will be hurt and think herself unwelcome. If she arrives unannounced like this, it isn't our fault if we are filthy."

So, clad in our dusty overalls, with muddy shoes and grimy hands we descended the terraces and met the

Queen and Princess Victoria, grown bored with waiting indoors, advancing to meet us through the rose-garden. They were heartily amused at having caught us unawares, cleansing our hen-houses, but not in the least shocked by our odd appearance.

Princess Victoria, especially, loved the unconventional. One day a leak in our roof was reported to me. I donned my gardening suit, green corduroy breeches and tunic, and climbed up to the old Admiral's main-deck to shovel the snow away before it could melt and filter through to the ceiling beneath. It was a glorious sunny afternoon, and from my dizzy height I saw John emerge into the garden with Princess Victoria and another woman who proved to be Miss Violet Vivian. I took immediate shelter behind a chimney-stack, hoping that John would not betray my presence; but evidently he had, for suddenly I heard Princess Victoria's voice calling to me—

" Peggy ! I know you're up there. Come down."

Poking my head around the chimney-stack, I excused myself, for I could not curtesy in breeches, and a bow from a woman would look odd.

" Forgive me, Madam, I can't. I am not suitably attired."

" Come down at once, Peggy," she insisted. " I long to see your breeches."

There was nothing for it but to go down, and, feeling very self-conscious, for in those days few women wore breeches, I presented myself before our guests.

" *Very* picturesque and becoming," commented Princess Victoria. " I shall buy a costume like that for myself and walk in it down Bond Street."

And once, when we gave a tea in our garden for some factory girls, and Queen Alexandra and Princess Victoria arriving unexpectedly found me dancing with the girls on our lawn to the strains of a gramophone, Princess Victoria confided to me when I returned to the Shelter-Deck where John was refreshing our visitors with ices—

" Peggy ! I *long* to come and dance too."

Our Royal visitors always seemed to catch us unawares, and I must chronicle the most amusing incident of all. The Court was going to be in residence at Windsor for Ascot, and, of course, John was expected to be in waiting. We were leaving Admiral's House the next morning, and had sent two of the servants ahead of us to prepare our quarters under the Norman Gateway. All day long I had been packing clothes and preparing to shut up the house. The weather was unusually warm, and I was longing to finish all my odd jobs and then have my bath and slip on a *peignoir* for dinner, for I felt both hot and dirty. John had long since escaped to the garden, and was happily splitting logs with great skill on the rubbish heap near the garage ; work he particularly loved, having learned it from the foresters of his home at Castle Hill. " It's the prettiest sight to see an expert fell a tree, Peg. They cut a notch in the trunk, drive in a wedge, and they throw that tree to an inch of where they wish it to lie," he told me. I had been out to inspect his prowess with the axe, and had found him collarless, clad in an old grey-stripped pyjama jacket of flannel (long since filched from his wardrobe by me because too ragged for respectability, but evidently rescued and still beloved). A grimy hand had swept across a sweat-bedewed face, leaving its mark on brow and cheek ; but its owner was blissfully unconscious of this, and pointed triumphantly to a pile of neatly split logs : " To keep my Peg warm in the winter. I'm working for her."

I kissed the cleanest bit of the face that I could find, and went back to my packing ; and while I was addressing the last luggage label in our little blue Wedgwood room overlooking the road, I heard a great car purr up to the front door. Peering through the curtains I saw, with consternation, the beloved form of Queen Alexandra. Sitting beside her was a strange lady and opposite them sat Princess Victoria.

Now what was I to do? I had learned that the Queen
and Princess Victoria would only be amused by my
untidy appearance, but the stranger by her side—who
was she? I had just time to escape upstairs to wash
and brush up, but was it fair to leave my husband,
unwarned, on the rubbish heap? No, it certainly
was not.

I fled past Morley, who was marching through the hall
to open the front door, hissing in his ear as I passed
him: "It is the Queen. Put Her Majesty in the drawing-
room and I will come to her in a minute," and out I
rushed into the garden. Reaching the rubbish heap, I
signalled frantically to the forester, whispering hoarsely:
"Queen Alexandra, Princess Victoria, and a Strange
Personage."

The forester merely smiled at me and went on chopping
wood. I dared not raise my voice more urgently, because
only the garden wall divided us from the waiting car,
but I repeated my whispered warning, emphasised by
frantic gestures.

John grinned more widely, and saying, "Quite a good
joke, darling," posed and neatly split another log. While
he was wasting precious moments like this, I began to
pull out the remaining hairpins from my hair, thinking
that if I loosened it entirely I could recoil it the quicker
once in the security of my bedroom, and while doing
so I again desperately repeated, "John, DO come. It
really IS the Queen."

When at last I did make him believe me, his eyeglass
fell out, and he exclaimed—

"My days! I must wash and get a collar on," and
together we hurried down the garden path—to meet
Queen Alexandra, Princess Victoria, and a severe-faced
lady coming out of the garden door.

Well, there we were. And that was that. The Queen,
laughing heartily at our appearance, stood on tip-toe and
kissed me on both cheeks, then stroking my hair she said—

" Oh, such beautiful hair. I come upon an idyll. Adam and Eve in their garden."

Then we were presented in turn to a foreign Grand Duchess, who had been lorgnetting us up and down with icy eyes, and whose expression became every moment more and more scandalised. After this, the Queen asked us to show them our garden, and as she walked ahead with me I begged her to excuse John for a moment in order that he might wash his smutty face. He hurried off, leaving me to be scorched in the rear by that lorgnette as I showed the Queen our roses, the giant wistaria which formed a tent over the door in the wall leading out on to the Heath ; the tunnel through which Dick Turpin is alleged once to have escaped his pursuers ; the bas-reliefs in the verandah placed there by Sir Gilbert Scott, who once inhabited Admiral's House, and the ancient wooden plaque of Jupiter with bare nubbly knees grasping, as I used to think, a bunch of fine leeks, until John told me it was meant to represent a thunderbolt.

Had I been alone with the Queen and Princess Victoria I should thoroughly have enjoyed this impromptu visit of theirs, for both of them were so naturally kind and so full of fun that no one could help being completely happy and at ease in their company. But that critical lorgnette behind me, spying out all my defects, made me miserably conscious of my unconventional cloak of hair, my stained overall, and my bare legs and sandalled feet. I was thankful when John reappeared. He had washed his face and put on a collar, but had not had time to don waistcoat and coat. He still wore that disgraceful pyjama jacket, which now looked incongruous as well as shabby, allied with the clean collar.

After a very short time the Queen suggested to her silent guest that it was time to return to Marlborough House if they were not to be late for dinner, and we all walked towards the house.

John, by this time entirely at his ease and forgetful

of his attire, went to the front door, opened it, and stood
at attention, bowing with his best Court bow as the Queen
and the Grand Duchess passed him. I caught a glimpse
of the startled expression upon the chauffeur's face, which
suddenly began to twitch in an ungovernable fashion
so that its owner, to hide it, bent over the bonnet of the
car and feigned to be busy upon some fictitious detail.
The footman turned a lovely shade of puce, and his hand
shot up to hide his mouth. They had only seen my John
before clad in the conventional top hat and frock coat.
This proved too much for me. Something inside me began
to wobble and heave. I'd simply GOT to laugh—or burst.
Like the footman, no longer could I control my mouth,
which began to quiver. Seeing my little black kitten
in the hall, I caught it up and buried my working face
in its fur, but above its furry body Princess Victoria
caught sight of my dancing eyes, and then we both beat
a precipitate retreat into the inner hall where, safe from
that lorgnette, I fell upon an old oak chest and rocked
and rolled in silent laughter while she leaned against the
wall, tears of mirth coursing down her cheeks.

Next day we received a charming letter from the Queen
saying what a delight it had been to her to see us in our
sylvan setting, and a little note to me from Princess
Victoria saying the same thing, ending with "but our
foreign guest just drew the line."

I should think she did, lines and circles expressing
gigantic disapproving lorgnettes.

Arrived at Windsor, a message was brought to me by
one of the royal footmen saying that the Marquis de
Soveral would be glad to know when he might wait upon
me in the Library. Always he sought me out whenever
he was a guest in the Castle, and I enjoyed his visits
enormously, for he was so amusing, and his beautiful
manners were such a joy.

We met in Queen Elizabeth's Gallery, and when he
had kissed my hand in his own inimitable manner, he

told me that he had a message for me from a common
friend. When I looked mystified, he gave me a hint as
to this friend's identity. " Her name begins with A,"
he said, his eyes twinkling. " She sent you her love,
and she told me of an Arcadian idyll ; of a nymph cloaked
with her own bright waving hair. . . ."

" Oh, you needn't go on," I interrupted him. " I
know *exactly* what I looked like on that occasion," and
we both laughed heartily as I gave him *my* version of
Queen Alexandra's surprise visit.

To make me feel more comfortable about it—he was
a past master of putting people at their ease—he told
me of an odd adventure that had happened to him when
he was the only guest of the Empress Eugenie at
Farnborough.

" It was summer time and hot," he began, " and the
Empress told me that I might choose my own room. I
chose one at the end of a long corridor, to be the more
solitary, a room opposite a bathroom. The next morning
I went across to have my bath, and, when ready to return
to my bedroom, found that I had forgot—my dressing-
gown.

" Well, it was a very hot morning, and so I thought
to myself, why not ? I will walk across the corridor
with my bath-towel as cloak. I opened the door, stepped
out into the passage—and met the Empress on her way
to the Chapel to say her prayers. What happened then ?
I lose my head. Instead of going quickly back into the
bathroom and shutting the door, I stop still and make
her my best bow. The Empress she lose her head—she
stop still and make me her best curtesy. . . . I laugh
now—I did not laugh then. . . ."

So like him to tell this delicious story against himself,
because he felt that I, also, had been taken at a disadvantage. No wonder the Marquis de Soveral was so
universally popular.

Looks, he had none. Charm he had to an extraordinary

degree, and the Windsor house-parties were never the same
when he ceased to make one of them.

XXXVI.

A very precious friend who came each week to Admiral's
House was our kinsman, Adrian Fortescue. We found
him in a curious way. A lady one day asked John if she
might see the Royal Library. Her request was granted,
and while my husband was showing her the treasures
stored therein she told him that she had lately met his
cousin, Adrian Fortescue. John denied having any
such cousin and remarked that many people called themselves by his name who had no real right to it. It was
true, but in this case he erred. Some days later came an
envelope addressed in so beautiful a hand that it seemed
a crime even to slit the envelope. It might have been
inscribed by some missal-decorating monk of the Middle
Ages, and wondering much as to the identity of the
writer, John, having at last opened it, turned at once
to the signature—Adrian Fortescue. He read the letter
through, then read it again. After which he twinkled at
it before handing it to me.

It was a very rude and angry letter, but, having read
it, I admitted that its writer had every cause to be indignant, for the little conversation in the Library concerning
him had been repeated, and it seemed that he was indeed
a veritable Fortescue. " We were cousins in the fourteenth
century," the writer asserted. " Mine is the elder but the
undistinguished branch. It did, however, remain loyal
to its King and its Faith, which is more than yours did."
There followed a genealogical tree, and details of the
family history proving beyond doubt that Adrian
Fortescue's assertions were correct.

Far from being annoyed by this letter John, always
a just man, was remorseful, and also his curiosity was

greatly piqued, as was mine. We longed to meet this unknown kinsman who was so beautiful a calligraphist, and then and there John wrote him an abject apology and begged him to show his forgiveness by coming to see us at Admiral's House.

Unluckily for me, on the day selected by Adrian, I had business appointments in Lower London. It was a cold gusty autumn day, I remember, and wrapping myself in a three-caped highwayman's coat, which I wore with high leather Russian boots, I strode down towards the tube station.

Coming up Holly Hill I met a strange figure wearing a voluminous Bavarian peasant's cloak which flapped in the breeze, and a wide clerical hat—almost a sombrero in form. Under it was a broad strong face from which two extraordinarily intelligent and alive eyes swept me from hat to heel with an amused gleam. I suppose I looked almost as unusual a figure to him as he looked to me.

Somehow I knew this must be Adrian Fortescue, and when, pulling off his hat with a curious foreign gesture and holding it against his chest, he asked me the way to Admiral's House, I knew that I had been right in my guess. I made myself known to him and apologised for the unlucky chance which prevented my being at home to receive my new cousin.

" That seems to me to be a great pity," he observed bluntly, staring at me as I turned to go on my way.

" You'll find Cousin John awaiting you with bended repentant knees and a tongue full of honeyed apologies for his insult," I mocked him gently over my shoulder ; and he blushed and chuckled as he replaced that exotic hat. A nice person, this Adrian Fortescue, I decided.

He came again, and yet again. We discovered him to be, in spite of his early middle age, a man of immense learning. He was a marvellous linguist, and joyed in mastering abstruse and difficult tongues and dialects.

He knew and loved the desert and its tribes ; had travelled in the East disguised as an Arab and once had to kill a man in self-defence. He was an expert on old Church music, on the liturgy, ritual, and vestments of the Roman Catholic Church, of which he was now an ordained priest ; a very good water-colour artist besides being an erudite scholar with a comprehensive knowledge of the classics ; and he appeared to have read every book that ever was written from abstruse scientific works to trashy modern novels which, when sleepless, he devoured at the rate of three a night.

Adrian, though a purist in language when writing, talked schoolboy slang, an oddly attractive habit in one so learned. From his ordinary speech one would never have dreamed that he was, as John described him, " One of the ablest men in Europe."

" Adrian has more brains in his little finger than I have in my whole body," he would state emphatically.

We were told that Adrian was considered to be very much of an *enfant terrible* in clerical circles, for he delighted in doing and saying unconventional things. He avoided with horror all social functions and publicity.

" I went to Westminster yesterday, but I smelt Bishops and fled away," he once confided to me. When he did meet dignitaries of his Church, he seldom could resist trying to shock them ; often, in his contrary mischievous way, deliberately expressing views that were not his own.

Though a man of so brilliant intellect, he was never given an honoured position in his Church. Perhaps the Powers that Were considered that his writings were of such value that only as priest of a country parish would he have time to pursue his literary and research work. He dedicated his translation of Boethius to me, a great honour of which I am very proud ; but most of all I value my book-plate, designed by him, the Fortescue arms, azure shield, a bend engrailed argent, plain cottised or, and the crest.

" I threw a tape measure on the table as a model for that curly mantling," he told me, and when I said that it was the most beautiful book-plate that I had ever seen he said : " Ah, you see, I put love into it. They are my own arms." He was as proud of being a member of the Fortescue family as they should be of their connection with him.

It was just before Christmas of the year 1922 that I received a thick envelope addressed to me in Adrian's matchless script. I opened it eagerly, but, after reading a few lines, the sunshine of the morning was blotted out and I sat in a quiet darkness of the spirit.

Adrian, our strong vivid Adrian, feeling unwell for the first time in his robust life, had visited a specialist who had given him sentence of death—it might be a slow and hideous death. . . .

" Afterwards I walked about the streets filled with people doing their Christmas shopping. And all the time I heard the splash of the ferryman's oars. . . ." So he wrote.

It was decided that an operation might save him, but, mercifully, as those who loved him believe, he died from its effects and so was saved the misery of a maimed existence.

Oh ! Adrian . . .

XXXVII.

John and Ada Galsworthy, our neighbours, living in Grove Lodge, once the home-farm of Admiral's House, were a constant joy to us. John G. and John F. were great friends, in spite of the fact that neither could read the other's books. Perhaps the fact that both were Devon men, and both loved horses and country life, linked them together. Anyhow they would tramp forth together for long walks on the Heath, and I gathered from John F. that they never lacked subjects of conversation.

We used thoroughly to enjoy their *chic* little dinners,

presented to carefully selected guests of the type we liked best. We dined out but seldom, for John was always tired on Windsor days or after writing history all day, and ceaseless anti-poison treatments exhausted me. But when we dined with the dear Galsworthys, we had only to nip out of our front door into theirs, for our houses were divided just by a wall.

The only other house in Hampstead that we frequented familiarly was that of Sir Edward Elgar. When he was ' trying out ' a new composition he invariably asked us to make one of a chosen audience of friends, chiefly musicians. Once there was a very long pause between these invitations, explained later by Lady Elgar, who told us that her husband had been ill, and, when convalescent, seemed to have lost all desire and inspiration to compose music. He buried himself down in the country and sawed and split logs all day in the woods surrounding their cottage, and the subject of music was never even mentioned. Lady Elgar was in despair, because usually his mind was so fertile and prolific that he wrote scores by day and by night. Even before breakfast he would compose, and she told me that one morning as she came downstairs she heard the most triumphant chords crashing from the music-room. Stirred by the inspiring melody, she went in and asked Sir Edward what was that wonderful thing he was playing.

" Only nonsense," he replied. " I was merely beguiling the time until you came down to breakfast ! "

" But it was a most WONDERFUL tune you were playing, Edward. You simply MUST publish it. The public will go mad about it as I have."

And they did. The melody he composed that morning was " Land of Hope and Glory."

Now, in this period of lassitude, all desire to compose seemed to have left him, and Lady Elgar became more and more discouraged.

Then one morning he suddenly said : " Order a piano

to be sent down to me at once." Just that and no more. Forthwith she telephoned for a grand-piano, and, from the moment that it came, Sir Edward played and played and wrote like one possessed.

Now we were to hear the result of this feverish labour for the first time. I put on a flame-coloured dress in honour of the occasion, and when I entered the music-room Sir Edward rushed up to me, caught me by both hands, and said : " You *dear !* You put it on for me." Landon Ronald was there, Albert Sammons, Alfred Salmond, and Muriel Foster ; also Sir Sidney and Lady Colvin. Sir Sidney, a great friend of Joseph Conrad, told me that Conrad had an enormous admiration for John's writings, and that when he read of deeds of gallantry of the British Army during the 1914-18 war he always said : " They're living up to Fortescue."

And this delighted John, an enthusiastic admirer of Conrad's books.

On this evening, our host was in the highest spirits and had remembered my request, made long since, to be allowed to see all his Doctor of Music robes presented by Universities from all over the world. There they were, laid out upon the table in the billiard-room, their gorgeous colours glowing like a garden of exotic flowers. After that, we went into the music-room where, cushioned luxuriously upon a divan, we listened to that wonderful music for violin, cello, and piano. I shall never forget that intimate rehearsal in the great dim music-room where the light was concentrated only upon the little eager group of musicians around the piano at the far end.

Sometimes we visited old Lord Leverhulme at The Hill, just across the Heath. The curious mixture of treasures and trash that he had amassed never failed to interest John—a priceless old Master hung next to a crude modern picture of a nude figure, and the miscellaneous collection of chairs, of every period and nationality, drawn up in parallel lines so that guests, at tea, had to talk to each other over their shoulders or out of the sides of their mouths, or else shout across a gangway. Paralysing.

At dinner, which was always served at 6.30 P.M. because the old man rose at 5 A.M., worked strenuously all day, and often afterwards caught the night train up to Liverpool, the guests were as odd and interesting an assortment as the furniture. At the end of dinner our host would rise and give us toast after toast—rhymed or otherwise, and then we would all go into the drawing-room where gramophone records were played, and all who liked might dance ; the old man himself seizing one woman guest after another and romping with her through a prancing polka. He was a wonderful old man. He loved dancing, and later built a ballroom in his garden. We were invited to its opening, and, tired though we both were after a working day, John thought we ought to put in an appearance. And so we went.

A long oblong room hung with beautiful Aubusson tapestries was lit incongruously by many-coloured silk lanterns which revolved automatically by electricity, giving a most dazzling and giddy effect. The idea had been taken, we were told, from Ciro's night club. From a dais we looked down upon the dancers, and I soon spied our gallant host, clad in a black velvet Court suit with knee breeches and lace ruffles, dancing furiously with a small matron attired in black silk high-necked, long-sleeved dress, beaded around neck and wrists, her scanty grey hair twisted into a little button knob at the back. His white hair had been carefully oiled and plastered down, but the violence of his exercise had shaken it into feathers which stuck out straight at the back of his head, and from each feather hung a drop of perspiration. I had never seen anyone sweat in so odd a manner before. Both he and his partner, doubtless a friend of his childhood, were enjoying themselves hugely, as were all the dancers. But the atmosphere and those revolving lights proved too much for our weary heads, and after five minutes we exchanged a glance of suffering, and simultaneously rising to our feet threaded our way across the ballroom to the exit at the opposite end.

We were accosted there by an anxious secretary of Lord Leverhulme who begged us to delay our departure.

" We are both hard-working people like you," John confided to him, " and we long for our good warm beds. Will you make our excuses, please, to our host ? " and we thankfully found our waiting car in the shrubbery.

I did not then meet young Lady Leverhulme (now Mrs Seldon Long), later to become a dear friend, gentle, sympathetic, and understanding ; though she has since told me that she was there, too, on that occasion, suffering as we were from those twirling lights.

In spite of his overbearing tyranny there were likeable traits in old Lord Leverhulme, notably and pre-eminently his loyalty to his old friends, whom he never forsook when Fortune had whirled him high into the air on that wheel of hers which revolves as quickly as did his ballroom lanterns. If he did not spare others, he certainly never spared himself, for a more hard-working enthusiast never lived.

Little clever ' Eve ' who during the war cheered and intrigued the youth of England with her sparkling, cynical and often very vulgar letters in ' The Tatler,' lived in a tiny old-world cottage not a hundred yards from our door. I made her acquaintance first over our garden wall. I was puddling happily, watering an herbaceous border, when suddenly I felt that someone was watching me. Looking up I met the cheeky gaze of two brown eyes set in a fair-skinned face which had a slightly Jewish look.

" I'm standing on the back of a seat in The Grove," its owner confessed, " and, since you've caught me at it, I can't pretend that I wasn't having a surreptitious peep at your garden. I know it's not a ladylike thing to do, but it's your fault after all for making it produce such heavenly smells. Oooh ! I thought my nose hadn't deceived me—stocks—millions of them. What beauties. And ROSES—ROSES . . ."

" Yes, our stocks are rather wonderful, aren't they ? " I smiled back at her. " But," as she wobbled for a moment on her perch and clutched frantically at the overhanging branch of one of our beech trees, " the garden is better and more safely seen from within than from without. We have a perfectly good garden door, not even bolted, if you have time to walk through it."

She did walk through it, and Eve entered our Paradise. We became great friends after that, and I knew the real Eve who, like The Mother of all Living, was a very human woman. From her writings, gay, flippant, mocking, careless, few would have suspected that she had a heart—and a very vulnerable heart.

A man once said to me that Eve of ' The Tatler ' had done a great work during the war ; her brave and amusing letters had brought courage and laughter into muddy trenches and stinking dug-outs. Nearly every officer in the British Army read the Letters of Eve, and even though the more staid among the military may sometimes have been slightly shocked by her *risqué* jokes and flippant tone, one and all chuckled over them, and to laugh is very wholesome : " Laughter, that divine disinfectant, that heavenly purge," as the one and only ' Elizabeth ' of the German garden, so truly remarked in one of her books.

XXXVIII.

John's time was very much cut up by his job at Windsor. Many years before I met him the gigantic task of cataloguing and arranging the various collections under his charge was accomplished, and the machinery of the Library was so wonderfully organised that it ran on oiled wheels ; so that the King (Edward VII.), knowing

John's need to do research work, gave him permission to live in London except when the Court was in residence. When it was not, he went down to Windsor from London on several days in each week to supervise the mounting of valuable drawings and engravings in the Print-room, answer correspondence, take visitors over the Library, and very often the Castle itself, decide which new books must be bought for the Royal Collection and which re-bound ; find places for new historical treasures acquired by, or given to, the King or Queen ; and to do the myriad other odd jobs that fell to the Librarian and Archivist.

He had a horror of meals in restaurants and hotels, and so ' Odd,' as we called our Scottish cook because of her quaint ways and sayings, used to prepare and pack him up a delicious little light luncheon to eat in his office. He would trudge off, knapsack on back, to the Hampstead tube station, casting many a wistful look back at ' Animals ' and me before he turned the corner of the lane leading to Holly Hill.

Before marriage he had never travelled either in the Tube or in a 'bus, always a hansom or a taxi ; and never thought of journeying in a train unless comfortably ensconced in a first-class carriage. But the war and a wife changed his ideas and his habits, and he quietly renounced his former luxurious way of travelling and adopted that of the working man, assuring me that he found a ride on a bus a new and exciting adventure, and that the tube journeys amused him also. I wonder if they really did ? I know he missed his comfortable first-class carriages when travelling by rail.

Lunching with Consuelo at Sunderland House, we met two delightful American officers, Captain Edgar Wells and Colonel Grayson Murphy, who often afterwards came to see us in Admiral's House. We became very intimate with Edgar Wells, who was an ex-Dean of Harvard and extremely intelligent, and it was he who

asked us whether we should be willing to house American
naval officers who had come to London to de-code peace
telegrams. Among the number there were certain home-
sick boys who felt lost in hotels or hostels, and would be
far happier living a family life in a private house.

We gladly consented to house six in our three spare
rooms, but when Edgar had gone John turned to me and
said—

" I make one condition, Sweetheart—that *you* manage
these boys and keep them in order. They will listen to
a woman. If they misbehave in my house I should have
to turn them out. To avoid any unpleasantness of that
sort, I turn them over to you. Americans respect women.
They'll be quite tame with you."

I willingly undertook the charge and welcomed our
six next day. Fortunately we had just arranged their
bedrooms before being overtaken by a domestic crisis.
Morley was on holiday and the temporary parlourmaid
collapsed with threatened mastoid ; the cook cut her
hand so badly that she had to be taken to Hampstead
Hospital to be sewn up ; the between-maid was called
home to a sick mother, and on the morning after the
Americans arrived we were all awakened by sounds as of
howling wolves downstairs. Heads of startled Americans
protruded from every door. John and I hurried into
dressing-gowns and rushed down to the kitchen from
whence these sounds issued, to find our hefty housemaid
in the throes of an epileptic fit.

I had hoped for the help of our ' daily woman,' but
for some reason she failed to appear, and so John and I
and the gardener did the housework and produced luncheon
for our guests.

I can see John now, appearing with a leg of lamb and
a basket of vegetables he had bought in Hampstead,
and afterwards, eyeglass firmly in eye, sweeping the
stairs with the conscientious care he put into all his
work, insisting upon using the tea-leaves from my

' elevenses ' to keep down the dust, and afterwards dusting around with a damp duster. Somehow we managed that luncheon, and fortunately only three of our Americans had to be fed, for they worked in shifts from 5 A.M. till 5 P.M. It took me some time to grasp who was working and who was in bed.

At the very beginning I told them that I should always be in the Wedgwood Room at ten o'clock each morning to hear complaints. I said that I should put a writing-block and pencil in the hall so that they could write down their plans for each day, that I might know how many of them would be in for luncheon and dinner. I gave them each a latch-key and told them that I didn't care at what hour of the day or night they came home so long as they did not disturb the household. And I impressed upon them that if they were ever in any doubt as to their own sobriety, I should prefer them not to come home until their heads were cool and their legs steady.

A chorus of " Sure ! " told me that I was understood.

My rules were observed after a fashion. One or other of the boys came to the Wedgwood Room at ten o'clock every morning, not to voice a complaint, but just to talk to his ' English Mother,' the name they soon found for me. That writing-block in the hall was written upon, but few of them ever kept to their original plans. Johnny S—— would write that he could not be in for luncheon, but would be back for dinner. He would arrive at 1 P.M. bringing with him three or four friends expecting to be fed ; and at dinner time we waited for him in vain.

My greatest difficulty was to keep these American boys warm. Accustomed to hyper-heated rooms at home, they shivered before our log-fires—coal and coke being severely rationed. I piled blankets and rugs on their beds, but, even so, the youngest boy discovered more in my linen-room, and I found no less than eight blankets on his bed.

They were very naughty at first about lighted cigarette-ends which they left burning on tables, bookcases, and shelves; until I discovered in a china-shop some ash-trays with the legend—

" Who burned the table-cloth ? " inscribed upon them in gold. These I left in their bedrooms and the careless-ness ceased at once.

On Thanksgiving Day I hardly expected any of them to come home to dinner. Nevertheless I ordered a huge turkey, and after a long search managed to find cran-berries for its sauce. I had been out all the afternoon, and, returning late, was surprised and touched to see six naval caps arrayed in a line upon the old oak chest in the hall.

Dinner was a great success, until the very end when a toast for relatives in America was proposed, and suddenly the youngest of the boys, the only son of his mother, and very, very young to be so far from home on Thanksgiving Day, choked and fled from the room.

After a little while I made some excuse and followed him upstairs, knocked at his bedroom door, and entering saw, with a tightening of the heart, a tumbled heap of bedclothes that heaved up and down to the accom-paniment of strange muffled sounds. " Johnny ! " I called softly. " Johnny, dear." After a little while a rumpled head came forth; I bent towards it, and was suddenly grasped convulsively around the neck by two thin arms. The English mother did her poor best to replace the mother in America.

One of the boys, a Gold Key of Yale and very brilliant, adored and venerated John, who grew very fond of him and would talk to him by the hour. The boy devoured John's books late into the night, and when their work in London ended and our sons went back to America he was one of those who never forgot to write to John every Christmas.

At one moment we had a vacant bed and someone in the Meteorological College asked us if we could take in a

young man working there. We consented and he came,
a very worthy but pompous and 'superior' young Scot
who did not mix at all well with our effervescent Americans.
One day our parlourmaid came to me in great distress
and said that Mr Grant (the Scot) had asked her to darn
the seat of his trousers which really needed a patch.
What should she do ?

Next morning, lying in bed, John suddenly began to
chant—

> " We're in trouble over Grant's pants ;
> They're not so very stout without,
> They're wearing very thin within,
> They'll have to be re-lined behind.
> In such an awkward place disgrace
> Would follow should the hide inside
> Peep out into the air, all bare . . ."

I can't remember any more of this improvisation,
poured forth without a moment's hesitation. Never
was there such a rhymer since Hood ! Marjory was staying
with us then, and I rushed upstairs to recite this pearl
to her before I forgot it. She, in her turn, repeated it
to the most dare-devil of our American sons who, of
course, shared it with his companions. Thenceforth,
whenever the unfortunate Scot appeared, he was greeted
by a murmured chorus—

" We're in trouble over Grant's pants," &c. (Grant
pronounced Grannt, American-fashion), the rhythm beaten
out with feet and hands.

John gave the boys some glorious days at Windsor
when he took them over the Castle from basement to
Round Tower. They were particularly thrilled with the
engraved portrait of Daniel Parkes hanging in Queen
Anne's Closet. The boys were very proud to know that
the messenger who brought the despatch telling of the
victory of Blenheim was American born.

One day Edgar Wells came to Admiral's House and
asked us if General Biddulph, of the American Army,
might see the Castle under John's guidance. The Court

was not in residence ; our little flat in the Norman Gateway
was in curl-papers, and so we decided to order luncheon
at a restuarant, take it down with us, and have a picnic
in the Gatehouse. Edgar told us that the General had a
partiality for Italian food, and so I raked Soho for the
best Italian restaurant and ordered luncheon for five
to be prepared and packed ready to be called for at nine
o'clock next morning.

When General Biddulph, Edgar Wells, Colonel Grayson
Murphy, John, and I, in a superb American Army car,
drove into the neighbourhood of Soho it wore a particularly sordid and depressing aspect. Unshorn, dark-
complexioned waiters in filthy aprons were sweeping
doorsteps and scurrying along with trays full of dirty
coffee-cups and broken bread—evidently foreign residents
of Soho had their *petit dejeuner* carried in to them from
the little restaurants nearby. The one which had been
recommended to me, and which had looked attractive
when I had entered it to give my order the evening before,
looked dreary and not too clean in the morning light.
Through the open doorway we could see chairs and
tables stacked in heaps, while an olive-skinned youth
sloshed dirty water from a bucket over the floor. I
began to feel slightly apprehensive.

The chauffeur entered the restaurant to ask for my
luncheon-basket. There was a long, long pause during
which, no doubt seeing my nervousness, Edgar Wells
and Grayson Murphy made gay conversation. We seemed
to wait for an eternity until at last the smart chauffeur
reappeared carrying a very small paper parcel which
he handed to me with a salute.

I felt myself crimsoning—

" I ordered a luncheon-basket for five," I said to him.
" This must be a mistake. Would you please ask again ? "

The manager had not yet arrived, nor had the head-
waiter, but some underling assured the chauffeur that
this really was my parcel. I watched John screw in his

eyeglass and peer at that parcel. Then he looked across at me and those wild eyebrows shot up into his hair. I merely elevated one of mine. There was no time to fetch more food from another restaurant, for the General was keeping to a strict time-table, hence our early start.

That dreadful little parcel, with grease seeping slowly through the white paper, humiliated me all the way to Windsor, and when we arrived at Norman Gate I urged John to start with our guests on their tour of the Castle, and excused myself from accompanying them on the excuse that I must open our flat and prepare the luncheon.

The moment they had vanished I rushed into our tiny kitchen and feverishly unpacked that miserable parcel. Inside it I found five little cardboard trays filled with a disgusting mixture of chopped sardines, cold potato, &c., reeking of garlic and covered with a sloppy sauce. Under these was a larger cardboard tray filled with soggy macaroni smeared over with tomato sauce and lumps of congealed cheese.

I looked no further. Gathering up the ends of the paper, I took it out of the front door and asked the chauffeur to throw it all away and then to come back at once. When he returned, grinning, I told him that I must commandeer the General's car for half an hour in order that he and his officers should not go hungry, and he drove me down into the town of Windsor, where I raided the best restaurant for food, which I brought back with me to the Castle in covered dishes.

When my party returned at one o'clock, foot-sore and cold, for it was a bitter winter day, they found a fire blazing in our little hexagon room and a savoury smell of hot food. I sat them in comfortable armchairs and fed them upon rich creamy soup which I had heated up in our kitchen, chicken *en cocotte*, and other delicacies. The General was too polite to make any remarks, but his whole face expressed astonished bewilderment. COULD

this feast have been contained in that insignificant parcel ?
Edgar murmured in my ear : " You're a witch," and
John, as he helped me to serve the second course, snatched
a surreptitious kiss in the kitchen and whispered : " Mine
is a wonderful woman." And so our day at Windsor was
retrieved from disaster.

Our American sons were always complaining that
prices in London were so high. None of them came from
rich families, and, as Christmas approached, all were
anxious to send home presents from London. I arranged
to take them with me on a shopping expedition, so that
I might act as adviser and protectress, for I feared they
were being exploited. It was a very tiring afternoon,
for all six wanted my advice at the same time. My
married son would rush up to me with two diminutive
woollen bootees for a new-born babe perched on two
large fingers, and, twiddling them in the air, would ask
if those would fit a big boy of two years old, while another
son would wave a jewelled handbag before my eyes
and say, " Wouldn't this be swell for a dame ? "

" Far too expensive—and I don't like it very much,"
I discouraged him. " Now *this* is what *I* should like."

" Say, your taste's good enough for me," and the less
expensive article was bought.

I was kept rushing from department to department
of that big Store, and I did manage to save those boys
a considerable sum of money and yet content them with
their purchases. But when, at last, we were all safely
outside its doors, I had a hard fight to prevent them carrying me off by force to the most expensive restaurant in
London, there to *fête* their English mother in return for
the help she had given them. Only by telling them that
such a feast would render my work of the afternoon
null and void, and that it would make me perfectly
miserable, could I dissuade them from carrying out this
plan.

I missed them dreadfully when they all sailed back

to America, and so did John; and I treasure a little
silver cigarette-lamp inscribed 'from your American
sons' among my most precious possessions. I have
also kept an ancient battered tin cash-box which was
sent to me from a New York office filled with 'candies,'
bought by little Johnny's father, " as a small thank-offering
for your kindness to our boy."

XXXIX.

Now that I had more free time, Consuelo roped me in
as Hon. Secretary of the Women's Municipal Party,
about which she was very keen. She said it was pre-
eminently women's work to fight the bad housing conditions, combat infant mortality, and insist upon good
and sterilised milk. I had to visit clerics of every de-
nomination in Hampstead, interest them in our project,
and persuade them to lend their church halls for our
meetings. Then I had to find good speakers, and, horror
of horrors, I often had to speak myself.

Public speaking was an agony to me in spite of my
stage training, but because of it I could disguise my
terror and appear perfectly at my ease, having learned
my speeches by heart. But for days beforehand I could
neither eat nor sleep properly, and John dreaded these
functions as much as I did, for I became an irritable
distraite companion.

Consuelo came up to 'Animal's' to open the inaugural
meeting of the Hampstead Branch of the Women's Municipal Party, held in our drawing-room, and of course
captured her audience at once.

The last speech I made for the Women's Municipal
Party finally discouraged me from platform speaking.
I had taken enormous trouble over it, mugging up my
statistics of infant mortality, carefully verifying my
housing details, rehearsing my impassioned words to a

haggard wild-eyed ghost of myself reflected in the mirrors of every room. I was far too nervous and shy to repeat it before so eloquent an orator as John.

When the awful day came upon me I recited my speech to a packed audience in one of the suburbs of London. Many of its members were mothers of the working class ; the very women we were so anxious to persuade to bring their babies to the Infant Welfare Centres which were just then being started. I pointed out to them the dangers that beset their children from careless diet and insufficient knowledge of hygiene, and, lest my tone should appear patronising, I gave them an instance of ignorance and inexperience in a more sheltered sphere of life than their own. I told them the story of a friend of mine, Lady— well, it wouldn't be fair to give her away—who was taking her nurse and baby with her on a trip to East Africa. One day the Nanny was too seasick to bathe the baby and this hazardous task fell to its mother for the first time. She managed very fairly well, successfully preventing the baby from bashing its brains in when, as is the pleasant habit of babies, it suddenly stiffened itself in ecstasy and kicked its little slippery body backwards. She fished it out of the water without dropping it and then proceeded to blot it—her Nanny having told her that babies must be blotted dry and not rubbed. When the powdering stage was reached, she found a bottle of what she supposed to be talcum powder, and shook a generous supply over the little body, never realising, until the powder began to fizzle in all the cracks, that she had inadvertently used Eno's Fruit Salt.

A flood of laughter from my delighted audience swept me off that platform and I drove home, happy that I had not made too great a fool of myself and devoutly thankful that my ordeal was over.

Next morning I studied my newspaper to see if my propagandic statistics had been faithfully recorded and was aghast to see, in ' leaded caps.,' a paragraph headed

THE BABY FIZZLED. *Only* my ridiculous little story had been chronicled by the Press.

After this, I decided that since I could not be taken seriously I had better cease to speak on public platforms, and I think John was very thankful.

XL.

John's sunny study on the second floor, with its three windows set in the curved south side overlooking the rose-garden, was a perpetual joy to him, in brilliant contrast with the slim dark little room he had had in Brompton Square. His beloved bookshelves lined the walls of his new study to half their height, and engravings of his soldier-heroes were hung above them.

Mr Cribb, his marvellous cartographer, would come here, and together he and my historian worked for hours on end. I think little Mr Cribb was very nearly as proud of the History of the British Army as I was ; and every time that John brought out a new volume, he presented his cartographer with some silver object with his name, the autograph of the donor, and the number of the new volume engraved upon it.

Faithful to my promise to his doctor, I invaded John's study punctually every day at eleven o'clock with some sort of fortifying drink—Ovaltine, egg-nog, &c., which John called his ' boozle.' Very soon even the cook and the butler spoke of this drink solemnly as " Your boozle, sir." When Mr Cribb came, two boozles were served in the study, for, once these two men were inside it, one never knew at what hour they would emerge, tired but generally triumphant.

John had tried to visit the scene of every European campaign which he described, but in general he could only make good his local ignorance of many places far beyond the sea by buying every map of them that he

could find, and heaping the whole mass of them on Mr
Cribb. Then, together, they compared old maps with
modern surveys, and finally Mr Cribb produced the beautiful maps which adorn the History.

" The difficulties which he had to overcome were
enormous," John wrote in his final tribute to Mr Cribb,
who, alas, died before the last volume of the History was
finished. " His geographic knowledge was immense ;
his craftsmanship masterly ; his draughtsmanship superb ;
his patience never-ending ; his industry and ingenuity
unwearied ; and finally an invaluable quality to me—
his enthusiasm for the history of the Army was un-
quenchable. Never had historian a more able, conscientious, and unselfish colleague."

I like to think that modest little Mr Cribb, busy, I am
sure, making maps of the campaigns of Michael and his
Angels, still conserves his enthusiasm for ' A History of
the British Army,' and has time to peer through those
large spectacles of his at these glowing words, written
by the pen of the historian with whom he once worked
so long, so loyally, and so lovingly.

XLI.

During these two happy years spent at Admiral's House,
the household was governed, as I have said, by ' Odd,' our
Scots cook-housekeeper. She came from Ballater, and
had been brought up by a wonderful mother, full of the
quiet wisdom and dignity so often found in the Highlands.
' Odd ' was still young when we found her, brimming over
with energy, intelligence, and humour. I can see—and
hear—her now, training the younger maids as she, herself,
had been trained by her mother, to scrub and clean to
the strains of " The Campbells are Coming." No one
could slack to that brisk and heartening tune. She had
a genius for economy, and in spite of the restricted rations

during the war, contrived to make delicious cakes with half an egg, and dainty dishes seemingly out of nothing at all.

But in spite of our great happiness, life became increasingly difficult as post-war taxation became heavier, and one day John, who had become very silent of late, told me quite simply and quietly that he doubted whether, after all, he would be able to finish his History. It might be necessary for him to take to journalism, or to writing shorter and more popular books, to supplement our diminishing income. In the preface to his next volume (Volume IX.) he should warn his soldiers that this volume would probably be the last.

A great surge of rebellion arose within me after the first moments of still despair. The History MUST be finished. I refused utterly to bow my head to Fate however bloody that head might become, and I made it do some hard thinking during the night-watches.

John was elected President of the Royal Historical Society at this time, and his inaugural speech was yet unprepared when he was struck down by influenza. I had a milder attack, but was too busy to go to bed. The Secretary rang up in a state of agitation when he learned that the new President could not deliver his lecture, and asked if I could possibly find some manuscript chapters of the forthcoming volume of the History (Volume IX.) which he, the Secretary, could read to the audience instead.

I suggested to John that I could do that for him, having had my voice professionally trained, and he agreed with relief, not knowing that I was running a temperature.

So I muffled myself up in a fur cloak, put on a large velvet poke-bonnet under which I could hide if I made any blunders, and set off.

The Secretary received me very kindly, but apologised that I must be kept waiting. The Society had just heard the news of Lord Bryce's death, and one of its distinguished members must first give tribute to the personality and life-work of so great a man. My heart sank into my shoes, for I had screwed myself up to platform-point, and now I must sit on the staircase outside (I refused to enter the lecture-room until the dread moment arrived for my reading) shivering with fright and with my courage oozing away.

When at last I entered that room, I was placed before a lectern with rows of learned greybeards under me and a terrifying table of pressmen on one side, and I began to read.

Before I had finished I was very glad indeed of the shelter of that poke-bonnet; for I had not had time before starting to read the chapters John had selected, and they dealt with the extremely embarrassing condition of barracks in England—particularly in the married quarters—in the year 1832.

On the journey, going or coming in the tube, in my feverish agitation I somehow lost a very valuable gold cigarette case given me as a wedding-present. Luckily it was insured, and the insurance money proved very useful to us later. When I got back to ' Animal's ' that night, my temperature was normal. Fright had quelled my fever.

Volume IX., with its sad little preface, was published soon afterwards. Soldiers all over the world wrote imploring their historian to give them another volume. Veteran officers assured him that the Army would be lost without its text-book; I had a letter from Mr Arthur Balfour saying that " it would be a National calamity if the work were intermitted." Lord Bryce, once acting as Chairman for one of John's lectures, had described him as " the greatest living Military Historian." Then came my suggestion. What little savings we had we would put into a business—of some sort—and I would run it for the History.

John was the most gallant gentleman I ever met. He

knew that I had no business experience whatever, but his confidence in me was so supreme that he was perfectly willing to risk his small savings in any project I might elect to hazard. His eyes had been very tiresome, and the dread influenza germ had twice attacked him, so we decided that we would go for a short and inexpensive sea-voyage to set him up again and to give us time to think things out. Sea-passages were difficult to get at that time, just after the war, but a dear old friend of mine, Lady Gray Hill, wife of Sir John Gray Hill, the shipping lawyer, said that she could get these for us on the Booth line to Portugal. John objected that we could not afford the trip, but Fate had played into my hands on the day when I had deputised for him at the Royal Historical Society, and I was able to crush his objections to the cost of the sea-voyage with the weight of the insurance money paid to me for that lost cigarette-case.

XLII.

Just before we started on our trip to Lisbon, Stavy Ilchester came up to ' Animal's ' to see us, and as we dined together in the rose-garden we told him of our coming adventure.

Stavy became discouraging. He told us that we should be devoured by live-stock in the Portuguese inns and probably poisoned by oily cookery in dirty pots and pans.

Nevertheless we started, and, while trying to identify our luggage among the bales which were being perilously swung aboard and dumped into the hold by cranes, I became conscious of the near presence of a man surrounded by three eager girls in their teens. I noticed that he was staring at us rather intently, and when John suddenly gave a cry of content as he spied his trunk dangling in the air, his name conspicuously painted upon it in large white letters, this unknown man moved closer to us, took off his hat, and said—

" I thought I could not be mistaken. You are John Fortescue. My cousin, Stavy Ilchester, told me to look out for you on this boat." And then Sir Herbert Cook presented us to his elder daughter, Vera, and two girl friends of hers. His wife, he told us, and the male members of the party who had been invited, were prevented from sailing at the last moment.

Having made our acquaintance, he pleaded with us to join his diminished party and to come and stay with him in his Palace of Montserrate.

" But you don't know us at all," I warned him. " Probably in a few days you'll hate the sight of us. Wouldn't it be safer to wait until the end of the voyage and then see if you care to repeat that very kind invitation ? "

But he said that we should be conferring a great favour upon him by coming, and told us how thankful he would be to have a woman to look after his maidens, and a man to solace his loneliness. Couched in so charming a way, his invitation could hardly be refused, and when he repeated Stavy Ilchester's warning as to the lively condition of Portuguese mattresses in country inns and gave us further grisly details about the lack of sanitation in the country, I could only be thankful to accept his offer of hospitality when I remembered that John's health was still in a fragile state.

I shall never forget our arrival in Cintra. Sir Herbert Cook had been made Visconde de Montserrate by King Manöel, and was therefore a Great Personage. The Mayor and citizens had all turned out in their very fusty finery, greasy black broadcloth decorated with chains and huge floral buttonholes, to greet him ; the town band was massed on the platform, and the moment we appeared blew forth the most dismal blasts and moans that I had ever heard. Sir Herbert's Portuguese agent had come down to act as interpreter, and he informed us that these depressing sounds were intended to reproduce the English National Anthem.

Three shabby open carriages, garlanded with flowers and each drawn by a pair of moth-eaten mules, had been hired to convey us to the Palace of Montserrate.

At every bend of the road we found more town officials, more and more citizens of Cintra all anxious to kiss the hand of the Visconde and to give tongue. Pretty girls pelted us with camellias, municipal grandees made unintelligible speeches, and local musicians deafened us with music. Our progress was consequently leisurely in the extreme.

We reached the palace at last, white and cupola'd like an Arabian Nights building—reconstructed in a fantastic way by Sir, Herbert Cook's grandfather who had bought the place in a ruinous condition, and, being a great botanist, had transformed the garden into a thing of beauty, filled with rare plants from all parts of the world which grew to Brobdingnagian proportions.

That visit to Cintra seems to me now like an exotic dream. I had never travelled farther than Belgium, Ireland, and the Isle of Wight, so that I was excited as the girls. It was thrilling to enter the arcaded corridors of that white palace and to find a fountain playing in the central hall surrounded by exotic lilies and to hear its plashing as one lay in bed; to dine in that long room canopied with faded flame-coloured silk, flanked on all sides by huge negroid figures bearing baskets filled with clusters of real Muscat grapes; to go out into the garden at night and sniff the heady scent blown from the white trumpets of giant datura; to pick sprays of jessamine with blossoms as big as montana clematis; to swing in a hammock in that enchanted garden and watch the bare-legged gardeners clad in black shorts, white shirts, and emerald green jelly-bag caps turned up with scarlet, sweeping the paths with blossoming branches, or irrigating the grass by letting loose a cataract of water from a great stone basin and guiding it to its destination by paddling in it and wiggling their bare toes.

All through our Cintra visit, whenever we were alone together, John and I had continued to discuss my plan of opening a shop in London.

Sir Herbert Cook was, of course, a well-known business man, and I felt that he, of all people, could give me advice upon my projected business scheme, and one day I broached my subject and asked him if he thought that a complete amateur might yet succeed in business.

He looked at me sharply and then said : " If you put *yourself* into it. Yes."

I told him that I had no false pride and intended to devote myself to my work if I began it. He suggested house-decoration which, in those days, was not so overdone as it is now, and thought that it would be a good idea for me to take back with me some old carved Portuguese beds and find some ancient brocades—exclusive, arresting things to catch the imagination of the rich London public.

He was very anxious to back my venture because he considered that its object—the History of the British Army—deserved help and encouragement, but my independent spirit rejected this kind offer. I wanted to bear the burden and heat of the day alone with my historian. However, at his urgent plea, I promised Sir Herbert that if I were ever in any difficulty I would ask his help first of all since he had already proved by this spontaneous and eager suggestion of his that he was our very real friend.

Some weeks later I found myself installed in a tiny second-floor flat in Knightsbridge with my Portuguese beds and a stock of lovely Italian brocatellos, velvets, and silks, which I had purchased from a famous Italian who, having made his fortune in London, had sold his remaining stock to me and retired to Italy. My lease did not allow me to advertise, but I had some circulars, beautifully written by Adrian Fortescue, reproduced and broadcasted among my friends.

One incident which touched me deeply I must record. I had a letter from Mr Bumpus, the well-known bookseller in Oxford Street, telling me that if I would send him a supply of my circulars he would send them out with every advertisement, bill, and receipt of his own, and so make me known to his vast *clientèle* and save the (to me) enormous expense of postage. John, who had many valuable books from the Royal Collection re-bound by Mr Bumpus (who was also an enthusiastic admirer of the History), had spoken to him of my adventurous little enterprise, and, to help John and the History, he made this extraordinarily generous offer which I shall never forget.

Before I started my house-decoration business our bank manager, who happened to be a Devon man, tried hard to dissuade me from it. He pointed out that I had no business experience whatever, and should be always handicapped by *Noblesse oblige* and by remembering the things that ' are not done '—which he told me often *were* done in commerce. " Business," he said in his paternal way, " often means sharp practice and always means ruthless competition. I fear you will continually be taken at a disadvantage."

And here, at the very outset of my commercial career, was Mr Bumpus's open-hearted—and handed—letter. I must say, now, that everywhere in the trade I found the same kindness and chivalry. At first my purchases in the wholesale trade were tiny—a few buttons, cords, and tassels for the cushions I was making—a yard or two of silk for lining curtains. But always I was treated as though I were London's leading house-decorator, with the utmost consideration, deference, and respect, so that my humble shopping expeditions were a joy to me.

Life, from the time that I ' opened ' in my small flat, became strenuous. I would arrange my household affairs

with 'Odd' at Hampstead, do a little private secretary work
for John, and then hurry down by tube to Knightsbridge.
Arrived at the flat, I would polish the windows, sweep the
floors, dust the curios that I had collected, display my
brocades to best advantage, then brush my hair, powder
my nose, and wait, with a beating heart, for the bell to
ring announcing a customer. And, miraculously as it
seemed to me, that bell did ring—and went on ringing.
My Italian brocatellos were really beautiful and exclusive,
hand-made, the designs copied from old palaces, mon-
asteries and cathedrals, and people were 'letting go' a
little then after the long repression and rigid economies
of those years of war. The business proved an instant
success. I went through agonies over the arithmetic
part of it because, unfortunately, figures were left out
of my composition. When it was necessary to calculate
the price of—say—$12\frac{3}{4}$ yards of brocatello at so much,
I either appealed to the man of the purchasing party
(if happily there was one) to do the sum for me, or made
some excuse to vanish into my little office where I rang
up some patient friend in the City to implore him to do
a quick calculation. The only records I kept were in a
day-book, where I entered details of orders and prices
quoted, scratching off each completed order with a
triumphant PAID when the account was settled; and
in my cheque-book, wherein I added my gains to my
balance and subtracted my expenditure upon counterfoils.
And so I wobbled along somehow.

Just at this time Marjory married Archie Arbuthnot,
Colonel of a Gurkha regiment, a widower with a ready-
made family to which, the following year, she added a
little daughter, Deborah Faith, who became the light
of her grandfather's eyes.

And all Mrs Patrick Campbell's sad prophecies as to
the success of Mervyn's marriage with Stella came
true. . . .

To occupy his troubled mind and help him to forget

his broken health and heart, John and I had suggested that when he was invalided home from East Africa, he should be our guest at Admiral's House and help CINTRA with her accounts, which, for a time, he did, until his loneliness and longing for the East overcame him and he went back to East Africa—to return to us no more.

John wrote an epitaph for him which is recorded in Great Bealings Church—

" A strong man and a gentle. He learned the tongues of many strange tribes that so he might know their hearts and govern them with righteousness.

" His work being ended, he laid him down to sleep in the land of the people that he loved. . . ."

XLIII.

After three months, the business threatened to overflow the flat in Knightsbridge, and it was necessary to start thinking about larger premises.

The work was hard and tiring, and sometimes at the end of the day I was quite exhausted after hauling heavy rolls of brocade out of a great Italian wedding-chest, a beautiful gilded thing with the arms of the family to whom it had belonged carved and emblazoned in lovely dim blues, reds, and greens. It was very capacious, that *cassone*, but it was also very tall, and sixty-yard rolls of brocade are of a tremendous weight. I would have to heave these out, unroll, and display them one after another to a critical or capricious customer, and then, when she had departed, roll them up again, creaselessly, and replace them in—as I learned to call it—that cursed *cassone*. Also, being unable to afford an errand-boy or girl I had to deliver all my orders myself, climbing up and down motor-buses, travelling in tubes, or walking to my customers' houses carrying heavy boxes or bulky packages, which I always delivered at their back doors. I well remember that on one occasion a cousin of John's, whose house we had never yet visited, bought from me a series of rare wine-glasses. When I took them to his back door, he and his family were having luncheon, and I asked the odd-man who answered my ring if I might see the butler. He left me standing in the area and called to the butler—

" There's a person wishes to see you, Mr Hubbard," and a portly dignified man came out of the pantry and peered in my direction. I explained my business and told him that, as the wine-glasses were rare and valuable, I should prefer, if he would allow me, to unpack them in his pantry and in his presence. Then, if I had accidentally broken one on my journey in the tube, he could not be blamed and mine would be the responsibility. He gave me a quick look, bowed very low, and led me into his own room where I unpacked the glasses, all of them intact. Then he himself escorted me to the *front* door, and with the grave courtesy common to the best butlers said : " May I call you a taxi, Madam." I took that as a very great compliment, for he had not an idea who I was, yet deemed me worthy of an exit by the front door, escorted by himself.

Next day the purchaser of the wine-glasses called to thank me for their delivery and said—

" Why on earth didn't you tell Hubbard to let us know you were there ? We'd have been so delighted if you had lunched with us. You've never yet seen our house."

" You have delightful kitchen premises," I complimented him, and when he looked surprised I told him of my visit and the courtesy of his butler.

" Hubbard can scent a lady a mile away," he replied. " But why on earth did you go to the back door ? "

" Because I never intend to mix my social and business life. In the trade I am CINTRA, the business woman, and I mean to behave like one when on business bent."

I had called myself CINTRA because it was when staying

out there with Sir Herbert Cook that I had finally taken
my decision to go into trade ; and also because I wanted
to succeed on my own merits or not at all. I knew that
if the Press found out that I was running a business to
help finish the History, they would make a ' story ' out
of it, and I was finding that personal and private recommendation was proving quite as efficacious as publicity
and advertisement. Customers began to ask me to make
cushions and coverlets, &c., for them instead of merely
buying lengths of material, and so, becoming bold, I
engaged a little woman to come and work for me on the
top floor of Admiral's House. Also, as the average
customer seemed so helpless and unimaginative, always
wanting my lovely silks and never knowing what to do
with them if she bought them, I copied a little picture
frock from a Watteau fan. This I hung in my diminutive
showroom, and a lovely woman in search of brocatellos
for her old castle in Kent, pounced upon it to wear at
the Devonshire House Fancy Dress Ball. It was admired
and other women came to me for picturesque frocks.

I loved suiting the different types of women with
gowns and I found many who were brave enough to flout
fashion for their individual style. I became busier than
ever, and my return to Hampstead in the evenings was
generally very late, for relations and friends, thrilled by
my new venture, would come to the flat after business
hours to have tea in my office and hear how I was getting
on. Even staid people who had at first strongly disapproved of the wife of a member of the King's Household
starting a business, came to see my little flat in curiosity,
and came again and again afterwards because my work
there fascinated them.

One of my most enthusiastic supporters was Adrian,
who would look in on his way from The British Museum.
He would swing into the flat in his Bavarian peasant's
cloak, fling his queer wide-brimmed hat on a divan, and
start poking around and fingering my exhibits with his

lively vivid interest and curiosity, pelting questions at me about them, and about this and that, until I would lure him from the showroom with the promise of toasted crumpets in my office. He was as greedy as a schoolboy over his tea, and if I knew when he was coming I used to lay in a large stock of chocolate cake and cream buns which he voraciously devoured.

Between buns, and while I poured out cup after cup of tea for him, he, in his turn, poured out to me all his parochial worries. He was the most generous and unpractical man alive. He gave all his substance to needy parishioners, and, having no fixed stipend but only the voluntary contributions of a poor parish, was always in difficulties about his church expenses and in despair over his inability to raise enough money to meet them. When he first confided this to me, I suggested that he should design book-plates for my customers and illuminate little aphorisms on parchment or vellum to be used as book-markers, &c. This he did most exquisitely, handing them to me with a sardonic grin, and I was able to get him many orders and so ease his financial burden. In his simplicity, he thought me the most marvellous business woman the world had ever seen, and once advised his Cardinal " to let Peggy Fortescue run the diocese for him."

One of Adrian's great joys at this time was to persuade me to go down to Letchworth to spend a Saturday afternoon with him and meet all his pet parishioners. John came with us once, but ever after funked Letchworth and its charming ladies. He was not a social man. Like all bachelors, Adrian was terrified of his housekeeper, who, as is the way of housekeepers of single men, tyrannised over him, and so, I am sure, to avoid having to feed me himself, he would arrange a series of visits for me : " I want to show off my cousin (with delight he had discovered that I, also, was his blood-cousin, ancestors of his and mine having married in a later century than the fourteenth. He was nearer kin to me than to John), the famous CINTRA, in Letchworth. You don't mind, do you? We're to make a triumphant progress around the Garden City this afternoon, and must devour many buns. Oh—I *knew* I'd forgotten something—I never ordered the town band to meet you at the station."

John Tweed, the sculptor, was another of my visitors to the flat. He delighted in my beautiful materials, and, seeing the success they had, he once ruefully suggested that I might display some of his nudes among them and perhaps sell them for him. His nude statues were those I liked least, particularly the studies of women, who, to my mind, were too massive and muscular, and so huge that I doubt if one of them could ever have entered my tiny flat. For it was very tiny—only three rooms— and now that customers came in clumps I was finding my showrooms very inconvenient, and I told John that it had become imperative for me to have larger premises, now that it seemed safe to take them.

We chose a small ground-floor shop in Sloane Street, for those that I had consulted in the trade assured me that a show-window caught the eye of many chance customers and increased business. But just as we were on the point of signing the lease for my new premises, we were very nearly crushed by one of those fantastic pieces of ill-luck that have haunted an otherwise perfect married life.

XLIV.

I came into John's study one morning to say good-bye to him before he started off to Windsor and I for Knights- bridge, when I happened to notice a patch of damp about the size of a half-crown on the wall behind his chair. I pointed it out to him.

" Even though we have a full repairing lease, darling, I don't think that small spot need inflame your conscience," he laughed. I remarked, sententiously, that small spots sometimes became large spots if not taken in time, little knowing how soon that truth was to be proved. I got our builder to come up the moment after John had gone off to Windsor. The builder did not like the look of that spot, and sent for some workmen who poked a little exploratory hole in the wall. They went on poking until the hole became a chasm. They found enormous fungi in the hollow between the outer and inner walls, and woodwork crumbling away with dry-rot. Apparently a window had been bricked up during the days of the window-tax, but only with one thickness of brick, and for a hundred years the rain had been beating through those porous bricks and their crevices, undiscovered. During the years, the trouble had spread silently across the walls and floor of the room on the second floor, which was now John's study. Indeed, his great desk and writing chair had been placed immediately above a beam which was very nearly eaten away by dry-rot.

In a few hours the room was practically demolished, and a gaping void showed the drawing-room beneath. One of the maid's rooms on the third floor was destroyed likewise and part of the roof. A central heating pipe had stopped the mischief eventually ; but the wreckage was terrible, as would be the cost of repairs.

I watched the destruction going on until I was obliged to flee and hide myself in my bathroom, feeling terribly sick. My imagination had already foreseen what this ghastly misfortune meant. I knew that most of our little reserve was sunk in my business, which must now be crippled just as it was beginning to succeed and to expand ; and, worst of all, I knew that I had to deliver this awful blow to John when he got back from Windsor.

I delivered it while he was peacefully having his after-tea cigarette downstairs. I had kept him from going up to the shell that was once his study until he was a little rested and refreshed. He whitened, and one of his long nervous hands began to caress his chin in the way he had when disturbed. Then he quietly threw back his head and said in a matter-of-fact tone (which did not deceive me in the least) : " Well, darling, there the matter is—and it must be faced." A thing I admired profoundly in John was the way in which he faced trouble. Difficulties, problems—even disasters—seemed to stimulate rather than discourage him. He had, *in excelsis*, that quality he most admired in the British soldier—the refusal to admit defeat, which so often turned what seemed to be defeat into victory.

Our repairs estimate came to over £3000.

' Odd ' was marvellous. She begged us to dismiss all our staff at the end of the month save for Morley and herself, saying that it was useless to pay wages and keep servants in a practically demolished house, and that she would cook as usual and clean up after the workmen. As I was out all day until evening, and John at Windsor several days a week, we felt that ' Odd ' and Morley might be able to manage together, with a woman to come in to do the scrubbing, but when I suggested this extra help to ' Odd,' a look in her Highland eye told me that she intended to do that scrubbing herself and so save us the precious ' bawbees.'

I worked all day at the flat and John continued to write history, using our Wedgwood sitting-room downstairs for his work ; and, as I cut lengths of brocatello, designed cushions and table-runners, &c., packed and delivered my parcels, my brain worked ceaselessly at our new problem.

At length I had an inspiration. We would borrow money and buy Admiral's House, and, instead of taking on the Sloane Street shop, I would transfer my business to Hampstead and trade there.

I went down to the City to consult Sir Herbert Cook, who, though always neck-deep in his own important business there, was never too busy to give me some of his time.

"Well, what can I do for Madame CINTRA?" he smiled at me, pushing aside a mass of papers, and then I told him of our house-disaster and of my plan to buy the old house and trade in it. He considered that it was sound business to buy the house, on the condition that the amount spent upon the repairs was knocked off the purchase price. But he received my idea of removing my shop from Knightsbridge to our own home very gloomily. "You'll never get people up to the wilds of Hampstead. Better shut up shop," was his advice. But I was mulish and determined. I would now concentrate upon designing frocks. I would court publicity in future and run ' The Romantic House,' the old Admiral and Dick Turpin, for all I was worth. I would give dress shows in our lovely garden. I would MAKE people come up to Hampstead.

Needless to say, my wonderful John became infected with my enthusiasm for the new idea, and backed me up. He had no doubt whatever of the success of the new venture. His unbounded confidence in me gave me confidence in myself.

There followed a period of miserable discomfort after this momentous decision was made. We lived in a cloud of musty brick and cement dust in an icy house half open to the sky. ' Odd ' continued to be wonderful. When she had dismissed her staff, with the exception of old Morley, she proceeded to do practically the whole work of the house because he, having been suddenly erupted out of his groove, became doddering and dismayed. She tore up stair-carpets, enveloped furniture in dust-sheets to protect it as far as possible from the all-pervading filth made by the workmen ; scrubbed the stairs daily (a despairing and useless job as it seemed to us), and, though deprived of her kitchenmaid, yet still contrived to prepare delicious meals and to cook like a *chef*. My heart used to ache when I came back from the flat at night to see the hot, begrimed little figure that was now our ' Odd,' in place of the spotless one we had known clad in its immaculate white dress, apron, and cap. But we loved the gallant, grubby little 'Odd' even more than the smart one, for we knew that she was working selflessly and ceaselessly to help us in a bad crisis of our affairs. I had confided the whole calamity to her and I found her Scots sense and loyalty a tremendous help and comfort.

My poor Historian went on writing doggedly all through this nightmare time. I had fitted up the Wedgwood Room as a writing-room, and we lived and ate in this one room. It saved 'Odd' work, and, when I came home in the evenings, she served us a dainty little dinner on a round table before the fire.

In the meantime I had consulted surveyors and experts, who said that the house was sound as a bell save for this one section of it where the damp of years had filtered through. We therefore decided to buy.

I began to think out the transformation of the house into business premises. We would keep the ground-floor for our own private use ; the second-floor, comprising John's study, dressing-room, and bathroom would remain private and sacred to him ; the drawing-room on the first floor would become a showroom, various spare bedrooms could be fitting-rooms, and the whole of the top floor, workrooms.

At that moment I still had only one small woman to put into those spacious rooms, and she became a joke when the business was formally opened at Hampstead and an L.C.C. Inspector came to inspect them. While questioning me downstairs she asked me how many machines were employed in my rooms, and when I said "One," she inquired how many hands worked it. I replied : " One pair of hands and one pair of feet." She looked puzzled and asked to see my workrooms, and I led her up those tall staircases to the top of the house where my one solitary little woman was working my only sewing-machine, alone in a vast room.

I shall never forget that Inspector's face nor how she

laughed in a quiet helpless manner. It appeared that she had been informed that I was running a factory, manufacturing wholesale goods, and that the whole of our top floor was filled with machinery.

XLV.

During those weary months while the house was being reconstructed, my one fat little worker and I laboured ceaselessly to make enough stock for a goodly display when the moment came to transfer the business from Knightsbridge to Admiral's House. I had to design cushions, bedspreads, coverlets, shawls, and Italian picture-gowns ; select the materials and trimmings, then make my instructions for their putting-together, fool-proof, before going down to my flat to run the business there. I never minded leaving my little woman alone to make things for stock, but it was agonising to be obliged to leave her alone with an order. The flat was too small to contain a workroom, so that I was forced to leave her by herself at Admiral's House all day long, and I always dreaded a muddle or a disaster if by any unlucky chance she should have misunderstood my instructions.

We had one really terrible tragedy when once she deliberately disobeyed my strict orders. I shall never forget it because it was my first bitter experience of the necessity of taking full responsibility for the blunder of another.

A distinguished customer one day appeared at the flat with an enormous cylindrical parcel under his arm. Opening it, he unrolled upon my floor a wondrous strip of antique yellow velvet beautifully embossed and embroidered with flowers in reds, blues, and greens. It measured at least five yards in length, and though the colour was dimmed with years the material was quite unblemished. He told me that it was an ancient Chinese prayer-mat in an extraordinary state of preservation, and very rare and precious. I had already decorated his studio with Italian curtains and cushions, and he told me that only to CINTRA would he entrust his treasure. He wanted it to be cut in half, the two pieces to be joined together and the whole lined to make a bed-cover.

At first I absolutely refused to do it. I said that I should be terrified to cut anything so lovely, and I told him that the work of alteration could not be done under my constant supervision, since my only worker was in Hampstead and I must remain all day at the Knightsbridge flat.

My visitor argued that it was really a very simple thing that he had asked me to do; that I could cut the velvet now, in his presence; we could then join the design symmetrically, and all my worker would have to do would be to seam the two pieces together by hand. I explained that if we sewed together two pieces of stiff velvet there would inevitably be a ridge in the middle of the bedspread and to iron it flat would certainly mark the velvet. He assured me that he did not mind having a ridge and agreed with me that the velvet must on no account be ironed. In the end he over-persuaded me to undertake the alteration, and departed, all confident smiles, leaving his terrible prayer-mat, already cut in half, upon the floor of my showroom.

I had to hire a taxi to take it up to Hampstead where next morning, in fear and trembling, I pieced the sides together myself, selected a heavy black ribbed silk as a lining, and gave the square to my worker telling her to seam the two pieces together by hand, imploring her over and over again NOT to iron the work when she had done it, however unfinished and lumpy it might look. She swore not to touch the velvet with an iron, and I went off to the flat where I had a series of important appointments.

All that day I worked with an undercurrent of apprehension swirling in my mind, and I was thankful when closing time came.

Directly I reached Admiral's House I galloped upstairs to the workroom, not even waiting to poke my head into John's study to see if he had returned from Windsor, so great was my anxiety to see that finished bed-cover. My worker had gone home, and there, folded upon a chair, was the precious strip of Chinese velvet. Hastily I unfolded it—to find the central seam a silver ribbon where the fool-woman HAD both steamed and ironed it, and, lower down (*of course* on the plain yellow background where it was most conspicuous) was the complete form of a flat-iron marked in water-stain where, seeing the mess she had made of the seam, she had evidently in panic dropped the hot iron, enveloped in its wet cloth, upon the velvet.

I leaned against the table staring at that bedspread and feeling physically sick. Its owner wanted it back at his studio by 6 P.M. the next day, in time to display his treasure to a crowd of guests he was entertaining that evening.

What could I do ? Hire a car and drive round London until I found an expert cleaner who might be able to repair the damage. With weak knees I descended the staircase and looked into John's study, hoping to find him and longing for his comfort. But I found him fighting an important action, and I could not paralyse operations with my own personal bomb, and during dinner I had to act with all my might so that my tired Man should not suspect the agony of anxiety within me.

Next morning, very early after a sleepless night, I telephoned for a car and then drove round London for hours trying to find a cleaner who would undertake this awful job. The flat remained shut all day, for not until 3 P.M. did I find a French cleaner in Putney who would attempt the work. Then I had to wait for two hours while it was being done. At five o'clock I went to fetch that unfortunate bed-cover. It was finished—but the cleaning had but freshened the yellow background and the coloured embroidery, leaving the water-stains more evident than before.

There was nothing left for me to do now but to confess the whole tragedy to the owner, and I resolved to drive back to Hampstead and there write him an abject letter. I felt that it would be unfair to visit him in person with my tear-sodden face and swollen eyes, which might prevent him from damning them heartily, as I felt he had the right to do. I told him this in my letter, in which I said that although I had given strict instructions that the velvet should not be ironed, my worker had disobeyed me, but I realised that mine was the responsibility since she was in my employ. If he could suggest any reparation or compensation for the damage done I should faithfully fulfil my obligation, but that I, personally, knew of no adequate reparation to be made for the ruin of a possession so precious.

A reply to my letter was sent back by the same messenger. The owner of the converted prayer-mat merely requested that I would bring it back to him myself immediately. I do not know when I have been more terrified or more humiliated, but I hailed a taxi and drove in it to Chelsea with that terrible bed-cover. I rang the studio bell and the door was immediately opened by the man himself.

First he took from me the heavy package and threw it carelessly upon a table ; returned, and holding out both hands drew me into the studio. Then looking at me gravely, he said very gently, " It is only an inanimate thing that is damaged and you are spoiling eyes that are precious. It is not worth one tear. *People* matter in life—not *things*. If ever such an accident happens to me I hope I may be brave enough to write as fine a letter as you have written to me.

" Now let us examine this poor piece of stuff." He

unrolled it and displayed the awful mark, more conspicuous than ever by artificial light. I stood miserably dumb. Then he laughed lightly, tossed the velvet aside, and said gaily : " I shall say that those are the marks of the Empress of China's little knees when she knelt for her devotions. It is a prayer-mat, you know."

When I pleaded for punishment of some sort and said that I should feel so much better if he would only curse me a little, he said that the one act of reparation that he demanded was that I should come to his party that night as guest of honour with my husband. " I want to present the wonderful CINTRA who has decorated my studio so beautifully."

I protested that with red eyes, a swollen nose, a headache, and a heartache, I should be but a ' damper ' to his feast ; but he insisted, and when John and I did make our appearance, he led me round his studio, introducing me to all the important people present, and praising my work. A perfect example of the behaviour of a very great and chivalrous gentleman that I can never forget. These are the things that one remembers always in one's heart.

XLVI.

I decided to open the business at Hampstead with a garden-party and to display a selection of frocks. John composed some special verses to advertise my wares. He was a wonderful rhymer and always celebrated any venture of mine with a *rondeau*.

> " A pretty frock. Since Mother Eve entwined
> A skirt of leaves, and draped it to her mind,
> And Adam, gazing, said, ' I think it's made
> The least in life too full; and is the shade
> Just what it should be ? See if you can find
> A paler leaf or two; don't change the kind ;
> Vary the tone. And should the skirt be lined ?
> No ? Then, to work ! By noon you must parade
>   A pretty frock ! '

266

> "Through Ages Fashion, changeful as the wind,
> Plays Adam's part, now seeing and now blind,
> And lovely colours side by side are laid
> And lovely lines with cunning art displayed
> Until, behold ! A masterpiece designed !
>   A pretty frock."

A mob of people came and the roads around the house were choked with cars. I was surrounded by interested journalists who had at last discovered that CINTRA was the wife of John Fortescue, the Military Historian. I was obliged to explain to them my reason for opening a business, for some of them appeared to think that it was merely the whim of a rich and hitherto idle woman, and that it was wrong of me to take the bread out of professional mouths. When they realised that my intent was serious, they all became sympathetic and charming, and from thenceforth the publicity they gave to my venture proved an enormous help.

Gradually the house-decoration became submerged in dressmaking. I had much difficulty in getting a punctual and adequate supply of brocatellos from Italy. I had orders to decorate complete houses with them, and one lovely old castle in Kent, but I had to refuse the orders, not having enough materials in stock and being unable to promise a date when more would come in. The general slump began, and then no one could afford to do up their houses. Knowing that women must continue to clothe their bodies, I now concentrated chiefly upon clothes, choosing exclusive and beautiful materials and designing each gown to suit its individual wearer.

When the traveller for that great artist Bianchini brought me his range of wonderful but very costly French brocades, silks, and velvets, I asked him if I might buy only *one* dress-length of my favourite samples and pleaded that these might not be sold to other London dress-makers. The traveller, a big Scotsman, who later became a staunch friend and supporter of CINTRA, twinkled at me and said that to keep a material exclusive to one firm it was necessary to buy the whole length of it. No fabric that he showed me cost less than 30s. a yard, wholesale price, and some of the lovelier *lamé* velvets were four, five, or six pounds a yard. Impossible for CINTRA, just starting in the dress business, and with at present very few customers for clothes, to afford to buy complete rolls of material of thirty or sixty yards, and my whole idea of exclusiveness would be defeated even if I could.

So I made a sporting proposition to be laid before Monsieur Bianchini. I said that his materials were so beautiful that they deserved to be treated individually ; for, as I played with one lovely supple fabric after another, each told me the one and only way in which it ought to be treated. I suggested that I should choose one length of material and design one gown worthy of it, to be sub-mitted to Monsieur Bianchini himself. If, when he saw it, he considered that I understood and appreciated his stuffs as they deserved, would he in future allow me to buy single dress-lengths of those materials that he had sold only to Paris and America, so that my selection would never have been seen before in London ? In this way I could become his client and could always give my customers exclusive designs and materials which they would see worn by no one else.

The big traveller chuckled, but consented to submit my proposition to Monsieur Bianchini. Knowing the great artist, he had hopes that my rather cheeky suggestion might ' tickle him to death.' In any case we might try.

I therefore chose a marvellous length of *lamé* satin which I will attempt to describe. One side of it was of the sleekest softest black satin through which were woven silver threads and sprays of vivid nasturtium flowers in tints of vermilion, orange, and yellow, giving the effect, when the satin caught the light, of dew-wet flowers. The reverse side of the material was one shimmering sheet of silver splashed with vivid colour, where the ghost-flowers showed through it. I draped this upon myself, taking care to display the silver sheeny side in the winged sleeves and floating train of the model I designed for the personal eye of Monsieur Bianchini. He was enchanted with it, and deemed me worthy thereafter to use his materials in the way I had asked. So that, henceforth, I could design original gowns for those of my clients who would allow me to make clothes that suited their individual type instead of slavishly following the prevailing fashion. Thus I gradually developed an exclusive business, and, as it grew and prospered, I was able to engage a cutter and fitter, an army of work-girls, and some pretty showroom assistants.

XLVII.

The spring of 1922 was a particularly unhealthy one. Our doctor told us that in nearly every house in Hampstead someone was ill, in most cases dangerously ill, with horrible forms of influenza, gastric and pulmonary. He worked day and night and hardly had time to eat or sleep. John caught cold after cold. Hardly had he recovered from one than he would catch another germ from either a member of the Library staff, our own servants, or in tubes or trains. In the end the doctor persuaded me to let him have injections against no less than seven forms of influenza. But he was very much pulled down, and when, in March, he received a very cordial letter from his old friend Horace Smith-Dorrien, who was at that time Governor of Gibraltar, inviting us both to visit him there, I saw at once that the idea of a short sea-voyage, followed by a holiday in the sun, appealed to John as keenly as it did to me. The business had been doing very well, and I was very tired. When John demurred that this trip would be an unjustifiable expense, I argued that we must look upon it as a health-investment, and that after a little change of scene and

air we should both work better. Craftily I told him that
I dreaded the work of the coming season, with Ascot,
the Courts, &c., ahead of me. Immediately he began
to waver, screwing in the eyeglass and scrutinising my
face attentively. Finally he kissed it and said : " My
gallant woman shall have her holiday. We'll go." The
only way I could ever get him to do anything good for
himself was to persuade him that he was doing it for me.
In return for his capitulation to my wishes, I promised
him that our adventure should not cost us a penny. I
would take with me a small selection of seductive tea-
gowns which I would somehow sell in Gibraltar and so
pay our fares. This I immediately did, for on arrival
at Government House, pretty Lady Smith-Dorrien
came into my room while I was unpacking and said :
" I *do* hope you've brought out some of your lovely gowns.
I want some badly, and there are several women staying
here who are dying to have a CINTRA model." Before
I had finished my unpacking, my bedroom had become
a showroom with lovely ladies trying on my tea-gowns,
all of which were sold in half an hour.

That visit to Gibraltar stands out in my memory very
vividly. John was enchanted to be with his old friend
Horace once again, and they discussed the late war far
into the night. The name of Lord French recurred
frequently in these conversations. The military defences
of the Rock also intrigued John greatly, and he made a
tour of them with the Governor while I visited the shops
and drove about with the Governor's lady, her adopted
nieces, Gabrielle and Celia Palmer, and members of the
house-party. Every night there was a dinner-party or a
dance at Government House. Ships came into harbour,
and their officers must be entertained ; Sir Horace, Lady
Smith-Dorrien, and the girls were all keen lawn tennis
players, and the tennis courts and fives courts were
always occupied.

Celia Palmer had a tame monkey which, unfortunately,

had taken to drink. Before we arrived it had been the cause of much disturbance in Government House because, before its vice had been discovered, members of the staff had come under suspicion when bottles of scent had been found empty in the ladies' bedrooms, and whisky and brandy bottles were depleted of their contents. Inky whiskers eventually betrayed the thief after it had visited the ink-stand in Sir Horace's study. He gave orders that in future it must be confined to kitchen quarters and never come above stairs.

One day, on returning from a drive, we heard the sound of a very angry voice at the end of a corridor where was situated Sir Horace's office. He was, it seemed, in one of his famous rages. " That b—— monkey," was distinctly audible and " Celia ! Where is Celia ? " Poor Celia paled. We drifted towards the noise and found a furious Sir Horace standing in the doorway of his room. With a violent gesture he invited us to enter. It looked as though swept by a whirlwind. The floor was strewn with torn papers, a bottle of ink had been upset in the midst of them, pens, pencils littered the floor.

" That d——d monkey of yours, Celia ! I'll have it shot ! I forbade you to let it come upstairs. Look at the merry hell it has made of my office. God knows what important papers it has destroyed. It may be responsible for a war. . . ." Suddenly his eyes became fixed, and then began to twinkle ; the words died on his lips, which began, unaccountably, to twitch. We followed the direction of his fixed stare directed towards a corner of the room where a camp-bed had been placed so that on nights when he was working late he could sleep in his office. There, lying between the sheets, its head nuzzling into the pillows like a human being, lay that wicked monkey. By its side lay an empty whisky bottle, and clutched in a small paw was—believe me or not, this is the truth—an empty bottle of Aspirin tablets. . . .

This extremely human behaviour of the monkey's

undoubtedly saved its life. Instead of being shot at dawn, it was presented to a ship, and the last news heard of it was that every night in the Officers' Mess it drank them all under the table.

We returned from Gibraltar brown-skinned and refreshed by our little adventure, and laden with gaudy beads of every description which John had found for me in some of the quaint shops on the Rock, and with which he intended to make necklaces for my dresses. Instantly I was plunged into preparations for the spring season, and, in addition to making fresh models for stock, I had to design and make a special consignment to be sent out to Gibraltar, so eagerly had the few tea-gowns that I had taken out with me been seized. We had a very hectic spring.

XLVIII.

We decided to spend our summer holiday abroad, following John's theory that real rest can only be obtained by crossing the sea, and we had been wondering where we should spend it until Charles Fortescue came to stay with us for a night, and told us of a delightful spot in Brittany, on the farther side of Dinard—St Jacut-de-la-Mer—situated on a peninsula between a lovely estuary and the open sea. He and his family had stayed in St Lunaire, on the opposite side of the estuary, and had often walked across it at low tide to St Jacut, where they had lunched in an old windmill, converted by a clever Parisienne (who was also an excellent cook) into a restaurant. He thought she had a bedroom to let in the windmill, but we could always write to her and find out. I did. She had. We took it.

We crossed over to St Malo on a sweltering day, and, arriving at the wrong moment for the tide, had to wait hours to get in. And having got in we found that we had lost the ferry, and had to wait still longer, being devoured

by clouds of midges. John consoled himself with recol-
lections of the great Châteaubriand, and I gazed with
horror into that pit where living *langoustes*, kept for sale,
tore at each other with thousands of waving claws.

But when we reached St Jacut we were compensated
for that journey. Madame gave us an excellent meal
and then led us up a wooden ladder, outside the mill,
to our bedroom at the very top, a delicious circular room
with windows on all sides overlooking estuary and sea—
wooden floor, white-washed walls, two little beds, two
chairs, a chest of drawers, and a table. Severely simple,
but clean and comfortable.

Inwardly I prayed for fine weather, for it would not
be very amusing to be obliged to climb up that outside
ladder in rain or a gale. But during the whole of our
visit the blessed sun shone upon us, and I think John
thoroughly enjoyed climbing down in the mornings, clad
in pyjamas, can in hand, to fetch water from the well
which Madame afterwards heated for his tub. To get
to the well he had to dodge an irritable donkey whose
diet of thistles seemed to have frayed its temper.

I was mad to get down to those wonderful shell-strewn
sands, to wade across to one of the many rock-islands
which studded the sea, and the very first morning, clad
in a mauve sun-bonnet and overall, my feet bare, I started
off on a voyage of discovery by myself while John was
shaving—always a very serious ceremony with him, for
he prided himself upon his beautifully shorn chin (and a
little, I think, upon the beautiful chin). At that early
hour I had the sandy bays to myself, and I raced along
the wet sand, singing as I ran. The pools left by the tide
were incredibly beautiful, filled with waving seaweeds
and sea-anemones of every hue, and everywhere upon
those stretches of golden shimmering sand were delicate
shells of every size and shape. I wandered on, entranced,
till at length I found myself in a lonely isolated bay,
and was rather startled to see the rough figure of a man

appear from the great rocks and advance towards me.
He wore the clothes and *béret* of a Breton fisherman,
but his huge frame and fierce face rather alarmed me.
He came close up to me, staring at me with very blue,
rather wild eyes. Then with a sudden courtly gesture
he doffed his *béret* and said softly—

" *Je baise vos petits pieds, si belle que vous êtes,*" bowed,
and moved slowly away, leaving me silent and amazed
by so beautiful a compliment, so beautifully expressed,
and from so unexpected a quarter.

John was as keen as I to get down to the shore, and,
when he saw me whip off my sand-shoes and race into the
sea, he called out wistfully : " I can't follow you down
there, Peg, for I shall ruin my shoes."

" Take them OFF ! " I shouted.

" But I can't walk about in socks," he protested.

" Of course not. You take them off too," I yelled.
" You're going to paddle."

" But—I've never done such a thing in my life," he
demurred.

" Then high time you began," I cried, and was delighted
to see him sit down, strip off shoes and socks, and join
me on the wet sands.

Thenceforth I had a hard job to persuade him to put
on shoes again. He developed a passion for paddling,
and spent happy hours prawning with me or collecting
shells with which I intended to make flowers and dress-
ornaments.

Walking through a field of ripe corn at sunset one
evening, we met a strikingly handsome woman with an
adorable face walking with a young golden-haired girl.
My eyes met those of the elder woman, and for one moment
my glance held hers. In that moment I knew that I had
found a friend and kindred spirit, and that we should
meet again and be friends.

When we regained our *Moulin*, we found a very gay
party of young people wearing fancy dress, dancing in

the restaurant. Madame had hired it for that afternoon.
We remained outside and watched the scene through the
window. There were two very lovely girls there, one
with hair the colour of pale Florentine gold, worn
clubbed, like a Shakespearean page, with a square-cut
fringe over black pencilled eyebrows and huge yellow,
black-lashed eyes. She was dressed in a black velvet
doublet and hose which suited her to perfection.

The other girl looked as though she had come from
Devonshire. She had a warm cream-and-roses skin,
large soft blue-grey eyes, dark lashes, and a shock of
bronze-gold curls. She was a little over-plump, but that
was a fault of youth and did not spoil her fresh loveliness.

" John ! I MUST have them to wear my frocks at CINTRA
dress-shows," I breathed ecstatically in his ear.

Presently a slim boy with a sensitive face came out,
and, addressing us in beautiful French, apologised for
having monopolised the restaurant for a few hours to
celebrate his birthday, and begged us to honour him with
our company. Madame had told him that we were lodging
in the windmill.

And so it was that we made the acquaintance of the
Vicomte de X. and the two lovely girls, both of whom I
secured, later, as mannequins for my Moonlight Dress
Parade in our Hampstead garden.

The plump child with those lovely grey-blue eyes and
chestnut curls was Betty Stockfeld, who has since made
her name upon stage and screen.

We invited the boy and the two girls to luncheon with
us next day ; their parents called upon us, and in their
turn invited us to tea at *L'Abbaye* where they were all
staying, and there it was that I met again the woman
with the adorable face whom I had first seen in the corn-
field—Nell Toohey, an Australian, and now my very dear
friend. John grew very fond of her too, rejoicing in her
keen sense of humour, her intelligence, and downright
candour. She could never learn French, and when,

after her first night at *L'Abbaye*, the Reverend Mother asked her if she had slept well, she replied : " *Nong, nong, j'ai dormi avec un mauvais matelot.*" Hardly the confidence to make to a Mother Superior, but of course she meant *matelas*.

XLIX.

Our holiday was over all too soon. I wanted to prepare for the autumn season, and John was never happy for long when divorced from his work ; and so we travelled back at the end of August.

The business continued to expand and to prosper. At intervals I gave shows, and the most important of these was a dress parade held on a night in June of the following year, in our lovely garden. I laid down strips of sky-blue carpet on the grey paving-stones of the rose-garden, and we tied fairy-lamps to all the rose-trees and Chinese lanterns to the taller trees. Mr McDermott, who was then Director of the Everyman Theatre in Hampstead, lent me limelight lamps, which I hid among huge bushes of lilac and syringa to cast cross-shafts of light upon my mannequins as they drifted among the roses and masses of white foxgloves. I engaged a string quartette, led by the sister of Miss Isolde Menges, to play dreamy music while hidden in the ' shelter deck ' (our open-air bedroom on the first floor) ; and I collected all the loveliest girls of my acquaintance, among them my two Brittany beauties, to wear the glittering brocade gowns and cloaks and the diaphanous tulle and chiffon picture-frocks which were all that I intended to show.

My husband, CINTRA's tame poet, composed the following *rondeau*, which was printed on all the invitations :—

> " In CINTRA's garden sweet the roses blow,
> And rest is there and peace ; while far below,
> Like droning of five million human flies,
> The hum of distant London swells and dies

> And dies and swells, in ceaseless ebb and flow—
> The hum of men who hurry to and fro
> And seek and seek—for what they hardly know,
> But there is calm 'neath silent summer skies
> In CINTRA's garden.

> "There lanterns dim, 'mid music soft and low,
> Shall guide the living flowers as they go
> Arrayed in CINTRA's loveliest draperies,
> Till dazzling light reveal them to your eyes.
> Come, gentles, see what one fair night can show
> In CINTRA's garden."

Of course we went through all the preliminary agonies
that everyone suffers on these occasions. The weather
had been wet for weeks beforehand, and facetious
journalists hinted that people invited to CINTRA's evening
party had better bring with them umbrellas and hot-
water bottles. Insurance companies rang me up counsel-
ling me to insure against inevitable rain ; but I refused to
be damped beforehand. My worried John wondered
how anyone living in England ever had the courage to
give an open-air entertainment, but gallantly hoped for
the best.

My party fell upon the one fine night of the year.

When eventually I emerged, clad in my magnolia-
tinted georgette draperies with a trail of red roses slung
from my waist, daylight had faded, and flickering fairy-
lights twinkled all over the garden.

The guests began to arrive, received first by my showroom assistants, pretty girls whom I had dressed in
mediæval frocks of Italian-red brocade girdled with gold,
their hair bound with golden filets studded with gleaming
red stones. They looked like human roses as they flitted
about among the rose-beds.

I had invited about one hundred guests, but over three
hundred came. One woman wrote 'Thirty' against the
question 'Probable number of party' on her invitation
card—and she brought thirty friends.

We weathered another crisis at the outset. The rose-garden was to be my stage, and was accordingly wired very carefully with cables reaching from the house to my hidden limelight lamps. I implored my first guests not to risk walking there, but the flood of people arriving overwhelmed me, and soon they were streaming all over the rose-garden. Of course they stumbled over the cables and disconnected them, and for twenty agonising minutes I wondered if the whole lighting effect would be wrecked. However, Mr McDermott and his henchmen worked gallantly to repair the damage, while Miss Menges and her maidens played delicious music to keep the audience patient, and very soon he was able to give me the signal to begin my dress parade.

It was a pretty show though I say it. One lovely girl after another, clad in shimmering, glittering garments drifted out from the vine-clad verandah into the garden and ' meandered with a mazy motion ' among the flowers to the strains of soft invisible music. Beams of different-coloured light followed my ' living flowers,' and oh ! my relief when the first beam beamed and I knew that Mr McDermott's efforts had been successful.

There was a little white Greek-pillared temple in a dark corner of the garden. In this I posed figures at intervals, suddenly illumining it to reveal them. Each girl had been carefully rehearsed in some small action, the better to display her frock and to give a little life and movement to the scene. The greatest success was perhaps my little silver bride—the child with the pale gold hair that we had seen dancing in the old windmill in Brittany dressed in black velvet doublet and hose. I had persuaded her mother to allow her to wear frocks for me at my next London show. I shall never forget the vision of her little silvery figure drifting slowly in a beam of white light, her tulle veil floating round her like a mist amid the roses and tall white foxgloves.

I eventually sold that bride's frock to a persistent American at 1.30 A.M. the next morning when my guests

were at last departing ; for long after the dress parade
was over they lingered among our flowers.

John was quite as thrilled as I was over the success
of our evening, and for an hour after the departure of
the last guest we sat in our open-air bedroom gazing out
over the rose-garden watching the hundreds of little
fairy-lamps wink themselves out. The garden looked
fay-haunted in the silence of the small hours.

> " In CINTRA's garden sweet the roses blow
>   And rest is there and peace . . ."

I quoted softly.

L.

In spite of his labours alone in his study where the
History was growing apace, in his leisure hours my Man
always found time to help me with my business in every
kind of unusual way. He composed *rondeaux ;* the word-
ing of circulars ; often helped me with the draping of a
gown, for he had that unerring eye for line and colour
sometimes found in a man, and, when found, always
superior to that of a woman. Frequently he made just
the suggestion for which I was searching, and when I
was too tired to be capable any longer of judging an
effect, he would damn it heartily or praise it, and so give
the final decision.

He always wanted to make the ornaments that he saw
me and my staff making, and would thread artistic necklaces, which were then the fashion, stringing the beads
of Venetian glass, gilded or coloured wood, and sometimes
of non-precious stones such as crystal, amethyst or lapis,
upon Chinese cords ; spacing the beads with military
precision, infinite patience and concentration, and always
with success. I would find him seated in an armchair
in our Wedgwood Room before a table strewn with boxes
of beads, cords, tassels. and beeswax ; eyeglass fixed

into an intent eye, as though he were a General arranging
the disposition of his troops to best advantage.

A fashion came in for leather flowers, and he would
collect any odd scraps, cut to waste, from the binder at
Windsor, and then with pencil, compass, and scissors,
contrive flower-petals and leaves for my use. And I
really do believe that he enjoyed it all immensely, for
he was keen to hear every detail of the day's business
when the blessed moment came for our little *tête-à-tête*
dinner in the evening when my work ceased for an hour.
For our peaceful evenings were now things of the past.
After dinner, instead of taking up my embroidery needle
while John read aloud to me, I was forced to take up my
pen to write letters, do designs, or wrestle with accounts,
while he patiently worked at his canvas-work or read to
himself, interrupted from time to time when I asked
him to verify the addition of a customer's account or to
calculate a workgirl's wages at so much an hour.

Often, as the hour grew late, and I, doubtless, pallid
and nervous, for always I was handicapped by that cursed
war-poison and continual treatments, he would grow
desperate, rise to his feet, and insist that I go to bed. I
would protest that I had not nearly finished my work,
that customers were awaiting designs, patterns, and
estimates which *only* CINTRA could supply. He would
damn the customers, the designs, the patterns, and the
estimates in no half-hearted manner, saying that his
wife's health was the only thing that mattered to him.
Over-strung and weary, sometimes I would be goaded
into irritable defiance and continue doggedly to work.
Whereupon he, tired out after a long day at Windsor
or from concentrated writing in his Hampstead study,
would sit down again in his chair with a frantic sigh of
exasperation and say, " Very well. Then I will sit here
and wait until you have finished." This, he knew, would
conquer me, for his health meant more than all the world
to me, and torn between my duty to him and my duty

to the business that I had created for him, I should be obliged to shovel my papers into a drawer and drag myself upstairs to bed.

Later, as the business developed rapidly and my work and responsibilities increased, I was driven to deceive him. When he suggested that it was bedtime, I agreed with docility, went upstairs, undressed, got into bed, and, when he had sunk into the deep sleep of a weary man, I slipped on my dressing-gown and stole downstairs to start my work anew.

As I have said, the business grew and prospered, and, of course, I found it exhausting, for, if one works up a personal business as I did, not even the Archangel Michael will serve instead of CINTRA. All my customers insisted upon seeing me for my designs ; that *I* be present at their fittings, and they flatly refused to see my representative when, later, I could afford to appoint one. So I spent my time between showrooms and fitting-rooms and workrooms, often wishing that we did not live in a vertical house with 172 steps to reach the top floor. It was always when in my bath, safe from interruption, that I thought out new ideas for clothes ; and the best cloak that I ever designed was first draped upon myself with a bath-towel. But inspiration came from birds and flowers—anything one saw. A magpie in flight—winged tea-gown of black and white ; sweet peas in bloom, and at once one saw a filmy *negligée* of mauve chiffon posed over pink ; or pink over lemon yellow ; a snowdrop piercing through glittering snow inspired a bridal dress of white and silver with girdle of green and garland of tender spring leaves ; even John Galsworthy's car, manœuvring from garage to gate, left a wonderful design for embroidery with its geometric wheel-tracks on the snow. I found a clever girl who could draw the designs that I fashioned with fabrics upon myself ; and an artistic cutter and fitter to watch me as I played with the materials before a big mirror, and who taught me what was makeable and what not.

I learned a valuable lesson very early in the day when I went to the distribution of prizes at some big College of Design. Lady Duff-Gordon, the famous ' LUCILE,' had been asked to present the prize for the best evening-dress design and then cut it out in brocade and pin it into dress-form upon a mannequin.

She arrived, with one of her lovely girls, and, having presented the prize to a proud and blushing young designer, she began to cut and to pin. The mannequin stood, in profile, upon the stage and we watched with admiration the clever fingers of LUCILE slash and drape the material, achieving lovely folds and lines and a sideway-swirling train.

Loud applause from the audience when she had created this beautiful gown from the winning design. She smiled a trifle maliciously and then bade the mannequin turn completely round to display the other side of the model. We saw a hip-length of *crêpe-de-Chine* knicker and a slender silk-clad leg. The designer had drawn a lovely but unmakeable model which had only one side; the width of material, which swept around the body and fell in folds of drapery on the left side, was not wide enough to cover the body on the right side farther than the waist.

There was a breathless silence, and then loud titters from the audience, and that poor prize-winner blushed ever more deeply as LUCILE discoursed upon the necessity of designers learning the practical as well as the artistic side of dressmaking.

After this, I took care to study it carefully and always to ask my cutter if my designs were practicable. She would say: " Start playing with the stuff, Madame, and I will see how your ideas can be carried out," and so we worked together, and I learned to be practical in my work.

Very often I had to attend at customers' houses, and John decreed that I must have a car. We found a little second-hand French car which we bought from a chauffeur,

who in his turn had bought it from another chauffeur
whose master had left it to him in his will. I knew nothing
of cars, nor did John, and neither of us were mechanically
minded, but we guessed that a chauffeur's car was pretty
sure to have its engine in good condition, and so it proved.

'Billy,' as we named my shabby little *coupé*, had a
wonderful engine, but he had his disadvantages. He
had no self-starter ; his petrol tank was under the seat,
so that one had to remove a heavy cushion to fill it ;
and to turn on the petrol it was necessary to take up the
floor-boards under which a little tap was concealed. This
contrivance at least made it quite safe to leave ' Billy '
outside customers' houses for any length of time, for no
thief could ever have discovered the way to start that
car. It even defeated the complete staff of one of the
great garages behind Piccadilly where I left ' Billy ' one
day while lunching with a friend at the Berkeley. The
lunch being very good and the coffee excellent, I lingered
longer than I had intended, and then suddenly realised
that an appointment loomed near. My companion
suggested that I should ask a page to telephone to the
garage and tell someone to bring ' Billy ' round to the
Berkeley. It was a wet wintry day, and in this way I
could remain luxuriously in the warm hotel, and much
time would be saved. I waited, and waited, and waited
until, becoming impatient and anxious, for I prided
myself upon always being punctual for business appointments (though John said I never was for anything else),
I telephoned through to the garage myself. A hectic
voice replied to me. It was the foreman who, learning
my identity, asked desperately : " Would you please
come to the garage, Madam. No one here can find out
how to start your car. It's in pieces in the yard and all
my men are having a try."

On that occasion I was very late indeed for an appointment, but I left a dozen laughing men behind me when
I left the garage in my rebuilt ' Billy.'

LI.

I was getting more and more tired. My nights were
not always good after a painful treatment, or when I
had heavy bills for merchandise to meet, wages to pay,
a bank balance running low, and customers were slack
in settling their accounts. I thought an overdraft a
shameful thing, and, during all those years, I never once
asked my bank manager 'to oblige me.' When I told
my accountant of this dread of mine, he laughed heartily
and informed me that I was probably the only dressmaker
in London at that bad moment who did not live on an
overdraft.

This curious sharp young man whom I had lately
acquired to come in once a month to balance my books
thought me, I know, a little mad, for to him it was sheer
madness not to snatch every halfpenny one could for the
business. But when he first arrived I told him firmly
that he must never take off discount from my wholesale
firms unless I really *had* paid cash for my order or settled
my account within the month of grace. He disregarded
my orders, and, at the end of that bad year, told me
triumphantly that he had saved me a substantial sum
in discounts. I stared at him, knowing that I had scarcely
ever been able to pay my heavy bills for materials
punctually. More often had I been obliged to plead for
patience and to pay them in instalments.

I questioned him closely, and he admitted with a grin
that he had succeeded in 'snatching' a number of overdue
discounts either at quarter-days when every firm is too
busy to notice such details, or by trading upon the fact
that I was a good and honest customer who would always
pay in the end.

I do not know when I have felt more furious. Then
and there I made him sit down and write cheques for all
those stolen discounts to be returned to those firms from

whom he had filched them in my name. And I, myself, wrote personal apologies to each, explaining that this had been done without my knowledge and against my express orders.

I had a most grateful letter from the London Director of the famous French firm of Rodier, who asked if he might publish my letter in 'The Drapers' Record,' as it was the very first instance in his long experience of any firm refusing stolen discount. Pathetic.

But although my balance at the bank often dwindled alarmingly and caused me great anxiety when I had heavy expenses to meet, always, at the worst and blackest moment of apprehension, as the end of the week drew near and I was faced with the necessity of paying an army of workgirls with an insufficient sum lying in my account, some blessed cheque would come in from a dilatory customer and the situation would be saved. Then I would call myself a faithless woman and repeat to myself over and over again : " You know your business CAN'T fail because you are doing it for the History."

Certainly it developed and prospered very rapidly, and, when superintending my humming workroom, I used to look back with amusement to the days when that crowded room contained only one fat little woman working in solitary state.

I loved all my girls. They worked so loyally and with such enthusiasm, particularly during the spring season when we were inundated with orders for Court gowns and Ascot frocks. Then the pressure became so great that I used to work *with* them, putting finishing touches to a Court train or helping them to pack up dresses while a taxi waited at the door to convey a messenger with a Court gown to some thrilled *débutante*.

On one occasion when I was invited, myself, to a Court Ball, I had designed my dress weeks before, and had given the design and material to my head worker ; but we had so many orders to complete for that Ball that I

soon gave up the idea of going myself, and told her not
to attempt to have my dress made. On the actual day
we were rushed to death. For some reason that I cannot
now remember, the Ball had been postponed, and then
put on again, so that dresses that had been laid aside
for more pressing orders had to be finished in a hurry.
It was a tropically hot day in June, and I ordered iced
lemonade to be sent up to the workrooms to refresh us
all. When the last layer of tissue-paper had been spread
in the last box, I felt thankful that there had been no
time to make my own gown. I was so weary and hot
that all I longed for was a bath—and bed.

When at last I tottered down to my bedroom, there
on my huge four-post bed was laid out the loveliest gown
all ready to put on.

My girls had sworn that ' Madame ' *should* go to the
Ball and wear a new dress, and they had worked in their
free time to make it.

Tired though I was, of course I had to go. I could not
disappoint those dear girls who had worked so hard for
me. In the end, John and I found it rather amusing to
recognise CINTRA gowns as they sailed into the ballroom,
though now and then I had a mad desire to rush up to
the wearer and put a finishing touch, or tear off some
unsuitable head-dress that marred the effect of my design.

LII.

Some months after this I received a letter from a
great friend in New York who had attended my evening
dress show in the rose-garden, telling me that various
Americans who had been present had suggested that I
be asked to bring over a collection of evening gowns and
cloaks and to give a Show in the Plaza Hotel in aid of
the soldiers and sailors of America. They promised to
arrange the whole thing for me. All I should have

to do was to bring over the models and stage the performances.

John was dead against this plan. The mysterious microbe was still rampant and was gradually undermining my strength, and the painful experimental treatments to scotch it were even more exhausting than the malady itself. I never had time to rest and was always overtired. He feared that this American business would prove too much for me.

I, on the contrary, was keen to embark on this new venture. If successful, it would prove a splendid advertisement and enlarge my business connection. I had always wanted to visit America. So I argued with John, who at length reluctantly yielded to pressure from home and from America, and it was decided that we should go over for six weeks.

There followed a wild rush of preparation. I knew that I must strike an original note in America, for every Parisian designer visits the United States with his or her choice and *chic* models. As John put it : " CINTRA's clothes must be *chic*-erer." A whirl of activity raged in Admiral's House.

My secretary, Annie Macleod, known to us as ' Mac,' a dear Scotswoman, who looked very incongruous clothed always in her perfectly cut Scotch tweeds and brogues as she moved among the feminine frivolities I was inventing, strode about the house with long lists of figures in her hands, and somehow managed to keep her sleek boyish head. Hers was the awful job of pricing the models in dollars for wholesale and retail sale, and of making foolproof price-programmes for Madame.

I found it simpler to live in a kimono for six weeks beforehand, for it could be more quickly thrown off when I wanted to design a dress by winding materials about my own body. Each dress had to be made in duplicate, so that I should leave my London showrooms well stocked in my absence ; and all the delicate confections prepared for America had to be packed tenderly in layers upon layers of tissue-paper, with all their accessories such as girdles, head-dresses, underslips, &c., numbered with the same numbers as the models to which they belonged.

Finally we, and our baskets of merchandise, embarked on the *Caronia*, one of the smaller boats going to America, but all the better for that. We had a very rough voyage, but, fortunately, neither John nor I minded this. He was never so happy as when at sea, and I am perfectly all right in any kind of weather, provided that I can lie down and close my eyes. Then I enjoy the swinging of a ship, but, if I try to walk the deck and see waves towering above me and deck-rails rising and sinking, I get instantly giddy and wish for death. On the *Caronia* I might have been able to rest had I not been so terrified of embarking on this venture in a strange land without the support of my loyal staff and workrooms. But I was already suffering the agonies of nervousness which I used to feel before the first night of a new play, and the days seemed interminable and the nights even more so. However, at last we reached the mouth of the Hudson, and, in the small hours, I disturbed my husband's rest by rushing at intervals to the porthole of our cabin to see if the Statue of Liberty was yet in sight. I had been told that even before dawn I should see her, illumined by the huge torch that she holds in her right hand. But not until breakfast was over did a sympathetic American passenger rush up to me and say : " Say, Ma'am ! You can now see the Statue of Liberty way off in the mist." And then I saw her in the far distance ; that towering figure looking like a tiny white ghost.

The mist rather spoiled our view of New York as we approached ; but I received an impression of a fantastic Dream City which looked as if it had been built by a giant's child with a gigantic box of bricks.

With the quarantine officers, the gentlemen of the American Press also came on board in their legions, carrying more cameras than I have ever seen in my life. We were run to earth in our cabin and urged to climb up on to the top deck where the photographers awaited us in formidable serried rows ready for action ; the front rows kneeling so as not to block the view of those behind them.

When the papers appeared next day I was horrified to see the appalling grin with which they had immortalised me. It was the result of a command of the leading reporter : " Now, Ma'am ! Bust your best smile ! " which of course thoroughly upset my gravity.

We had one very bad moment when our passports were examined. John was born in Madeira, from whence he was transported to England at the age of six weeks in the company of a goat which provided him with daily milk. This, in the view of the United States officials, constituted him a Portuguese subject, and they were doubtful if the Portuguese quota was or was not already complete. If it was, then he could not be permitted to land.

I shall never forget John's horror and indignation. To be mistaken for anyone but an Englishman was, to him, an insult ; and then the possibility of being either sent home or shut up in Ellis Island while I underwent the American ordeal alone, sent him nearly frantic. However, after much discussion, it was decided that, as he would only be in America for six weeks, he might be allowed to land. And land we did, thank God, together.

On the dock were many American friends, including one of our ' American sons,' who had come all the way from Arkansas to greet us. They had all sent us radio greetings during the voyage.

Our first host and hostess, Mr and Mrs Francis Rogers, met us very cordially, but with a look of concern upon their faces, which was explained when they had to break the news to me that, during our voyage, the American duties upon gowns and luxury accessories had been raised ninety per cent. We were faced with the necessity of depositing a thousand pounds with the Customs before I could take out my models. I could take them into New York as ' samples ' if I liked, and then the price of unsold dresses would be refunded to me when I embarked again for England.

This was, of course, the only thing to do. But where was the thousand pounds to come from ? John started nervously fingering his chin and I, though I had withstood the storms of the Atlantic, felt very sick.

Nellie and Frank Rogers gallantly came to the rescue. She and her husband would guarantee the money, which she was certain would be more than reimbursed by the sale of my lovely gowns. That business settled, she then turned to matters social, producing two engagement-books, one for me and one for my husband. Each day and hour was filled with strange fixtures for us both. Every moment had been mapped out for us both before we landed, and we each had to study assiduously our ' books of words,' trying to learn our ' dates ' and the names of the people who were entertaining us. The learned people, Societies, Universities, and Clubs, all wanted John to feed with them and to discourse on abstruse subjects, and the frivolous people wanted me.

Before we left the docks, I saw my CINTRA baskets whirled off to the Customs House where they would be held in bond until they had been examined, and then we, in our turn, were carried off in black-and-white taxis to the house of our first hospitable host and hostess.

The next few days seemed to be one long Press interview. The first reporter I saw asked me to tell him whether short skirts or long skirts would be worn next season. I replied, " It depends upon the leg."

He stared at me with an open mouth which gradually stretched into a grin, and then he said thoughtfully : " Say ! there's something in that."

"A very great deal," I assured him grimly.

The next man came up and asked me if gowns should be sleeveless or not.

"It depends upon the arm," I answered.

He looked equally taken aback, and then, turning to the crowd of others, said : "Say, boys ! Here's a noo stunt. Something out of the good old rut. Gather around."

One of them asked me to expound my views on the coming fashions, and I told him that I was the last person in the world to give them information of that kind, being a Fashion Anarchist. I then launched forth into a diatribe against fashion, and preached a little sermon on individualism in dress. Apparently I was the first woman to cross the Atlantic tilting against tradition, and, judging from the pages and pages of publicity given to CINTRA, her views, and her gowns, the Gentlemen of the Press were, to use their own expression, 'tickled to death.' To me it is so very obvious that a designer should evolve a dress suitable to the type of each individual woman who seeks his, or her, aid, regardless of the dictates of Paris, that the enthusiasm and comment my extremely commonplace views evoked in New York came as a never-ending surprise to me, until I realised that New York was entirely conventional.

My great anxiety was to get my baskets through and out of the Customs. I found that I was booked for a *matinée* and evening Dress Parade in the Plaza Hotel, New York, and for two more in a theatre in Philadelphia a week later. There was very little time in which to make preparations, but I was assured that the ladies of New York had fixed up everything.

Having always arranged every item of my Dress Shows myself and having had much experience by this time, I knew the enormous amount of preliminary work entailed and the immense importance of meticulous detail if all were to go swiftly and smoothly as dress-parades should go, and I wished that the Committee of twenty-eight amiable amateurs who were arranging them for me now would come to see CINTRA and take her into their confidence. The *one* business woman who was supposed to be responsible for all executive functions, or in other words 'to run the Shows,' was, I learned to my dismay, seriously ill—sick unto death as it unhappily proved, and she never appeared at all.

I realised that I must quickly bestir myself to get my baskets out of the Customs, and that the most urgent thing for me to do was to go to the Customs House myself and hustle the officials, for I had been warned that there was a danger that other consignments might come in and be taken through before mine.

Accordingly, I hurried down early next morning in company with a professional dressmaker, considerately found for me by my hostess, who knew to what treatment my gowns were liable, and realised that I should need help in that Customs House after the examination of my models was over.

We were taken into an enormous barn-like building where I presented my baggage forms. Casual clerks, chewing gum, badgered me about from pillar to post and seemed to think it quite impossible for me to have my baskets that day. At last I impressed upon them the urgency of the case, and they led me into a vast hall piled up with baggage from which my CINTRA baskets were unearthed. A dusty giant was detailed to unpack and to examine their contents, and, to my horror, I saw my beautifully packed models fished out of their masses of tissue-paper, roughly shaken to discover if any contraband gold or jewels were hidden in their folds, and thrown upon a pile of sooty sacks. Another man, dustier if possible than the first, was fetched to sew huge cardboard labels on to the delicate gowns with a packing-needle and string. Then the large tin Customs sample-seal, like a pill-box, was snapped on in a conspicuous place and the number registered ; the dress also being sealed with the black finger-marks of the sempster.

Having heard much of the independent character of the Americans, like Agag I decided to walk delicately. I said tactfully : " I can't bear seeing a man doing a woman's work. Won't you let us do the sewing for you while you do something more important ? " The man grinned gratefully and handed me the needle and string. We used fine thread which the dressmaker had taken care to bring with her, and sewed the remainder of those hideous tin sample-seals *inside the linings* of the dresses.

When he had unpacked and examined about five models, my dusty giant suddenly held one aloft, turned it round and round, eyed it critically, and finally walked off with it to another and larger shed. Wondering what could possibly be contraband about that particular frock, after an astonished pause, I followed him. He was standing amid a crowd of equally grimy men and displaying the dress. As I joined them I was just in time to hear him say—

" Say ! Isn't this a peach of a gown ? "

So that was all. He was actually admiring my design. I told the men how glad I was that a few American citizens liked my work because, in a few days, I should be exhibiting my dresses to an audience of New Yorkers ; that, frankly, I was terrified, knowing what beautiful models were brought over from France every year. Whereupon one of the packers remarked : " Say, Ma'am, you can knock spots off Paris ! " And my nice giant further encouraged me by saying : " Don't you let 'em put it over you, Ma'am. You can put it over *them*—like a tent."

Finally the great chief of Customs came up, and, having looked over my models, said that they were the best that he had seen pass through the Customs in all his twenty-three years' experience. (After the Plaza Shows I heard that he and his wife had attended them both.)

The examination over and the dreaded repacking of

the models finished at last, my tribe of grubby men shook me warmly by the hand, and, wishing me all the luck in the world, promised to think of me on the great day of the Show.

This peculiar, and so un-English incident, gave me great encouragement, and, in the jargon of the Americans, " Sure I needed it before I was through."

LIII.

Once safely through the Customs, I then had to transfer the models to the Plaza Hotel where the Show was to be held in a few days' time. The manager had reserved me a dressing-room in which to store them, and had had a special lock put on to the door to which only he had the key. Nothing could exceed the wonderful kindness of every member of the staff of that vast hotel, from the manager to the hall porter. It struck me as very strange to see the amazement on the face of an American when he was thanked. A waiter brought me some coffee one day and naturally I said, " Thank you." He was turning away, but returned and asked : " What's that, Ma'am ? " I replied : " I only said ' Thank you.' " He stared and then said in a wondering voice, " Same to you," which struck me as so odd.

During those first days, John refused all invitations and reserved himself entirely for me. Without him, I do not know how I could ever have got through the work that had to be done—the unpacking and ticketing of the models and the complete revisal of my wholesale and retail price-lists. He spent hours and hours with me in that suffocatingly hot dressing-room adding on the additional duty and translating the result into American dollars—with a variable exchange. When I thanked him, almost tearfully, for his help and support, he just screwed in that eyeglass and looked at me with surprise, saying quietly : " But I only came out here to be of service to my brave Woman."

I found that one member of my invisible and unknown Committee had conceived the brilliant idea of inviting all the big furriers, jewellers, milliners, and stores of New York to exhibit a specimen of their goods with a CINTRA model, on payment of the sum of 300 dollars, the name of each firm to be announced with the exhibit as the mannequin appeared on the platform. A magnificent way of increasing the sum of money we hoped to amass for the Soldiers' and Sailors' Fund ; but I discovered, to my consternation, that the lady who had had this inspiration apparently had not known that I was only showing evening dresses and cloaks, for she had accepted tweed and broadtail overcoats, leather hats, &c., to be shown with my models. I was faced with disaster unless I could somehow get suitable goods and accessories substituted for this incongruous collection of stuff.

Since I had been pledged to exhibit these American accessories, I insisted upon my right to see and choose them myself, and I was obliged to make a hectic tour of twenty-five Stores (which took me two whole days) demanding interviews with the head of each firm. And no one who has not tried to get an immediate interview with a commerce king in New York can ever realise the difficulties that beset me. My hostess and the other members of the Committee were far too busy to accompany me on these expeditions, and had it not been for the kindness of a New York taxi-driver I should never have got anywhere.

The first one I hailed was placidly chewing gum. He rolled it into a safe corner of his mouth and just said, " Where'll I take yer ? " very abruptly, and resumed his chewing. Instantly I threw myself upon his mercy. I said : " Well, I'm a poor fool from England and I shan't know if you drive me to Virginia, so I will put myself

entirely in your hands, and you shall look after me."
He stopped chewing, gave me one look to see if I were
pulling his leg, then, seeing that I was in earnest, he just
said, " Right, Ma'am. You've said it."

I then gave him a list of all the shops I wished to visit,
and he got into the taxi beside me (*not* dipping the flag
until our consultation was over), licked the stump of a
pencil, and proceeded to number my shops in the order
in which we should pass them, to save me time and
money. He explained that the avenues ran north and
south and that the streets ran east and west, crossing
the avenues. A very easy system once you grasp it.

Then he drove me to each shop in turn, always insisting
upon accompanying me in the elevator up to the 103rd
floor, or wherever I had to be whirled, and, when I
eventually emerged from my interviews, he was always
awaiting me on the landing quietly chewing gum or
smoking a cheroot. He was as a father to me. At the
end of the afternoon I gave him my purse and said :
" Now you'd better take what you ought to have, for I
don't yet understand your American money." Whereupon, having snapped up the flag so that the meter ceased
to register, he once again entered the cab, and, sitting
by my side, gave me a little lesson on the American
currency, telling me the exact fare that I owed him and
no more.

" Where do *you* come in ? " I asked him, smiling.
" Well, you ain't no call to give me a cent, Ma'am,"
he said, " but if you want to, the usual thing is 10 per
cent "—which in New York is the minimum tip. Needless
to say he got the maximum one, but he obviously didn't
expect it. We ended by shaking hands warmly on my
host's doorstep, and he told me about his little daughter,
who was on the ' Movies,' and promised, if he could,
to bring her to see me at the Plaza. He was a most
delightful person, and every driver we met was equally
kind. We had heard so much of the incivility of the

New York taxi-man, that it is a delight to me to
testify that I have never been more courteously and
chivalrously treated than I was by this much-abused
type. It has pleased me since to hear Americans who
had visited London speak just as enthusiastically about
our taxi-men.

I shall never forget those visits to the New York shops,
nor the choosing of those gorgeous accessories. I selected
long chains of marvellous pearls, a few diamond rings,
glorious fur coats worth thousands and thousands of
dollars ; fans of enormous ostrich feathers and Paradise
plumes, jewelled head-dresses, vanity cases and hand-
bags. I managed to persuade those managers who had
already supplied unsuitable goods to be shown with my
models to substitute something even more 'stunning'—
their favourite word—which would harmonise with my
evening gowns. This they eagerly did, and in every case
we parted friends for life, and I left them purring.

But what anxious and exhausting work it was ; and
in what a strange and bewildering world I found myself.
Still, I suppose it was a very salutary experience for me,
this visit to New York. English people are apt to pride
themselves upon their independence and self-sufficiency,
but when I first arrived in America I felt as helpless as a
child and just as small.

If I could have taken active part in the arrangement
of my own Shows, or at least have known what was
being arranged, I should perhaps have regained my
English calm and efficiency, for by this time I had really
learned my job, and, in London, difficulties merely stimulated me. But here in New York, I felt as nervous as
a cat.

The day of the Shows was drawing ever nearer, and I
began to agitate for an immediate rehearsal. I said that
in England I sometimes rehearsed and timed a Dress
Show twenty times before its actual public performance.
I was informed that in America they 'got a hustle

on ' ; my plodding and painstaking English ways were ridiculed ; and I was assured that all would be right on the day.

Still, I felt so unhappy about it all that I persuaded John to shirk some evening engagement and to come to my aid.

So together we stayed at home that evening, and at his suggestion I rang up every member of my Committee to get the information I craved. Many of them were out, but I learned from one of them that a rehearsal was arranged for the next day—a dress rehearsal and a Press rehearsal—with photographs—*at the same hour*.

Ye Gods !

I also learned that fifty well-known American actresses had consented to act as mannequins for the afternoon performance, and that the Junior League, a band of *débutantes* who help certain charities during the winter season, would wear my frocks in the evening.

I was aghast.

How long interval would there be between the performances, I asked ; knowing from past experience that models must be adapted to their wearers.

" Oh—perhaps two hours," I was informed.

Had dressers been provided ? I inquired anxiously.

Oh no, the girls could help each other ; and the Junior League were sure to bring their maids or relations to dress them, I was assured.

Would there be ample accommodation for all these fifty ladies, *and* their maids and relations ? I asked. How many dressing-rooms would the management of the Plaza give us ?

One big one, was my answer.

I could only foresee—CHAOS—and waited apprehensively for the *one* rehearsal next day.

Well—it was very funny. I see the humour of it now. Both sets of mannequins had been called to rehearse at the same time and in the same place. When I entered that dressing-room, I was confronted by one hundred very charming and lovely young ladies already fighting over the fifty frocks that I had provided. It was a case of might is right. The Gentlemen of the Press were there in dozens, awaiting the appearance of the mannequins in the big ballroom. As each strong successful girl secured a dress and put it on, she was seized upon by a Press Photographer and swept off—somewhere—never to appear again.

Of course we never had a rehearsal. We never got near the stage. I never knew which of the ladies were the professional actresses nor which the Junior League *débutantes*. I was giddy and very near tears, and I needed all my courage not to abandon my models and flee from America with John on the first homeward-bound ship. Only the thought that my CINTRA business had been created to help him to finish his History, deterred me. I MUST—somehow—make a success of this American venture, and it would be wickedly ungrateful to leave our kind hostess in the lurch after all her hard work over my Shows. In her, I had one very efficient and keen helper who was also a loyal and enthusiastic friend, but she, being the moving spirit of a hundred and one charities and 'Movements,' knew that the time she could give me must be limited, and this was why she had secured that one commercial woman with full professional training and experience, as Chairwoman of my Committee. It was no one's fault but everyone's misfortune that this competent woman's health had collapsed on the very day that our ship docked.

LIV.

The dreaded day came at last. The golden ballroom of the Plaza Hotel was filled with three thousand gilded chairs, a stage had been erected at one end of the room draped with black velvet curtains which, when parted in the centre back, displayed a hidden miniature staircase also covered with black velvet. A little black rostrum was arranged on the right-hand side of the stage, down by the footlights, for CINTRA herself, who was to act as Mistress of the Ceremonies ; limelight lamps had been placed in the gallery at the far end of the ballroom opposite the stage, and the orchestra was to play immediately beneath the stage, screened by a jungle of palms and exotic flowers.

The manager of the Plaza had most kindly allotted me a suite of rooms for the occasion, and so I dressed myself early in the fantastic gown I had designed for myself. It was a swathed, sheath-like, sleeveless, dress of black chiffon velvet with an exaggerated train ending in a point. From one bare arm, just above the elbow, hung a long black chenille tassel with an acorn-top of brilliants. My head was capped with a close-fitting black velvet turban from which two long ostrich feathers, held by a diamond star, curled to my waist. I wore one huge marquise ring of brilliants, diamond buckles on my black velvet shoes, and I carried a slender black-tasselled stick with a diamond knob.

Mine was the first entrance. I had to pose between the parted curtains at the back of the stage, walk down the staircase to slow music, meander across the stage, and finally take up my position upon the rostrum from whence I must formally open the proceedings.

Needless to say, I had implored John to compose me a short introductory verse which I might recite instead of making some conventional speech, and he had immediately complied with a little *rondeau* which began by gently mocking the alien-papers we had been obliged to fill in before landing in New York, and the very odd questions we had to answer as to our bodily and mental health, powers of self-support, and religious and political convictions. I still remember the first eight lines of it—

" An alien in New York ! Oh hear me swear
    Full fifty dollars in my purse I bear.
    Sound, crimeless, sane am I ; no anarchist
    (Save against fashion) ; no polygamist—
    Husband have I but one—Nor is't my care
    With speech or bomb to blow into the air
    The President and Congress—Spare, oh, spare
    One who for four short weeks would fain exist
    An alien in New York "—&c., &c.

In this way I introduced myself, standing with the usual knocking knees upon my rostrum.

I was given a wonderful reception ; after which I posed immovably and waited for the entrance of the first mannequin, for I was to announce the name of each model ; of the girl who was wearing it ; and of the firms providing accessories, as each girl appeared through the curtains. A prompter was posted behind me, hidden by the black velvet curtains which screened the back of the stage. She was very necessary because, as the Show had never been arranged or timed, the first girl who happened to be ready was pushed on. So that I never knew who was going to appear, or in what.

My life was further complicated by the fact that my prompter would whisper to me that Miss Someone was appearing in such-and-such a model, wearing So-and-So's pearls. I would announce these facts in a resonant voice to the enormous audience and constantly feel a dig in the back, then hear an agitated voice hissing behind me : " Oh NO ! I see she's changed the pearls for Somebody Else's diamonds," and then give me yet another name. The corrections became so numerous that I feared the exhibiting firms would be foaming and furious, and at last, partly to appease them and partly to justify myself to the audience who could not hear the prompter's revisions, I said to the sea of faces—

" Ladies and gentlemen ! Forgive me ! This is really not my fault. I can only imagine that the accessories provided by the New York firms to be worn with my dresses are *so* lovely that the ladies are fighting over them in the wings."

A roar of applause and laughter, and the situation was saved. I heard afterwards that the firms concerned were enchanted with the muddles, for, whereas they had paid three hundred dollars each for their names to be mentioned from the platform *once* during the performance, owing to the corrections, each of them was announced and their goods described about six times.

The lovely ' Dolores,' the famous Ziegfeld star for whom I had designed stage-dresses for the American production of 'Sally,' was undoubtedly the fairest of the fifty beautiful actress-mannequins. Although playing to crowded houses in Philadelphia, she yet found time to come over and help me by wearing some of my models. Her slim height, graceful leisurely movements, statuesque poses, and wonderful willowy walk produced roars of enthusiasm from the audience whenever she appeared, and the presence of so famous a star contributed enormously to the success of the Dress Parade. For, miraculously I thought as I remembered the total lack of rehearsals and detailed preparation, the *matinée* was a tremendous success. We had a splendid audience ; they applauded each item vociferously as if at a popular play ; and afterwards I held a little Court of artists, authors, pressmen (of course), actor-managers, movie-stars, Jew financiers, business men, and the usual crowd of women. I had more compliments on my work than I had ever received in my life, and the nicest of all was this one : " The gowns look as though they were designed by a sculptress and not by a dressmaker." I loved that, because draperies were our strong point. I was very happy, and if only my loyal staff of workers at Hampstead could have been there too, to share in the success they had helped to make, my cup of happiness would have been full.

The *matinée* successfully over, there was still the evening

performance to come, and so, having set my professional
helpers to the work of altering the gowns to fit another
set of wearers, I went to my suite of rooms, tore off my
dress, put on a *peignoir*, and rang for some of that heavenly
American coffee. Whilst waiting for it, I thought I
would open the big windows, for the over-heated rooms
were stifling me. With a great effort I managed to push
up the double windows, but was scared by the result.
Apparently a tornado had arisen during the *matinée*,
and in two instants the ends of the sheets were whipped
from the great bed and flapping like sails, the curtains
threshing the walls, and everything that was not anchored
in that room was flying about in the air. The waiter,
appearing at that tempestuous moment and seeing my
frantic efforts to shut the window again, quietly put
down his tray of coffee and sandwiches and came to my
aid. When we had closed the window I sat on the untidy
bed and gasped. Did these cyclones often occur in New
York? I inquired anxiously. Then he informed me that
no wind had arisen, but that little exhibition I had just
seen was caused by the terrific draught of air between
gigantic buildings. It was always like that, and no one
on the first floor could ever open a window.

So I drank my coffee to steady my nerves and quietly
stewed in the fug until John came to visit me. He had
promised to station himself during the performance in
the gallery at the far end of the ballroom with the limelight men and to report to me faithfully, afterwards, as
to audibility, visibility, and the general effect of the Show
as heard and seen from the most distant point.

" Was it all right ? " I asked him eagerly at once.

" I never saw my Peg look more wonderful," was his
answer.

" But the Show ? " I pressed him impatiently. " How
did it go ? The audience seemed to like it, but OH the
agony and the muddles ! Were they very apparent ? "

" I only saw my Woman," he replied softly. So I

had to find out from others how my Dress Parade had struck them.

An hour and a half later my bedroom was invaded by a flushed and indignant young lady — one of my *débutante*-mannequins who rushed in to implore me to arbitrate in a discussion as to whether she or her best friend should wear a certain dress. My troubles had begun again.

I went down to the dressing-room.

Contrary to my expectations I thoroughly enjoyed the evening Show, and so did John, who told me afterwards that he perambulated the huge ballroom, its balcony and its gallery, to watch the proceedings from different angles, so that he might, this time, give me a faithful report of his impressions of the Dress Parade as a whole.

Some of my nervous apprehension had worn off, for I had realised that things *did* get themselves done—somehow—in New York. As a matter of fact the Junior League is a very highly disciplined body. If a girl joins it, she really has to work hard and to attend rehearsals of any Show they are doing. There is a Seasonal Captain whose orders must be obeyed on pain of expulsion, and this Captain had organised private rehearsals, taught the *débutantes* how to walk, to curtesy, and how to display a dress. American girls are very intelligent and daring, and also very lovely, and as each girl appeared and did some original little 'stunt' of her own, suitable to the frock she was wearing, I found myself wanting to applaud her from my rostrum. For instance there was the dance frock—very fluffy, young, and diaphanous, which I called 'Primavera.' The child who wore it had a head of short golden curls and an apple-blossom complexion. She floated in through the curtains and improvised a really lovely joyous little dance, looking the embodiment of spring and displaying my dance-dress to perfection. She was encored twice.

My bride appeared with a gigantic shower-bouquet of lilies-of-the-valley (at one dollar a spray) provided by a proud mamma. The orchestra struck up a wedding-march and she walked demurely to the footlights, turned, and walked back to the black velvet platform steps where she knelt for a moment with her back to the audience, showing every detail of my bridal gown and its train quite perfectly. I was so grateful to her because I was rather proud of the train of that dress. That Dress Parade had all the elements of surprise and delight for me, the Designer ; and I enjoyed every moment of it, never knowing what I should see next. It was really a most excellent Variety Show. My great triumph was that afterwards, in the dressing-room, each mother of each *débutante* asked me to reserve the frock her girl had worn, for they were all coming to buy them at my sale of models at the end of that week.

When all the sales were registered, the presentations made, the compliments paid and acknowledged, my *débutantes* and their attendant cavaliers finished up the evening by dancing in the Plaza ballroom which had been swiftly denuded of its chairs, and CINTRA, triumphant but utterly exhausted, was driven home to bed. The final scene of this tremendous day was not so picturesque. CINTRA, having no feet left to stand on, taking off her shoes at the foot of her staircase, painfully dragging herself up to her bedroom with the aid of husband and banisters, and sitting down to rest on every landing.

But I felt that the weariness was well worth while, for I had the satisfaction of knowing that I had not only been the means of helping the soldiers and sailors of America, but had more than recouped my expenses for journey, brocades, and workmanship, by the immediate sale of those fifty gowns and cloaks. I felt tired out, but so happy in thinking that my success would help the completion of the History.

LV.

John had accompanied me to America with the single idea of looking after me. He wanted to be at hand to support me in this new enterprise and to save me all he could. This he did in every possible way. I can see him now, toiling up those endless staircases in the Plaza Hotel laden with frocks, taking them up from the dressing-room to the wardrobe-room, his patrician head just emerging above the billows of brocade and tulle ; indefatigably pricing them and translating pounds into dollars for my lists. But, of course, the moment it was known that he was in America he was besieged by learned Societies and Universities, all wanting him to be their guest of honour or to lecture to them.

An American officer whom he had met in England was very keen for him to address the students of West Point on Armistice Day (which happened also to be the day of my sale of models), and afterwards that we should return to his house as his guests. John, loving youth, and particularly young soldiers, consented to talk to the boys and refused to accept any fee. I always attended his lectures, when possible, and it was arranged that I should rush down to West Point the moment my sale was over and join him there.

On the morning of the 11th of November I was awakened by the tempestuous entrance of my hostess. She came into my bedroom, white and agitated, brandishing a copy of ' The New York Times.'

" Isn't this perfectly monstrous ? " she fumed. " What does it mean ? "

I took the newspaper from her and read in huge leaded captions that my husband's lecture at West Point had been cancelled—the first we had heard of this. In a long and offensive article John was accused of abusing Americans while enjoying their hospitality ; and, particularly, of criticising their conduct in the Great War.

My head whirled. During the war, as I have said, we
had entertained young American officers, lodging as many
as six at a time. We loved them, and, apparently, made
them very happy with us, for to this day they call us
their 'English parents.' We had also thrown open our
house and garden to hundreds of American Rotarians
and had given them, as I thought, a very good party.
John had written a charming little *rondeau* for their
invitation cards, and we had tried to be kind and hospitable. And only three days ago I had given two Dress
Shows in aid of the American soldiers and sailors. What
could this accusation mean?

Reading on, I realised that some malicious person had
dug out a volume of reprinted lectures which my husband
had given in Oxford (the Ford Lectures of 1911) in which
he criticised the character and conduct of Americans
(an unforgivable sin in America, " a country too young
as yet to be able to stand criticism," as a leading American
woman once remarked to me). This book of lectures
is entitled ' British Statesmen of the Great War,' and
' the Great War ' had been ignorantly—or mischievously—
read to mean the German war just over; whereas the
lectures dealt with the Great War of 1793-1814. Almost
incredible, but true.

Long after we returned to England we heard the true
story of what actually happened about that West Point
lecture, and it is foolish and fantastic enough to be
interesting.

We happened to be in New York when, owing to the
Irish troubles, there was an anti-English demonstration
all over America. A venomous Sinn Fein editor in Boston
saw his opportunity to dig up John's old volume of
lectures and to make mischief. Senator Weekes being
absent, this man telephoned to West Point and read an
extract from ' British Statesmen of the Great War ' to
a terrified Adjutant, who was asked whether, now, he
considered that this man Fortescue, who could so abuse

America and criticise the conduct of Americans *during the late war*, was a fit and proper person to address young American cadets on Armistice Day ?

The Adjutant, quite evidently scared, and not having the book in question to refer to, telephoned to Senator Weekes, who was staying in Washington. The Senator never having heard of the book and unable to get a copy, at once ordered the lecture to be cancelled ; and we read of its cancellation for the first time in ' The New York Times ' on the day itself. No word came, or has ever come, from Senator Weekes himself.

The more poisonous section of the American Press tried to infer that my husband's criticism and censure of America and Americans were expressions of the King's opinion, as my husband, being a member of the Royal Household, must be in close touch with the King. Rumours of this row in America were cabled over to England, and the Admiral's House telephone bell never ceased ringing. One reporter asked ' Odd,' our Scotch housekeeper, if she happened to have a copy of her master's new book, ' British Statesmen of the Great War.' She replied that her master had not published a new book for some time, but that she had just been dusting a book with that title, and she was sure that it was an *old* book. She was asked to go upstairs to his study and to verify the title and the date of its publication, so she scuttled away and then informed the reporter that it was indeed an old book of reprinted lectures published in 1911. The reporter was enchanted, laughed heartily, and told her that she had given England the laugh over America for such an ignorant blunder ; actually to have mistaken the Great War of 1793-1814 for the Great War of 1914 was too delicious. The matter was dismissed with a few sarcastic comments by the English Press ; but we, in America, the victims of that ignorant blunder, did not find it either amusing or delicious. The pressmen of New York were even more eager for details than those of England. The house in which we were staying was besieged by journalists, all of whom had attended my Dress Shows and given me enthusiastic notices in their newspapers. Others telephoned from early dawn until midnight. It seemed simplest to invite them all to the house at the same hour and to confront them *en masse*. This we did, and they arrived at 9 A.M. and surrounded John, who looked like a noble stag at bay amid a pack of hounds. But these were kindly intentioned hounds : they had liked my Shows ; had given them pages of eulogy ; and I had made friends with them from the moment when they posed me for my photograph and asked me to " Bust my best smile." Now they were on the scent of a good story, ' copy ' that would feed the voracious American public for at least a week ; but one and all were obviously sorry that the publicity they would give to this new sensation must crush all CINTRA'S success in America. They were quite evidently anxious to eradicate or minimise the bad impression these mistaken articles in the newspapers had given of my husband's character. None of the men had seen or even heard of the book from which the damning paragraph had been quoted ; but one and all tried to get him to say that ' The New York Times ' had misquoted and exaggerated what he had said. He sat in the midst of them, quite unshaken, smiling courteously, and repeating over and over again that although he had not a copy of the book with him, he was of opinion that the paragraph had been quoted quite accurately ; that these things *had* happened in the past ; that America had *not* played the game ; concluding with the words : " My practice is, has been, and shall be, to tell the truth without fear or favour. Even to please you, gentlemen, I cannot alter historical facts."

Sadly they went their way. They realised better than we did the effect this affair would have upon our American visit, and they doubtless knew that their editors would never print those last words of my Historian.

When the last man had gone, our host, who had been present, walked up to John and said quietly—

" I should like to shake you by the hand, sir. It has been a privilege to watch the behaviour of an English gentleman with his back to the wall."

After this, our dear hostess suggested that it was time to go over to the Plaza for my sale of models. I raised my eyebrows and merely said : " Wouldn't it be rather a waste of time ? " She smiled rather tremulously. She had worked very hard for the success of my Shows and was very anxious that I should reap some reward for my labours as well as the soldiers and sailors of America ; but she knew in her heart that all my promised sales were ruined.

However, she insisted that as the whole episode was founded upon a fantastic blunder, we must not skulk indoors but carry out the original programme. So over to the Plaza we went.

Of course none of the *débutantes* who had asked for their dresses to be reserved for them came to fetch them. The models were all arrayed attractively in the great ballroom with the names of their would-be purchasers pinned to them. In place of a crowd of excited buyers there were only the manager of the Plaza, who had been consistently kind and charming to me from the outset, and who was now genuinely concerned for me ; and a few friends of Nellie Rogers, who came to prove that they, at least, were loyal and did not believe the calumnies about my husband that they had read in the papers.

For the first half-hour no one appeared. Nellie had to go home for an interview, and her friends, having duly admired the dresses and striven to encourage me, accompanied her. I was left alone with my rejected models in that vast room. The waters of desolation flowed over my head. The irony of it all ! I had made this great effort to help John with his History, and the enterprise had been wrecked by an historical fact chronicled by him !

I should get the duty money, paid to bring in my models, refunded, when I took them out of America again, unsold, so that I could repay that thousand pound loan. But when I reached home I should be faced with heavy bills for materials and ornaments, the price of which would have been more than covered by the sale of the models in America. My great triumph in New York had now been completely annulled.

Well, we stayed in New York until the end of our visit in spite of the suggestion in the newspapers that we had been told to leave the country.

Our social programme was yet far from complete, and we wondered how many of these engagements might now be cancelled. The entertaining of us by official bodies, The English-Speaking Union and so forth, was over, but friends of our American friends had been eager to do us honour, and, to their credit (acting as they did against public opinion), they gallantly fulfilled their offers of hospitality. It was galling, however, to be eyed coldly by certain of their guests, who were barely civil when introduced to us, for John's explanation to the Press was never published.

Frank and Nellie Rogers merely emphasised their kindness and courtesy towards us although, doubtless, they suffered much adverse criticism for still harbouring us under their roof. Indeed, we were told afterwards that they had received a letter from a Sinn Fein leader threatening to blow up their house with a bomb unless they ejected us from it.

Our visit to them was very nearly at an end, and would terminate with my Dress Shows to be held in Philadelphia, organised by Dolores, who was playing there in ' Sally,' and an exceptionally charming lady of Philadelphia, Miss Frances Griscom, in aid of the Charlotte Cushman Club. This was a lovely little hostel for touring actresses, founded curiously enough by a staid old Quaker lady. Returning from some of her good works one night, this old lady was accosted by a pretty girl with a scared, tear-stained face, who asked her if she knew of respectable rooms where she might lodge. The girl added that she was a touring actress and that she had walked for hours in search of a lodging, without success, and was terrified that she might have to spend the night wandering about the streets of Philadelphia. Charlotte Cushman—all honour to her—found the girl shelter, and was so much shocked to think of the plight she was in, that she then and there founded a tiny residential Club for touring actresses, consisting at first of but two bedrooms, and when she died she endowed it with her small fortune. This was the origin of the now flourishing Charlotte Cushman Club of to-day, and I speak from bitter experience when I say that I heartily wish that such a residential Club existed in every English town that possesses a theatre.

Needless to say, I had been delighted when asked to give Dress Shows in aid of so deserving an object as the Charlotte Cushman Club, but now I wondered sadly whether even the energy and enthusiasm of the lovely Dolores who was staying in it at the time, and of Miss Frances Griscom who was to be our hostess in Philadelphia, could succeed in even half filling the theatre where my dress parades were to be held. Miss Griscom had had a photograph of Dolores in the daffodil-yellow Spanish lace dress, one of those that I had designed for her to wear in 'Sally,' reproduced in colour as a poster which was plastered everywhere in Philadelphia, Dolores herself canvassed for tickets among the audiences witnessing the nightly performance of 'Sally,' in which she was playing, and Mr Ziegfeld kindly gave his permission for her to wear the dresses I had designed for her to wear in that play, during my dress parades.

John and I, meanwhile, had been transported to the Griscom country house, a delightful place with quiet spacious rooms and great open fires. It was set in a large park where deer grazed peacefully under ancient

trees. We might have been in England. It was such a
rest to be free of the constant shrilling of the telephone
bell; such a comfort to be mothered by a white-haired
maid who had been with the family thirty years. As
an American girl remarked to me: "In New York it's
always 'How many dollars have you got?' and
in Philadelphia it's only 'Who was your great grand-
mother?'"

Our hostess and her brother, both keenly pro-English,
gave a delightful dinner in our honour, asking a few
intelligent Americans to meet us. At the end of it they
all drank John's health, and expressed regret and shame
for 'the late deplorable incident.' In return, I quietly
repeated the *rondeau* he had written for the Rotarian
garden-party we had so lately given at Admiral's House.

> " The Herring Pond ! 'Tis deep and wide,
> And, in close comradeship allied,
> America's and Britain's sons
> Sleep sound on its foundations.
> These were the men who fought and died
> That truth and honour might abide,
> And laughed at death, so they denied
> To stealthy over-weening Huns
>   The Herring Pond.
>
> " So let them sleep, securely ride
> Our peaceful fleets upon the tide,
> Hushed is the thunder of the guns.
> So rise to Heaven our orisons
> That goodwill reign on either side
>   The Herring Pond."

I thought that this simple *rondeau*, written after the
war and long before this ill-fated visit to America, would
prove more eloquently than any words of mine the
injustice of the allegations against my Man and of his
treatment in America. My feelings nearly overcame
me before I reached the end of the second verse, but I
got through it somehow, and everyone present rose from
the table, again drank John's health, and shook him
warmly by the hand.

We did have a fair-sized audience for the dress parades, and those who were present showed great enthusiasm. Dolores, in her 'Sally' gowns, brought down the house, and, when she made her final appearance, she led me down to the footlights to share the applause. Afterwards, in the dressing-room, she acted as saleswoman and mannequin for those who had been interested enough in the models shown that afternoon to wait after the *matinée* and ask their price. To my consternation, I saw a large lady descend upon Dolores, who had shed her last frock and was standing slim and lovely, in a silk chemise, and say to her, " Try on that green and silver gown for me, my girl. I thought it cute."

To my relief and gratitude, Dolores, instead of eyeing her haughtily, smilingly slipped on the dress, postured in it, expatiated upon its line and the beauty of the fabric, and eventually sold it for me. She was wonderful.

LVI.

We returned to New York for our final week, staying this time with Colonel and Mrs Grayson Murphy. We had known him in London during the war; CINTRA, with the aid of her Librarian husband, had stocked the library of his new house, and it was he, an old West Point cadet, who had arranged that famous lecture John was to have given there on Armistice Day. Now we were to be his guests.

The rest of my days in New York were taken up with business interviews. I was asked to dress two films, and the manager of a forthcoming theatrical production called one morning at 9 A.M. and asked me to improvise a Spanish dress, there and then, to give him an idea of what I could do. I rushed up to my bedroom and hastily draped a Spanish shawl around me, fixing its folds with pins. Luckily he admired the result, and wished to engage me as his designer on the spot, but I realised that this would mean 'staying over' until March, and so, of course, could not accept any of these offers, as all my London clients were waiting for me to design their spring clothes.

Then I had to rebuff and to avoid various persistent Jewish gentlemen who pursued me with business offers, wanting the sole agency for CINTRA gowns in the United States. One of them even got past the imported English butler—a great feat—and I found him, pen in hand and contract all ready for me to sign, waiting for me in one of the drawing-rooms when I emerged from a big farewell dinner-party. My host, smoking a long cigar and ostensibly looking at pictures in the adjoining room, was in reality listening to the eloquent proposition which was being made to me. I had come out of the inner drawing-room to answer a telephone call (the telephone never ceases from troubling in New York, and the weary are never at rest). My host drifted towards me, and without looking at me murmured, " Cintra ! If you sign anything before I look through it I'll never forgive you." I signed nothing and I dismissed my Jew.

We embarked on the *Mauretania* next day.

We had a long and a very rough crossing. I was so tired that I stayed in my bunk and slept through most of it. John was very joyous. He prowled about the decks in the worst weather, hanging on by his eyelashes, and then came below to gloat over the marvellous picture of his wife actually resting in bed.

I was a very shabby person when we embarked, for I had sold all my personal American outfit ' off my back ' before I left. As these were my own clothes, they had paid no duty, and could therefore be sold more cheaply than my show models. Not every woman in America is a millionairess. These sales, and the sums realised for certain of the less expensive models I had sold in New York and Philadelphia to my hostesses and a few of their friends, just paid our fares.

I had a very hard struggle to regain my solid footing when I returned to London. Business had stood still in my absence. Although I had left duplicate models at Admiral's House and a competent staff to carry on while I was away, all my customers preferred to wait until CINTRA came back from America and could design something individual for them. I had to redouble my efforts and work by day and far into the night to retrieve my financial position and pay my waiting bills.

LVII.

Just at this time Guy, my second brother, became engaged to Judith Upton. He found her in Sussex, and, after a very short acquaintance, wisely captured her for himself on the summit of one of the Downs. Judith was in every way the daughter-in-law dreamed of always by Daddie. We were to discover later, to our joy, that she was possessed of a sense of humour pungent as the turf of those Sussex downs, and a quick tongue which, though never malicious, was very often acidly, but justly, critical and always apposite. She was very active and energetic and a great talker; very excellent for the quiet slow-spoken Guy. He was of the salt of the earth; she would provide pepper—as well as sugar. We were all very happy about this engagement, and, of course, I at once suggested that my wedding-present to her should be her bridal dress and bouquet which I myself would make.

It was a straight mediæval gown with a square neck and golden girdle, and its long winged sleeves and veil were of an almost primrose-tinted chiffon. I made her a sheaf of arum lilies; the pistils of the lilies were to emphasise the golden note struck first by her heavy knot of hair. She had brought so much sunshine into our lives by becoming part of them, that I wanted her dress to be emblematic.

Daddie married them, and it was a happy little wedding. Guy wore his war-khaki uniform and looked quietly radiant.

John and I stayed the night with Mummie and Daddie in little Kitchen Court before returning to our work in London early next day, leaving the beloved parents happy because they knew their son's future to be in safe keeping.

For some time there had been talk of the advisability of a CINTRA branch in Lower London for the benefit of lazy ladies who found Hampstead too far for them to come for fittings during the season ; and now I and my staff decided that the moment had come for the further expansion of the business. John saw the trade advantages of such a step, but he had become more and more nervous about my health, which was steadily deteriorating. The mysterious poison had attacked me in several places, so that sometimes I had to undergo as many as three minor operations in a week. This sent him frantic, because there was no possibility of rest for me either before or after them. They had to be endured with a local anæs-thetic, or none at all, and be fitted in between my daily multiplying appointments. He argued that if I moved the business down to the West End, I should be busier than ever, and though, of course, he was glad of the success of my venture, he dreaded the extra work for me, and the fact that I should no longer be working more or less under his surveillance in Admiral's House. I argued that at any rate I should be nearer the various specialists who were trying to help me, and I promised to find a flat where I could have a private room with a large divan in it so that I could retire thither for rest between appointments. I knew that the divan would never hold my reclining body, but the idea of it comforted him ; and the thought that he would no longer be able to *see* me overworking, consoled me enormously, because I knew that whether in the north or west of London CINTRA could find no rest while her business prospered.

And so, after some difficulty, I once again over-persuaded John ; and then began my search for suitable premises, which I eventually found upon the second floor of number 28 Sackville Street. The rooms were large, airy, and sufficient for my purposes ; and the situation quiet but central.

Best of all, a lift brought me and my staff and customers up to the second floor.

When all was prepared, I asked John to announce the new venture in verse. He twinkled and retired for an hour to his study, emerging triumphantly with this *rondeau*—

> " In Sackville Street at number twenty-eight
> Is CINTRA found, yes CINTRA, who of late
> Kept shop at Hampstead. Now her work to crown
> She is descending to the lower town.
> To southward, pent within its walls too strait
> Roars Piccadilly, like a stream in spate.
> To North runs Vigo Street, demure, sedate.
> Betwixt these twain hath CINTRA set her down
> In Sackville Street.
>
> " Here, gracious ladies, CINTRA doth await
> Your coming, yours who best appreciate
> The grace of line and hue in every gown
> Which CINTRA fairly claims to be her own.
> She welcomes you to number twenty-eight
> In Sackville Street."

I didn't have to await the coming of the gracious ladies for very long ; their cars soon blocked Sackville Street and we were, as I had anticipated, busier than ever. Our first excitement was a late telephone call to Admiral's House from an agitated lady who had been for some time organising a *matinée* at the Hyde Park Hotel in aid of some pet charity of Princess Louise, Duchess of Argyll, who had promised to be present. The chief attraction of the afternoon was to be a Dress Parade arranged by a famous but temperamental dress designer who, two days before the *matinée*, telephoned to the Organiser to say that she had not been feeling well for some time,

nor in the mood to design. In short, the Dress Parade
that she had promised to provide could not take place.
Princess Louise, desperate, asked the Organiser to strive
her utmost to fill this blank in her programme. The
lady protested that it was Saturday, that all business
houses and dressmaking establishments closed at 1 P.M.,
and remained closed until Monday morning, and the
matinée was advertised for Monday afternoon. No one
could be expected to organise a dress parade over the
week-end. Princess Louise suggested that her Organiser
should ring up CINTRA and beg her to achieve the apparently impossible and so save the situation, and I got her
message at noon on Saturday afternoon, just before my
workrooms closed.

Rashly I promised to provide *something* in the way of
a Show, provided that it were explained to the audience
that this ' something ' had been improvised during the
week-end in response to an emergency call. Then I
rushed upstairs to find ' *Ninon*,' my head worker, and
to consult with her as to what we could produce at such
short notice.

Luckily we had some very lovely models already made
for stock, and I planned some *tableaux vivants* representing
seasons and sports of the year, and we rummaged in
cupboards to dress them appropriately. I was less nervous
on this occasion, because I felt that not much could be
expected of me in a day and a half—the complete day
being a Sunday.

John once more composed me a short rhymed speech
(which unluckily I forget) to explain the situation and to
excuse any shortcomings in my Dress Parade, and,
when I had delivered it from the platform, Princess
Louise, sitting in the front row, very graciously sent me
up her own bouquet of red roses.

This hastily improvised Show went off very well, and
some weeks afterwards a messenger came to Sackville
Street from Kensington Palace, asking me for patterns

of brocades because Princess Louise wished me to make her gown for the coming Court Ball. She chose a very lovely one of silver and black, and then came the day fixed for the fitting and I was asked to go with my fitter to the Palace.

I shall never forget that hot summer day. I was very, very tired, and the fitting was fixed for 6.30 P.M. when my workrooms would be closed. *Ninon*, to my horror, suddenly showed signs of collapse. Perhaps it was nervous excitement caused by the prospect of fitting a Princess of Royal blood in a Palace, combined with the heat of the day, but towards closing time she came into my office with a bright yellow face and glazed eyes to tell me that she feared that it would be impossible for her to go to Kensington Palace that evening. This was appalling, for I had but one fitter and that appointment must be kept at all costs. A friend who was having tea with me in my room, kindly offered to lend me her car and chauffeur to convey me and the poor *Ninon* to the Palace.

She packed us, with our dress-box, into her huge Rolls Royce and bade her chauffeur drive us to Kensington Palace. At length we arrived there, and he was driving up to the front entrance in great state when I horrified him by asking to be taken to the back door. He stared at me incredulously, and I had to explain to him that I had come on a business errand and must go in by the trade entrance.

We were admitted by some underling of the Palace and pushed into a little housekeeper's room from whence we were soon summoned to Princess Louise's bedroom on a floor above. She greeted me with a scolding. Why had I come to the back door? And once again I explained that to-day I was CINTRA, the dressmaker, and behaving as such.

The fitting was long and the room ill-lit. I had to hold an electric candle, taken from its sconce on the wall, to enable the Princess to see her own reflection in the

long mirror, while *Ninon* pinned and fitted the gown that
I had designed. Sheer terror of being overcome kept poor
Ninon normal during those two hours, and at length
we emerged from the bedroom, having satisfied a new
client and without having disgraced ourselves in any way.

LVIII.

CINTRA's ' tame poet ' wrote her an *extravaganza* to
send out to her customers, partly as a Christmas greeting,
but chiefly to impress upon their minds the address of
her new business premises in Lower London. Incredibly
quickly he produced it, and it had such a success and
charmed so many with its fantasy and impudence that I
must quote it. It was entitled—

CINTRA AT OLYMPUS.

" It struck the chief director of the Dinky-Pinky press
  That to interview the goddesses and print their views on dress
  Would be interesting copy, and would break some novel ground,
  And would send his circulation flying upward with a bound.
  So an eminent reporter, who was said to have some brain,
  Was sent to Mount Olympus on a special aeroplane,
  And he found a tattered label while he loitered at the gate,
  With the legend, ' CINTRA, Sackville Street, at Number Twenty-Eight.'

" Queenly Juno first received him, and she said, ' There's no denying
  That married life with Jupiter was sometimes very trying.
  He hadn't got the taste and the discernment that he might,
  That Danae was very plain—Europa was a fright.
  But all's completely altered since I got some lovely gowns ;
  He loves me, never leaves me, never thunders, never frowns,
  Never looks at other women ; and I owe this happy Fate
  To CINTRA, her of Sackville Street, at Number Twenty-Eight.'

" He then approached Minerva, and he got his flimsy ready ;
  And she said, ' No doubt you've heard that I'm a very learned lady ;
  But what could endless learning, boundless knowledge profit me
  Who began to feel my stoutness to a terrible degree ?
  Now see how skilful use of line in this most lovely dress
  Has given me back my figure and my former shapeliness !
  That CINTRA is an artist ; she's wonderful ; she's great !
  You know her place in Sackville Street ; at Number Twenty-Eight ? '

" And then spoke chaste Diana : ' I'm inflexibly severe
To foolish erring mortals, but—Endymion's a dear.
He's a shepherd and he's badly off ; with wool and mutton low,
And at last Olympia races he dropped a lot, I know :
But he bought me such a tea-gown, such a dream in line and hue,
Such drapery, such harmony, with " Di, dear, that's for you,"
And I've found out that he got it at a very modest rate
From CINTRA's shop in Sackville Street, at Number Twenty-Eight.'

" Then next came smiling Venus : ' When I rose up from the sea
No bathing-dress had been supplied for pretty little me.
But Vulcan didn't mind it ; and a certain God of War
Said, " Clothing, Venus ! Nonsense ! You look better as you are."
And—well you know the scandal ; it has reached your earthly flats,
For Olympus hums with gossip, and all goddesses are cats !
Still, I think the undraped business has been overdone of late,
So I'm off to CINTRA, Sackville Street, at Number Twenty-Eight.'

" Then last came little Iris, with her gauzy wings aflaunt,
(And he noted on his flimsy, ' Such a dainty *débutante !* ')
' Oh ! Are you the Daily Female ? Did you want to see my frocks ?
Look at this one ; just the colours of the loveliest hollyhocks !
Look at these—I've got a dozen—they would make a poet's themes :
In design and form and colour ; they are simply, simply dreams !
Don't you long to see me wear them ? Oh, I see you cannot wait !
Give my love to CINTRA, Sackville Street, at Number Twenty-Eight.'

" And the eminent reporter crushed his flimsy in his hand
And at twenty miles a minute he flew back to the Strand,
And the interview was headed in enormous leaded ' caps ' :
' FASHIONS CHANGING IN OLYMPUS.'
' UNDRAPED STYLES COMPLETE COLLAPSE.'
' CHASTE DIANA LOVES HER TEA-GOWN.'
' WHERE DOES VENUS GET HER UNDIES ? '
' LITTLE IRIS COMES TO SACKVILLE STREET ON TWO SUCCESSIVE
MONDAYS.'
' QUEEN JUNO AND MINERVA ARE COMING DOWN IN STATE
' TO VISIT CINTRA : SACKVILLE STREET, AT NUMBER TWENTY-EIGHT.' "

After this, CINTRA's clientèle became more varied and
picturesque every day. I was asked to design dresses for
the stage ; and Continental and Oriental visitors thronged
my showrooms. Eileen Forbes Sempill, Sir John Lavery's
daughter, brought me bevies of little Japanese ladies in
gay kimonos, all wishing to be Europeanised. Eileen,
loving to see them in their kimonos and dreading to see
them attired in the clothes of London, which she knew

would ill become them, brought them to me in the hope
that I could persuade them to wear something suitable
to their type. These Japanese clients exhausted me more
than all others because of their AWFUL Oriental impassivity
of countenance. Not a flicker of enthusiasm or disapproval
ever changed their mask-like faces. It was like showing
one's goods to wax dummy figures. I brought out gown
after gown for their inspection, and apparently they were
quite indifferent to all. It was always a surprise to me
when Eileen, their patient interpreter, would tell me
after half an hour's hard work : " Madame So-and-So
would like that tea-gown "—or that gown, or that cloak.

I shall never forget the visit of one little Japanese
lady of high degree who was brought by Eileen to Sackville
Street with her child of four years old (sex impossible to
distinguish, for it looked exactly like a Japanese doll,
swathed in its gay kimono with its round head and square-
cut fringe of sleek black hair) and a nurse carrying another
baby Japanese doll. While the mamma impassively
stared at dress after dress, shown to her by *Ninon* in the
front showroom, I, soon discouraged by that Oriental
immovability of feature, had escaped to my Cave-room
where I watched, fascinated, the ex-baby, seated upon
the black velvet cushion on the floor decking itself with
the barbaric jewellery displayed thereon and staring at
its reflection in the great mirror before it. The nurse
stood in the doorway holding the diminutive Japanese
doll in her arms and making queer clucking sounds to it.
Suddenly it began to squeak, and the nurse glided away
with it to the front showroom where I followed, to find
her in earnest conversation with its mother. Soon Eileen
came to me and asked in a whisper if there was any private
place where the mother might give the baby its tea, for
it would continue to squeak until fed. I suggested the
Cave-room—it seemed their proper setting—and promised
that I would allow no one to enter until the sacred rite
had been performed. The little Japanese mother took

her baby from the nurse, climbed the black velvet dais, and seated herself with native dignity upon the gilded throne under the jewelled Persian lamp. I shut the door and left those two to their happiness.

At that moment our old friend Charles Cust called to view CINTRA'S new premises. I took him round the flat and then gave him tea in my room.

" Where is this famous CINTRA'S CAVE I have read so much about ? " he asked me, licking his fingers after devouring buttery crumpets as fast as I could toast them for him. " You didn't show it to me. Why not ? "

I confided to him the lovely scene that was being enacted there at that moment, and his whole face grew soft.

" How beautiful. If that doesn't bring luck to your place I don't know what will," said that confirmed bachelor, rather wistfully, I thought.

But my personal luck was ' out.' The poison was spreading alarmingly. Sometimes I felt so exhausted that I seemed disembodied ; or that my body was just an empty ache ; and my spirit, still full of energy, despised it as a tiresome incompetent thing, not strong or vital enough to accomplish the orders dictated by the mind. Maddening, when John needed help so badly and the History was yet uncompleted ; and frightening, too, when even strange customers began to remark upon my fragile appearance.

It would be fatal for the business if the rumour spread that CINTRA was ill, for I knew that this report would instantly become exaggerated into an announcement that I was giving up—or had already given up—my shop.

My throat had been troubling me a good deal—what a bore one's ' vile body ' can be, and how right Saint Paul was so to describe it. John implored me to visit yet another specialist, who discovered new and strange microbes with long legs and whiskers living in the recesses of my throat—" that d——d poison " again. After consultation with the other doctors who had been treating me, he urged an immediate operation. So it was decided that I should be put into a private room in the St John and St Elizabeth Hospital in St John's Wood, just opposite to my surgeon's private house. " Then I can run in before breakfast and cut you up," he informed me callously.

He performed the operation quite beautifully, so the nurses informed me some time afterwards, all of them dazzled by his speed and skill.

I was very happy in that little hospital. Everyone spoiled me from the trained nurses to the nuns. Even the Reverend Mother provided ash-trays so that my male visitors might smoke, and came herself to see me every evening, bringing peace and calm with her as she quietly entered my room in her white habit and smiled gently and humorously down upon me. Extra vases had to be bought to hold a small part of the wonderful flowers showered upon me by my relations, friends, and work-girls, and the surplus beautified the public wards and the hospital chapel.

LIX.

When I was strong enough to be moved, sea-air was prescribed to brace me up again, and the doctors suggested my native air of the East Coast. But here John took a firm stand. He said the only hope of my regaining strength was to put at least the width of the Channel between me and my CINTRA business, otherwise he knew that I should be incessantly worrying about it and plaguing him to let me run up to London or allow *Ninon* to come to Suffolk to report progress to me. I had loved our holiday in Brittany. To Brittany therefore he would transport me. His Harrow fag, Horace Annesley Vachell, had written a book about Pont Aven. We would first go there, and, if we didn't like it, could find some little place on the coast near by.

" Brittany has no drainage system. The worst place to choose for someone recovering from a throat operation," croaked one.

" Much safer to stay within the reach of her doctors," advised another.

But John, surely having seen a gleam in my eye when my beloved Brittany was mentioned, remained firm to his original plan. Brittany it was to be. " I know my Woman will be happy there," he said to me.

Before we started he had a private consultation with my doctors. I was only told that a course of treatment and a diet had been prescribed for me to follow while I was away. In reality the doctors had told him very definitely that it was a case of the demise of me or of my CINTRA business, and, confronted with this decision, John had briefly remarked that " the business could go to hell."

Somehow he contrived to hide his consternation behind the mask that a hyper-sensitive man learns to put on to conceal his deeper feelings from the world. I only noticed that he appeared anxious and preoccupied, but then my delicate state, the unexpected expense of the operation, and the fact that he was to be hoisted out of his working groove, seemed sufficient to explain this ; and I mentally resolved to work harder than ever upon our return from Brittany, to make more money and to gain him the leisure he so needed to complete the History.

Pont Aven was a failure. The hotel that Mr Vachell had made so famous by his book, ' The Face of Clay,' was now utterly spoiled and tourist-haunted. And our first night was rendered hideous by the strains of the *binious* (a terrible form of bagpipe, ever after described by John as ' the b——y *binious* ') because we had inadvertently arrived on the day of the annual *fête*.

We found a little hotel on the coast, not far from Pont Aven, near a lovely rock-studded bay where I enjoyed delicious bathes. The hotel actually possessed a good chef, and we could choose our fish from a great tub near the kitchen door, daily filled with fresh leaping fish of every kind which were afterwards grilled over a charcoal brazier.

The delicious sea-bathing and open-air life (for the weather was perfect and we lived out of doors) gradually restored my strength and energy so that one morning I felt that I must soon go home and start work again.

I had heard of a very clever Parisian cutter and fitter who was anxious to come to London and learn English. For this reason she was willing to come and work for me at a moderate wage. It seemed to me a good idea to run up to Paris and interview her in person, so, over our morning coffee, I broached this idea to John.

To my intense surprise he, who had always been so keen on my CINTRA business and had hitherto enthusiastically backed all my enterprises, remained silent.

"But, dearest, I am quite recovered now," I urged. Still silence.

"But, John, only the other day—before I went into hospital—you agreed with me that it would be an excellent idea to engage this Frenchwoman."

With tightly compressed mouth, he took his pipe out of his pocket and began slowly and carefully to fill it.

As I watched those long fingers packing in the tobacco and looked at that bent head, suddenly with a blinding flash of intuition I knew the truth. But *he* must confirm it or I would never believe it.

"You are NOT going to tell me that I must *close my business?*" I whispered.

"Thank God, Sweetheart, you have guessed it," he said quietly, "for I had not the courage to tell you."

A block of ice seemed to drop on my heart. I became coldly businesslike.

"Very well. Then I must wire to *Ninon* to meet me in Paris, and we can arrange for the final sale of models and for the letting of 28 Sackville Street," I said.

With a great sigh of relief he rose and, kissing me gently as he passed, went down to the hotel office to send off the telegram.

I do not remember anything of that day. I only know that in the night, too tortured to sleep, I slipped out of the hotel and pounded for miles along the shore until, reaching a wild and desolate spot, I flung myself face downwards upon the sand-dunes and fought out my battle alone. Defeat seemed like the bitterness of death. The History was not yet finished, and I had built up that business to help John with all my vitality and love. Henceforth I was only to be a burden and an expense to him.

I believe my absence frightened him terribly, for he told me afterwards that, suddenly realising that I had gone, he went out with a lantern searching for me along the cliffs, fearing that in the darkness and my desperation I might have stumbled and fallen over. I ought to have fought that battle quietly in my bed, but at that moment I needed movement, the help of a wild wind—and solitude.

A few days later I met *Ninon* in Paris, and there I gave her instructions for a final sale for closing the business and dismissing my dear girls. I was very much stronger in health, but that ordeal I could not face, personally, then. We could not trust ourselves to be alone together, *Ninon* and I, and so we met only in public *cafés*. We had both been so proud of the CINTRA business.

And so it was done. . . .

For six months afterwards I had to live the life of an invalid, embittered by CINTRA inquiries and orders which still flowed in from customers and friends who, for some reason or another, did not know that my business was closed. One morning I opened a long official-looking envelope covered with impressive seals and Indian stamps, to find therein an order for eighteen State gowns from Lady Reading, then *Vice-Reine* of India. She told me that the metal tea-gowns she had bought from me before leaving England had never tarnished, even in the heat and damp of India, and therefore she was sending me a more important order. Tragically I handed the letter to John, and then asked him if he would help me to make a great bonfire of all my CINTRA books, designs, and newspaper notices : " It will be easier for me to forget," I told him. " And from the ashes of my failure we can perhaps grow roses."

" Don't feel bitter, Sweetheart," he begged me very gently. " Every experience in life has its value. Without your stage training you could never have built up CINTRA, and you will find that the great study of human nature you have had while running this business will one day prove precious to you."

And so we made our bonfire. . . .

LX.

Soon after the closing of CINTRA, ' Odd ' received the bad news that her mother in Scotland was very ill. ' Odd ' adored her mother, and we saw that she could never be happy away from her. We needed her, as ever, but it was kinder to let her go, and go she did.

We had a very hard winter that year. The heights of Hampstead were covered with snow and the ponds were frozen. Everyone in London seemed to be tobogganing on the slopes of the Heath or skating on the ponds, and offended swans, finding their water frozen hard and invaded by two-legged beasts, wandered about, furious and disconsolate, not knowing where to go. One morning Eve called for me and persuaded me to toboggan with her, and, whilst shooting down hills and colliding with thorn bushes, I suddenly saw our ' dotty ' old gardener with his toothless wife disporting themselves in like manner upon tin tea-trays. I laughed so much that I fell off our toboggan into a snow-drift, and when I got home to Admiral's House I felt so much exhilarated and amused that I seized a pencil and tried to describe in words our enjoyable but somewhat undignified morning.

John came in later bright-eyed and pink-nosed leading by the hand Marjory's little step-daughter Sheila who was grizzling over a grazed knee. He had taken her for a walk on the Heath and she, seeing other children sliding on the frozen ' Leg-of-Mutton ' pond, must needs slide too. John, an expert slider in his boyhood, becoming exasperated by the child's clumsy efforts to keep her balance, could not resist giving her a demonstration of how such things should be done, and, gallantly striding out upon the ice, had led the sliding procession of all the little hooligans of London, Sheila doing her best to imitate his movements. Except for the grazed knee, they appeared to have enjoyed themselves immensely, but I was rather apprehensive lest an observant photographer—for there were hordes of them at Hampstead that day taking pictures of the unusual phenomenon of winter sports in Hampstead—should ' spot ' John sliding on his pond, and that I should see pictures of him in the act under large headlines in the ' Daily Sketch ' or the ' Daily Mirror '—

" KING'S LIBRARIAN IN JOYOUS MOOD " or " THE HISTORIAN OF THE BRITISH ARMY ON HOLIDAY." Instead, I saw in the ' Evening News ' my own account of the winter sports in Hampstead, because, when he had read my bubbling story of our morning's adventures on the Heath, he had laughed immoderately ; and, thinking that others would laugh too if they read it, he had sent it off, secretly, to the ' Evening News,' telling them only to print it if they considered that it had genuine merit. They gave it a prominent place the day they received it, and I knew nothing about all this, until, meeting the companion of my adventure on the Heath, she tackled me for describing her in print as ' a staid matron of my acquaintance.'

This was the beginning of a new era for me. I realised joyfully that if my first idiotic bit of writing could be deemed worthy of immediate publication, I might still perhaps help John by earning money with my pen. And suddenly the desire to write and the delight of writing was born in me. Deprived of the means of self-expression with lovely fabrics, I now found that I could paint prose-pictures and pour out my thoughts and observations upon paper, and I went on writing.

The day the postman brought me that first cheque for the winter sports article was one of the happiest of my life. Breaking my strict rule never to enter John's study when he was working unless to bring him his ' boozle ' prescribed by the doctor, I went in now and laid the cheque silently upon the page of history that he was writing.

Startled from intense concentration upon his subject, not even realising that this outrage of interruption had been perpetrated by his wife, he first frowned fiercely, looking at the cheque with abstracted and exasperated gaze, then dragging himself out of the past with an intense effort he suddenly grasped what that slip of pink paper meant to me—to us.

Pen dropped from long fingers, eyeglass from eye, and that lovely ' special ' smile dawned in the brilliant eyes as he looked up at me and held wide his arms.

Military operations were temporarily held up.

My next little triumph was when Sir Owen Seaman, editor of ' Punch,' accepted an article I wrote " In Defence of the Mongrel." Someone had suggested in ' The Times ' that all mongrel dogs should be exterminated and only pure-bred dogs allowed to survive. At once I thought of the gay galaxy of mixed breeds which disported themselves so amusingly on Hampstead Heath. Always, when we walked there, we were adopted by a mongrel of sorts who insisted upon escorting us, and John delighted in the sports of these delightful freak-dogs as much as I did. Hampstead Heath would never be the same were

these dear Pomerollies, Spalmatians, Aberdoodles, and
other fascinating mixtures exterminated. I was spurred
to describe them in their defence. And Sir Owen wrote
to me in his own hand to thank me for my little story,
and to tell me that he intended to illustrate it. It was
illustrated by the famous E. H. Shepard who, I have
since been told, spent hours deciding which end of which
breed he should illustrate—the Spalmatian—the head of
a Spaniel and the tail of a Dalmation ? Or vice-versa.

Encouraged by the honour and glory of acceptance by
' Punch,' I wrote odd articles on anything that occurred
to me and sent them in to ' The Times,' in the diffident
hope that they might perhaps be printed in the last column
of the Court Page where queer articles often appear.
They were.

The ' Evening News ' started asking me to write upon
given subjects ; the ' Daily Chronicle ' did likewise.
Other papers followed suit. My journalistic friends who
had been so much intrigued by CINTRA's Dress Shows,
her Cave and her garden-parties, started ringing up to
find out her views on this or that for a symposium ; and
thus editors were reminded that the Winifred Fortescue
who had suddenly burst into the journalistic world had
once been CINTRA, the dress-designer and house-decorator,
and they wrote to her from time to time asking her for
an article on these subjects. ' The Times ' engaged me
to write their " London Fashions."

And so, from that moment I became busy and much
happier. Once more I could be of use to John instead of
an expense and a drag. In print, I could still help my
débutantes and those women who wanted advice about
their clothes and houses. I must put my feet up for the
prescribed hours of rest, but now, instead of lying inert
and despairing, I could take with me a pencil and a block
of paper and scribble away the days, weeks, and months
of what would otherwise have been for me a longer and
drearier winter than Hiawatha's.

LXI.

After seven months of coddled physical inaction I began to 'sit up and take notice,' so that in the spring of 1925, in the month of April when lambs begin to waggle their tails, a proposal from the editor of the 'Morning Post' that I should inaugurate a Women's Page, made me wag mine. The Women's Page was only to appear on three days a week. I might choose my own contributions, and all I, personally, was asked to do was to contribute one leading article and one original dress design weekly and to edit the pages. I should have my own private office in the 'Morning Post' building so that on the days when my pages were being set up I could supervise them in my own room. Most of my work I could do at home. It should not be exhausting.

And so I accepted the post.

I was very keen to make my Women's Pages fairly intelligent, not only dealing with problems of clothes and complexions. It seemed to me that the 'Morning Post,' essentially an Empire paper, should represent the women of the Empire and their work. But, for the first issue, not having had time to get in touch with any possible contributors, I was obliged to furnish all the material for my page myself, in addition to an original design and the leading article. Somehow I managed this, and went down to my office in the 'Morning Post' building, where I was handed over to a very severe-looking grey-haired man who had been alternately Day Editor and Night Editor on the 'Morning Post' for many years, Mr William Hutcheon, who, I was informed, would teach me how to set up my page.

This important personage shook hands with me coldly but courteously, eyeing me with a very distrustful canny Scotch eye.

However, he soon found out that his charge was both

333

docile and diffident, eager and only too willing to learn all that he could impart ; and then, gradually, he unbent. He brought me a flat brass measure, marked out into column, half-column, and quarter-column lengths, with CINTRA engraved upon it. This, he told me, was my ' badge of office.' Next he telephoned up to the print-room to ask if Mrs Fortescue's copy was ready, and presently a ' printer's devil ' in a splashed white coat appeared carrying in his hands yards of printed strips of paper with the ink still wet from the printing press.

Next Mr Hutcheon spread out an old copy of the ' Morning Post,' and then taking those long strips of paper (my various articles and paragraphs) he began to cut them apart from each other and to piece them together, like a puzzle, upon the page before him until every column was filled either with my writings or with advertisements, and the page was fully ' set up.'

As he snipped and selected, he laughingly remarked that authors seldom realised that when their articles were placed in the most important position upon the page it was often not because of the merit of their work but because an article of that particular length happened best to fill in that particular vacant space.

The Women's Page arranged to his satisfaction, Mr Hutcheon (who had steadily become more and more human) was actually persuaded to stay and drink a cup of tea with CINTRA.

The hot tea, and perhaps my prattle, thawed that Scotch reserve a little, and, when he finally rose to depart, the little friendly grin that accompanied a hearty handshake told me that I had gained a friend, for which I was very, very glad, for, in the way of me, I had liked him the moment he entered my room, and I had wanted his friendship.

When we had finished our tea, Mr Hutcheon warned me that I must stay awhile in my office in case of possible changes or last-minute additions to my page. Sometimes, at the eleventh hour, some important advertisement might come in which at all cost must be inserted, even though it meant cutting out a complete article.

So I stayed on after he had bidden me a kindly farewell, and, sure enough, very soon after his departure, there was a loud knock at my door and there entered a ' printer's devil,' hot and ink-splashed, flapping a wet page, to tell me that some firm had withdrawn their advertisement for this issue, leaving a blank which would take 400 words to fill. The paper was just going to Press, and would I please, with all speed, produce 400 words to fill that blank.

I had no reserve of articles, and so had to think of some subject and swiftly to produce those 400 words myself, which I *somehow* did, with the ' printer's devil ' waiting in the room.

I found that I was not strong enough in health to run a household, help John, and also produce pages of a newspaper. Realising that my new salary would enable us to engage a housekeeper, I decided to advertise for one at once and to relegate the machinery of the house to her.

Through the ' Morning Post ' I found little Mrs Smith, one of those old-fashioned housekeepers, now, alas, almost extinct, who were the salt of the earth. She appeared one day, very trim and severe in a tight-fitting black dress with white bands around throat and wrists, a large gold watch suspended by a solid gold chain from the belt which encircled her neat waist, her ' Alexandra fringe ' curled and netted under an eminently respectable toque. Looking at me with large blue eyes which gazed at me frankly through owlish steel-rimmed spectacles, she sat (after much persuasion), her tiny black-gloved hands folded in her lap, and asked me to give her details of the situation.

I liked her at sight, and felt certain that she was the woman for me if I could only persuade her to come.

But those clear honest eyes compelled me to equal
honesty.

" If you come here, Mrs Smith, you will have a very
hard time at first until you get things straightened and
organised. The house is in an awful condition, and I
haven't time to cope with it all." Encouraged by her
smile, I poured forth the story of my illness, the closing
of CINTRA, ' Odd's ' sudden departure, and so on. " I
haven't even yet had courage to transform the house
back again from business premises into a home," I confessed to her. " Before we discuss anything you had
better see for yourself the mess we're in and then you
can decide if you feel like tackling it." And I took her
upstairs and threw open the door of the dismantled
drawing-room, wherein were piled rolls of material,
cardboard boxes, Italian cushions, and all the surplus
stock left over after the final sale.

" Tch—tch—tch," clucked little Mrs Smith.

" There is worse to come," I encouraged her. " The
higher we go the worse it is," and I led her upstairs and
showed her the dusty fitting-room and then the huge
empty workrooms on the top floor, lined with dreary
dummies clothed only in sackcloth, some of them still
wearing paper patterns pinned to their lifeless breasts.
It made me feel physically sick to visit this Morgue, once
filled with chattering, laughing workgirls, now dusty,
silent, and sad.

Perhaps little Mrs Smith, whose heart proved to be as
large as her body was small, realised some of the bitterness
that I was feeling, for she suddenly smiled through those
steel-rimmed spectacles a very lovely smile.

" If you find my references satisfactory, Madam, I
should like to come to you," she said regarding me steadfastly.

My life was now completely untroubled by domestic
care. I had given Mrs Smith a small office in which she
kept and balanced household accounts, interviewed the

cook, lectured the housemaids, and washed and arranged the fruit for dessert. Her bedroom was on the second floor overlooking the garden, and here, in the afternoons and evenings, she sat darning stockings most marvellously (I still treasure one she mended, as an example of the finest and most delicate needlework I ever saw), or reading quietly to herself. When I turned the corner leading into The Grove on my way home from the office at night, I loved to see her lamp in the window, like a beacon. It gave me such a sense of peace and security to think of that loyal, quiet little woman with her steadfast eyes, sitting up there as guardian of our house and of our interests.

John was devoted to her and she to him. Every evening after dinner he would go to her office to invite her to come and take a cup of coffee with us, and if she were too busy over her accounts he would carry out a cup to her office. I can see her now sitting in that prim attitude of hers, erect upon the very edge of an armchair in our Wedgwood Room, beaming at John's query : " Well, Mrs Smith, and how's things ? " as she sipped the coffee she so loved.

Once, on a rare free afternoon, I asked her if she would care to go to a ' Movie ' with me, and was surprised to see a flush of pleasure in her face and a glitter in her eye as she accepted my suggestion with the greatest animation. We went and had a lovely time together. Staid Mrs Smith became almost girlish, and finally, while devouring a chocolate *éclair* in a *café* after the performance, she produced a very surprising snapshot of herself, when young, riding upon a camel.

" I went to Egypt with my mistress when I was only seventeen. I shall never forget that journey, for she had a premature *accouchement* in the train, and, as we were alone, I had to deliver the baby," the little woman informed me as calmly as though telling me that she had found green peas in the market that morning.

" But had you ever delivered a baby before ? " I asked.
" Oh no. I was only a child and had been very carefully
brought up. I hardly knew how babies came," she told
me. " I was very much surprised as you may imagine,
Madam, but common-sense told me what to do." A
jewel of a woman, Mrs Smith.

One morning she knocked at my bedroom door, and
when I bade her enter came in with a perplexed expression.

" I am sorry to disturb you so early, Madam," she
apologised, " but there is a Hampstead doctor downstairs
who wishes to see you urgently—I think it must be an
accident case. There is a poor boy with him with a
bandaged head."

I hurried into some clothes and went downstairs to
find a strange man standing in the hall with a very queer-
looking boy, dirty and ragged, his head bandaged on one
side and beyond the bandage a mop of unkempt hair
standing straight on end. Two wild eyes stared at me
with a terrified expression and the sullen mouth hung
open.

" I am Dr X., Mrs Fortescue," the man introduced
himself. " I came to speak to you about this boy. Now,
Charles, old man, there is no need to be frightened here.
Can he go out into your garden while I tell you about
him ? "

I gave ' Charles ' into the care of Mrs Smith and took
the doctor into my Wedgwood Room.

" Forgive me for coming here like this without first
asking for an appointment," he apologised, " but this is
a very sad case. Charles was brought into the Hampstead
Hospital with his head split open and I have attended him.
It appears that the boy's mother is dead and his father
is a drunkard living on the dole. Charles is only half-
witted, but sane and good enough not to want to be like
his father, and so one day he ran away from home, and,
having no friends, sought work for himself in Hampstead.
As bad luck would have it, the first person to whom he

338

applied was a miserly and brutal woman. She offered
to take him in and let him work for her in exchange
for his keep, and she made him do the whole work of the
house and garden and every kind of menial and degrading
job. Naturally, never having been house-trained, he was
clumsy, and one day when he broke something, she broke
his head with a spade. He just had strength and sense
enough left to stagger and crawl to the hospital, where
I found him in a fainting condition on the steps. We've
had him in hospital for six weeks, and I brought a case
against the woman, who had to pay heavy damages to
Charles. I am to be his banker and guardian, and I've
put the money in a bank as a nest-egg for him. Now I
want to find him a home and some work—any light work
with a little pay to foster that germ of self-respect.

" Now, Mrs Fortescue, could you possibly take the boy
and use him in any way ? "

We were already fully staffed, and I must confess
that I am not partial to the half-witted. But the story
was very pathetic, and I was touched by the courage of
the boy. Luckily John was at home that day, and so,
telling the doctor that I must first consult my husband,
I went upstairs to his study. John came downstairs
with me and we all went out into the garden where we
found Charles standing in sullen, scared silence, and
Mrs Smith, having failed to make conversation with him,
staring at him through her spectacles with baffled compassion in her eyes.

When we appeared, the poor boy shrank against a wall
and instinctively put up his arm before his face as though
about to be struck, and that gesture finished me—and
John.

" Oh John, we've GOT to have him and make him stop
looking like that," I whispered.

" Poor devil, I suppose so," said John resignedly. So
the doctor departed leaving Charles with us.

" And what do we do now ? " I asked Mrs Smith.

" Give him a good bath," said Mrs Smith, sniffing the air. She took Charles away, and soon, from the servants' bathroom, I heard the sounds of running water, then splashing. The voice of Mrs Smith could be heard speaking from outside the door—

" Charles ! Have you washed your neck ? "

" Yes, Ma'am."

A pause. . . .

" Charles ! Have you washed your feet ? "

" Yes, Ma'am."

" Between the toes."

" Yes, Ma'am."

And finally—

" Charles ! Have you washed your *ears* ? "

" Yes, Ma'am."

The dialogue ended and after a time Mrs Smith came to my room to report that Charles was now clean. " I was about to say ' from head to toes,' Madam, but his head still leaves much to be desired. There is nothing for it but that I must wash it myself," she said with disgust and decision.

When this last rite was performed, she returned once more in a state of consternation—

" Madam, neither you nor I considered Charles's clothes. They are nothing but rags—and filthy at that. All this good washing would be wasted if we put him back into them. Besides, he would not be presentable."

Of course Charles must be reclothed ' from head to toes,' and so I gave Mrs Smith permission to go out and buy the boy a complete outfit. Çharles in the meanwhile sat in the warm bathroom enveloped in a huge bath-sheet, tearing at a large beef-sandwich with wolfish teeth and gulping down a cupful of hot chocolate.

So it was that Charles became a member of our house-hold. Mrs Smith, whom he feared but adored, adopted him as her special charge, taught him how to eat and speak politely, employed him in various ways and took charge of his earnings, doling him out a small weekly sum to spend how he liked. She gave the central heating into his care and taught him how to clean the big furnace from clinkers and to stoke it. He was so terribly proud of this responsibility that he could hardly be torn from the stoke-hole, and, thinking that he needed fresh air to build up an undermined constitution, I gave him weeding jobs to do in the garden for me.

A friend had given us a rare collection of rock-plants which were our especial pride. John and I made a rock-wall and bank, and we planted these lovely things ourselves. The path beneath and around them had become weed-grown after the winter rain, and so one day I gave Charles the job of tidying it up. He eagerly set to work at once, promising to have it finished when I got back from the office. Clad in blue overalls, his unruly hair, as always, standing on end, having defied all Mrs Smith's efforts at combing and plastering, I left him hoeing that path as though his life depended upon it.

It was late when I got home and too dark for me to inspect Charles's work; but next morning John and I called him and asked him to take us out to see it.

The path was clean and bare of weeds. The rock wall and bank were equally bare of plants. . . .

" When I'd done that path I 'ad a go at the wall an' the bank," said Charles proudly. " You can't see nuthin' green there now, can yer, Ma'am ? " asked Charles, his whole face lit with pride.

John and I exchanged a swift, agonised glance. Controlling myself with a frantic effort, I said quietly: " Where did you put all those weeds, Charles ? " with a wild hope that I might yet rescue some of my less fragile rock-plants.

" I *burned* 'em on the rubbish 'eap," he told me, bursting with righteousness because, for once, he had faithfully followed Mrs Smith's injunction always to be thorough in his work.

Of course I praised him. How could I have dunched the poor boy, so proud of his first job of work for me ? And after all, it was partly my fault because, although I had certainly *only* told him to weed the path, I had not thought of telling him not to touch the wall or bank, because it had never occurred to me that anyone could mistake rock-plants for weeds. Excess of zeal on Charles's part—a good fault anyway. And fortunately both John and I possessed a sense of humour. I looked whimsically at him, and that divine twinkle dawned behind the eye-glass. The situation was saved, and so were the feelings of poor Charles.

LXII.

Much as I enjoyed my work for the ' Morning Post,' I, like my fellow-journalists, could not help being aware of an atmosphere of anxiety and unrest. Conferences were being continually called, and were in progress all day long ; directors with furrowed brows invaded the building ; editors were nervous and irritable. The old order was changing and giving place to new ; new wine was being put into old bottles, and we all anticipated the inevitable result. We ' extras and innovations ' soon became aware that the paper was in difficulties, and that our tenure of office would probably be short. Older members of the staff also began to realise that their long-tried services were becoming superfluous. That period of the ' Morning Post's ' history was turbulent and full of anxiety and apprehension.

The Editor told me that I might take my three weeks' holiday in August if I could arrange for someone else to do my work during my absence. I decided to leave it already done, so that all Mr Hutcheon would have to do would be to set up my pages for me with materials already supplied.

John had a desire to visit Germany again. He thought

that as nearly seven years had passed since the Armistice
was signed, much of the bitter feeling against England
would have died down, and perhaps, in the Black Forest,
where we intended to stay, the peasants would have
already forgotten it. The doctors had prescribed mountain
air and climbing for my health.

We went *viâ* Cologne and the Rhine. In Cologne the
anti-English spirit was uncomfortably evident, and one
night there sufficed us. Nearly everybody has sailed
down the Rhine, so that I need not describe that almost
theatrical scenery with its incredible castles perched on
wooded peaks. John enjoyed the Rhine wines he drank
at every landing-place, and then, in response to my plea
to see Heidelberg, we spent one magic night there, dining
on a terrace perched high above that lovely winding river,
and then went into the Black Forest.

Our hotel was placed near the highest waterfall in
South Germany, and from our bedrooms we heard its
eternal roar. By day we climbed high up into the forest,
clad in sweaters, corduroy breeches, with peasant hooded
cloaks slung over our shoulders in case of rain. We bathed
in forest pools, ate wild raspberries, and John drank
Kirsch liqueur made from the fruit of wild cherry trees
growing around the isolated farms ; and we breathed in
that wonderful resin-scented air and talked to little round-
headed boys and flaxen pig-tailed maidens who ran out
of their wooden houses to wave us a friendly greeting.

It was all very peaceful and very beautiful, but I was
disappointed to find that my new 'cure' of climbing
mountains only made me feel more tired. When we came
in from our long expeditions, I was good for nothing, but
could only lie exhausted upon my bed.

When we reached home I found a letter from the Editor
of the 'Morning Post' regretting that its finances could
no longer stand the additional salaries of the 'extras'
of which I was one. My job was over after only six
months' duration.

It was a very sad situation, not so much for me, for I had learned to prefer ' free-lance ' journalism and could still make money that way; but for older members of the ' Morning Post ' staff who, a few weeks later, were swept away by the new economy campaign after many years of hard work and faithful service. " In one week seven members of the staff holding positions of responsibility and trust passed out into the chilly night. They included, alas, the ' Morning Post's ' first Night Editor," —I quote Mr Hutcheon's autobiography, ' Gentlemen of the Press,' for he, also, was among those whose services were no longer required. But I had made a faithful friend, to whom I shall ever owe my affectionate gratitude for the help and encouragement he gave me then and since. He was always so sure that I could write a book; was for ever spurring me on to make the effort; and no one rejoiced more over my success than he. Now I have lost him too. God rest his loyal soul.

LXIII.

The question for us now was retrenchment. John and I, after many consultations and much searching of the heart, decided that we must sell Admiral's House and find some smaller dwelling in the country. John had always vowed that he would resign his post as Librarian and Archivist to the King at the end of twenty years' service. The twenty years would expire next year, and then he would be on the pension list and we could certainly no longer afford to live in so large a house requiring so many servants. Could we afford to keep our dear little Mrs Smith ? No, we most certainly could not, and there lay ahead of us (but thank Heaven not for many months) the sadness of breaking this news to her. Charles, poor Charles also, must be placed in some happy home, for we should no longer be able to afford either luxuries or superfluities.

I began to plan ahead, and, almost at once, I visited Hampton's and had a long talk with our staunch friend, Captain Amery Underwood, who had first found, and then let, my CINTRA premises in Sackville Street for me, and had helped us with our housing problems and those of our friends so often in the past. He had been a keen soldier during the war, and, like all soldiers, had a great veneration for the Historian of the British Army, coupled with real respect and affection for John Fortescue, the man.

I was received in Hampton's offices as though I were the Queen, and Captain Underwood consoled me by his confident assurance that if we put Admiral's House, with its romantic history, on the market we should get a fancy price for it.

There remained the necessity of finding another home *before* we sold ' Animal's,' partly because of John's thousands of books, many of them books of reference which he must consult, and which could not be stored if we should happen to sell Admiral's House at once, but chiefly because his work must on no account be interrupted for a long time. He would have to give at least six months' notice to the King before he resigned from Windsor, and, in the meantime, he was anxious to finish jobs that were already begun in the Print-rooms and Library. When his successor was found he would have to be ' shown the ropes.' His work would be comparatively easy, for John had already done the heavy work of sorting and reorganising during his twenty years of office ; but a new Librarian might well be somewhat overwhelmed by suddenly being put in charge of a hundred and fifty thousand books, and about the same number of engravings ; eighteen thousand drawings, and six collections. This would entail for John a long sojourn at Windsor and would give me the chance to manage the removal from ' Animal's,' and our installation in a new home, without disturbing him.

That new home was yet to be found, and I must confess that the prospect of finding it and of leaving our dear ' Animal's ' appalled me.

LXIV

We had endless discussions as to where we should search for a little house in the country. I rather hoped to be in Sussex near Mummie and Daddie. I longed to be able to wander in bluebell woods and to climb those high Downs and breathe the wonderful air blowing from the not-far-distant sea. But the History was not yet finished, the train communications from Sussex to London are so bad, particularly from the neighbourhood of Petworth, and John must be within easy reach of London, where he would be obliged to go for his research work. At length we decided upon Hertfordshire. The air there is good, and the northern approaches to London for a car are so much better and clearer than those of the south. Also Cambridge and its great Library would not be far distant.

We found a little converted cottage upon the estate of the Roman Catholic College which stands in its own spacious grounds, outside Ware, just about thirty miles from London along the Great North Road. It was a dear little place, with the enchanting name of ' Little Orchard,' derived from its paddock filled with fruit trees. It stood at the end of a *cul-de-sac* lane ending with a gate leading into grass fields and a farm (which afterwards supplied us with wonderful milk from Jersey cows and cream at sixpence a pint), and the cottage commanded a typical Hertfordshire view of rolling fields and little copses.

It was sunny and compact, healthy and dry, and near London. Documents and doctors would be easily accessible. It would serve its purpose. It was ' to let,' but we dared not take it before selling Admiral's House.

The President of the College promised to give us the first refusal and kindly agreed to discourage other would-be tenants.

I realised that a married couple indoors and a gardener without (three small cottages—one already let, went with the property) would be all the staff we should require, and this was perhaps the greatest attraction of Little Orchard.

We first saw it in early autumn when apples were reddening on the trees, and, soon after this, the Hampstead agent of Messrs Hampton urged us to put Admiral's House up to auction. I protested that this was a dangerous season in which to try to sell a house, for, supposing that there were no bidders, there would afterwards be long months when the weather and our lovely garden would be at their worst. When interested people came to view the property they would see a bleak and bare garden— if November fogs permitted them to see it at all—and surely they would go away discouraged. The agent persisted that purchasers always like to acquire a property in the autumn, since they could, at that season, plant anything they liked in the garden and make any alterations they fancied to the house so that all would be in readiness for their occupation in the late spring. Still I argued that, in my opinion, the property had better be put up to auction in the late spring, so that in case of a failure to sell it there would still be many months when the garden would be looking glorious with a profusion of spring flowers, daffodils, narcissi, and bluebells under the beech-tree hedge ; then lilies-of-the-valley, wistaria, white foxgloves, stocks, and a riot of roses. Even in September and October there would be Michaelmas daisies, dahlias, and late roses, for the herbaceous border looked its best during these months.

But no. I was overruled. John, though at heart agreeing with me, remarked : " It's no good buying a dog and then barking oneself, Peg. These people must know their business better than we." And so, eventually, he gave his consent for the house to be put up for auction at once. It was a grave decision for us because the fee would be £100.

All through that anxious day of the sale, John wrote history doggedly in his study, and I was like a cat on hot bricks, so nervous and restless that I could settle to nothing. When I knew that the sale was over I hadn't the courage to telephone to Captain Underwood to ask the result. I felt that I should prefer to hear the news, good or bad, from his lips, and so I got into the car and drove down to St James's Square.

One look at Captain Underwood's face as I was shown into his office told me that his news was disastrous. He had no smile for me, only a look of grave concern.

There had not been one bid for the house. I had never been able to share his roseate views of the possibility of Admiral's House fetching a fancy price, and I had felt horribly apprehensive of this very result all day. He was as disappointed and disgusted as if the house had been his own, and simply could NOT understand why it had not been immediately snapped up. He had advertised it freely. 'The Times' had given its romantic history a full column—and yet—NOT ONE BID.

I had to break the news to John on my return. A tightening of the lips, a contraction of those 'startled prawn' eyebrows, a swift look at me full of concern to see how I was taking it, and one long hand caressing that beautifully shorn chin.

Then, the eyeglass shaken out, the tense figure relaxed in its chair ; a shrug of the shoulders ; a whimsical smile and a lift of the eyebrows—

" Well, darling, there the matter is."

And there the matter was—until December, when an enterprising estate agent called upon us to ask the price of the property. At once I asked him what he intended to do with it, for we had so often been told what a fortune we might make if we pulled down the old house and built a gigantic block of flats upon that wonderful site, the highest point in Hampstead. But we would never even contemplate such an act of vandalism, and, when our would-be purchaser assured us that he would keep the house intact, we finally sold it to him with such furniture that we should not require or could not use in Little Orchard. It never occurred to us that anyone could be so wicked as to cut up *the garden* into building plots, which is what this man eventually did. The old house itself was sold with only the rose-garden and the lawn above it. Two modern villas, built upon the upper terraces, now stare into its windows. RUINED. Even now I can't bear to think of it. *Tout passe.*

LXV.

That removal from Admiral's House nearly finished me—those stairs. . . . Mrs Smith was invaluable. She packed and packed—and still she packed. One night we went on working until midnight and then were astonished by a sudden clash of bells and hooting of sirens. "A fire !" I exclaimed.

"No, Madam," reassured Mrs Smith. "New Year's Day." I had completely forgotten it. I suggested that we leave our packing and go downstairs in search of some form of reviving fluid in which to drink the health of the New Year and of each other. I found some vermouth for Mrs Smith, and she brewed me some China tea ; then we pledged each other wearily. After this I insisted that she should go to bed, but she refused to go unless I, also, stopped work ; and we each went to our respective rooms.

I waited until she was safely inside hers and gave her time to get into bed and fall asleep ; then I crept into the drawing-room and continued the packing we had left. Suddenly the door opened softly and a tiny figure wearing a white linen nightgown with long sleeves and a high frilled neck, a long pigtail of grey hair hanging down its back, and large reproachful blue eyes staring at me through steel-rimmed spectacles, stood in the doorway.

"What are you doing out of bed, Mrs Smith?" I demanded of her sternly.

"That is the question I came downstairs to ask *you*, Madam," she retorted crisply.

"I only wanted to finish this big trunk," I pleaded like a child caught in an act of disobedience.

"Then I will remain here and help you, Madam," she stated firmly, and we packed the trunk together and had finished by 2 A.M.

John was working equally hard at Windsor, burning 'rubbish' in the great furnace which heated the Castle. Long afterwards, when the History was triumphantly finished, I suggested that its manuscript should be given to the family archives at Castle Hill, his home, and accordingly John wrote to my brother-in-law to ask him if he would like to have it. He replied that one day it would have a commercial value and should belong, by right, to John's wife. I answered that if it were mine, even if starving, I could never sell the manuscript of the History, and I preferred to know it safe at Castle Hill for all time. And so John had an old uniform-case repaired to house the mass of manuscript, and one morning we started collecting it from various shelves and boxes. It was then that I discovered that the MS. of two or three of the volumes was missing. I questioned John carefully— he was sure that he had emptied his office at Windsor, and I knew that nothing remained of his at Admiral's House. I telephoned to the faithful Barry at Windsor and asked him to search the office again, but he found nothing. And then, in the evening, John suddenly looked at me with a twinkle and said : "I remember now, Sweetheart, I burned a lot of manuscript in the Castle furnace."

I stared at him in horror. " There was such a mass of stuff to bring here," he said. " I thought I'd lighten the load."

The actual day of removal from Admiral's House was marked by one funny incident amid hours of misery. It was raining, of course. In my experience it always rains for removals. The first van was drawn up to the front door, which was consequently open, and a damp and icy wind wailed through the house lifting straw and sheets of newspaper as it swirled and eddied through the dismantled house. The Abomination of Desolation had come upon us. I was trying to telephone in the hall when I became aware of a small smirking man standing before me and bowing repeatedly. The wind had evidently blown him in at the open door. When I had hung up the receiver he addressed me—

" Excuse me, Madam," he began in guttural accents, " but I came to beg the favour of your custom."

He handed me his commercial card, and, reading his name, I realised that he was the German greengrocer and fruiterer whom we had left because his prices were too high and his merchandise bad. I had never met him personally, but when Mrs Smith complained about him I had authorised her to find someone honest to supply us. Now here he was in the flesh—a great deal of flesh.

" I always supplied The Honourable Mrs Fortescue with vegetables and fruit and she was always delighted with my produce," he proceeded oilily. " She . . ."

" *I* am Mrs Fortescue," I answered smiling, looking him full in the eyes.

He had the grace to withdraw swiftly and silently with a quick bow of apology, and enough humour to see what a fool he had made of himself in taking me for the new purchaser of Admiral's House. This episode refreshed me not a little on a day of severe trials.

LXVI.

John had come up from Windsor to support me through
our final exodus from dear 'Animal's,' and when the
last van had departed we got into our car to drive to
Ware, intending to stay the night at a comfortable hotel,
once an old country mansion, which had been recommended to us there. A fine sleet was driving across the
Heath as we left 'Animal's,' standing tall and pale in
the dusk, its blank windows looking like sorrowful staring
eyes as we abandoned it to its fate. As we reached Barnet
a cold fog descended upon us ; so thick that John, muffled
to the ears in a huge overcoat, had to get out and guide
me step by step, for I could not see the hedges bordering
the road. He tapped the banks with his stick and shouted
directions and encouragement to me. When at length
we reached the hotel outside Ware, where we had booked
rooms for two nights, we were greeted on its doorstep
by the distraught manager who confessed to us that he
was bankrupt and the hotel in the hands of the Official
Receiver, who, it seemed, could receive anything and
anybody but us.

We urged that our rooms had been booked a fortnight
since, and John asked the manager why he had not then
told us of this dire probability. The flustered man
admitted that he had always hoped against hope that he
might be able to tide over his difficulties.

There was nothing for it but to return in the fog to the
next town where there were hotels. It was already late,
and we were very tired and very hungry and very cold.
Our luck was out that day, for we chose an old-fashioned
hotel with no comforts of any sort. We were given a huge
bedroom, cold and damp as a vault, and when a fire was
lighted in the tiny grate the long-disused chimney refused
to draw and we were soon choked by acrid wood smoke.
All the hot dinner dishes were ' off,' and we could only

get some tough cold meat and some fossilised cheese to eat. I dared not ask for the hot coffee for which I longed, knowing, from the sample of the fare already offered, that it would be blue poison. As I could not stop shivering, and John's fingers were quite dead, I suggested that we should go upstairs and creep into that catafalque of a bed. I rang for the chambermaid, a dreary female wearing squashed slippers, gave her my hot-water-bottle to fill, and when she returned with it I literally fell into bed, exhausted. The sheets felt icy cold, and I feared damp, and so I draped John's Jaeger dressing-gown over them lest we get rheumatic fever. Just as I was beginning to thaw there was a queer sensation by my feet, ONLY the hot-water bottle leaking and the bed soaked—the final straw—oh Day of Woe.

There were no spare sheets and blankets to replace the wet ones. We had each to sleep on hills at either edge of the bed, continually rolling down into the humid valley between. The only thing that helped me at all as the sleepless hours of that long night dragged by, was John's marvellous vocabulary of expletives, amassed from brothers in the Army and Navy and merchant skippers and Colonials during his voyages and travels abroad, varied by some intensely original ones of his own ; the final stream cascading forth when, next morning, the top of the ancient wardrobe crashed to the ground as he tried to pull open the door.

Together we saw our furniture stacked into the garage and out-buildings of Little Orchard, where it would have to remain until the structural alterations to the house were finished ; and then we drove off to Windsor, there to stay until the work at Little Orchard was fairly advanced and I could go back alone to make the house habitable for John, who would be free in March. He now struggled with the mass of George IIIrd's papers—thousands of them —which he had discovered mouldering in a cellar in London and which the King wanted him to read and sort, pre-

ferring that the family affairs of the Royal Family should
first be seen by a man of discretion who was also a member
of his own private Household. This was terribly heavy
work for John in addition to his preparations for departure
from Windsor. When he had finished the preliminary
task of selection he was obliged to employ a legion of
devils to help him to transcribe, translate, and put in
order this colossal mass of material (many of the documents
rendered almost illegible by damp and mould)—a twenty-
year job if it were done properly. But now only a rough
interim catalogue could be made of them, and an overtired man was maddened daily by the mistakes made
on the typescript which, where possible, he must check
and correct. I longed for the moment to come when he
would be free to concentrate only upon his own great
'History of the British Army.'

From Windsor I drove down to L.O. (as we soon began
to call Little Orchard) to supervise the workmen and
to plant bulbs and flowers in our garden, and in March
I took down two of our ex-servants to help me settle in.
Dear little Mrs Smith had left us, very tearfully. She
had pleaded to stay with us, without salary, but in the
smaller house we had only room for two working servants.
She found a situation in an historic house in the North,
and we placed poor Charles with kind people in the South.
I felt lonely indeed without them.

I was far from well and sometimes felt quite
frightened by my weakness and light-headedness. I
had to go up to London two or three times a week for
very trying treatments, and I began to wonder if I should
ever find a doctor who could scotch this mysterious
poison.

The prospect of a visit from Mummie and Daddie in
April to house-warm L.O. cheered me considerably. Our
landlord assured me that the orchard would then be alive
with dancing daffodils. Daddie adored yellow, and to
please him I hung curtains of golden Italian brocatello

(relics of CINTRA) against pale grey walls and emphasised
the gay golden note in the bedrooms. Then one day I
had a letter from Marjory telling me that she had been
summoned to Petworth to help Mummie nurse Daddie,
who had caught a bad chill, had a high temperature, and
a frightening cough. She promised to tell me if I were
needed. Nevertheless I felt that Daddie was far more
ill than they were telling me, and my mind filled with
apprehensions. As in all crises of our affairs I thought
of Guy, whose name should have been Peter, the Rock
upon whom we all leaned. I rang him up and found
out that he was just as anxious as I about Daddie, and
just as dissatisfied with the reports that we were getting.
He told me that he intended to go at once to Petworth
and judge for himself the gravity of Daddie's condition.
I had to go up to London next day for three different
treatments, and I arranged to be in my Club at a certain
hour so that Guy could telephone to me there and tell
me the truth.

His news, when at last I heard his quiet calm voice
speaking from Sussex, justified them all. Daddie was
dying. I must come AT ONCE if I were again to see him
alive.

Exhausted from my treatments, sick and terrified by
this news, the world went black for a moment. With a
fierce effort I regained my self-control.

I said I would come at once, and feverishly searched
an A.B.C. for trains—one had just gone ; the next was
a slow train, and I should have to change and wait at
Horsham. I must risk punctures and drive down in
my car.

I leaped into it, drove furiously, and at last reached
the little courtyard from which the house got its name.
A lamp had already been lit in the hall, and, for the first
time, I noticed that the framework of the glass panes of
the front door formed a great black cross.

Daddie had been fretting to have all his children around

him ; wondering if his strength would last until I came. Our agony lasted for several days.

As always, he was marvellously patient and unselfish, never complaining ; afraid that his coughing must be disturbing the sleep of our neighbour ; always begging us to leave his room ; to go out into the spring sunshine and take Mummie with us.

Each post brought humble offerings from the poor of his old parish—eggs broken into an omelette through insufficient packing, half a pound of butter bursting through its package and sticking to the letters in the postman's bag, a fowl from the most indigent people in the village. These would be deposited upon the doorstep, with bunches of faded wild flowers from the children of the neighbourhood. (Mummie had put a little notice on the front door begging people not to ring the bell.) Everyone who had ever known him loved him and shared his suffering and our sorrow.

When the end was near, the doctor gave him morphia that his passing might be painless, and we kissed him farewell in his sleep. But, almost miraculously, as though he felt our great longing once more to hear his beloved voice, he returned from that dark shore where he was waiting to embark on his last voyage, and very early next morning he summoned his children. As we knelt round his bed, with a great effort he took a hand of each of us, and, placing his own upon them, solemnly and clearly blessed us.

Then he lay back on his pillows with closed eyes. Presently we heard him whisper—

" I have fought a good fight—I have finished my course—I have kept—to the best of my poor ability—the faith."

It was not in his humble heart to complete the sentence : " Henceforth is laid up for me a crown of righteousness."

Then, after a long pause, he said : " I have tried to be an English gentleman." And so he died.

We laid him to rest in the tiny churchyard of Burton, the smallest of his 'cathedrals,' as he had always called his three 'little, lost, Down churches'; a lovely place set in the heart of a beautiful park amid the Downs of Sussex. His last journey was travelled between hedges of blossoming blackthorn, the air pungent with the smell of gorse-bloom, the sun shining upon the massed flowers sent by all who loved him, the air ringing with the triumphant song of birds.

As they brought him to the gateway of the churchyard, two baby lambs gambolled across the path to meet him, as though to welcome him to the Land of Eternal Spring.

LXVII.

John was obliged to rush back to Windsor for the Easter visit of the Court, and I returned, alone, to Little Orchard, there to continue my work. As I entered the house a workman was hanging the golden curtains designed to give pleasure to Daddie. I turned sharply away and stared across the orchard, filled now with the yellow daffodils Daddie had loved. Pain everywhere. . . .

John, anxious about me, and unable to leave Windsor, wrote imploring me to come to him, at any rate for a few days. I went. But nothing could help me very much just then. . . .

Early in June, Little Orchard was ready for occupation, and I had found a competent married couple to look after us. I installed them, taught them their duties. The Court was again at Windsor for Ascot week and John at his post. Directly the Castle was empty, he wanted me to go there and help him pack books and possessions before he left the King's service on 30th June.

One evening, on my return from a day in London, on entering L.O. I heard the telephone bell shrilling in the hall. Taking up the receiver, I was greeted by a queer muffled voice saying that it was speaking from Windsor Castle. It was the voice of our temporary cook, who was looking after John during the Ascot visit. In broken tones she told me that she had just rung up to tell me " that I was no longer Mrs Fortescue." My senses reeled for a moment and then I gasped out : " What do you mean ? WHAT has happened ? "

" I've just been sewing a star-thing on his coat ! " the tearful voice went on. And then I realised that my husband had been given another degree of the Victorian Order by the King, and, in my relief that nothing awful had happened to John, I ejaculated : " Oh, is *that* all ! " which remark quite evidently shocked our cook.

In this manner was I informed that my husband had been given the K.C.V.O.

Later, he told me that he had been out for a walk in the Great Park, and, coming in hot and tired, found various members of the Household, besides pages and footmen, all searching for him.

" His Majesty is awaiting you in his room," was shouted at him, and he was not even allowed to go and change his dusty clothes or make himself tidy, but was hurried to the King at once.

He found the King alone ; was asked to kneel ; a sword was borrowed from the officer on guard, and King George, graciously thanking his Librarian for his twenty years of service to King Edward and himself, touched John's shoulder with it, and then bade him rise and go away to telephone the news to his wife that she was now Lady Fortescue. John tried to get our Hertfordshire number, but it was engaged. He had barely time to have his bath and scramble into his Household uniform to dine with the King, so he deputed his cook-housekeeper to telephone the news to me when she could get through— and that was how she did it.

Towards the end of June I joined John at Windsor and together we struggled with yet another *déménagement*.

On the last day of the month, having bade farewell to his tearful staff, the Librarian entered each room of the Library with me, where he stood silently looking around it for a moment ; climbed the narrow stairway leading down into the Print-rooms, each of which he visited in turn. Then turning his back upon them he kissed me very solemnly, and we went out together. With the shutting of those doors he closed, also, a long chapter of his life.

Quietly he got into our little car and we slipped away.

LXVIII.

Although always regretting our dear 'Animal's,' we grew fond of our new home after a time. Little Orchard had its charm, and it was beautifully quiet : John enjoyed its peaceful view of pasture-land. And, when a cocker spaniel was added unto us, he and 'Mr Smee' (called after the sentimental pirate in 'Peter Pan') went for daily walks together, when Mr Smee regularly poached in our neighbour's preserves, and John, The Sportsman, turned a blind eye if a VERY occasional baby partridge was laid at his feet.

A friend who had for some time watched me dragging about with weary feet and whipping myself into a state of forced energy, asked me to go up to London to consult yet another doctor who had studied medicine in every capital of Europe, and now, in advanced years, was only interested in so-called 'hopeless' cases. He begged me to go over to Paris, there to consult the doctors of the Pasteur Institute who specialise in microbes.

When John consented to this new experiment, he wrote to medical friends in Paris to prepare them for my coming, and I went there at once, alone. Although they could not find the cause of the poisoning, they suggested that I should remain in Paris to undergo new treatments, which I did—returning to L.O. to live an invalid life, broken only by periodical visits to Paris for another course of treatment.

During this time John worked hard at the History, safe from outside interruption. He was now writing Volume XIII.—the last. He came downstairs to meals, sometimes silent and abstracted, fighting battles all by himself. Sometimes he was animated and loquacious, when he would explain an action to me and tell me of what he had been writing. There were days when he would look white and stern, hardly addressing one word to me throughout the day, and then I knew that he was recording some ghastly administrative muddle that had caused his beloved soldiers suffering and privation, and I felt as sad and anxious as he did.

When, after two years, I was allowed to live a more active life, I managed the small house and large garden ; superintended the bottling of our fruits and the rearing of our poultry ; rushed up to London in my little car to do advisory work for a silk Firm which I had engaged to do the moment my health permitted. On my free days I scribbled articles for newspapers in our blue parlour.

We were saved from social interruptions by a curious accident. Our butler-house-parlourman-odd-man had been a tram-conductor before the war, and was quite untrained when he came to us. His wife acted as cook. Shortly after their engagement I had to go over to Paris for another treatment. Callers were beginning to arrive at L.O. before I went away this time, and, when I returned after six weeks, I asked our house-parlourman if any had come during my absence, for I could find no cards anywhere.

" Oh, I *burnt* them things," he announced proudly. " I knew Your Ladyship wouldn't like them little white tickets cluttering up the place."

The ticket habit. As tram-conductor his business had been, at the end of each day, to sweep up and burn all stray tram-tickets.

When I told John of this awkward state of things, he twinkled at me deliciously and remarked that evidently a Special Providence watched over historians. But afterwards the Historian's wife occasionally had moments when she felt hot all down her spine on meeting her neighbours at friends' houses and not knowing whether or not they had called upon her and their call had been ignored. A facetious friend suggested that I should publish an explanation in the local papers. But who would have believed it if I had ?

Anyhow this excessive tidiness of our man-servant aided the completion of the History.

LXIX.

During these years Mummie, our ' Little Beloved,' had been striving to live on alone in Kitchen Court. Her health was not good, and we all saw that she was perfectly miserable there ; so restless that she could never remain for more than a week or ten days in the little house where she and Daddie had been so happy together. Then she would flee to Sutton Rectory to be with Aunt Eva ; or to one of her children. In turn, we implored her to come and live with us, and time and again one or other of us thought that we had at last persuaded her ; and then she would say—

" Daddie always hoped that, if he had to leave me, this little house would be my safe refuge."

John often said to me : " Have patience. Things will sort themselves somehow. I can well understand Doña's reluctance to part with her independence."

But we saw that, although she still clung to little Kitchen Court because of its associations and the happy memories of the past, she could now hardly bear to live there without Daddie. . . .

Her life had really ended with his, and only a gallant

little ghost of her remained with us for three years after he went away.

Then she followed him. . . . And so we lost our ' Little Beloved ' too.

> " He first deceased—she for a little tried
> To live without him—liked it not—and died."

LXX.

" Darling, I believe the d——d thing's done ! " These words arrested my steps as I entered John's study one morning in October, and so startled me that I nearly dropped the egg-nog drink that I was bringing him. He was sitting at his great desk fingering some sheets of manuscript with slim nervous fingers.

I knew that ' the d——d thing ' could only refer to the really blessed thing, his ' History of the British Army.' I knew that for the last few days he had been, to use his own hunting term, ' running for blood.' But even so, I could hardly believe that his thirty-six years of struggle and ceaseless toil were over (for he spent six years in research work before he began to write the History), and that the thirteenth and last volume was actually FINISHED.

I set down the egg-nog drink upon his desk and kissed his tired face. I could find no words to express what I was feeling ; indeed I felt as dazed as he looked. He picked up the tumbler, drank vaguely, rose, and went blindly out of the room, so did not see the tears coursing down my face. I had watched that gallant struggle going on for so long. I had shared it since our marriage in 1914. I had seen the toll it was taking of his precious health. The work brought in less than a halfpenny a line, less than the pay of a private soldier without emoluments ; for a military history, with original maps, is costly to produce and therefore costly to buy. He could have made far more money by writing for the Press. But the great work must be finished or neither of us could be happy, and for payment he had the gratitude of soldiers all over the world ; wonderful letters telling him that his book was the only one consulted by the General Staff ; letters thanking him for the help given to the writers ; begging for another volume ; consulting him about various actions of various regiments in the past ; asking him his opinion on every possible detail of matters military in the present. This had been his incentive to go on writing. As he wrote in the preface of Volume IX. in the year 1920—

"Next I owe much to those officers, distinguished and undistinguished who, from time to time have written to me from all parts of the world, asking for a new volume. Many of these will write no more letters and read no more books ; yet not the less, but rather the more, shall I strive to give them what was their desire. It is for them that I have laboured gratefully for the best part of a quarter of a century ; and for them, if it be possible, I should wish to labour still."

And so he had laboured on for another nine years, and at last—AT LAST—his great History was finished, FINISHED—FINISHED.

I had been warned to prepare for a big reaction when the History was at last ended ; that my husband might become *Nunc dimittis-y* and feel that with its completion his life-work was done. So, during that last month, I had bought him a divine spaniel puppy to tease him, bite his feet, and keep him busy mopping up pools. I called her ' Topsy ' because she came from Turvey and was inky black, and, as though she knew my purpose in buying her, she devoted herself to him from the first moment ; shadowed him, assaulted him with rapturous love and licks, invaded even his study where she sat at his feet under his great writing-desk. Like all spaniel puppies, she looked like a sad saint and was really a devil

of mischief, and only that morning she had nearly caused
a scandal in our household by removing John's bedroom
slippers, one by one, and placing them under the cook's
bed, carefully replacing them by a pair of the outraged
woman's, which I found under *his* bed on the lower floor.

With relief I saw, from his study window, that outside
on the lawn he was caressing and reproving Topsy for
this improper action. Already he had forgotten that he
had just accomplished a longer task than that of Gibbon,
and, thank God, was neither pompous nor theatrical about
this great feat of endurance. Just his simple, diffident
self, entirely occupied in playing with his beloved puppy.

Some weeks later he placed some printed pages in my
hand. They were the preface to his last volume, and, in
the final paragraph, I saw that he had dedicated the
History to ME. . . .

" And there is she, nearest of all to me, who, in defiance
of pain and sickness, has fought incessantly to win me
the leisure for completion of my task, and by sheer courage
and resolution has prevailed.

" I had not the presumption when I began this history
to inscribe it to anyone, illustrious or obscure. I could
not have inscribed it to her, for she was then a child of
whose existence I was for many years to remain unaware.
But, now that it is done, I dedicate it with loving thank-
fulness to my wife."

When I could speak, of course I protested. The History
should be dedicated to the Army for whom it was written,
and not to me. He quietly stated that he had done quite
enough for his Army.

" But for my Woman the History would never have
been completed."

I felt, and shall always feel, that this honour was too
great for me, although, of course, it made me the proudest
woman in the universe. After all I had only done what
any other wife worthy of the name would have done in
striving to help my Man. The History was like a child

to us both, and it was only natural that both parents should love it and work for it.

MAGNUM OPUS. These words formed a headline in 'The Times' the morning after the last volume of the 'History of the British Army' was given to the world, and all the other newspapers wrote of it in the same strain. We were flooded with Press cuttings which, to my indignation, I found carelessly thrown away, unread, in my historian's huge waste-paper basket. Feverishly I rescued and read ; but I could not persuade him to read one of them.

" After all, darling, it is only the opinion of one man," he said as I pressed him to read the first glowing tribute. " If the book is worth anything it will live. If not, it will perish." At this time he wrote to our dear old ' Mac,' once my secretary at ' Animal's,' who had typed two volumes for him out of pure love for him and his History : " So that little job is finished." And, being finished, he dismissed it from his mind. But through mine continually throbbed the noble words of his concluding paragraph, which he put into the mouth of ' the historian of the dim future '—

" The builders of this Empire despised and derided the stone which became the headstone of the corner. They were not worthy of such an army. Two centuries of thankless toil could not abate its ardour ; two centuries of conquest could not awake it to insolence. Dutiful to its masters, merciful to its enemies, it clung steadfastly to its old simple ideals—obedience, service, sacrifice."

And I knew that a vast invisible army of dead soldiers, whose friend and champion this man was, saluted him as he laid down his pen.

LXXI.

John had always said that when the History was finished he would go to bed for a year. Instead, he at once started upon another book. The Royal Army Service Corps pleaded with him to write their history. He had always had an immense admiration for the Service, and, of course, knew more about it than anyone living, but he was terribly tired and I could feel nothing but dismay when he told me that he had accepted the job. Although he gave no other reason for his acceptance than that the work would interest him enormously, and that he would be glad to put on record the splendid work done by the Corps, and especially by General Seldon Long, its Head during the war, miserably I knew that it was chiefly to ease our financial position. Once again, because of my health, I had been obliged to give up my advisory work in London, and journalistic work is precarious in the extreme. I was always being asked to write articles for magazines and newspapers, but, after exhausting treatments, I sometimes had no ideas or, if I had ideas, no strength with which to express them. My doctors' bills were the heaviest items of our expenditure, and it was very bitter to me to feel myself a burden upon the husband I had tried so hard to help. One day I could not help pouring out all this pent-up bitterness to him.

"Don't, Sweetheart, I pray of you," he said gently. "My Woman has been so gallant in working for me. Now it is my pride to work for her."

But every day I noticed how deadly tired he looked when he came out of his study, and I heard the heavy sigh he gave as each post brought him masses more material to sift.

One evening he was sitting in his armchair in our blue parlour after dinner, intent upon a chair-cover he was working in *point de Flandres* for my room. Generally he would gossip with me happily as he played with the silks and wools, trying colour-combinations and asking my opinion. To-night he sat with furrowed brow and his lips pressed together in a firm straight line. He was taking no joy in his work ; his thoughts were elsewhere, and I could see that they were unhappy thoughts. He looked white and weary. Suddenly he looked up, caught my anxious eye, and, throwing his work aside, said in a desperate voice—

"Sometimes I wonder if I've been a d——d fool voluntarily to put my neck into the yoke again. After thirty-six years at last I finish a grinding job, and, almost at once, in my old age, I undertake another."

I sprang out of my chair. "John, you're to give it up. I *insist* upon your giving it up. You only undertook it because of me, and I can't and won't bear to see you getting more and more tired. Yes, I know what you're going to say: 'We need the money.' D——n money. What do we care for it? All I care for is your precious health. If we can't afford to live in England, then we'll go abroad. You always said you'd like to go and live in the sun when the History was finished. I said I wouldn't go while Mummie was alive. There's nothing to keep me now.

"Let me go and see General Long. You have nearly finished the first volume dealing with the South African War. That period you knew intimately. Let some man who has fought throughout the war of 1914-18 tackle the second volume."

He seemed struck with this idea; but he didn't like it.

I telephoned to General Long's house in Maidenhead and asked if I might come there to see him on private business. I was at once cordially invited by Mrs Long to go there next day and stay the night. The General could pick me up in London and drive me down.

When I met him next day, the General was suffering from toothache, and asked me if I would mind waiting for him while he visited his dentist on the way down to Maidenhead.

Not a propitious moment to deliver my blow—for blow I knew it must be. I became even more nervous, for I must now wait until the poor General was through his dental ordeal and had had dinner quietly in his own home before I broached my subject.

When we reached Maidenhead we all had a happy little dinner on the terrace overlooking the river. The garden, which was Mrs Long's pride, was bright with flowers of every hue, and the lawn a vivid green. She, herself, was at her vivacious best and full of Irish humour, so that the interval of waiting before my self-imposed ordeal did not seem very long.

After dinner she said gaily: " And now for your important business with B.D. (her *petit nom* for General Long). Perhaps you had better go with him to his study."

I went—and at first haltingly, and then in a rush, I explained my mission.

Instead of the outburst of irritated disappointment and indignation which I had half expected (and should completely have understood), the General, who had listened to me patiently with an inexplicable smile on his face, merely leaned back in his chair and said quietly—

" Yes, Peggy dear, I heard from John this morning. Of course it is a very great disappointment to me and will be to my brother officers, but I *quite* understand and John mustn't do anything that might injure his health."

" John wrote to you ? " I gasped. " He had already told you ? "

" Yes," beamed the General. " He told me the object of your visit, and said that he considered it to be more 'straight' to write to me himself because he hated the idea of sheltering behind a woman's skirts."

OH . . . !

So that was that, and the rest of that evening was spent very merrily by us all cruising up and down the lovely reaches of the Thames by moonlight in the General's motor launch, and munching chocolates of which he always kept a generous supply for the delectation of his guests. Dear B.D.

Just after my visit to Maidenhead we were obliged to dismiss our married couple.

Then began the wearisome "We are two in family. We live in a small labour-saving house" business; but fortunately I soon found a young couple who were eager to come to us. The man had been one of the under-chefs on the *Mauretania*. In spite of his twenty-eight years he had already made forty voyages on different ships, had tired of the restless life of the sea, and was anxious to find a place in the country where he could remain always with his wife and small five-year-old son, Billy.

During the summer our male cook made himself useful in a number of ways. He adored doing odd jobs in the garden, rushing out in his immaculate white clothes to clip a hedge while some dish was simmering; mowing the lawn, feeding the hens. One morning I looked out of my window and saw him on the top of a ladder, tying up a creeper, his fair hair blown on end.

" You look about eighteen, Dent," I called out to him, and he laughed up at me.

Five minutes later there was a knock at my door and a voice said, " It's Dent, mi-lady. I came up to say what I ought to have said at once. If I look young it's because I live in Your Ladyship's perpetual sunshine."

Amazing remark from one's cook, but treasured in my memory still with the beautiful compliment of the Breton sailor.

Dent was the only cook we ever had who positively revelled in his cooking. Always he was pleading with me to invite guests to luncheon or dinner so that he might have more scope; and then he would produce a really chic meal, even designing appropriate menu cards himself which afterwards he begged to have autographed by our guests. When John's eldest brother came to luncheon, I asked him to sign the menu (decorated by Dent with the family arms, copied from my book-plate) to give our chef pleasure. He at once complied with my

request, but later, when I gave the card to Dent, he stared
at it with a look of blank disappointment—

"But, Your Ladyship, he's only written ' Fortescue,' "
he blurted out.

"Because that is his name," I retorted.

"But he's an Earl. He hasn't *put* Earl—and now
none of my people will ever believe it ! " Dent explained
naïvely.

LXXII.

While John was completing Volume I. of the Royal
Army Service Corps History, I wrote numerous letters
to friends living in the South of France, asking for their
advice as to the best locality in which to search for a
permanent home. I explained that, if we came, we should
have to dig up our roots from English soil. Once having
gone abroad we could never afford to remove ourselves
and our possessions back again to England ; nor could
we contemplate an annual visit there. It was therefore
of vital importance to us to choose a healthy place which
would not be too hot in summer. I threw myself on their
mercy, and my last stipulation was that wherever we
eventually settled, it must be within reach of a really
good doctor.

We had been reading many of W. J. Locke's books,
including ' The Town of Tombarel,' and it seemed to me
that Provence would be the ideal place for us. Accordingly
I wrote also to Mrs Locke who, though unknown to me
then, would, I was sure, give me the information I wanted.
She very charmingly asked me to tea in her London house,
and listened patiently while I plied her with questions.
She had lived in Cannes for years, and she strongly recommended us to search for a house in the environs of Grasse,
where an abundance of water and groves of old olive trees
gave coolness and shade during the hot summer months.
There, she assured me, we could comfortably remain,

being always sure of cool nights and a breeze by day during *la grande chaleur* which, unless one lives *in* the sea, is so exhausting on the coast.

" The best doctor in Europe, Doctor Brès, lives outside Grasse," she concluded, as her final convincing argument in favour of that locality.

Consuelo, and Jacques Balsan, whom she had married some years before, happened to be in London and I went to see them. I knew that Consuelo would give me sound and sympathetic advice, and having, herself, a lovely place in Eze, would know the climate of the hills.

I found her shivering over a fire in a fur coat on a grey afternoon in May. She was enthusiastic about life in the South of France.

Both of them echoed the advice of Mrs Locke—the locality of Grasse would be healthiest and best—and when I received a letter from Lady Trent, who has an estate in Cannes and to whom I had also written for counsel, saying exactly the same thing, we decided to try to find a house up in the mountains of that region.

John being too much occupied with his book, which must be finished before we could leave England, we decided that it would be better for me to go out alone to Grasse to search for a house.

Before leaving Cannes for Jersey, Lady Trent had driven up to see a friend of hers, Ralph Conway, who lives in Magagnosc, a village beyond Grasse, and had taken with her my letter.

" This woman has thrown herself upon my mercy," she told him. " I have to leave for England, so cannot help her in her search for a house. But something must be done about it, and I leave her in your care. You know this part of the world better than I."

So that when I arrived this kind man and his sister adopted me, told me of a tiny property hidden amid olive groves on the border of Grasse which they thought perfect for our requirements, drove me to see it, besides many others, and, by their warm-hearted greeting and generous help, made me feel at once that I would love to live in this neighbourhood.

Never shall I forget one heavenly hot evening in June spent in their company. Seated upon the great wall of their garden over which cascaded pink roses and geraniums, I stared in wonder at the marvellous view of mountains and olive groves before and below me. Suddenly a tiny spark of fire flashed amid the roses, then another above my head ; soon the whole garden seemed fay-haunted. At first I thought that my host had arranged a new system of electric lighting to delight his guests during an *al fresco* entertainment, and I gave a joyful cry, for the effect was so beautiful.

" Fireflies," he said, smiling. " They always come in June." Fireflies ! They, alone, were reason enough to live in this place. Soon the whole landscape was starred with their tiny lights. They flickered amid the dim olive groves ; they lit the roses as they flashed past ; one even perched upon my shoulder. The other guests went indoors to play bridge, but I sat upon my wall, entranced, until the last firefly had darted away into the darkness. Oh lovely, lovely land.

I saw so many properties, each fascinating, and every one of them having some new attraction, that I grew bewildered. Then there was the question of price. The moment that I grew interested in one place, the proprietor of another offered to lower the price of his or to throw in old Provençal furniture. One would be too large for our requirements and would need much upkeep, but—the price was very low (perhaps for this reason) ; another was perfect from a picturesque point of view, but was in a semi-ruinous condition ; the next was lovely but too isolated ; the little Domaine that Mr Conway had first found attracted me greatly, but would be far too small to hold our furniture and all John's books ; otherwise it would be ideal ; a fertile cultivated garden, its terrace walls in splendid condition and lined with prospering vines ; matured fruit trees of every kind, and the property bounded by a small olive grove. But the cottage only possessed four tiny bedrooms, a bathroom, kitchen, and entrance hall. If we bought it we should have to build—and build rather extensively. I funked making so big a decision alone. After all, John would *have* to be disturbed. He must come out and make the decision. I could not take so heavy a responsibility upon myself, and so I telegraphed to ask him to join me.

He came, rather out of temper on arrival because he had so much to do at home ; but in half an hour he succumbed to the spell of this enchanted land, basked like a lizard in the sun and became even more anxious than I to find a home here and install himself within it with as little delay as possible.

We visited five or six properties which, by the process of elimination, I had selected as ' possibles,' and of these he was immediately most attracted by the sunny little Domaine I have already described. He found its greatest advantage to be a drive up to the front door of the cottage, for the only approach to most Provençal houses is either a rough cart-track across a valley or rugged steps ascending or descending the side of a mountain.

" We shall have to build on a wing, a library-dining-room with two large bedrooms over it," said John with the decisive look in his eye of one who had already completed a purchase.

" Can we afford to do that ? " I asked. " Have we enough margin ? "

" With the pound at 124 we should do it easily," he replied, " and we can write a few articles to pay for extras."

So I saw that he had made up his mind, and, in a few days, we had agreed to purchase the little Domaine from its owner, a Belgian Count. The Count was not then in residence, so that we were allowed to visit our new property daily. We gloated over it. We sat on its terrace walls and ate luscious peaches from ' our ' trees while planning the enlargement of the house, and I insisted upon visiting the place by night to see if we, also, should have fireflies—to me a very important item. There were myriads of them, and then I knew that we had found our Paradise.

John was as excited as a boy over this, our final adventure, and, having sweltered through the preliminary formalities of buying a property in Provence—hours spent in the stuffy offices of land-agent and lawyer—he was agog to get back to England and start packing up. I pointed out that we had not yet disposed of L.O., and probably could not come out again to France until next quarter-day. In the meanwhile we could make a plan for the enlargement of our Provençal cottage and consider estimates of cost. If we did this speedily, the building should be well advanced by the autumn, and we could perhaps camp in the existing part of the house on our arrival.

We travelled back to England on one of the hottest days of all, and that night our *wagon-lit* was like an oven. I took the top berth, being more likely to sleep than John, whose habit it was, if sleepless, to stretch his legs in the corridor. He would be able to slip out there more easily if he occupied the lower berth. At last I fell into an uneasy sleep, and was woken in the small hours by a curious sound. Turning on my head-light and peering over the edge of my berth, I was almost electrified to see my husband, clothed only in his eyeglass, seated upon the edge of his berth, devouring the peaches we had brought with us from the Domaine, and chuckling to himself.

I burst out laughing and he looked up at me with a beaming face wet with peach-juice.

" I never would have believed it if anyone had told

me that at the age of sixty-nine I should be sitting in a wagon-lit in my birthday-suit, devouring peaches at three o'clock in the morning," he remarked with that delicious twinkle dancing in his eyes.

LXXIII.

The next hectic three months I can more or less skip. The remainder of the lease of Little Orchard had to be disposed of, and, in the midst of packing and making lists for the insurance of our possessions (every picture, our silver, clothes, and personal possessions had to be listed and valued separately), the telephone bell would ring and the voice of a house-agent would inquire whether Mrs Snoflipoof or the Duchess of Pernoffka might come down to see the house. I would break off from what I was doing, frantically arrange flowers in all the rooms to make them look more attractive, and hide the mass of papers I was sorting or the clothes I was packing, to be ready to receive these people. Sometimes they came, but more often they lost their way, or it began to rain, or some unexpected social engagement prevented their coming, and I would curse the waste of time. However, at last two parties of enthusiasts fell in love with L.O. and bartered for it over a week-end, the loser hating the winner—and us—for evermore. But now our minds were at ease and we could concentrate upon uprooting ourselves from England.

In September, we bade farewell to our dismantled house and our lovely autumn roses and we drove to Ware in my Morris car. This was our last drive in gallant ' Sir William,' and we both felt quite sad about it. At Ware station I handed him over to the agent who had promised to find him another home, and I thought that I had seen the last of my dear little car.

We bundled all our mass of luggage and ourselves into

the train, and hardly had it moved out of the station when I had what John called ' one of Peg's panics.' In the pain of parting from ' Sir William ' I had left the leather case containing our passports and tickets in his pocket. . . . !

This quite shattered us, for our train arrived in London only just in time to allow us to catch the boat-train at Victoria. We were both wondering what on earth we had better do, when the train slowed up at the next station, and there, sweating on the platform, was our Morris agent, brandishing my pocket-book ! Splendid man, he had raced the train, knowing that it would stop at the next station, and he and ' Sir William ' had saved the situation.

LXXIV.

While staying in Magagnosc we had met Mr Marshall Hall, cousin of the renowned barrister, and he had told us of a ' kind English lady ' living in Grasse who was ready to allow us to store our furniture in the lower floor of her house, which she had converted into a flat. This we might use until our own house was ready for occupation. We told him that we had arranged to store our furniture in London so as to endure but one removal of it, and that all we now sought was a temporary refuge for ourselves. He wrote to us just before we left England to tell us that this same benevolent lady, Miss Pearce, was willing to let us her furnished flat for a nominal rent.

What a very kind old lady, we said to each other as we composed a grateful letter of acceptance.

So we, and our mountain of personal luggage, drove up to the door of her big villa in Grasse, both of us rather dreading our first meeting with this kind but unknown old lady. I pictured her as the typical English spinster who settles abroad and occupies herself with good works, kind but garrulous, and I was so weary after our *déménage-*

ment and the long journey that I felt quite unable to cope with her.

We were greeted on the doorstep by a tall laughing girl—probably a niece of the old lady, I decided. She wore an ancient tweed skirt and a blue shirt open at the sun-burned throat. Her hair was clubbed and a square fringe surmounted straight eyebrows and a pair of rascally blue eyes which challenged ours and took our measure in one straight smiling glance. In appearance she was a mixture of Joan of Arc and du Maurier's 'Trilby.' We both liked her at sight and I felt that the English Colony in Grasse would be the richer and the gayer for her presence. I hoped that she would prove to be a permanency. She greeted us frankly and cheerily; seemed to be in no wise appalled by our stack of heavy luggage; was sure that we must be tired out and would prefer to go straight to our flat to wash and rest. We should find a quite passable temporary servant installed; and our kitchen cupboards already stocked with groceries. "I ordered all the necessities of life," she told us. "You can buy your own luxuries. I know the market and the shops here and you don't, so that I thought it would be easier for you if I got in your first supplies."

I asked her name and found to my intense surprise that SHE was the 'benevolent old lady' we had conjured up in imagination. Why had we imagined that she was old? Is it so rare for young people to be thoughtful and kind?

We stayed in 'Trilby's' flat for nearly four months, visiting our Domaine daily to supervise the workmen. I cannot call those happy months, for hardly had we arrived than the pound sterling collapsed—a disaster for us. Our dreams of a leisured life in the sunshine were shattered; my promised work for the English newspapers came to an end before it had begun, for it became unpatriotic to write of foreign countries. England and the English must be advertised and boosted to tide over this

377

financial crisis. John, who had hoped at last for some
rest and freedom from pecuniary anxiety, must now
take up his pen again at once and work harder than ever.
Worst of all, we had signed the contracts for the enlargement of our new home. The house, being built on the
slope of a mountain, it had been necessary to dig away
two lower terraces and to substitute masonry for earth
to support the new wing. These foundations were already
made, and the existing property looked as though an
earthquake had disturbed its peace. There was nothing
for it but to go on. More capital must be taken out to
pay our debts, and we should thus be impoverished further.
In the meantime John was fretting because he was once
more divorced from his books, which were all in a London
warehouse ; and he was also anxious about me. I was
suffering from over-fatigue and reaction. It is heavy
work digging up one's roots from English soil. Also I was
perturbed in mind because the work at the Domaine was
constantly being held up by bad weather. We had given
orders for those foundations to be made before we arrived,
but we found out that no Provençal will take an ounce
of responsibility, and, though we had passed estimates
and plans directly they were sent to us in England in
August so that the work might be well advanced by the
time we came out to Provence in September, we found
on arrival that nothing had been started. The old Italian
entrepreneur who was building for us promised that the
work should be finished and the house ready for our
furniture by Christmas, but first the November rains and
then unusually sharp frosts delayed the work, and when
at last our furniture arrived from London in gigantic
vans none of the new rooms were ready to receive it. I
have described elsewhere that agonising arrival of our
furniture at the Domaine, but I omitted the awful *con-
tretemps* of its arrival in Nice. Before leaving England,
John had spent two solid hours locking drawers and
labelling keys with labels of untearable parchment specially

procured for this purpose. He had handed over forty
keys to the foreman of the removal firm which had been
recommended to us, so that there could be no difficulty
with the Customs at Nice. The foreman said that he
would travel to the South of France *with* the furniture
so that he could unlock any drawers or cases the Customs
officials wished to inspect. Imagine then our horror and
consternation when we received a telegram from these
officials informing us that our vans had arrived in Nice
and demanding the keys. We replied that they were in
the possession of the English foreman, whereupon we got
another very fierce telegram telling us that as we were
withholding our keys and obstructing the Customs examination, the locks of our furniture would be forced.
Further, we were commanded to appear before a tribunal
of Customs officials to explain our conduct.

Our removal firm had let us down badly. They were
under contract to collect and deliver our furniture ' from
door to door,' but had merely sent it over, unescorted,
to Nice, where they had put the job of delivering it to the
Domaine into the hands of a dumping firm which did
not even undertake to unpack and place the furniture
which it dumped.

We had to drive over to Nice in pouring rain to face
the enraged Customs officials. John, who was suffering
from tired head-nerves and consequent deafness, was
obliged to leave pleas and explanations to me, and my
French in those days was far from fluent. We found
our furniture all tipped out into the yard of the Customs ;
ancient locks of Chippendale cupboards, Sheraton chests
of drawers, and bureaus, forced open mercilessly and
their contents spilled out upon the dirty platform. I
never witnessed a more chaotic or depressing spectacle.
When I had talked, explained, gesticulated, and pleaded
we were at length allowed to depart after payment of
a heavy fine, and seeing our furniture permanently
damaged. I was so blind with rage, misery, and weariness

after this ordeal that in driving back to Grasse I lost the way, and we found ourselves benighted among pine-woods, driving endlessly along precipitous roads which, for all I knew, led directly to cliffs and the sea. Eventually we met a little man in a little car who, in answer to my despairing cry of " *Monsieur! Monsieur! Au secours! Nous sommes perdus,*" stopped his engine and began a voluble explanation of the route to Grasse. I was deaf as well as blind with weariness by this time, and, evidently seeing my vague and dazed expression, he suggested going ahead of us and giving us a lead through these black woods to the main road. He then tore ahead at a speed so frantic that I was hard put to it to keep his rear-light in view as I speeded after him, hurtling round hairpin bends, sweating with fright lest I skid over a precipice or lose sight of that red guiding star.

Eventually we got home, the journey from Nice having taken nearly five hours instead of forty minutes.

When, after every kind of complication, we had received our furniture (wrapped by the Customs people in our best linen sheets and pillow-cases to save trouble) and had stored our possessions into the few available rooms of the old cottage, and into garage, hen-houses, and rabbit-runs outside, we received a telegram from our removal firm in London saying—

" Keys in tobacco tin in Van 306."

As both vans had been gone from us for four days, we searched, indoors and out, for that tobacco tin—although the telegram was a little late to be of any use to us—and eventually discovered those unfortunate keys at the bottom of an old Dutch milk-can under a box of toilet paper, some old snow-boots of John's, and other oddments.

John, being honest and kind-hearted, had, unfortunately, sent an advance cheque to this removal firm. They had written telling us the date our furniture would be shipped and asking for an immediate payment for the removal before the money exchange shifted any more. So all that was left to him to do was to write vitriolic letters to them, and to turn the atmosphere of the Domaine blue with his picturesque curses. That did us both some good, but our scarred furniture remains as a perpetual reminder of that awful day and night.

We moved into our new home directly we had made the old section of the house habitable. The tiny existing *salon* had to contain John's huge writing-desk and my writing-table, besides two armchairs, a large chesterfield, and other furniture. We had to eat in the diminutive hall which opened into the kitchen, and all day we were obliged to listen to the barbaric music of masons, carpenters, and plumbers, and were powdered white with cement dust which blew into windows and filtered under doors. Even in these noisy and miserable conditions, John continued doggedly to write, shutting from his mind the deafening din of the workmen and writing, writing, writing, until Emilia summoned us to luncheon in our little hall. More than ever I encouraged him to spend hours in the open air, weeding in the garden, but although I provided a pneumatic kneeler and begged him to work gently, I noticed that he simply could not help putting as much force and energy into his gardening as he put into everything he did. He fought his weeds as frantically as he fought Fate. But he did great work in the garden, and I prompted Hilaire, our old gardener whom we had taken over with the property, to enlist John's help in cleaning off suckers from vines and tomatoes and in tying up Cos lettuces to make them ' heart up '; work which could not be done violently.

Our neighbour, Princess Torre Tasso, told me long after the event that she came to call upon us one day, but seeing John seated alone on the ground of an upper terrace, wearing an enormous Provençal straw hat and a beatific smile as he tied up his lettuces, she felt that it would be sheer cruelty to disturb him, and so turned round and crept away unseen. What marvellous tact.

We did not take leave of our warm-hearted but leisurely workmen until the month of May, but during this first enchanting spring—for life *out of doors* was enchanting— I, also, worked hard in our garden, sowing seeds and planting so that our little Domaine might soon be embowered in flowers.

We learned new and strange superstitions and methods of gardening in the South of France from Hilaire, whose Rabelaisian humour was a continual refreshment. There was so great an abundance of vegetables and fruit in our garden that we were obliged to sell the surplus to an hotel in Grasse, and I can see John now, clad in blue workman's overalls and the enormous straw hat, conscientiously preparing his vegetables for market, washing them in the great stone *bassin* on the top terrace, selecting carrots, turnips, and onions of the same size, and tying them into neat bundles of ten, in the cleanly and methodical French fashion.

When the workmen had sadly waved their last farewell and we were left in real possession of our lovely little Domaine our happiness knew no bounds. The peace and loveliness of our surroundings soaked into our tired spirits and we began to revive. By day, hot sun and a blaze of colours ; the warm, clear, flower-scented air. At night the silence broken only by the sound of hidden streams, the queer chorus of joyous mating frogs in the valley, and, later, by the song of nightingales throbbing their hearts out amid the dim olive groves. It was all so new to us and so beautiful that whatever we were doing, we had to stop and stare at some effect of light upon a mountain or some strange insect in the garden. Each day was filled with lovely or amusing sensations, experiences, and discoveries.

We had tried three *bonnes-a-tout-faire* while living in ' Trilby's ' flat, and, after three disappointments, had found Emilia ; a gay and sturdy little Italian who seemed thoroughly to enjoy cleaning up the mess indoors. At once she took complete charge of the Domaine and of us, and with her coming we felt that we really were established at last in our new home and could begin TO LIVE.

LXXV.

Indeed we did begin to live—and to love—every moment of this new life, and, although we had been plunged suddenly into endless and unforeseen difficulties and worries, John never once regretted the step we had taken. Always he said, sweeping long arms in an enveloping gesture towards the beauty and the profusion around us—

" Darling—in spite of everything I'm damned glad we came."

This constant assurance fortified me to bear a heavy load of anxiety. Had he once deplored the fact that we had effectually burned our boats so that not even a little dinghy was left to carry us across the Channel back to England ; or had he railed against our cruel luck ; that would have broken my spirit. But he wrote contentedly every morning in his *Galerie ;* he revelled in the good, cheap wines of the country, the olive oil, the Parmesan cheese (so expensive in England, and out here the cheese of the peasant) ; he was thrilled when our black Bresse hens laid eggs and our white *Vendée lapine,* given to us by Jacques Balsan, or the Chinchilla lady rabbit left by the Count, produced large families ; and when our queer pigeons with their feathered trousers hatched their eggs. The friendliness and quaint sayings of our peasant neigh-bours touched and amused him ; he enjoyed enormously making his daily tour of the terraces to inspect the pro-gress of our vines and fruit trees, fetching me out of doors to be introduced to every new opening bud of the flowers we had planted together ; to watch a hawk-moth piercing his beak into their hearts ; a stray locust perched on a post ; a praying mantis in his startling green coat

erect on hind legs, fore-legs pressed together as he chirped
his orisons ; gorgeous dragon-flies chasing each other
over the great stone basin like streaks of blue flame ;
and, most wonderful of all, the fireflies at night, which
we watched together as we sat under the pergola of
wistaria on the little stone-paved terrace above the rose-
garden after dinner ; listening to the tremendous voices
of little green tree-frogs.

Above all, John loved those little *tête-à-tête* dinners
in the garden. Emilia would trot up and down the stone
steps from the kitchen below, bringing *Monsieur's* favourite
dishes, cooked in her inimitable Italian way ; and, when
they had all been appreciated and removed, came the
quiet moment of coffee and cigarettes. *Monsieur* always
made the coffee himself from a delightful machine we had
brought with us from England, in which one watches
the amber coffee bubbling cheerfully. When it was made
and he had poured out mine and then his own, we would
sit quietly and happily talking, or just gazing at the
sea of roses before us in their lovely mountain setting,
until the last firefly had flickered away into the dim olive
groves, and we had counted the eleven lights of Magagnosc
on the opposite mountain. Then we would retire to his
Galerie where he read aloud to me while I embroidered or
knitted until bedtime.

We found that in Provence it is possible to be poor
with dignity, for the more one does for oneself the more
one is respected. Also, the loveliness of the scenery and
the caressing warmth of the sun soothe frayed nerves
into tranquillity. It is impossible to worry for very long
at a time in Provence. During the daytime one starts,
but the train of harassing thoughts is always interrupted
by some amusing incident, and at once one's troubled
mind is eased by laughter. The climate, also, helps one
to throw off care. Winter in England is a drear and
depressing thing, beginning in November and lasting
really until April. In Provence one can hardly date it,

for always there are flowers and the sun never deserts us for long. Spring comes so soon ; almost treading on the skirts of summer.

John, being a chilly mortal, basked in the sunshine as luxuriously as the lizards on our garden walls. It gave him joy to see a rose floating in his finger-bowl at dinner on Christmas Day ; to find a purple carpet of violets on the top terrace early in February ; and it inspired him, when writing, to look through the great arched door of his *Galerie* at a gay pageant of scarlet tulips, marching like battalions of his red-coated soldiers, down the grass-slopes leading to our front gate.

New ways and customs always interested John immensely. Nothing would satisfy him until Emilia took us down to the *Grand Marché* in Grasse when she went there to get her household provisions. We all drove down there in *Desirée*, my new Fiat car, and he accompanied Emilia to every stall, was introduced to every vendor of her acquaintance, and came home bursting with odd information.

Emilia, being tiny and fat, was immensely proud of conducting *Monsieur*, very tall and thin, around the market. She pattered along by his side, her head just reaching to his elbow, carrying her beloved *filet* and *Monsieur* her basket. Now and then she shot up a street so narrow that they could barely walk abreast ; pointing out ancient houses, wonderful old iron-work for which Grasse is famous, and peering under dark arched doorways to show him beautiful stone staircases.

Then, another day, he would suggest a mountain expedition, and he and I would drive off without any fixed idea of where we would go ; losing ourselves frequently along mountain tracks, but always finding some new and lovely scene, or strange wild flower—a scarlet lily on the slope leading to Callian ; a rare orchis ; some brilliant-plumaged bird the like of which we had never seen, or some curious formation of rock, such as the huge layered boulders which border the road by Tourrettes.

"This country must surely be volcanic," John would remark; "that curious formation of rounded hills and layered stones; the lovely colours in the rocks—rose, green, ochre; the sudden rifts and ravines."

The little towns, perched on the very tops of mountains, built there to avoid Saracen raids, and the endless walled terraces of vineyards or olive trees climbing to great heights, intrigued him vastly.

"God, the industry and patience of these people," he would remark. "Think of the centuries of work these walls and terraces represent. How on earth did they drag up their material to that height? And what a military position! Absolutely impregnable. They could roll down stones and pour boiling lead on to the heads of climbing assailants, and, of course, that is what they did.

"But drought was their most formidable enemy—you see that village up there has been abandoned—lack of water certainly."

He was the most fascinating companion, for his knowledge was encyclopedic, his eye missed nothing, and very often he became gay and adventurous as a schoolboy, so that it was impossible to believe that he was past seventy.

On holiday, he became a joyous boy, and no one could have recognised in him the stern preoccupied man whose working life was almost monastic in its simplicity and severity.

Some time after the beginning of our normal existence in our little Domaine, kind Lady Trent invited us to one of her innumerable parties in Cannes; this time to meet officers of the Mediterranean Fleet. We drove down to 'Springland,' where we were introduced to the Commander of the great aeroplane-carrier, the *Glorious*, and he, and some others, begged John to go to sea with them to witness their manœuvres. He adored the sea, and I

thought that this little change might do him good, so
that when they appealed to me to persuade him to go
with them as far as Naples, I encouraged him to accept
their invitation. I knew that he was longing to go, but
felt reluctant to leave me to cope with the furnishing
and arranging of the new wing of our house alone. However, this was work to which I was well accustomed,
and his absence would enable me to arrange his *Galerie*
so that it would be ready for him upon his return.

Before he left, I asked him to place all the soldier-
portraits of his Generals, mezzotints, and line-engravings
upon the floor of the *Galerie* in their periods and positions :
Marlborough and his bewigged Generals ; Clive, Stringer,
Lawrence and the Indian heroes together ; the Peninsular
men ; and so forth, so that I could make no mistake in
the hanging of their portraits. There were fifty of them
and they had been stored for nearly eight months, so that
frames and glass were filthy.

I drove him over to St Maxime, where the *Glorious* was
anchored outside the port. We were met by a Lieutenant
who took us out to the huge aeroplane-carrier ship in
the Captain's motor launch, and I saw my Man safely
installed in a comfortable cabin. Then, when I had
been shown over the ship, given tea, and my pockets
stuffed with illicit tins of cigarettes, I was conducted on
shore again by an officer and a ship's mechanic, who had
orders to go over the engine of my car to see that nothing
was wrong before I started on my journey to Cannes,
where it had been arranged that I should dine and spend
the night with Lady Trent.

It was visiting day on the *Glorious*, and, owing to the
fact that someone else had commandeered the Captain's
launch at the hour fixed for my departure, I was already
late in starting back, and had to drive faster than I liked
along that dangerous serpentine coast road.

As I entered the dining-room of Springland the guests
were just taking their places. Mine was next to the

Admiral of the Fleet, and I told him that my late
arrival was entirely due to the charming hospitality of
his officers.

Next day I rushed back to Grasse to grapple with
the arrangement of the house, and spent a very busy
week.

Hardly had I finished the *Galerie* when the telephone
bell shrilled in the hall, and Lady Trent's butler informed
me that Sir John had arrived at Springland and was
waiting for me.

It was a very weary and rather disappointed man that
I took home. The weather had been too bad to permit
of night manœuvres, and the terrific din of aeroplanes
continually landing upon the steel decks of the *Glorious*
had hurt his ears intolerably. Also, though admiring
all the modern inventions and the wonderful way in
which all work was carried out, he was depressed by the
substitution of machinery for the hand-labour of sailors,
and deplored, with the officers, the fact that the Navy
was fast becoming mechanised.

As usual, he began to revive as we approached his
beloved Domaine, and, arrived there, I immediately led
him upstairs and prepared his hot tub for him while he
undressed. I didn't want him to see the *Galerie* until it
was lit up and dinner ready to be served therein.

His room really did look lovely as we entered it together.
A great fire of olive logs was crackling in the open fireplace
at the apsidal end, and our round table, standing upon
its circular green carpet, was laid with white napery,
glass, and silver. I had arranged a bowl of floating red
roses in the centre, lit invisibly by the radiance of
the hidden lights within the three arched mirror-lined
niches above it in which my collection of glass was
displayed.

Tall standard lamps with apricot silk shades cast a
glow upon old bindings of books at the other end of the
room, and shone upon the faces of his ' Gallant Company '

388

portrayed above them. They looked very fine against their background of buffy-cream wall.

John stood quite still, screwed his eyeglass into his eye, threw back his head, and surveyed my work critically. Then—

" I repeat again ; mine is a very wonderful woman," he said softly. " A great success, Sweetheart. How well my soldiers look."

And then slowly he reviewed his ' Gallant Company,' touching and adjusting their frames lovingly as he toured the room.

" Curious face, Wolfe's—profile like the flap of an envelope, long imperious nose, and no chin at all. Able chap that."

" Dear old Abercrombie—I'm so fond of him. . . ."

" What an arrogant fellow Baird looks with his imperious outstretched arm. That white charger of his is completely out of drawing, but effective all the same. . . ."

" And old Granby—always portrayed without his wig. Do you know why, darling ? Because it fell off in action, and when the battle was going against him and his men were inclined to panic, suddenly they saw the sun shining upon the bald head of their leader far ahead of them, and they rallied round it."

" John Moore—a great hero of mine. What a fine man he was ; he had everything—ability, looks, and personal charm, and he conquered pain, and died slowly, in great agony, with a smile on his lips, thinking of his officers to the very last."

Emilia entered fussily with two little bowls of soup and he had to leave his soldiers, but all through dinner his eyes were wandering along the walls of his *Galerie*, saluting each member of his ' Gallant Company ' in turn, and his lips smiled happily throughout the meal.

" You love my soldiers, Sweetheart ? " he asked, as so often he had asked before.

LXXVI.

It was a very happy thing to see John seated at his great writing-desk in his *Galerie* next morning working, at last, under comfortable and quiet conditions, pacing up and down the long room at intervals, pipe in mouth, able once more to consult his precious books, so long packed away and inaccessible.

Even the heavy bills for building, which now began to come in, had not the power to mar completely those first happy months of occupation. They would furrow his brow and cause him an hour or two of moody restlessness, then he would square his shoulders, set his mouth into a grim line, and remarking to me, " We must write, and write hard for our bread, darling, that's all there is about it," would take up his pen again and drive it furiously until subtly interrupted by me by some urgent question concerning the arrangement of our garden which would lure him out of doors.

I had always admired the way difficulties and disasters only served to stimulate him to fresh effort ; his gift of such intense concentration, that nothing could upset a train of thought ; now I marvelled at the extraordinary ease and fluency with which he wrote, writing rapidly in his beautiful hand, with hardly a correction, what I called ' his inevitable prose.' Latterly he would write a vivid article or a forceful review which would have taken an ordinary man a fortnight to compose and polish for Press, in only an hour or two. Always they were accepted by enthusiastic publishers, and he would bring their letters for me to read with a little quiet smile of content.

He began to write his reminiscences, afterwards christened ' Author and Curator,' about this time, with happy interest. For this I was thankful, for I had always dreaded that one day I might be called upon to write his biography,

and I knew that I could never remember in detail the mass
of work he had accomplished whilst arranging the Library
and the six collections under his care at Windsor. He
read it to me, chapter by chapter, and the only criticism
I could make was that he made nothing at all of the
gigantic task of writing 'A History of the British Army,'
which had eaten up thirty-six of his best years. I felt
that his soldiers would like to have known how he accomplished it against desperate odds. But no, he seemed to
think nothing of this great achievement.

"The book is DONE—for what it is worth," he would
say to me and dismiss the subject.

The demand for articles about life and the activities
of the English in a foreign country had died the death,
and the market for my work seemed closed. John said :
"Blackwood liked the articles you sent him when we were
in England. Why not send him some about our queer
happy life here ? It will all be new to his readers."

And so I climbed up into my Tower and began to write
an account of our adventures whilst moving in to our
Domaine.

When it was finished, a few days later, I carried it down
to John, who had had his bath, and, dressed for dinner,
was sitting in his *Galerie* doing his canvas-work, happily
embroidering a lovely design with slim deft fingers.

I gave him my sheets of pencilled manuscript, and then
pottered about the *Galerie* rearranging the flowers and
casting nervous glances surreptitiously at him as he read.
He was a wonderful but severe critic, and I was just
waiting to see whether he would be amused or damn
my work with censure or faint praise. Suddenly I saw
him begin to shake with silent laughter until the eyeglass
fell out. The chuckling continued as he read and I became
reassured. Finally he handed me back my scribbled
pages, saying—

"*Good*, darling, it runs along. All your people are
alive and kicking—your narrative is fluent and vivid. I

hadn't realised how funny it all was. I suppose the agony of it was too great at the time. Send it to Blackwood, Sweetheart—he'll take it all right. In my opinion he'd be a d——d fool if he didn't."

This was high praise from John, who then encouraged me to write a series of articles about our life in Provence.

There was endless material, each day provided more and more. I never went into the town of Grasse, nor even into our garden or kitchen, without some quaint experience or hearing and seeing something touching or amusing. And so, in the intervals of housekeeping, gardening, letter-writing, and doing secretarial work for John, I scribbled up in my Tower, always bringing the results to be vetted by him in the evening. He never changed a word, though he frequently corrected my punctuation (always a difficulty with me), and sometimes, though rarely and then triumphantly, my spelling.

We lived a curious kind of life—a mixture of civilised and purely peasant days—driving down to the coast to attend a few—very few—social functions, and spending the rest of our time writing, and working in our garden.

Hilaire, our gardener, was a continual joy. It was thrilling to watch his Provençal methods of sowing seeds, irrigating the garden, tending his vines and his olive trees, and our beasts and birds.

He was extraordinarily keen, and, as the summer advanced and *la grande chaleur* fell upon us, he would come at five o'clock in the morning to water the garden before the heat of the sun became fierce, and long after our dinner-hour we would see his faithful form watering in the cool of the evening.

But I have described Hilaire and our garden and Emilia and our queer housekeeping in that series of articles suggested by John, which were afterwards reprinted in book form by Mr Blackwood, who christened the small volume ' Perfume from Provence,' so I will not repeat myself.

We decided to spend our first summer in Provence, although we were warned that nearly all the English colony fled to higher altitudes, or went home during *la grande chaleur*, which generally begins in mid-June and abates in mid-September.

Having only just left the chilly climate of England, we were looking forward to a heavy dose of heat, and were anxious to watch our grapes ripen and to eat our own melons from the half-acre of different varieties sown by Hilaire in open ground.

We did not find the heat excessive, because Grasse being heavily planted with ancient olive trees, there is always abundant shade, and the Domaine is situated near to the little mountain torrent *Le Riou*, and between many natural springs which cascade into the great *bassins* of near-by estates and overflow into the valley, so that everywhere one hears the sound of hidden water, gurgling and rippling downhill.

Also, when enlarging our house, we had taken care so to build the new rooms that they had windows on either side to ensure a continual draught of fresh air blowing through them in summer.

The heat, when it came, was dry heat, which is easily supportable if one remains indoors in the middle of the day when the sun is fiercest. In July, I, who had always secretly pitied those who found a *siesta* after luncheon necessary, was very ready to throw off most of my clothes and flop down upon the divan in my Tower for an hour or two. Refreshed by iced tea, I was then able to don my workman's overalls and go out to help Hilaire water the garden until dinner-time.

John revelled in the heat and surprised me by his energy. He would write every morning and go for mountain walks after tea ; or attack weeds in the garden with his usual ferocity, always with a smile of happiness upon his face. . . .

I love to remember that smile and to be sure that

during his short life in Provence nothing had power to shake his inner happiness and content; neither the financial cares that beset us nor the sickness that was so soon and so unexpectedly to maim him. He had, at least, the joy of a new adventure in a lovely land before that last long trial of endurance was sent to test his strength.

Many months of severe illness; of slow recovery and discouraging relapse, taught him a gentleness with others, and patience under endless inhibitions and the indignities of the sick-room, that were foreign to his nature, for, if he had a defect of character, it had been, perhaps, an impatience of illness in any other than his wife, and a resentment against any form of imposed restraint. He learned to bear all that had to be borne, and even to joke about it; helped by the understanding of a very wonderful French doctor and a little nurse who loved him.

LXXVII.

He became suddenly and terrifyingly ill and Doctor Brès rushed him to a French hospital in Cannes; the English hospital being closed during the summer months. His spirit remained indomitable. After the first crisis was safely passed, he awoke from the deadly sleep of coma with a heartening " Damn " upon his lips because he found himself too weak to leap at once from his bed.

And the very next morning his nurse came to me and said: " Lady Fortescue, your husband kept asking me all night for paper and a pencil. Of course I didn't give them to him for I wanted him to sleep—and in any case he is too weak to hold a pencil. What can he want them for ? "

" *To write*—he is fretting because he can no longer write. Give him his pencil and his paper, Sister, he won't be able to write but it will comfort him to have them near him."

She gave him his paper and his pencil before she went off duty, and then came to me, in wonder, to tell me that weak and ill as he was, he had, through sheer force of will, forced himself to write five words. Those five words formed part of the opening sentence of a masterly article, entitled " What is War," which appeared, weeks later, in 'Blackwood's.' Painfully he wrote a few words each day, then rewrote them, and when after a period of months that article was finished and handed to me to send to England, for the first time I dared not read a composition of John's, so sure was I that it *must* fall far below his high standard of work. When it was eagerly accepted, published, and acclaimed as one of the finest things he had ever written, this little triumph did more good than all his medicines. Once more he had become a wage-earner.

John's deep-rooted prejudice against all doctors was overcome during the first visit of Doctor Brès, who examined him very minutely and then said—

" *Monsieur, je suis contente de vous.*"

" That is what Napoleon said to his soldiers," whispered John instantly.

" That is why I said it to a military historian," replied Doctor Brès, that wonderful psychologist, and ever afterwards John was devoted to him.

A few days later Doctor Brès told me that, the danger past, John would recover more quickly if I took him home. The Sirocco was scorching us in Cannes, and up in our mountains the air would be cooler and he could be fed upon *bouillon* made from our own fresh vegetables. He would certainly be happier in his own little Domaine, and he needed every encouragement that could be given to him just then.

Knowing the difficulty of controlling my restive Arab horse, I told Doctor Brès that I refused to be responsible for John's convalescence unless I had the doctor's written orders with which to control him. Five minutes later I was presented with a large sheet of instructions headed—

CONSEILS MILITAIRES.

" *Le poilu*, Jean Fortescue," it began, and continued by detailing all the medical treatment that this private soldier was to follow. At the foot of this document the doctor had written :

Signé,

BRÈS. *Général.*

Because his orders were given to him as to a soldier, John followed them with perfect obedience, and my admiration of Dr Brès became ever more profound. Nevertheless, with a sick terror, I dreaded our return to the Domaine, for no nurse could be spared from the hospital and John was as weak as a kitten. He was so precious, I so inexperienced in nursing, and Doctor Brès had warned me that my Man would always now be " *Très, très fragile.*" While I was thinking of this awful responsibility, one of the nurses came in to tell me that a gentleman was in the waiting-room who wished to see me. Wondering who this could possibly be, I went out, and to my great joy found Charles, my brother-in-law. He had had my last despairing letter and had rushed out.

We got our patient home safely, and into his own spacious green bedroom, wheeling his bed close to one of the great arched windows so that he could gaze at his favourite round mountain backed by silvery olive groves and the distant sea. He was so happy to be back in his beloved Domaine and to be greeted by the beaming and voluble Hilaire and Emilia, who were enchanted to have their dear ' *Monsieur* ' with them again, and at once he began to revive. It certainly was much cooler in Grasse than in Cannes, but, even so, the heat during the day was

intense. After his first conventionally attired appearance
at luncheon, Charles pleaded my indulgence if he removed
his coat and ate in his shirt-sleeves. The next day we
neither of us bothered to dress ourselves formally, but
with one consent came downstairs, he in a silk dressing-
gown worn over pyjamas and I in a kimono worn over
my nightgown, both of us with bare feet thrust into
slippers.

It was such a tremendous relief to have the dear sane
solidarity of his presence at that time, and to be able to
go out into the garden to do some watering, leaving him
lying upon a *chaise longue* within call of John, ready to
go into his room for a little gossip or to fetch him anything
that he might want. But I could not enlist Charles to
help in the garden while I was on duty. Once, indeed,
he did offer to help Hilaire with the heavy watering, which
must be done morning and night during *la grande chaleur*.
He was posted upon the terrace, below John's *Galerie*,
and given a hose to water the seed-beds on the terrace
below. But the hose had lost its spray, and to manipulate
it for light watering was an art not quickly acquired.
It was necessary to put a thumb or a finger-end half
over the end of the tube to control the gush of water,
so forcing it into a fine spray, and a beginner was likely
to squirt the water into his own face before he learned
the trick of directing it where he willed. This Charles
did once or twice, and I heard muffled execrations rising
upon the evening air; after which the silence was
unbroken save by the soothing sound of whispering water.
But in the morning, when I saw Hilaire, he beckoned
me mysteriously aside and hissed into my ear in toothless
Provençal the sad news that ' *Monsieur le Général* ' had
washed all Hilaire's precious pansy plants clean out of
the earth. I suppose that poor Charles became bored,
or that the beauty of the evening made him vague,
and so he forgot that water, descending from a tank
six terraces above him through a narrow hose, unless

properly controlled becomes a dangerous element with such pressure behind it.

John looked forward eagerly to the visits of Doctor Brès, and I loved to see the animation in his face, see his arms flung out wide in welcome as he cried, " *Bon jour, mon Général !* " and the reply, " *Bon jour, mon Caporal,*" for, after the successful journey home and several well-disciplined days without relapse, Doctor Brès had promoted the *poilu*, Jean Fortescue, to the rank of *Caporal*. When the medical examination was over, they would talk happily together for half an hour, and the doctor's good company helped John more than many tonics.

Another welcome visitor who enlivened John was General Sir Aylmer Haldane. He had always had an immense admiration for John Fortescue as the Historian of the British Army ; now enormously increased for the man, himself, when he saw his dogged determination to continue to earn money with his pen though handicapped so severely by illness. He told a friend that it was the most pathetic and gallant thing he had ever seen, to watch John, so frail and ill, writing, writing, writing ; refusing to admit disability or defeat, fighting fiercely against desperate odds to straighten out our financial position and to pay his debts. To me, the General said that John reminded him always of his (and John's) favourite hero, Sir John Moore, and that he never thought of the one without recalling the other ; the same charm, courage, and endurance ; the same indifference to physical pain.

Hugo Wemyss, an old bachelor acquaintance of John's, lived in a little *maisonette* contained in the ancient home-farm of *Château Malbosc*, just above us, belonging to a dear French friend of mine, Gabrielle de Croze, who was also a tower of strength at that time. He had often visited the Domaine and enjoyed gossiping with John about old friends in England and amusing episodes of their youth. He preferred to come on Emilia's day out, when he helped me make tea and toast cosily in the little kitchen. He was a great comfort to me during those months and months of grief and anxiety. Often, as I drove in to Grasse to do the marketing, I would see his picturesque figure sitting on a bench beside the road clad in blue linen workman's trousers, a Breton *béret* pulled over that noble head, his thin figure sometimes wrapped in a voluminous peasant's cloak, a string bag clasped in one beautiful hand. Dressed as a peasant, he always looked a king. His very blue eyes would light up and he would doff the *béret*, displaying the thick silver-white hair smoothly brushed back from the high brow. He had the manners of John ; a perfect old-world courtesy, so rarely found to-day.

LXXVIII.

John, as a convalescent, was far easier than most men to keep happy and amused. He would write for half an hour at a time, then pick up his loved canvas-work. Then he would read his 'Times' or an Oppenheim 'thriller' lent him by a neighbour. He hated being read to, for he said that it seemed so slow to him—his mind flew ahead of the reader, finished the sentence long before it was read aloud, and then, being bored, wandered off on a train of thought of its own—so that one of my few accomplishments was useless to amuse him.

It was a great day when at last he was allowed to go out into his garden, and a greater still when he was permitted to sit on a rug on the ground and to dig weeds out of a low wall. He was thrilled, when strong enough to mount the stone stairways and visit his vines with Hilaire. Already he was looking forward to taking part in our *vendange*, and soon was helping Hilaire to remove leaves which shaded the great clusters of grapes from the sun.

Directly we began to resume our normal existence, Charles went back to England.

Before his illness John had begun to write his autobiography. His reminiscent talks with Charles had revived many memories of their youth, of Castle Hill, their Devon home, of Harrow, and, later in life, their journeyings together in Europe, visiting old battlefields and verifying positions of troops ; so now was a good moment to begin writing remembered episodes and making notes for the book. I encouraged him to start again, thinking that such writing would amuse and could not tire him. In the evenings he read to me what he had written, and our happy tranquil life together amid these heavenly surroundings was renewed.

" He will always be very, very fragile." Those words of Doctor Brès haunted me, and I realised their truth as I saw how easily John tired.

But very gradually his strength came back. A loved niece of his, Joyce Carew (daughter of Arthur Fortescue), came out to cheer his convalescence ; and in September our friends and neighbours returned. John enjoyed taking ' little doddles,' as he called his short walks through the olive groves outside the Domaine, and soon he was strong enough to climb the ascent to Villa d'Andon and visit our kind neighbour, Mr McCoy, an American with a passion for books who had a fine collection of volumes and papers connected with the American War of Independence. John was able to decipher for him inscriptions written in old English on the fly-leaves of many of these books, and they talked happily together under the great plane trees of that lovely garden, while Mrs McCoy, a keen gardener, would show me her herbaceous border ; after which we would go into the old beamed sitting-room, once a kitchen, and devour the most wonderful teas. Mr McCoy would then visit John and study his library, and he would make a tour of our vines, discovering for us many table varieties we did not know we possessed, for he had studied vines since he came to live in Provence, and was also an iris specialist. I have many specimens that he gave me in my garden to-day.

Little Princess Torre Tasso, owner of *Château Malbosc*, was another delightful neighbour. During her summer absence she had given orders that the glorious carnations for which the *Château* is famous should be sent to us with the surplus fruit and vegetables, and it was a great thrill to see one of her gardeners, heavily laden, labouring up our drive, his head poking through a magnificent shower-bouquet of enormous carnations, mauve, pink, red, sulphur, yellow, and white. It took me an hour to arrange the spoil from the *Château* greenhouses.

We had not been long in the Domaine when someone told me that the famous ' Elizabeth,' who once wrote of her German garden, lived in Mougins. Since flapper-hood I had been a lover of her books and had thought that she was one of the few writers that I wanted to know. An artist, Vivian Guy, had told me that ' Elizabeth ' was anxious to meet John and me on her return from Switzer-land, and I had looked forward to this meeting enormously. She had written to ask me to tea during the week that I had had to take John down to the hospital, and I had left a message to be telephoned by Emilia to explain why I could not come. ' Elizabeth ' had then telephoned to the hospital begging me to go and stay with her during this anxious time.

Though I did not accept that warm-hearted invitation I can never forget it, and it made me all the more anxious to meet ' Elizabeth.' We three became friends, and her visits did much to cheer John's convalescence. He delighted in her quick wit and the outrageous things she said, looking at him the while with large innocent blue eyes from under a wide-brimmed hat. He admired her little short nose and her tiny feet, and said that his first impression of her was that of a slim girl of sixteen walking into his *Galerie*. Bless her, she walked into it as often as she could, realising my secret anxiety about John, and that her presence cheered us both.

LXXIX.

It would have been a very happy autumn and winter for me had I not been haunted by the fear that John might relapse. And in December the thing that I had so dreaded came to pass.

One stormy night he got out of bed, and, without waiting to put on dressing-gown or slippers, crept out of his dressing-room, where he was sleeping, and walked barefoot on the cold tiled floors of the corridor to fix a banging shutter. All this I heard some hours later. I had had a painful treatment and was sleeping the sleep of the exhausted. I was awakened very early next morning by a hoarse voice calling my name, followed by a crash, and, leaping out of bed, saw John lying unconscious in my doorway.

His pulse was alarmingly low, and in terror I telephoned to Doctor Brès's house, asking his maid to beg the doctor to come to the Domaine before he drove down to his consulting-room in Cannes.

He came at eight o'clock, and while examining his *Caporal* he looked very grave. Afterwards, alone with me, he told me that we must be prepared for anything, but that for the moment the only thing for so feeble a pulse and sub-normal a temperature was complete rest of mind and body in a warm bed. When the doctor had gone, promising to come again in the evening on his way home, John whispered weakly : " Darling, I am so sorry to have caused you this extra worry by my thoughtlessness ; but it is so d——d difficult to realise that one is old."

Difficult for hi⌐ and impossible for anyone else to realise that, for part of him would always remain an adventurous little boy.

For three days his condition never varied and I know that Doctor Brès feared most a collapse of the heart after so great a shock of cold. On the fourth morning, when I was feeding John, he suddenly looked at me with very brilliant eyes and whispered urgently—

" I must get up and straighten this financial muddle, but I am entangled in skeins and skeins of wool and I cannot free my legs and arms. Help me, darling—cut me free. For God's sake cut me free and help me to get up, or we are lost."

Delirium. . . .

Again I telephoned to Doctor Brès.

" I cannot come till this afternoon for I have several operations which I must attend this morning," he said. " But I will come as quickly as I can, and, in the meantime, I will send you an English nurse from Sunny Bank Hospital for it is not safe for you to be alone with him."

An hour later a dear little nurse was driven to our door in the hospital car, and in the late afternoon came Doctor Brès, who was completely puzzled by John's symptoms. There was no congestion in the lungs and no cough, so that it could not be pneumonia, but there was this burning fever, and tests showed later that he was full of B. Coli germs.

A night nurse was also prescribed, for his condition might develop into something extremely dangerous at any moment, and another telephone message to the English hospital in Cannes, late in the evening, was answered by the appearance at ten o'clock on a stormy night of a little brown-eyed nurse, very much like a perky robin, who introduced herself as ' Nell Burford.' Her personality instantly reassured me, for, tiny though she might be, she exuded confidence and competence.

I hope my welcome expressed the warmth and gratitude that I felt.

I had told Emilia to make me a bed in my Tower writing-room, above my bedroom, which must now be given up to the nurses as it communicated with John's. With my door open in the Tower-room I could still hear every sound in his, and I could creep downstairs to look at him whenever I liked.

Doctor Brès feared that John might develop typhoid, Maltese fever—even pneumonia. His symptoms were so baffling that diagnosis was impossible. At last pneumonia declared itself in all its horror, but then the battle became straightforward. Never in my life have I witnessed so many dawns. I did not draw the curtains of the three arched windows of my round Tower lest I should sleep too soundly, and when the first grey light glimmered into the room I rose and went out on to the roof-terrace, there to watch the coming of morning. I lifted up mine eyes unto the hills. . . . The vast expanse of rounded mountains before me; the sea of olive groves below me would gradually emerge from the early morning mists which wreathed the hills like swirling scarves, now hiding part of the scene, now revealing just the top of a mountain, so that it seemed to float in a white sea of cloud. The sky slowly became suffused with the soft shades of a moonstone, tender and mysterious; then the mist-wreaths curled upwards and formed little clouds which soon the sun, rising over the rim of the mountains, transformed into a flight of flamingoes soaring against a sky of green and gold. Dark cypresses, on the skyline, stabbed the red radiance of the dawn; a little breeze awoke and stirred the olive trees, turning their leaves so that they shimmered and rippled in silver waves across the plain.

After days and nights that seemed interminable the crisis passed, and Doctor Brès decided that only one nurse was now necessary. The day nurse had been spared from the staff of the hospital, whereas the little night nurse belonged to the visiting staff, sent to nurse outdoor cases, and therefore she remained with us and undertook day duty. From that moment this small

person began to mother and to manage us all, but she
did it so quietly and tactfully that even the bossy quick-
tempered Emilia and our high-spirited housemaid could
not resent her, for, although she gave the orders for John's
special foods and drinks, she herself went down to the
kitchen to fetch the trays, and, having seen that they
were covered with spotless linen and a little bowl of
flowers placed there to make the dull invalid food look
more attractive, she would carry those trays up to his
room with her own hands. She poured strengthening
fluids into me, insisting upon giving me soothing massage
when I could not sleep, for among other things she was
an expert *masseuse ;* and she even conquered grumpy
old Hilaire by praising his vegetables, as she begged the
best to make *bouillon* for his beloved *Monsieur.*

Her great ambition was to get John strong enough to
have his luncheon sitting in a chair in his bedroom on his
birthday. I had told her that the anniversary was on
28th December—Innocents' Day—" A singularly in-
appropriate feast for my birthday," as he always said.

On the day itself Dr Brès came very early, and after
the usual meticulous examination of his *Caporal* he gave
permission to his patient to get out of bed for a little
while.

John was as excited as a child. For some time he had
pleaded daily with his doctor to allow this privilege. His
little nurse tripped about his room, arranging the birthday
bouquets of flowers. With my help, she dragged in one
of the comfortable armchairs from the *salon*, piling
its back with cushions ; and then devoted herself to the
task of washing her invalid and wrapping him in woollens.
Between us we helped him out of bed and guided his
staggering steps to the armchair, into which he sank
exhausted, but beaming with pride.

A dainty little luncheon was prepared for him which
he thoroughly enjoyed, and then came the supreme
moment of the day, a few drops of the coffee he loved and

a few whiffs of a cigarette—the first for weeks. This was the birthday treat permitted by Doctor Brès.

I had gone downstairs to make the coffee, and the little nurse suggested that it could be enjoyed more comfortably in bed. John had been sitting up for half an hour and she detected signs of weariness. She helped him to his feet, and suddenly he gave a cry. "What *is* it, Sir John ? " she asked, startled. "A sudden sharp pain in my leg," he gasped. "A muscle unused for some time, I suppose," but his face had gone grey.

It proved to be a clot in the big vein of the leg—and a wandering clot.

John received the news that he must lie immovable, flat upon his back, for some long time, with the dreadful apathy of despair ; and Doctor Brès, seeing that look in his eyes—the look of a soldier who at last accepts defeat —swiftly decided that it were better to ignore the conventional clot treatment and leave this particular man a certain freedom of movement lest, constricted and confined, he pine away and die.

A hefty nurse must be found to help the little Sister to move him when necessary, but the special bed and sand-bags need not be used. I knew the reason of that expression in John's eyes. His brain was clear as ever now, and he knew the fearful cost of illness—the desperate state of our finances—and realised that if he must lie flat upon his back, writing would be impossible.

Our friends and neighbours were so wonderfully kind to me during those anxious imprisoned weeks ; sending flowers, fruit, and books for John ; coming to see me or writing and telephoning. One who never failed me during that awful time was ' Elizabeth.' In spite of her literary work, which she takes very seriously, shutting herself up every morning in her Garden Studio where her servants are forbidden to disturb her on pain of dismissal ; and of her numerous social engagements, which are the penalty of being a ' lion-ess ' (in her tiny case it ought to be ' cub '), she would come and share a toast-and-jam tea with me in John's *Galerie*, roving about from chair to chair as she munched—"I can't bear to feel anchored, Peggy"—making startling statements with an air of blue-eyed innocence, looking like a small ethereal child as she uttered worldly cynicisms, intended to rouse my mind from the lethargy of depression and to startle a laugh out of me. Almost daily she telephoned for news of John.

At long last John's daily prayer to Doctor Brès that he might be allowed to put foot to the ground was granted. For some time now the swelling of the leg had abated and 'Tiny,' as we had grown accustomed to call the little nurse, had been allowed to give gentle massage to restore the wasted muscles.

"He imagines that he will be able to put his foot to the ground, poor darling," she confided to me, "but he will find that the muscles have shrunk so that he can't. He will have to learn to walk all over again."

And when the longed-for moment came, and, supported by Tiny and Doctor Brès, John tried to stand up, he had the bitter disappointment of finding that one leg was very definitely shorter than the other.

That night his temperature flew up and he began to cough. An unsuspected remnant of clot, which should have dispersed long ago, had flown up into the lungs. Pneumonia again. . . .

Oh God of Pity. . . .

Once again we fought that awful battle, our powers of resistance and our remnant of courage weakened by months of strain. Doctor Brès came constantly. His vigilance never relaxed, his skill and encouragement were lavished upon 'that dear man,' for he had learned to love my Man as did everyone who really knew him.

Once more we won our battle, and, in the late spring, when his sister, Francie Gordon Duff, had come out from England to cheer John's convalescence, we had the joy of carrying him in a bath chair out into his beloved garden, ablaze now with the glory of spring flowers, and of seeing his beautiful frail hands caress the petals of flaming St Brigid anemones and slender tulips which bordered the drive of the Domaine. I shall never forget that slow and happy progress, Tiny fluttering on one side of his chair in her white butterfly veil, and Francie and I walking on the other, while old Hilaire proudly propelled it along the terrace ; Emilia and Lucienne chattering excitedly in rear—all of us anxious to point out new glories which for so long John had not seen.

The sun was so hot that Tiny permitted him to sit out of doors while he gossiped happily with Francie and to have his luncheon in the porch of the front door where, sheltered from the light wind, he could sit and stare at the tapestry of flowers before him. A glorious day for us all, and the harbinger of yet happier days to follow as his strength slowly but surely returned to him, and hope and joy to me. Soon he was learning to walk again, leaning upon Tiny, who clasped him around the waist, her head under his elbow, he was so tall and she so little. He became his own impatient irritable self, restive under restraint, eager to do more each day, chafing because his writing hours were severely limited ; indignant because his diet must still be carefully restricted and supervised.

" He's getting tiresome. *Such* a good sign," purred Tiny, and one day while she was giving him his massage I heard the sound of a resounding slap, then silence, then a shout of laughter. Going into his room I found John chuckling and Tiny with a very flushed face.

" What's happening in here ? " I inquired.

" Oh, Lady Fortescue, I am so sorry, but I really couldn't help it—he *is* so tiresome—he *will* try to help himself instead of relaxing. . . ."

" It's the first time in my life that I have been slapped by a woman, Peg," laughed John. " Why do you leave me in the power of this great bully ? " patting Tiny's correcting hand affectionately.

She adored him, and I delighted in their conversations, for she was hungry for information of every kind.

" How I should have enjoyed teaching that intelligent child," John said to me. " She is so very bright and receptive ; I could have made anything of her."

She had been brought up with a crowd of brothers and boy-cousins, so that she understood men even better than women, and was one of the very few people who could ever manage John. She bossed him most beautifully, and he nearly always obeyed her in the end, even though a short battle of wills and words might prelude his defeat.

Summer came and *la grande chaleur* was upon us. Though John rejoiced in the hot sunshine, he was nervous and anæmic from long confinement indoors. Tiny and I began to wilt. Doctor Brès prescribed a sea-voyage for his *Caporal*, and suggested that I should take him to England by sea. He wanted to break the atmosphere of invalidism, and said that only a voyage from home would give John back confidence. Tiny was anxious to see her family, and promised to travel with us to keep an eye on John if we went to England, and this decided me. I went down to Cannes and booked berths for the three of us on the Dutch boat *Baloeran*, sailing from Marseilles.

LXXX.

John was never so happy as when on a voyage. He adored the sea, even its storms and the feeling of freedom and escape given by ships. Only at sea could he be really lazy ; the knowledge that no letters could reach him and no telephone tease, rested him at once. He would lie in a deck-chair, not even reading, but just staring at the ever-changing sea, or prowl the decks for hours.

Tiny, an inveterate sightseer, was thrilled when our ship put into ports. She went ashore with the Head Sister (now Matron) of Sunny Bank Hospital, Miss Williams, who was likewise travelling home to England on leave. We four shared the same table at meals ; marvelling at the enormous quantity of food supplied, and the swift noiseless waiting of the Malay servants.

We had a calm passage, but were delayed by fog ; otherwise it was uneventful.

We went first to London where John had business with his lawyer, and where he was visited by his brother Charles ; lunched with his sisters Mary Bridgeman and Lucy St Aldwyn, all enchanted to see him looking so well after his long illness, and then we went down to the house of an old CINTRA customer of mine who had recently lost her mother and was living alone in a small manor-house in Kent. Here, in the peace of the country and the care of a devoted little friend, John spent the remainder of his time in England, tended by the faithful Tiny, who deferred her holiday so that she might watch over him. He corrected the proofs of various articles destined for ' Blackwood's Magazine,' and he tried to show his gratitude to our hostess for ensuring his peace and rest by frantically weeding her herbaceous border, which was in the usual state of late-summer overgrowth. Members of our respective families and many friends came to see us here, including our old friend Francis Oppenheimer, who brought with him his delicious new wife whom I loved at sight. With her young face, her apple-blossom skin, clear blue eyes, shining white hair and indescribable *chic*, she looked exactly like a figure painted upon an eighteenth century French fan. She looked altogether too good to be true, but, happily, wasn't. Something in her drew forth from me all the past agony about John, and the apprehensive future. When I had done, I marvelled at myself for having confided so spontaneously in someone I was meeting for the first time—only it didn't

seem to me like the first time ; I felt that I had always
known Janette.

While I was talking to her, John was confiding his
anxieties about me to Francis, asking him to become
my unofficial guardian and adviser should I be left lonely
and in need of help. In fact John and I were talking
each of the other the whole of that afternoon. I wonder
if those two dear visitors realised the comfort they gave
to us ?

Another friend we saw was our Scotch cook-housekeeper
of Hampstead days, our once-faithful 'Odd,' who was
now 'placed' in a village near-by. We drove over to
see her, and I have a happy last vision of her as she
kissed the hands of her old master in farewell.

During this visit to England I was obliged constantly
to go up to London to settle business affairs and visit
doctors, leaving John in the care of his hostess and
Tiny. Very thankful was I for the peaceful intervals
enjoyed in Kent, basking in the old-world garden or
helping with a canteen for hop-pickers, for the hop-
vines were being stripped.

LXXXI.

At last the day came when we must go home to Provence.
We bade farewell to a tearful Tiny, and were driven to
Dover where we crossed the Channel and got straight
into our *wagon-lit* at Calais, as Doctor Brès had impressed
upon me the risk of a return journey by sea for John
when the equinoctial gales were likely to begin.

It was the first time for many months that I had been
left in sole charge of my precious Man, and I was inwardly
terrified of the responsibility, because each of his serious
illnesses had come upon him absolutely without warning.
He looked splendid now, but I knew the danger of the
slightest chill or over-fatigue and—I knew my Arab horse.

Could I care for his health adequately ? Could I control him, restrict his diet and his terrible energy ?

Our journey was, however, a complete success. I had arranged that John's berth in the *wagon-lit* should be made up at Calais instead of at Paris, so that he got straight into bed the moment we entered the boat-train, and was able to rest during the long journey to Paris. So cheerful and refreshed was he when evening came, that he insisted upon dining with me in the restaurant car, after which he slept through the night and awoke beaming and hungry for his coffee and rolls.

He was as excited as I to see his first olive trees from the windows of the restaurant car, and he got more and more thrilled as we neared Cannes, where our car would be awaiting us.

Back in our own little Domaine, greeted by a dancing Hilaire and Emilia, he became a child again, and rather an over-excited child, for he rebelled against my depressing suggestion that he should go immediately indoors and lie down—he *must* first make a round of the terraces with Hilaire, to see his crop of ripening grapes—he wasn't in the least tired, he was " as fresh as a daisy."

He certainly did not look in the least tired — a pair of very brilliant eyes pleaded with me not to be ' governessy ' on this his first morning at home : " Come with me, Sweetheart, and see which of your flowers are in bloom," he cunningly cajoled me, with that irresistible smile irradiating a very brown face. Of course I weakly gave in, and went.

It was wonderful to watch him climbing the stone steps of the terraces with a firm assured tread. As I watched him, now, I found it difficult to believe that this was the same man who had crawled painfully along the level supported by Tiny and me only six weeks ago, and my heart rejoiced within me.

All through luncheon John was in the highest spirits, teasing me and chaffing Emilia who made every kind of excuse to invade the *Galerie* so that she might have glimpses of *Monsieur* as he devoured her dishes, and when the coffee tray was brought in he insisted that *I* should stretch myself upon the divan while *he* made the coffee and served me.

Those golden days of late September and early October shine in my memory with the radiance of the Southern sun, which blessed us every day. Only on the morning of our *vendange* did we have rain, to the bitter disappointment of John, who longed to cut his own grapes and whose ardour had to be restrained because of the downpour. But he superintended their weighing as before, sheltered by the porch.

He gloried in our autumn roses in the rose-garden and the blaze of dahlia-zinnias in the beds bordering the front terrace ; he revelled in the long drives we had together high up into the mountains, getting out to pick wild flowers or to picnic in a pine-wood ; the happy hours we spent working gently in our garden ; the 'little doddles' we took through the olive groves in the cool of the late afternoon, and best of all he loved our quiet evenings, he reading aloud to me as I worked, as of old.

Blood tests showed that he was marvellously better. So proud and excited was I by this joyful news that I immediately rang up Doctor Brès and told him that his *Caporal* had earned his stripe, for John had had the promise that if he came back from England in normal health, he should be promoted to the rank of *Serjeant*.

" He is longing to see his *Général*," I said. " Do please come and see how splendid he looks."

There was a pause, and then the very sad voice of Doctor Brès told me that his beloved wife was very, very ill and that he was taking her at once to Paris where she might have to undergo an operation.

For a long time I sat before that telephone in chilled

quietness, all my joy dimmed by the knowledge that our
' beloved physician ' was going away. If John should
need his skill he could not come. Tiny was in England ;
but a few days later I had a letter from her telling
me that she was sick of the English climate, and begging
me to allow her to finish her holiday in the sunshine of
the Domaine with us.

Very soon she was singing about the garden wearing
a gay little cotton frock and *espadrilles*, there being now
no need for that white uniform of sickness.

LXXXII.

Five happy days we spent together, lazy days of pure
enjoyment and glorious sunshine. On the sixth day John
woke early with severe abdominal pain.

" Only that cursed digestion of mine, my Peg. Don't
be uneasy. I'll go for a stroll with Tiny and walk it off."

When she saw the colour of his face she begged him
to rest. The morning sun was still very hot, and he
would be better lying on the divan in his cool *Galerie*.
But he irritably refused to be managed.

" I've lived with my bad digestion all my life, Tiny, and
I must be permitted to know what is best for it."

In that mood she could do nothing with him, and with a
resigned sigh she went upstairs to get her hat.

When they came back from their walk I was upstairs.
As Tiny went up to her bedroom I called out : " Is he
better ? "

" *Rotten*," she replied, and came into mine to tell me
that in all her life she would never forget that walk. The
pain and nausea had come on again and John had nearly
collapsed, but doggedly he had forced himself to walk
two kilometres of rough mountain road, leaning against
trees when the pain became almost insupportable, but
he had conquered it and got home—somehow. We

helped him upstairs and into bed, and Tiny tried every-thing to ease his discomfort. We telephoned to Sunny Bank to ask for the name of another doctor as ours was in Paris, and after many hours a car drove up to our door and a kind-faced old doctor came up to John's room. He tried to examine the abdomen, but John found it impossible to relax. All his life he had suffered from this inability to relax for even a moment. Directly he was asked to slacken his muscles, he became as stiff and hard as a board, and in the end, with a sigh of exasperation, the doctor gave up the attempt to locate that spasmodic pain, and said that we could only wait for other symptoms to develop.

For two days we waited, and then he suggested the advisability of a second opinion—that of a surgeon.

A surgeon came, and after a long examination and consultation with the doctor they decided that John was suffering from obstruction, or perhaps appendicitis. In any case it would be safer to take him down to Sunny Bank Hospital for observation. To leave him here, so far from the aid that could be given by doctors and a hospital, would be very dangerous.

Tiny feared that John would fiercely oppose this plan. He so loved his home and would dread a hospital ; but when I told him what the doctors wanted, I detected a look of relief on that pain-ravaged face. He had experi-enced what it meant to wait for long hours for the coming of a busy Cannes doctor to his aid.

" If Tiny can come with me and be my nurse I will go," he said quietly.

We telephoned to Cannes for a motor ambulance, and I had a glimpse of poor old Hilaire's horror-struck face as the great closed van marked with the red cross drove silently to our door. While the stretcher-men were rolling John in blankets and preparing to carry him downstairs, I flew into the kitchen to warn Emilia to wave a *cheerful* farewell to *Monsieur*, and then I rushed into the garden to find Hilaire. He was crouched down among his vines, tears coursing down his cheeks. Fiercely I told him that he must pull himself together and give *Monsieur* all the encouragement that he could. Choking, he nodded his poor old head in assent.

Emilia, with all the histrionic powers of the Italian, ran smiling out of her kitchen as the stretcher was carried through the hall, promising her *Monsieur* that she would prepare him all his favourite dishes in defiance of the doctors, when he came home in a few days' time. But Hilaire's smile was the grin of a tragic mask, and all he could say, over and over again, was : " *Cela me fait de la peine—cela me fait de la peine.*" John, whose suffering had been alleviated by drugs, could even smile at Hilaire's awful farewell.

" Poor old fellow. One might almost think he was assisting at my funeral," he said to me, and I actually contrived a laugh.

Tiny accompanied her patient in the ambulance and I drove behind with the things he would need in hospital, including, of course, a writing-case with paper, pencils, and pen, for he " intended to make a lot of money by writing when tied by the leg in hospital."

I calculated that this indomitable man had made no less a sum than £250 from his writings during those fifteen months of illness.

Tiny told me afterwards that all the way down to Cannes John kept asking her what places they were passing and telling her to describe to him the light on the mountains, the wild flowers in the fields. In his recumbent position he could see nothing for himself. He seemed extraordinarily happy, she said, amusing himself by composing a nonsense-rhyme to amuse his great-nephews. The end of it eluded him, but, suddenly, with a chuckle, he exclaimed : " I've *got* it, Tiny ! "

" Repeat it to me, Sir John," she begged, " or you may forget it."

" No, I shall have plenty of time to write it out while I'm in hospital," he said.

And so that whimsical ending was lost for ever. . . .

LXXXIII.

I can never forget the kindness of everyone in Sunny Bank Hospital. I was given a room on the first floor so that I could always be with, or near, my Man.

For three days John was ' under observation ' and given experimental treatment. He no longer suffered acute pain, only the misery of distension and an utter weariness. His family and mine offered to come out to us, but they had all seen him lately in England, and he was too weak to talk to them. An expensive journey with a grievous ending, and all to no purpose now. On the fourth day doctor and surgeon resolved to operate for obstruction, their decision being backed by a second surgeon whom I had called in consultation.

Tiny broke the news to John, merely telling him that the surgeon was going to perform a slight operation to relieve his dreadful discomfort, which was now so great that although all his life he had had a morbid dread of operations, now he almost welcomed one.

Before he was taken into the theatre I was alone with him for a few moments, and, as I kissed that beloved face, he looked up at me and said—

" Do you remember what *I* did when my precious woman was having an operation in Brompton Square ? I wrote a chapter of history while the surgeon was at work." Those brilliant eyes looked into mine with an unspoken request.

" You mean that you want *me* to write while you are in the theatre ? " I asked.

He nodded silently.

" Very well. I will try," I said, trying to control my voice.

Miss Williams, the Head Sister, told John that the doctor and surgeon had decided to perform the operation with only a local anæsthetic. Tiny looked at me with tragic brown eyes as I cried out, " Oh *no*—not *that.* . . ."

Miss Williams explained that the operation could not last longer than twenty minutes, and a local anæsthetic would save him all the miserable after-effects of ether. To me she whispered that the doctor was afraid of the lungs after pneumonia.

This was the worst horror of all for a hyper-sensitive man, and I knew that I, myself, could never go through such an ordeal. They wheeled him away, and, in obedience to whispered instructions from Miss Williams, a young nurse led me upstairs to wait in the privacy of her sitting-room.

Alone there, I took up a pencil, and, obedient to my promise, I tried to begin to write. I did contrive to cover half a quarto page—in two and a half hours—not a very creditable performance, but I am cursed with a vivid imagination—and they had told me that the operation could not take longer than twenty minutes.

At last I heard footsteps echoing along the corridor. They stopped outside my door. Someone knocked. I was asked to come downstairs. Grouped in the corridor outside John's room were doctor, surgeon, and Miss Williams, all looking ghastly. I could not speak, the strain had been too long and too great, but I suppose my eyes asked an agonised question, for, when the doctors entered John's room, Miss Williams told me jerkily that the surgeon had discovered an appendix abscess.

" An appendix abscess ? " I echoed dully.

" Yes. It had burst, and that is why we have been so long."

I forced myself to go into John's room, dreading what I might see. As I went in I heard him say : " *Merci infiniment, Messieurs,*" to his doctor and surgeon in farewell. Tiny was there and looked at me. The suffering in her eyes told me that she had shared that dread ordeal with him. John was propped up on his pillows, his face flushed, his eyes feverishly bright. He began talking excitedly at once.

" They cut me open in two places, darling. I'm afraid I did curse once or twice when they cut deep—but you see I didn't bargain on being cut open twice—I watched it all in the reflector of the great lamp above the operating table."

" *You watched it all?* " I whispered, horrified. " I think that would have killed me."

" I, on the contrary, found it extraordinarily interesting," stated this extraordinary man tensely.

They gave him morphia to make him sleep, and then Tiny came up to my room. She told me that, after an unsatisfactory X-ray on the operating table, the surgeon had opened up the left side, thinking that it was a case of obstruction. What he had found obliged him to cut open the right side, where he found an appendix abscess, evidently of long standing, for it was in almost a gangrenous condition. It had burst. Peritonitis.

LXXXIV.

Three days more. Whenever I went into John's room he was being given an injection of glucose or of saline— an interminable process—*goutte par goutte*—the only way left to us to nourish him. Now they gave him morphia, for, without it, he longed to sleep but could not, and the drug numbed the pain and discomfort.

Little Marion Leverhulme was staying in Cannes and sometimes she came up to the hospital and joined me in that weary waiting for the inevitable end of all this agony, for Tiny, who loved me as well as John, had long since told me the truth. He could not survive this last thing that had come upon him. If, by some miracle, he won yet another victory against pain and sickness, he would be for ever disabled. She knew that neither he nor I could bear that, and besides he was so weary of the struggle. Every day he said to me : " I am *so, so* tired, Sweetheart."

LXXXV.

On Sunday morning Tiny came to me and told me, very tenderly, that he was drifting away. In the afternoon, for five precious moments, he and I were alone together and he was conscious of my presence. He looked up at me with that special smile, and I bent over him and told him that I blessed God for every moment of our life together. He said—

" And I bless Him too. I don't know what I have done that He should give me such a wife. I fear I have been but a burden to her of late."

I told him that since he became ill he had seemed more than ever mine—my baby—dependant upon me for everything, and therefore doubly dear. He took my hand and laid it upon his heart, saying—

" Goodnight, my Sweet. Soon I shall be reading to her in our Domaine."

That was really our farewell, for afterwards he slept again and when he woke in the evening his mind was wandering. He was back, with me, happy, in his beloved Domaine.

" He's going," whispered Tiny. . . .

His face was so beautiful, the face of a young man, but carved in ivory—all the lines smoothed away ; an expression of awe and amazement in the eyes, which looked at some far-off vision, invisible to us—as though he were reading the answer to all the riddles of this earth with a wistful eager interest—and humility. I called his name and told him that I was there, close beside him, and he made a little stifled sound as though he tried to tell me that he knew.

After that he just sank into a sleep so peaceful that I hardly knew when it became eternal.

LXXXVI.

A wild storm was lashing the trees. All day it had banged doors and billowed curtains wildly into rooms. John had smiled at the confusion and had said, " I like it."

I had always known that his fighting spirit must swirl away in a storm. Now I stared out into the wind-swept garden through windows blurred with rain. There was an electric standard lamp in the street behind the hospital wall. Seen through the wire mosquito-screen of my window, it took the form of a fiery cross with a blazing central star. It was like a symbol to me. That fiery cross was what I had to bear; that brilliant star, the example of his courage which I must strive to follow.

Telegrams came next day from John's family and mine. They offered to come out to me, but there was nothing now that I could not do for him myself; and I felt that I could not bear to speak of him to anyone just then.

I had one deep comfort. A message from the War Office—

" The Army has lost a true friend and mourns an Historian whose works will inspire future generations as they have informed and encouraged the present."

That telegram went with me everywhere and was read and re-read. His soldiers loved him, and all over the Empire they mourned his loss with me. His life of labour, dedicated to their service, had not been lived in vain; his works would live after him. No more fitting epitaph could he have had than that telegram. Almost I could hear him saying—

" My days, darling, I had no idea the Army thought so much of me."

After all, his selfless labour had its reward, and surely, surely, he must know it. . . .

LXXXVII.

Knowing so well John's horror of the conventional panoply of death, I refused the public funeral that all were eager to give a famous man—wreaths, a procession in which the British Legion should join ; a service in the English Church in Cannes.

Instead, I arranged for a short and quiet little service to be held early in the morning in the tiny chapel of the hospital where he lay, resting at last. It should be performed by a Military Chaplain, and only I, and Tiny, who loved him and had fought for his precious life like a little soldier, should be present.

Our British Vice-Consul came to see me, and I asked him if he thought that I might cover John with a Union Jack,

" He is not a soldier, I know . . ." I began.

" If John Fortescue has not the right to a Union Jack, I know of no man who has," broke in the Vice-Consul, who had been, himself, an officer in one of the fine old regiments of the Line.

And so my Man had his flag.

These arrangements made, I telephoned to the Domaine telling Emilia to fill every room with flowers and to open wide the windows to let in the sunshine, for I was coming home. I had to go back to find certain papers wanted by the French authorities, and among them, in John's despatch case, I found a letter addressed to me in his familiar hand. Such a wonderful, wonderful letter. In it, besides many sacred messages to me, I read his last wishes—which in every case I had forestalled, save one, which must also be obeyed, an urgent plea that I should not attend the last rites of his funeral.

Hilaire and Emilia were in tears. They wanted to know the day and hour of the funeral, so that they might follow *Monsieur* to his last resting-place, carrying enormous *gerbes*. The telephone had not ceased ringing since the news had become known, Emilia said. All our friends in Grasse wanted to know the same thing, and every workman who had helped us to arrange the Domaine wished to walk in the procession. When I told her of *Monsieur's* last wishes, " swift, simple, and private burial," her face puckered in perplexity—a private funeral—the thing was unheard of in France. All who had known and loved *Monsieur* wished now to pay him their last tribute of respect. She was evidently deeply wounded, and old Hilaire was frankly scandalised by my arrangements. Knowing that John would not like his humble peasants to be hurt, I asked Gabrielle de Croze to translate for me a message which I then and there composed, explaining that, in life, *Monsieur* had always valued the loyalty and willing affectionate service that he had received. These things had meant more to him than flowers, which would fade in a day and which would cost money that, in these hard times, should be spent upon the necessities of life. This I published, unsigned, in the local newspaper, and Hilaire brought the paragraph to show me, saying that now he understood. . . . I asked both him and Emilia to pick a sprig of rosemary from the Domaine garden for *Monsieur ;* and this comforted them a little.

On the morning of John's last journey the storm still raged. Yet, during that last service, the sun blazed through a rift in the heavy rain-clouds and shone upon the Union Jack in a last benediction.

When the Chaplain had pronounced the final words of the blessing, " And give you peace, now, and evermore," I stole out into the garden and stared across a sea of olive trees, silver against an indigo sky, to a white ribbon